World War I
&
European Society

World War I & European Society

A Sourcebook

Marilyn Shevin-Coetzee
Frans Coetzee

George Washington University

D. C. Heath and Company
Lexington, Massachusetts   Toronto

Address editorial correspondence to:

D. C. Heath and Company
125 Spring Street
Lexington, MA 02173

Acquisitions Editor: James Miller
Developmental Editor: Daphne Zervoglos
Production Editor: Kathleen A. Deselle
Designer: Alwyn Velásquez
Photo Researcher: Linda Finigan
Production Coordinator: Dick Tonachel
Permissions Editor: Margaret Roll

Cover: *Return to the Front* by Richard Jack, 1917; National Railway Museum, York, England. Transparency supplied by The Bridgeman Art Library / Art Resource, New York.

Published simultaneously in Canada.

Printed in the United States of America.

International Standard Book Number: 0–669–33470–7

Library of Congress Catalog Number: 94–72565

10 9 8 7 6 5 4 3

This book is dedicated to our daughter, Michelle Hanna Shevin-Coetzee, in the hope that her generation will never experience the horrors chronicled in the following pages.

Preface

In our experience as teachers of European history, we have found that students are eager to learn about the past, especially through exploring documents. Working with historical accounts not only gives them a sense of accomplishment in having "done history," but also provides them with a vivid sense of what life was like for their predecessors. Such achievements are essential if students are to gain a well-rounded appreciation of the past.

Our objectives in this volume are to eliminate students' misconceptions about the First World War and to provide a convenient and accessible introduction to many aspects of this conflict that were previously ignored or underemphasized. We have selected the documents in this anthology to illustrate the principal themes of the social history of the war.

The volume's organization is relatively straightforward: there are four large thematic parts with an overall chronological thrust. Part I, The Challenge of Mobilization and Stalemate, begins with the initial responses to the conflict by newly mobilized soldiers, intellectuals, and ordinary civilians. Many personal accounts from the front then illustrate the growing realization that victory would be neither as swift nor as easy as almost everyone had assumed in the heady days of August 1914. The ways in which soldiers sought to accommodate themselves to persistent tedium and intermittent horror, the efforts to break the stalemate by means of technology (poison gas and aerial or submarine warfare), and events in theaters of war beyond Western Europe are all treated here.

Parts II and III deal more directly with the domestic experience of war, with the efforts of combatant societies to preserve cohesion in the face of unprecedented demands. Part II, Society Under Stress, documents the strain of preserving social order, the state's primary function, by maintaining a certain standard of living. Scholars conversant with the subject will find here a mixture of the familiar and the unfamiliar, with the expectation that the former will appear in a fresh light. Accordingly, the material conditions of the home front — such as availability of food and standards of nutrition — appear in the context of the other determinants of patriotic unity. Treatment of minorities, the role of religion, the ways in which notions of masculine and feminine behavior were embedded in the social order — and subsequently contested — are reflected in our choice of sources. Part III, State and Society in Crisis, more explicitly addresses the role of the state, including its intervention in the labor market and restriction of civil liberties, its expanded administrative presence, the penetration of bureaucracy in daily affairs, and the collapse of governments which, having demanded so much from their citizens, could not reward them with the fruits of victory.

Finally, Part IV, The Aesthetic War, focuses upon the war's artistic dimensions. For all its brutality, or perhaps partly because of it, the conflict stimulated a remarkable cultural response. This part brings together imaginative literature, art, and propaganda posters to illustrate the images with which Europe's writers and artists sought to evoke and comprehend this first total war. We have been interested particularly in supplementing the printed page with visual images to provide students with as comprehensive an introduction and, we hope, as nuanced an interpretation of the war as possible. In one sense, however, the war did not end in 1918. Not until a decade later, for example, were many of the great war novels published. The struggle to define and interpret the war's legacy and to find acceptable and meaningful ways to perpetuate the memory of that cataclysm, were issues of debate as intense as those of responsibility for its outbreak or for its conduct.

We have made a conscious decision to avoid sustained consideration of the tangled diplomatic course of the conflict and the equally tangled web of the Russian Revolution because, until recently, they have attracted more in the way of scholarly attention and therefore are adequately treated in a number of existing publications. Furthermore, focusing this volume as we have helps to preserve a high degree of thematic coherence, to make a distinctive contribution, and to keep this volume to manageable proportions. We hope that its use proves as rewarding as its compilation.

Many thanks are in order to the reviewers and other colleagues who helped us as the project unfolded. Reviewers who offered insights and suggestions were Daniel Borg, *Clark University;* Kathleen Canning, *University of Michigan;* William Irvine, *Glendon College of York University;* Sterling Kernick, *Western Illinois University;* William Keylor, *Boston University;* Allen McConnell, *Queens College of the City University of New York;* and Diethelm Prowe, *Carleton College.* Special thanks are due to Walter Simons of Dartmouth College for translating the extracts dealing with Belgium and to our former colleague, Sir Michael Howard, for his valuable advice. Thanks also to D. C. Heath editorial and production staff who contributed significantly to the final result: James Miller, acquisitions editor; Daphne Zervoglos, developmental editor; Kathleen Deselle, production editor; Alwyn Velásquez, designer; Margaret Roll, permissions editor; Dick Tonachel, production coordinator; and Linda Finigan, photo researcher. But while we have welcomed and benefited from the advice of many, the responsibility of the final product is our own.

M. S-C.

F. C.

Contents

Chronology

1914

June 28	Assassination of Archduke Franz Ferdinand of Austria-Hungary.
July 23	Austro-Hungarian ultimatum to Serbia.
July 24	Partial mobilization of Austro-Hungarian army.
July 30	Mobilization of Russian army.
August 1	Mobilization of French and German armies; Germany declares war on Russia.
August 2	German trade unions agree to support war.
August 3	Germany declares war on France.
August 4	German invasion of neutral Belgium; Britain enters the war against Germany.
Early August	Passage of Defense of the Realm Act (DORA) in Britain.
August	Sporadic anti-German riots in Britain.
August 26–30	Battle of Tannenberg (East Prussia).
September 6–9	Battle of the Marne.
Mid-September	Trench warfare begins.
September 20	France implements policy of industrial mobilization.
October 12	First Battle of Ypres.
October 18–19	Anti-German riots in Deptford, England.

November 1	Russia declares war on Turkey.
December 21	First German air raids on Britain.

1915

January	Introduction of food rationing in Germany.
February–March	Allied attempts to take the Dardanelles.
February–September	Intensive German submarine warfare begins.
March	Conclusion of Treasury Agreement with trade unions in Britain.
March 21	First German air raid on Paris.
April 8	Turkey initiates deportation and massacre of Armenians.
April 22–May 27	Second Battle of Ypres; introduction of gas warfare.
April 25	Allied land campaign against Turks in Gallipoli begins.
May 2–4	Russian retreat at Battle of Gorlice-Tarnow.
May 7	Sinking of the *Lusitania* by German U-boat.
May 8	Anti-German riots break out in England following news about the *Lusitania*.
May 23	Italy enters war on Allied side.
May 26	Formation of coalition government in Britain in which Asquith retains the office of Prime Minister.
July	Coal miners strike in South Wales; Munitions of War Act passed in Britain.
September	First Zimmerwald Movement Conference held in Switzerland.
October	Aristide Briand replaces Rene Viviani as French Premier.
Late Autumn	France recruits women laborers in earnest.

1916

January 24	Britain implements conscription.
February 21	Battle of Verdun begins (through December 18).
March	Clydeside Strikes in Scotland; Alexandre Ribot replaces Briand as French Premier.

April	Second Zimmerwald Movement Conference in Switzerland.
April 20	France implements policy of price control on vital necessities.
April 24–29	Easter Uprising in Ireland.
May 31–June 1	Naval Battle of Jutland.
June 4–October 10	Russian Brusilov offensive.
June 5	Start of Arab revolt against Turks in Hejaz; death of Britain's Lord Kitchener when his ship is torpedoed.
June 7–9	Anti-German riots in London following Kitchener's death.
June 12	Paolo Boselli replaces Antonio Salandra as Premier of Italy.
July 1–November 19	Battle of Somme.
November 7	Reelection of Woodrow Wilson as President of United States.
November 21	Death of Emperor Franz Josef of Austria-Hungary and succession of Archduke Karl.
December 2	Patriotic Auxiliary Service Act in Germany.
December 7	Lloyd George becomes Prime Minister in reconstruction of British government.

1917

January	Resumption of unrestricted submarine warfare by Germany.
January–February	"Turnip Winter" in Germany; food riots break out.
January 17	France initiates compulsory arbitration of wage disputes.
February 2	Britain introduces bread rationing.
March 16	Tsar Nicholas II of Russia abdicates his throne.
March 21–July 18	Germany launches spring offensive.
April 6	United States enters war against Germany.
April 16	Publication of infamous "Corpse Conversion Factory" propaganda in *The Times* (London).
April 16–29	Chemin des Dames offensive.
April 7–9	Anti-German riots in London following German air raid.
April 29	First mutiny by French army unit.
July 14	Resignation of German Chancellor Theobald von Bethmann-Hollweg and succession of Georg Michaelis.
July 31–November 10	Third Battle of Ypres (Battle of Passchendaele).

August	Third Zimmerwald Movement Conference in Stockholm; unrest in Turin, Italy, over lack of bread in stores.
August 1	Pope Benedict XV appeals for peace.
August 5	Act encouraging creation of nursing facilities for mothers in France.
August 6	Alexander Kerensky becomes head of Provisional Government in Russia.
October	Count Georg von Hertling replaces Michaelis as Germany's Chancellor.
October 24–November 10	Battle of Caporetto; Vittorio Orlando replaces Boselli as Italy's Premier.
November 7	Bolshevik overthrow of Provisional Government in Russia.
November 2	Balfour Declaration supporting establishment of homeland for the Jews in Palestine.
November 16	Georges Clemenceau becomes French Premier.
December 3	Lenin and the Bolsheviks sign armistice with Germany.
December 6	Finland declares independence from Russia.
December 9	General Edmund Allenby captures Jerusalem.

1918

January 8	Woodrow Wilson proposes his Fourteen Points as a basis for peace.
March 3	Russia signs Treaty of Brest-Litovsk.
March 21	Germany launches spring offensive.
May–October	Allied forces intervene in Russian Civil War.
July 16	Deposed Tsar Nicholas II and family are executed.
July 18–November 10	Allied counteroffensive against Germany.
Late September	Prince Max of Baden replaces Hertling as Germany's Chancellor.
October 3–4	Germany offers to make peace according to Wilson's Fourteen Points.
October 4	British and Arab forces occupy Damascus.
October 16	Austria-Hungary declares itself a federal state based upon nationalities.

October 28	German sailors mutiny at Kiel.
Early November	Revolutionary unrest in Germany.
November 3	Austria-Hungary sues for peace with Allies.
November 7	Kurt Eisner declares Bavaria a Republic.
November 9	Abdication of Kaiser Wilhelm II of Germany.
November 11	Armistice is signed on the Western Front.

THE FIRST WORLD WAR,
1914–1918

 ▬▬▬ Front lines, August 1914
 — · — Front lines, November 1918
 —— Line of trench warfare
 ······ Russian/German frontier, early 1915
 – – – Maximum extent of Central
         Powers' advance

 Central Powers at start of war
 States later ally to Central Powers
 Entente Powers; Belgium, Lux.
 States later join Entente
 States neutral throughout war

ATLANTIC

OCEAN

NORWAY

Christiania ⊗

North

Sea

DENMARK

Jutland

Copenhagen

GREAT
BRITAIN

Kiel

NETH.

Berl

London ⊗

Amsterdam

Channel

Brussels ⊗

Liége

English

BELGIUM

LUX.

GERMA

Seine R.

Paris ⊗

Berne ⊗

SWITZ.

FRANCE

R.

Rhine

ITAL

SPAIN

PORTUGAL

Madrid ⊗

Ron

Lisbon ⊗

Mediterranean   Sea

MOROCCO
(France)

ALGERIA
(France)

TUNIS
(Franc

| 0 | 400 | 800 Miles |
| 0 | 400 | 800 Kilometers |

THE WESTERN FRONT, 1914–1918

—— Boundaries, August 3, 1914	—— Limit of Allied advance and Armistice line, November 11, 1918
- - - Extent of German advance, September 1914	✳ Key battles and sieges mentioned in text
— — Hindenburg line, March 17, 1917	Allied and Associated Powers
⋯⋯⋯ Limit of German retreat, May 1917	Central Power
—— Trench warfare, 1914–1917	Neutral countries
▨ German gains, 1914–1917	
▧ Allied gains, 1914–1917	
—·— Limit of German advance, March–July 1918	

GREAT BRITAIN

Amsterdam

North Sea

NETHERLANDS

London

Passchendaele
Ypres

Brussels

BELGIUM

Liége

GERMANY

Rhine R.

Somme R.

St.-Quentin

LUX.

Arlon

Seine R.

Verdun

Marne R.

Paris

Château-Thierry

FRANCE

Rhine R.

0   100 Miles
0   100 Kilometers

Berne

SWITZERLAND

World War I
&
European Society

Introduction

Eighty years after its outbreak, the First World War remains a subject of abiding interest. As (arguably) history's first total war, it enveloped a multitude of nations, nationalities, races, and religions; produced new and more deadly weapons of destruction; altered traditional gender patterns; strengthened the power of the state; and unleashed revolutionary forces in Germany, Austria-Hungary, and Russia. In the four years of its duration, 1914–1918, eight to nine million soldiers succumbed to the fighting; many more were wounded and disabled. The total number of civilians killed is unknown but very high, especially in eastern Europe. The memory of war, for both surviving combatants and their families, lingered. Hailed by President Woodrow Wilson as the war to end all wars, one that would restore international and domestic stability and punish its instigator, Germany, the Great War instead ushered in decades of economic and political chaos, ultimately leading to dictatorship in Mussolini's Italy, Stalin's Soviet Union, Hitler's Germany, and a half-dozen east European states.

Library shelves are crammed with both popular and scholarly contributions about the war, especially concerning its diplomatic origins, the course of battles and life in the trenches, and the development of new, deadly military technology. But all of these issues depended on the ability of the various combatant nations to mobilize their civilian populations to sustain the war effort — to create a home front. Scholars have begun to explore particular aspects of home-front life, but surprisingly few have sought to take a broader comparative view of the subject. It is a commonplace notion that military service scarred the participants — emotionally if not physically — for life, as is so movingly rendered in the works of such articulate observers as poet and author Robert Graves and novelist Erich Remarque. But the impact of the war was felt in a no less profound way by those who remained civilians. The former British prime minister, Herbert Asquith, who endured in London a conflict in which his own beloved son, Raymond, had perished, remarked in November 1918 that the war had been "one of the greatest dramas in history" and that "it is not too much to say that it has cleansed and purged the whole atmosphere of the world." Somewhat less grandiloquently, author Evelyn Wrench summarized her sense of the war's impact on civilian affairs by noting that "when the fourth anniversary came, government control was so much a part of our lives that we found it difficult to jump back in our minds to the prewar world in which we lived in July 1914."

Perhaps the term "First World War" is misleading, because previous conflicts such as the Seven Years' War (1756–1763, known to Americans as the French and Indian Wars) and the Napoleonic Wars were truly intercontinental in scope, involving military action in the various European nations' colonial empires. In that case, the claim of the conflict of 1914–1918 to represent the first world war rests on the more slender thread of Japanese participation and the Allied conquest of Germany's African colonies. Nevertheless, both Asquith and Wrench were hinting at something more — that it was not so much the geographic breadth of the war that distinguished it from earlier struggles, but rather its social, economic, and cultural scope that marked it as the "Great War" or, more accurately, the first total war.

Indeed, one might argue that the military results of the war were short-lived. Within two decades the continent was at war again, in the second installment of what some historians have labeled Europe's "second Thirty Years' War." Moreover, in that Second World War, it would be two of the vanquished foes of the Great War, Germany and Russia, that would prove to be among the most formidable adversaries. In that sense, veterans of the First World War might well wonder what enduring military legacy their sacrifice had achieved.

It is, therefore, not in the battles and details of the various campaigns, interesting and informative as they are, that this book seeks to recover the meaning of the Great War. Rather, this volume is devoted to the impact of this unprecedented conflict as experienced by ordinary individuals at the front, in the trenches, and especially on the home front — in bread lines, munitions factories, strikes, or ceremonies and cemeteries to commemorate the fallen.

The war proved all the more significant because it did not conform to expectations. There had, of course, been extensive planning by military leaders throughout Europe before 1914 to prepare for a war; after all, such preparation was at the heart of their professional duty. Yet such efforts had focused on the intricate questions of quickly getting men into uniform and to the national frontier, as well as on strategic questions, such as the Germans' planned strike through Belgium (envisioned in the Schlieffen Plan of 1905) or the French Plan XVII to recover Alsace and Lorraine in a speedy thrust. Assuming that any war would be brief and decisive, military and government planners had given little thought to the equally vexing problems of mobilizing the domestic population for war. And so the various governments had to improvise; societies felt that improvisation all the more keenly, and as a result, the unanticipated social consequences of a seemingly endless total war were all the more profound. The lack of any prior comparable experience is one reason why the social history of the Great War proved so wrenching at the time and so fascinating in retrospect.

In 1914 as temperatures soared during one of the hottest summers on record in Europe, so too tempers flared. Lacking such conveniences as air-conditioning that late twentieth-century Europeans take for granted, and sweltering in heavy conventional fashions, the peoples of Europe were put to the test by both the torrid climate and events. The heat was an irritation, possibly a catalyst, rather than a direct cause of the First World War, the origins of which can be traced to deep-seated economic, military, diplomatic, and political developments. Ironically, the very technology that brought the continent closer together — telegraph, telephone, steamship — helped in the end to tear it asunder. Eventually long-term causes and short-term accidents combined to precipitate the war.

Tensions in Europe had been exacerbated by the imperial rivalries of the 1880s and 1890s, when the quest for raw materials, potential markets, military bases, possible destinations for the emigration of surplus populations, as well as for prestige prompted the race for colonial possessions in Africa and the Far East. The psychological effect of the falling profits of the era — the so-called Great Depression (1873–1896) — renewed pressure from industrial and commercial interests in the various European countries for colonial acquisitions to ensure their nations' exclusive gain at their rivals' expense. Colonial expansion, contend contemporary critics and subsequent scholars, yielded only meager tangible returns, yet the imperial race aggravated the competitive nature of state relations and threatened the preceding decade's fragile diplomatic equilibrium.

It was partly the need to sort out differences between colonial rivals and minimize probable friction that prompted the emergence of long-standing alliance systems. Certainly the Triple Entente of England, France, and Russia served the dual purpose of protecting each country's colonial ambitions from those of its partners (tensions between Britain and France, for example, had escalated over the Fashoda incident of 1898), as well as precluding the easy hegemony of the competing alliance bloc — the Triple Alliance of Germany, Austria-Hungary, and Italy. Originally the advocates of alliance diplomacy presumed that such links afforded members a degree of flexibility and influence over the excesses of their partners; by 1914, however, the reverse was the case, for the alliances threatened to escalate any local conflict involving one pair of powers into a general European conflagration.

Moreover, diplomats found their room to maneuver constrained by military leaders who themselves were responding to the technological advances that had reshaped not just the conduct of war but also the very preparation for it. With mass armies of conscripts and unprecedented quantities of equipment and supplies, mobilization was bound to be protracted, subject to intricate timetables. Once the carefully coordinated mobilization of hundreds of thousands of men, horses, and weapons had begun, it was difficult to stop. Only a strong-willed diplomat, politician, or monarch would be willing to defy military advice and invite confusion by delaying war preparations in the hope of finding a peaceful solution in one of the periodic local crises that punctuated the pre-1914 period.

The most serious of these crises was triggered — literally — by the assassination in Sarajevo of the heir to the Austro-Hungarian throne, Archduke Franz Ferdinand and his wife Sophie, on June 28, 1914. The assassin, Gavrilo Princip, a teenaged Serbian nationalist, shot the imperial couple as a gesture of defiance on behalf of the Serbs of Bosnia-Herzegovina, a province of mixed Serb, Croatian, and Muslim Slavic populations that had been annexed by Austria-Hungary. European opinion was shocked by this brazen act, but it did not regard it as likely to culminate in a continental conflict. Over the course of the next few weeks this impression proved illusory. First, the Austro-Hungarian government was persuaded that the government of neighboring Serbia had plotted the assassination in an attempt to seize Bosnia-Herzegovina. Diplomatic pressure to elicit from Serbia concessions or a confession of complicity inevitably entangled Slavic Serbia's protector, Russia, in the crisis. The second significant factor was that both Austria-Hungary and Russia were authoritarian monarchies facing domestic agitation for reform and in danger of fragmenting into their constituent nationalities. One seemingly attractive way of forestalling such an erosion of imperial authority was to achieve a quick and convincing triumph, diplomatic or military, over an irresolute rival.

Russia's proclivities on this score were reinforced by Tsar Nicholas II's determination not to yield, as he felt he had humiliatingly been forced to do in the past; Austria-Hungary's resolve was meanwhile strengthened by strong German pressure not to capitulate. The public and secret intricacies of the alliance system ensured that if Germany and Austria-Hungary went to war against Russia, France and possibly Britain would intervene. Yet Germany's military leaders, recognizing the difficulty of simultaneously fighting a war on two fronts, had in the Schlieffen Plan sought to alleviate the difficulty by deciding on a rapid strike at France through Belgium, discounting the prospect that the violation of Belgium's neutrality would ensure British intervention.

On July 23, 1914, Austria-Hungary issued an ultimatum to Serbia, couched in phrases so offensive that to have accepted it would have eroded the small country's sovereignty. Under the circumstances the Serb response was quite conciliatory but insufficient to preclude Austria-Hungary from declaring war on Serbia five days later. Russia responded by mobilizing, prompting Germany to do the same — and to declare war on Russia on August 1 and on France two days later. On August 4, after German troops had violated the Belgian frontier, Britain honored its treaty obligation to protect Belgian neutrality and entered the fray on the side of France and Russia, though strategic considerations for the safety of the English Channel had influenced the decision for war.

More than a concern for national honor brought Germany into the war, for a bitter economic and naval rivalry had pitted it against Britain for several decades. Germany's remarkable economic dynamism threatened Britain's industrial ascendancy, while Germany's colonial and naval ambitions commensurate with its economic achievement deepened the antagonism between the two countries. A growing fear of encirclement by the modernizing French and Russian armies and of socialist political gains and domestic tensions all influenced imperial Germany's elite in their decision to go to war.

By August 4 the Continent had plunged into an abyss. "The lamps are going out all over Europe," observed the British foreign secretary, Sir Edward Grey, on the evening of that long and somber day. "We shall not see them lit again in our lifetime."

The Departure *by B. Wennerberg, 1914 (Germany)*
(Imperial War Museum, London)

Part I

The Challenge of Mobilization and Stalemate

Sir Edward Grey's pessimistic assessment of the likely impact of the war jarred with many contemporaries' views. As the latter saw it, their countrymen greeted the mobilization process with immense enthusiasm and nationalistic fervor. War as Christmas, as a holiday, not a calamity to be mourned; as a spiritual release from the banalities of everyday life; as a transformation of the degeneracy inherent in modern culture through looking to a higher, common purpose — these were among the sentiments with which Europeans anticipated the coming conflict. In part, these suppositions drew strength from the mistaken premise, shared by all countries, that the war would prove something of a sporting match, brief and glorious, concluded by Christmas. Indeed, the link between sport and war was not entirely fanciful; an English public-school education assumed that training in team sports served as excellent preparation for the exercise of command. Sporting organizations, such as football clubs, helped to attract war volunteers, and officers were known to lead men into battle kicking a football before them. In Germany, too, the *Turnvereine* (gymnastic associations) aimed to strengthen individuals and the body politic alike. The idea of war as the greatest game of all even became a staple of propaganda posters. In Germany, such artwork depicted young, beautiful maidens handing flowers or beverages to soldiers departing by train to the front, or men, young and older, rushing to volunteer before they missed out on the fun.

Too, for some the frenetic energy of the early days of August may have seemed a welcome relief from the stagnation and familiar rhythms of daily life; others preferred the sense of higher purpose and national unity fostered by the war's outbreak to the domestic division and discord so characteristic of Europe during the prewar years. Wherever one looked, nations appeared embroiled in internal conflicts of their own. The British political system had faced severe challenges over the power and privileges of the House of Lords, the issue of female suffrage, Irish Home Rule, and the willingness and ability of British workingmen to bring the industrial system to its knees. Ulster intransigence, suffragette arson, and labor militancy all seemed to threaten the very ideal of peaceful compromise at the heart of British public life.

Meanwhile, French politics throughout the nineteenth century had been notoriously contentious and unstable, as conflicts persisted over the legacy of the Revolution, relations between the Catholic church and state, and the role of organized labor. On the eve of the war, nothing indicated that political life would grow any more settled. Bitter public debates broke out over electoral reform, taxation, and, above all, the introduction of longer terms of compulsory military service. Accordingly, France witnessed no fewer than six prime ministers in the two and one-half years preceding the war. Moreover, the assassination of the French Left's champion, Jean Jaurès, just days before the armies clashed in 1914, revealed that the Left's legitimacy still came into question.

The German domestic scene also boiled with discord, discontent, and dissidence. Germany's narcissistic emperor, William II, fancied himself an authority on all aspects of foreign and domestic affairs. Nevertheless, he spent long stretches of time aboard the royal yacht, *Hohenzollern,* surrounded by an eccentric circle of sycophantic advisers and admirers. The nation's political system was wracked by ideological, religious, and regional divisions, while a small but boisterous clique of extreme nationalists, outraged by the socialists' success and the parliamentary system's inertia, urged Germans to prepare themselves for battle against internal and external foes. Worker unrest, provoked by relatively low wages and abysmal factory conditions, only deepened the unease.

In Russia, despite the apparent monolithic authority of the tsar, political life was both restricted and unsettled. The autocracy still grappled with the impact of military defeat at the hands of Japan and the revolution of 1905, and although the regime had acquired some trappings of parliamentary government, no consensus existed for liberalizing reforms or reaching political stability. Political debate was not limited to proponents of autocratic reaction and their liberal critics, for after the turn of the century no European nation boasted more rapid industrialization than Russia. The world would soon witness the power of Russian factory workers, but even on the eve of the war, when St. Petersburg laborers launched a massive strike during the visit of the French president, the changing features of the Russian political landscape came into focus. That such changes were unfolding in a nation noted for its unresponsive, unwieldy bureaucracy and reactionary leadership provided further evidence of the growing polarization of Russian life.

Although Italy would not enter the war until May 1915, its leaders decided to side with the Entente for several reasons: they mistakenly believed that the conflict would be brief, that Italy would benefit both economically and politically from this alliance, and that their nation's participation would allow the government to quash internal demands for political, economic, and social reform. A country in which over half the population still labored at agricultural pursuits in 1914, Italy lagged far behind its European counterparts in social programs and industrial legislation. Poor living conditions, low pay, and heavy taxation provoked further resentment toward the government among Italy's working and middle classes.

Some historians have suggested that fear of accelerating domestic disintegration and anarchy played a key role in persuading politicians to embrace the idea of war. On this reading, European leaders calculated that only the unifying pressure of war could hold their fissiparous societies together. Certainly propaganda encouraged the notion of a community solidified in its newfound resolve to achieve victory. One British poster appropriately entitled "Are you in this picture?" depicted Britons from all social classes waiting in a long line to enlist in the army. Both the German slogan *Burgfrieden* (Fortress Under Siege) and the corresponding French concept of *Union sacrée* (Sacred Union) urged citizens, under pressure from external enemies, to put aside their differences and rally around the flag.

Yet this image of spontaneous, frenzied unanimity is incomplete and in some ways misleading. In fact, many European statesmen questioned the likelihood of national unity in a time of crisis and worried lest the outbreak of war only aggravate social unrest. To be sure, they harbored grave misgivings — unfounded in 1914 — about the potential threat of the socialist parties. So if some Europeans looked to the war optimistically, others viewed it through less rosy spectacles.

As the combatants' lack of military preparation came to light time and again, the more guarded responses to the outbreak of hostilities gained credence. In underestimating the duration of the conflict, the opposing nations, each confident of victory, failed to take measures to ensure a steady supply of food for both military and civilian populations and to stockpile raw materials for weapons and munitions. The British presumption that they could continue to conduct "business as usual" typified the initial response throughout Europe. Even Italy, which might have learned from the other combatants' inadequate preparations, sent ill-equipped and poorly trained units to the front in 1915.

European expectations of a brief conflict stemmed partly from the short, decisive campaigns of Prussia against Austria (1866) and France (1870–1871) that suggested that one power could defeat another with relative ease. Instead, military planners should have taken their cue from the American Civil War, which dragged on for four years with staggering casualties.

The first few weeks of campaigning in August 1914 conformed to expectations, as the various armies jockeyed for position and the German advance through Belgium rolled up huge territorial gains. An observer from the Napoleonic Wars would have recognized much of this conduct of war. Cavalry still cantered at the head of columns, soldiers trudged on foot, horse-drawn carts laboriously pulled supplies. But once the Battle of the Marne (September 1914) had stymied the German drive into France, war on the Western Front settled into a different and less recognizable mode: a prolonged and bloody stalemate.

That stalemate reflected the war's enormous emphasis on defense. Barbed wire, which had confined cattle on the U.S. Great Plains, proved effective in impeding the advance of fighting men. Machine guns used to deadly effect by imperialists in Africa and Asia now scored equal success against the soldiers of the European powers themselves. And the devastating bombardments of heavy artillery forced troops to burrow ever deeper into the soil merely to survive. By early 1915, parallel lines of German and Allied trenches stretched from the Belgian coast to the Swiss frontier.

Those trenches became a marked feature of the Western Front over the next three years and in their own peculiar way reflected the different nations' approaches to the war. The British, for example, appeared to rely on their alleged talent for improvisation. Because they persisted in viewing trenches as temporary, they reserved resources for offensive action instead. The French trenches, often squalid and uncomfortable, were little better. Many German emplacements, in contrast, exuded an air of permanence. Deeper and drier, they afforded relative comfort and protection from the incessant shelling.

Nevertheless, for trench dwellers of all nations, boredom became the other enemy, as soldiers filled periods of inactivity with mundane tasks such as delousing themselves and killing rats. Military leaders, however, knew well that offensive action kept morale high, and so, resolved to win the war promptly, they executed mass attacks on enemy lines. As casualties mounted, they grew only more determined to force a decisive breach through their opponents' trenches. As they saw it, the massive firepower now at their disposal offered an enormous advantage to the offensive, and they launched deafening bombardments before attacking.

Preliminary artillery fire negated any element of surprise, however. Furthermore, the constant shell fire devastated the once pristine countryside. The resulting pitted terrain between the trenches, a virtually impassable morass of mud, corpses, shell craters, and tangled wire, appropriately became known as No Man's Land. Strategists began to perceive a devastating contradiction between their initial dreams of a brief, glorious, and inexpensive victory and their soldiers' desperate attempts to win a few yards of blood-soaked ground at tremendous cost. They saw an appalling incongruity, a conflict that embodied remarkable technological innovation but that confined combatants to a primordial subterranean realm. Such contrasts fostered disillusionment, apathy, and disgust.

In the powerful novels that such cynicism inspired, the lingering image of the war centers on the horror of the trenches. Yet the intricate lines of trenches characterized the Western Front only. The Eastern Front saw more fluidity owing to the longer frontier and the lower concentration of firepower. Accordingly, the Eastern Front witnessed decisive battles, such as Tannenberg, that were extremely rare on the Western Front. Combatants also conducted operations in the Middle East, although the most spectacular of these, the amphibious Allied assault on the Dardanelles, proved a failure.

If strategic initiatives such as the Dardanelles could not break the stalemate, the adversaries still hoped to strike a decisive blow by using technological innovation. Of the new weapons of destruction, poison gas was surely among the most harrowing. Developed and used first by the Germans, chemical warfare debilitated its victims by either suffocating them or, more commonly, by damaging or burning their lungs. The use of chlorine gas for military purposes was the brainchild of Fritz Haber, a German chemist, Nobel Prize winner, and head of the prestigious Kaiser Wilhelm Institute in Berlin. After secret tests, German troops released chlorine gas for the first time in combat on April 22, 1915, in Belgium, near Ypres. The unfortunate victims, first French and Algerian soldiers, then Canadians, reeled in terror, and those who survived the assault abandoned their positions. German soldiers understandably hesitated to follow up their advantage, however, given the primitive state of gas masks and the gas clouds' notorious dependence on unpredictable atmospheric conditions such as wind and humidity. Aware of the demoralizing impact of chemicals on opposing armies, however, the Germans flirted with the idea of using zeppelins to drop gas bombs on Allied civilians but abandoned the plan for fear of retaliation by the French. The British and French produced their own gas shells for use at the front, and by 1917, chemical warfare had escalated further with the introduction of mustard gas. Yet although the quality of gas masks improved, they never afforded absolute reliability or protection. Thus gas became a permanent nuisance rather than a decisive weapon to break the stalemate.

The war at sea proved something of a stalemate as well, despite the tremendous sums that Germany and Britain had invested before 1914 in their respective navies. The British Admiralty, knowing that only its ships could protect the nation from starvation or invasion, pursued a cautious policy, while the German high-seas fleet, all too aware of Britain's numerical superiority, spent much of the war in port. The one major clash between the two rival armadas, the Battle of Jutland, erupted in May 1916, with inconclusive results. The Germans inflicted more damage than they sustained, but the British retained their control of the North Sea. From Britain's perspective, German commerce raiders such as the cruiser *Emden* constituted only a temporary irritant. A more sinister threat to the commercial lifelines on which Britain depended came from Germany's submarines, or U-boats. Indeed, no ships were safe from the small submersibles. The British luxury liner, the *Lusitania,* discovered this in May 1915 when a German torpedo shattered it, killing some twelve hundred passengers and crew. The ship's destruction, along with the resumption of unrestricted submarine warfare by the Germans in early 1917, would pull the United States into the war on the side of the Allies that April. For a time during the summer of 1917, it appeared that the heavy toll of merchant shipping exacted by German submarines might hamstring Britain's warmaking powers. By introducing the convoy system in which defenseless merchant ships were grouped together with naval escort, however, Britain ameliorated its losses and nullified the one naval weapon that might have swung the tide of victory to the Germans.

With the land war at a stalemate and enthusiasm for the conflict rapidly waning, the war in the air offered a ray of hope. Here, speed, technological mastery, and romantic heroism combined to present the prospect of decisive resolution. The aerial dogfights recalled the jousting matches of knights from an earlier era and stood in sharp contrast to the squalid, faceless struggles below. In reality, however, the planes were frail and unsuitable as heavy bombers, and they never made a definitive contribution to ending the war. Even the larger German zeppelins failed to resolve the conflict, despite the initial terror that their raids provoked, for they proved no match for protective barrage balloons, nimbler fighters, and, occasionally, strong winds. Although no evidence exists that the big bombers seriously jeopardized civilian morale (some initial panic in London to the contrary), military planners perpetually feared them. In truth, it was fighter pilots, rather than bombers, who garnered public adulation and respect, although the remarkable exploits of a handful of exceptional pilots do not typify the air war as a whole. Aces such as Germany's Baron von Richthofen, France's René Fonck, and Canada's Billy Bishop might shoot down as many as eighty enemy planes and inspire a sort of reciprocal chivalry among their adversaries, but the airman's daily contributions derived primarily from the less spectacular work of observation and reconnaissance.

Whatever their sphere of operations, most combatants battled the psychological strain of the war with a kind of grim humor, either recounted among friends or expressed in the various unofficial trench newspapers that blossomed during the conflict. One famous cartoon, depicting the conversation of two grimy French veterans, bore the caption:

"If only they hold out!"
"Who?"
"The civilians!"

Like much humor, this example struck a sensitive chord: the global conflict exerted such unprecedented demands that civilians at home would become as essential to the war effort as their besieged comrades at the front.

A. The Mood of 1914

1. MOBILIZATION OF FRENCH TROOPS

On the evening of August 4, 1789, the French National Assembly, by renouncing the rigid estate system that had hitherto divided French society into three corporate orders, helped usher in the French Revolution. That momentous event, like the mobilization of the armies of the French Third Republic 125 years later, aroused apprehension as well as great anticipation. Similarly, the ideals of liberty, equality, and fraternity espoused by the French Revolutionaries found resonance with their fellow citizens in 1914. The First World War, like the Revolution of 1789, initially produced a spirit of cooperation, brotherhood, and common endeavor. The mood evoked by the mobilization of French troops is expressed here by three Frenchmen: the first, a chaplain; the second, the well-known medieval historian Marc Bloch; and the third, an officer in the transport service.

a. Diary of a French Army Chaplain

On August 3rd, Belgium is required — by an ultimatum — to facilitate the German operations over her territory; she refuses, and, in her turn, sees her neutrality violated.

Excerpt from *Diary of a French Army Chaplain* by Felix Klein, Andrew Melrose, 1915, pp. 18–19, 24–27.

Then Germany officially declares War with France; England declares War with Germany; Austria declares War with Russia. From the Urals to the Atlantic, from the Balkans to the mountains of Scotland, with hundreds of vessels, with thousands of regiments, navies and armies are set in motion. In Serbia, in Belgium, in Russia, on the Algerian coast, towns are bombarded. And while on land the cannon already roar, the ironclads sail the seas, and the heavens are crossed by aeroplanes seeking news or carrying explosives.

Oh! that Saturday the 1st August, when the terrible seriousness of the situation was suddenly revealed to a people still but little anxious! That morning three whole classes, three hundred thousand men, receive individually the order for immediate departure. Heedless of all else, giving no backward glance leaving unfinished tasks begun, taking no precaution for the future, completely absorbed in the solemn present, they leave family, undertakings, business. *Veni, sequere me!* orders the Country, without further explanation, and, like those called in the Gospel, they follow; they go to the frontier, to battle, probably to die. The astonishing thing is that not one murmurs and many are enthusiastic; but the women weep, and the children they are leaving. In the streets, in the squares, in the shops to which they are already rushing for provisions, wives, mothers, sweethearts, make moan. At the stations, to which they have accompanied their men, they try, for their sake, to keep a brave front; but when they come back alone . . .

In the middle of the afternoon, at the summons of telegraph or telephone, all the town-halls, all the stations, simultaneously post up the order for general mobilization, which enjoins four millions of men, at the risk of their lives, to help the country in danger. And all answer: "Here we are!" and just consult their time-table to make sure of when they must start. . . .

Where, but a few weeks ago, could be found a more grievous spectacle than the first sittings of the new Chamber? And where, even in turning over the annals of many Parliaments, could be found a more admirable scene than that it offered on the 4th August; listening, silent as a tribunal of history, to the act of accusation drawn up, with proofs in hand, against those who had hurled twenty-five millions of men on to the fields of slaughter! And in this hot-bed of dissensions, quarrels, selfish desires, boundless ambitions, what trace remained of groups, of rivalries, of hates? Unanimous the respect with which the Presidential message was received; unanimous the adhesion to the Chief of the Government and his noble declaration: "It is the liberties of Europe that are being attacked of which France and her allies and friends are proud to be the defenders. . . . France did not wish for the war; since it is forced upon her, she will defend herself. We are without reproach, we shall be without fear. . . ."

And, without debate, with no dissentient voice, all the laws of national defence, with the heavy sacrifices they imply, are at once voted. The night of August 4th, just a hundred and twenty-five years ago, saw the end of Privileges; finer still this day of August 4th, 1914, which sees the end of our dissensions and our egotisms.

The fact is that we know ourselves no longer; barriers are falling on every side which, both in public and private life, divided us into hostile clans. A head committee is formed to guard the material and moral interests of the country without delay; to it the Government summons, side by side with those most technically competent, a representative of each party and the best known of its adversaries in the past — Briand, Delcassé, Millerand, de Mun, Ribot. In Belgium it is the same, or even better; the Catholic Government elects the chief Socialist Vandervelde as Minister of State to take his seat beside the venerable M. Woeste. With our friends no more than with ourselves, can political divisions reach the sublime level of patriotism. . . .

It is the same in private life, as I said. The relations between citizens are transformed. In the squares, in the streets, in the trains, outside the stations, on the thresholds of houses, each accosts the other, talks, gives news, exchanges impressions; each feels the same anxiety, the same hopes, the same wish to be useful, the same acceptance of the hardest sacrifices. Even the children say: "Papa is gone; he went to the War to prevent the Germans doing us harm."

The old proudly enumerate the sons, the nephews, the sons-in-law, the grandsons they have with the Colours; their own age prevents them from going, so they have enlisted in the Civic Guard. The women talk of the anxiety they are feeling for the dear absent ones, of the applications they have made to be admitted as hospital nurses. They tell us familiarly of the precautions against famine they are taking, their fear that milk may fail for the quite little ones; above all, of the possible invasion.

For, next to the field of battle where the men they love are slain, what is most horrible for women in war is the idea of falling into the hands of the enemy soldiers; the thought that in the absence of husband, brother or son, the house may be invaded, the home outraged by victorious brutes.

A woman of the people, to whom I was speaking of the imminence of the War a few days ago, astonished me by her calmness, all the more because she was aware that her husband would go amongst the first. The explanation was not long delayed.

"Happily," she said to me, "Serbia is far from here!"

When she understood that there was a question of a repetition — no doubt with better chances, but perhaps on the same site — the terrible duel of '70, she quickly changed her note: "Oh! Monsieur, the Prussians here!"

August 6th

They are not here yet. Neither from within nor without do things take the same turn as in the Summer of 1870.

While our mobilization goes on with the most irreproachable coolness, calmness and order, Germany, who wished to take us by surprise, in the execution of her principal plan comes up against a moral and material obstacle which was the last to be expected. Her famous sudden attack is transformed into a sudden check. By one action she turns against herself the human race and the first chances of the struggle. She begins the war by a crime against a people's rights and by a military loss. The violation of Belgian neutrality and the attack upon Liége may bring about — O justice of history and Providence! — the fall of the German Empire; a fine opportunity for that great law which makes the crime bring forth its own punishment to manifest itself.

b. *Memoirs of War*

One of the most beautiful memories the war has given me was the sight of Paris during the first days of mobilization. The city was quiet and somewhat solemn. The drop in traffic, the absence of buses, and the shortage of taxis made the streets almost silent. The sadness that was buried in our hearts showed only in the red and swollen eyes of many women. Out of the specter of war, the nation's armies created a surge of democratic fervor. In Paris there remained only "those who were leaving" — the nobility — and those who were not leaving, who seemed at that moment to recognize no obligation other than to pamper the soldiers of tomorrow. On the streets, in the stores and street-cars, strangers chatted freely; the unanimous goodwill, though often expressed in naive or awkward words and gestures, was nonetheless moving. The men for the most part were not hearty; they were resolute, and that was better. . . .

Very early on the morning of August 4, I left for Amiens. I went part of the long way between the avenue d'Orléans and the Gare de la Chapelle in a market gardener's wagon that a police constable had requisitioned for my use. Because I sat in the back, wedged between baskets of vegetables, the fresh and slightly acrid odor of cabbage and carrots will always bring back the emotions of that early-morning departure: my enthusiasm and the constriction that gripped my heart. At the Gare de la Chapelle, an aged, white-haired father made heroic but unavailing efforts to hold back his tears as he embraced an artillery officer. At Amiens I found an extraordinarily animated city, its streets predictably teeming with soldiers.

c. *On the Way to the Front*

1 August, Saturday

From the early hours, Paris is in turmoil, people still have a glimmer of hope, but nothing suggests that matters can now be settled peacefully. The banks are besieged; one has to queue for two or three hours before getting inside. At midday the doors are closed leaving outside large numbers of people who will have to leave on the following day.

In front of the "Gare de L'Est," the conscripts throng the yard ready for departure. Emotion is at its peak; relations and friends accompany those being called up individually. The women are crying, the men too. They have to say good-bye without knowing whether they will ever return.

At last at 4.15 in the afternoon, the news spreads like wild-fire, posters are being put up with the order for mobilization on them! It's every man for himself, you scarcely have the time to shake a few hands before having to go home to make preparations for departure.

(b) Excerpt from *Memoirs of War, 1914–15* by Marc Bloch, Cornell University Press, 1980, pp. 78–79.

(c) Excerpt from *A French Soldier's War Diary* by Henri Desagneaux, Elmsfield Press, 1975, pp. 3–5.

It's 5 o'clock, my mobilization order states: first day of mobilization — without delay. The first day is 2 August!

2 August, Sunday

Mobilized as a reserve lieutenant in the Railway Transport Service, I am posted to [assigned to] Gray. At 6 in the morning, after some painful good-byes, I go to Nogent-le-Perreux station. The train service is not yet organized. There are no more passenger or goods trains. The mobilization timetable is now operative but nobody at the station has any idea when a train is due.

Sad day, sad journey. At 7 A.M. a train comes, it arrives at its terminus — Troyes — at 2 P.M. I didn't bring anything to eat, the refreshment room has already sold out. The rush of troops is beginning and consuming everything in its path. Already you find yourself cut off from the world, the newspapers don't come here any more. But, on the other hand, how much news there is! Everyone has his bit of information to tell — and it's true! . . .

At last in the afternoon I catch the first train which comes along: a magnificent row of first-class carriages (a Paris–Vienna de-luxe; all stock is mobilized) which is going no one knows precisely where, except that it is in the direction of the Front. The compartments and corridors are bursting at the seams with people from all classes of society. The atmosphere is friendly, enthusiastic, but the train is already clearly suffering from this influx from every stratum of society! The blinds are torn down, luggage-racks and mirrors broken, and the toilets emptied of their fittings; it's (typical) French destruction.

At midnight, I am at Vesoul; nothing to eat there either; no train for Gray. I go to sleep on a bench in the refreshment room.

The most fantastic rumours are going around; everyone is seeing spies unbolting railway track or trying to blow up bridges.

3 August, Monday

At 4.28 I leave Vesoul and arrive at last at Gray at 6.30 A.M. where I put myself at the disposal of the commander called Mennetrier. I am sent to Thaon station to see to the detraining of the troops.

The Eastern Railway Company is a source of admiration to everyone, but we are not used to such slow speeds. (The average for a military train is 2.5 kilometres an hour.)

Morale is excellent, everyone is extraordinarily quiet and calm. Along the track at level-crossings, in the towns, crowds singing "La Marseillaise" gather to greet the troops.

The French women have set to it. They are handing out drinks, writing paper, and cigarettes. The general impression is the following: it's Kaiser Bill who wanted war, it had to happen, we shall never have such a fine opportunity again.

I don't stay long at Gray. At midday I catch the train again, am at Vesoul at 2.30, at

Epinal at midnight. The area is already full of soldiers and there are no provisions to be found.

Rumour has it that German planes are bombing Luneville. Epinal is protected by the searchlights of its forts. The weather is heavy and stormy.

4 August

After three hours' stop, I leave Epinal at 2.59 A.M. and arrive at Thaon at 3.25. It's pouring with rain. Nothing to eat and no rest. The troops' billets have to be prepared immediately for they will soon be here.

No newspapers, no news.

The Epinal searchlights rake the sky incessantly.

6 August, Thursday

At 2 A.M. I get one hour's rest. The next train is due at 3. The traffic is intense, with the same enthusiasm and the same slogans "Death to the Kaiser," "String the Kaiser up," "Death to the Boches." The same caricatures: pigs' heads in pointed helmets. Bouquets, garlands, flags.

At daybreak two convoys of wounded — already! — are announced, one of 400 for Epinal, the other for Thaon. According to reports, an infantry battalion has been decimated by machine-gunfire.

The whole afternoon, trains arrive every two hours, artillery and infantry. When the troops get out the local children shower them with flowers.

Still no letters or newspapers, we know nothing about what is happening.

11 August, Tuesday

The troops continue to arrive. Three companies are in front of us. A battle somewhere between Nancy and Epinal, near Sarrebourg is expected shortly. There is cannon-fire at Blamont and Baccarat.

Casualties are starting to arrive and sunstroke is prevalent; people are not so enthusiastic now as in the first days.

The Territorials and Reservists are now arriving. They are not as orderly as the Regulars. Then there are convoys, lines of carriages of every description and limitless baggage.

The H.Q. of the 13th Company has been set up at Thaon. How many non-combatants, what a burden they are! They have requisitioned everything in the surrounding area, and the troops have to camp in the open.

Organization too is not what it should be. There is a train bringing a convoy of administrative personnel. It has been travelling for twenty-nine hours, and has no fixed destination. The men have no provisions and have not eaten for a whole day.

2. BELGIUM ON THE DEFENSIVE

The following excerpt, based on the personal reminiscences of a former Belgian soldier, Jules Leroy, born in 1894 near Ypres, illustrates the chaotic atmosphere prevailing during the early days of the war. Despite its lack of preparation — Belgium had anticipated that Germany would respect its neutrality — the Belgian army fought bravely in the face of overwhelming odds.

It was real chaos at the barracks of Lier. This was a general mobilization, all classes being called up together; the army was not prepared for that. The people in charge could not manage it. One soldier was given trousers, the other a pair of boots, I got only a *capote* [an army coat] to wear over my civilian clothes. Nobody got all their equipment at one time. At roll call some showed up in civilian clothes, others had bits and pieces of uniform. We just wandered about. There was no training. There were not enough officers for that.

One day one of the officers called out: "Those of you who know how to cut down a tree, step forward!" There were four of us who could. We were sent to the fort of Walem, on the high road from Antwerp to Mechlin. In front of the fort there was a big square with poplars, which could provide cover for an approaching enemy. So they had to go. We were told to cut the trees with army material. Imagine, with those tiny army hatchets! Those pretty gray hatchets. We did what we could.

One day — we already knew that the Germans were approaching — we heard a shot from a German canon. It fell two hundred meters short. They were shelling us from Heist-op-den-Berg. After the third shot an officer climbed on the wall of the fort and yelled: "*Sauve qui peut!*" My friends asked me: "What is he saying?" I understood French and explained: "That means: Flee who can." We thought that the Germans were upon us and ran toward the other side of the road. I bet my *capote* is still there. I did not have time to fetch it. We fled westwards. By evening we were overcome with fatigue. We had lost two of our companions. I told Gilbert, my friend, how tired I felt, and he was too. "Let's rest for a while behind that hedge," he said. There the two of us sat down, out of the wind. Suddenly we saw something move, only twenty meters away. A bunch of soldiers lay there taking aim. We came closer, and suddenly one of them says: "But damn it: those are guys from Ypres! Get out of here, there will soon be trouble!" I said: "But where do we go?" — "Go north, to Antwerp." But by that time we did not know north from south.

Excerpt from *Van den Grooten Oorlog,* Jan Hardeman and Marieka Demeester, eds., trans. by Walter Simons, Malogijs, 1978, pp. 13–16.

Finally we reached the main road to Antwerp. In the distance a light was shining. At last, a house! We knocked on the door. "Come in." People were sitting around the stove. They were frightened. We asked for and were given bread, with coffee. I fell asleep. . . . At two in the morning, the man of the house woke us up: "It's time to go," he said. "The Germans will be here any time now."

We passed through Boechout, where we found a brewery. About forty soldiers were asleep on the sidewalk. The brewer arrived and told us we should feel free to drink all the beer we could. "I'd rather have you drink it than the Germans," he said. Some of us did as he said and drank too much. Gilbert and I only had a couple of beers. In Mortsel we joined a group of fifty to sixty men who didn't know where to go. Some had guns but had lost track of their company. Others, like us, were unarmed. And we trudged along, through Berchem, to the Scheldt River, which we crossed with the help of some bargemen. . . . We finally made it to Nieuwpoort, eating turnips and fruit. . . . There we sat down on the steps of a building. After a while the door opened and a nun appeared. She said: "Would you like some coffee?" We each got two sandwiches, and plenty of coffee. This was the convent of the Poor Clares. I will be grateful to them for all my life. They tasted so good, those two sandwiches!

3. A JUST WAR AGAINST ENGLAND

The German navy, upon which so much money and attention had been lavished, was widely acknowledged as a superb fighting force. Richard Stumpf, a Catholic sailor, served on the German battleship *Helgoland* for the duration of the war. His diaries testify to his initial enthusiasm for the conflict as a just war of retribution against Britain's economic jealousy and his subsequent disenchantment with the high-seas fleet's inactivity and incompetent leadership. A segment from his diary follows.

August 2

We are anchored at Wilhelmshaven Roadstead. We are about to go on war patrol today — real war patrol. Thus I wrote in my notebook on August 2.

Two rumors circulated everywhere at the time. One of them was that America was about to dispatch two billion dollars and two squadrons to our aid and the other asserted that Japan would give us moral support by demanding compensation for the war from Russia. The future was to prove both rumors to be nonsense. We got no newspapers or information until 5:30 that evening when the Executive Officer called us together again and set our minds at ease.

"The political situation," he began, "has deteriorated to such an extent that we must count on the outbreak of a war with England. All telegraphic communication with England has been cut off since four o'clock this afternoon. You must know what that means. Furthermore an English fishing boat was discovered cruising around Helgoland this afternoon. One of our cruisers the *Danzig* ordered it to leave. The boat refused and consequently *Danzig* took her into custody. It is certainly very suspicious that this Englishman was snooping around Helgoland. Hence you know now that we are facing a war with England."

All of us breathed a sigh of relief. The very thing for which we had so long waited and hoped, the thing we had yearned for and feared, had come true. There was no doubt that the real cause was jealousy over our economic progress. Germany had grown great, strong and wealthy. The quality of German goods had deprived England of a large part of the world market. The reasons cited by the English that they wanted to protect Belgian neutrality are ridiculous. Would she also have declared war on France if it had violated the Belgian border? However I don't wish to deal with events that occurred later. At that time Germany had not yet crossed the Belgian frontier.

I should like to add one more example to indicate how great the excitement was during those first days and how totally harmless incidents gave rise to the craziest rumors and suspicions. That evening while the starboard watch was busy painting camouflage, a great commotion arose suddenly and everyone ran to the top deck. There I heard that the *Oldenburg,* which lay next to us, had just fired five shots at English submarines. Some of the men insisted that they had seen and heard the shots quite distinctly. The next morning it turned out that none of our ships had fired. Twelve miles away, however, on the island of Wangerooge, a few blank shots had been fired!

At that time there was a general panic about spies. It was alleged that here alone eighteen of them had been captured and shot. I did not believe it. Then there was also the fear of enemy aircraft. The searchlights of some of the ships and of the coastal fortresses were continually playing in the air because of aircraft reports. The next day the newspaper announced that a bomb had even been dropped on the town hall. Later on this, too, was repudiated.

That same night while we stood at battle stations, we received a wireless message that our light cruiser the *Augsburg* had bombarded the Russian naval station at Libau, set it on fire and was now engaged in battle with [Russian] cruisers.

On the following day the official *Norddeich Zeitung* published the news that the French had already crossed the border. In addition, one of their planes had bombed the main railroad track near Nuremberg. As a result, the Kaiser had declared war on France. We had expected this news. It was inevitable. The center of our interest still focused on England's attitude. Would she merely rattle her saber again and sic the others on us? The next day relieved us of these fateful doubts.

At that time I often wondered whether there were any objective reasons for England's intervention. As far as I could tell, the governments, scientists and labor leaders of both sides had tried very hard to establish friendly relations between the two countries. How long ago was it that the English war fleet was received with great honor at Kiel harbor? A few days! We were to pay them a return visit at this very time.

Bitter thoughts rise to my mind whenever I recall that the cause of it all was prob- ably envy and petty trade jealousy. But then the Kaiser had told us that they were Germans like us, of the same race and of the same blood. Blood is thicker than water. And the English? — My country right or wrong! The pursuit of Mammon has deprived that nation of its senses. Can they actually believe that they can conquer a Germany which stands united behind its Kaiser with their soldiers whom they pay ten shillings a week? Can they believe that?

It is my opinion that they do not know what they are facing. They do not know our army and navy. They probably expect a repetition of the Boer War. One can for- give the French for going to war with us, the victors of 1870. And the Russians? They are an apathetic, stupid mob who do as they are commanded. That poor shadow the Tsar may not even know that he has broken his promises. Perfidious England, however, has stabbed us in the back with premeditation! This war is actually a racial conflict of the Germanic race against the Slavs, of culture against barbarism. Many prominent English- men understood this and have said as much. . . .

. . . It was our captain, Kapitän zur See Lübbert, who told us of the English decla- ration of war on the evening of August 4. "We shall show them what it means to attack us," he cried. "Look at our wonderful ships all around. They shall all fight to the last man and so long as they remain afloat. Down with our enemies! Death and destruction to all those who break our peace. Join with me in giving three cheers to our Supreme War Lord! His Majesty the Kaiser!"

4. HUSSARS ON THE MARCH

The German fleet epitomized the technological progress of the twentieth century; the hussars, the Austro-Hungarian light cavalry, with their elegant uniforms and splendid horses, evoked the spirit of an earlier age. The high expectations with which the cavalry mobilized were eventually dampened. In this war, mounted troops could not play the glorious and flamboyant role that had been their specialty in previous con- flicts. The Austro-Hungarian army as a whole was further hampered by the enervating combination of aging leaders and linguistic barriers, given that it drew recruits from the empire's diverse ethnic groups. The following selection by a cavalry officer de- scribes the process of mobilization and the spirits of his countrymen as they prepared for war.

Budapest, August 2, 1914. A crowd gathered in the doorway at the sight of the young cavalry officer packing his baggage on the cab. Big bustling crowd at the East Terminal. Hurry — almost disorder. At last I pushed a place for myself in the corridor of one of the cars and stood there until departure.

It was heartrending when the train pulled out. The women kept pressing their inflamed eyes with crumpled handkerchiefs. A father ran after his son as we rolled slowly

Excerpt from *Hussar's Picture Book* by Pal Keleman, Indiana University, 1972, pp. 4–6.

out of the station. A woman would have fallen if she had not been supported by the stranger next her.

On the way I had to listen to all kinds of hysterical stories and was glad when we arrived that night at Kolozsvár in Transylvania. I went to the hotel where we had all the comforts, this being still Europe — if a little ruffled.

The next evening, after a long hot journey in a luggage van, I reached Szeben and reported at the barracks. They don't make much of it — told me where I was attached and did not even look at me. In the afternoon I went out to the mobilization quarters at Erfalu. I slept the night in a peasant house, just as last year during maneuvers. After lunch some of us went out in the garden to rest. The August sun was pouring over the hill and the country vibrated in the heat. All day I had been constantly feeling that I was only on maneuvers.

Received materials. Horses, saddles, harness, men. Stood around and watched how that immense supply of war material was being marched up.

Went into Szeben and purchased what I still could. Received money from the Division Command. A major made a speech about the duties of an officer in tactics, discipline, administration . . . till eleven at night. All of us were sweating and swearing, for we were many and he kept on talking. Shouted for silence. An officer near me fainted and was carried out. But the major went on speaking. Nobody listened to him any more.

It was almost midnight when we were free and looked about for supper. Nowhere was warm food obtainable. I went into a café. There I met Barta, a regiment comrade who served with me at last year's maneuvers, and slept on the sofa in his hotel room because there was not a bed to be had in the whole town. Next morning I rode over to Erfalu and spent the day there.

We were summoned in the night. Marched off to board the train. We reached the station in the dawn. All morning the wagons were loaded. An old-fashioned second-class compartment car was given us officers.

We had lunch in the railway station restaurant. At the next table a lieutenant in the regular army was sitting with his fiancée. Poor girl, she had a sweet, delicate face. They sat there in such a depressed mood, not knowing whether to try to smile or to cry openly.

The train rolled out. I did not feel anything in particular.

We proceed from station to station. Music, torches, wine, deputations, flags. Cheering: "Hurrah for the Army!" "Hurrah, Hurrah!" Women and girls are burning in exultant fever. Civilians, shamed, receive us enthusiastically. I think, "much ado about nothing."

We arrive at Delatyn in Austrian Poland. Our major awaits us. We are assigned quarters. Vas, one of my cadets, and I get quite a nice little room with a railway clerk. Like a summer cottage.

On the 18th of August, there is a banquet in honor of the birthday of Emperor Franz Josef. Civilians and the intelligentsia of the town are invited. Most of them Poles. After the first glass of wine, the flood of toasts commences and does not cease until dark. We, the young ones, drink champagne. I go straight to bed.

5. The View from St. Petersburg

Russia's troops were the first to mobilize, but the process of preparing for war was no less chaotic as a result. The following selection, by an English clergyman, represents the view of a sympathetic, if sometimes bemused, foreign observer. W. Mansell Merry, a vicar of St. Michael's in Oxford, had accepted the invitation of the English church in St. Petersburg to serve as its chaplain during July and August 1914. Anticipating a restful summer abroad, Merry found himself engulfed in the maelstrom of war with little warning.

It is a fact that the through-journey to England *via* Berlin is no longer guaranteed; it is also undeniably true that both the "suisse" and the "dvórnik" at my own lodgings have been "mobilized" for possible service — but what about all the other rumours that are busily circulating? The Baltic is mined, we hear, and full of German ships; the English fleet has sailed westward under sealed orders; the Japanese have asked to be allowed to help us "to the last ship and man," should we be drawn into hostilities; the Serbs have scored a victory over the Austrians in the first battle fought; and a German descent upon Hango is imminently expected. How much of all this is true? Unfortunately, the gentleman, from whom answers to all my questionings were to be forthcoming, is unable through pressure of business to return home for lunch, so curiosity has to go unappeased; his wife tells me that she and her husband have been at work on the telephone practically all night, with the gleaning of very little news that is definite as the result of their long and tiresome vigil. However, three facts are certain enough amid all the "mélange" of current gossip; that Russia realizes that no honourable escape is any longer open to her from the duty of championing her fellow-Slavs of Serbia against the aggressive designs of Austria, although even at this eleventh hour she is offering to stop mobilization if Vienna will acknowledge Serbian sovereignty; that, in the event of hostilities being forced upon her, the campaign will be the most popular on which she will have embarked since 1812; and that, with an almost pathetically confident positiveness, she is relying on the whole-hearted co-operation in her undertaking, not of France only — for that is a foregone conclusion — but of Great Britain as well, the traditional foe of tyrants and bullies, the defender of the down-trodden, the friend of humanity, liberty and justice. This evening my English host and I have engaged ourselves to dine with a mutual friend at his country-house at Párgolovo, a most picturesque little village of dátchas some half an hour's run from Petrograd by rail, and a very delightful and refreshing time do we spend alike in the enjoyment of the hospitalities of his comfortable bungalow, and in acquainting ourselves with the beautiful lake and woodland scenery of its surroundings. On the drive back to the station quite an exciting adventure befalls us. Our dróshky is stopped in a dark and narrow lane by a huge crowd of "demonstrators," all carrying thick sticks and singing the National Hymn at the top of voices whose huskiness is readily traceable to the last public-house! The multitude close in all round,

Excerpt from *Two Months in Russia* by W. Mansell Merry, B. Blackwell, 1916, pp. 74–76, 78–79.

and one of their number, who acts as spokesman, requests us to inform him of our nationality, enquiring, moreover, why, on our hearing the strains of the Russian Anthem, we had not straightway uncovered our heads. My comrade, who speaks Russian like a native, replies chaffingly that we have not as yet heard anything approximately resembling the patriotic melody in question. This for the moment non-plusses our interrogator, who, evidently, has but little sense of humour. But he soon returns to the charge. "If," he shouts, "you do not tell us who you are and why you have kept your hats on, we shall upset you into the mud!" It is not always wise to rely too much on the sustained good temper of a Russian mob, so now the discretion of a soft answer is obviously the better part of valour. "Listen, all of you," cries my friend, standing up in the carriage, "we are both of us Englishmen born and bred, and if you'll start that hymn of yours again, and sing it properly, we'll stop here with our hats in·our hands as long as ever you care to keep it up!" The effect of this little speech is electrical. The crowd breaks into uproarious cheering; their leader leans over and kisses again and again both the hands of the lately suspected stranger; the familiar hymn bursts out afresh — this time with considerable approach to recognisable tune — and we both join in it heartily, erect and bare-headed, until the roysterers have had their fill, and, with a final round of applause, send us galloping off into the gloom to catch our homeward train by the barest possible margin.

Friday, July 31st

. . . All sorts of rumours reach us towards evening; that an English squadron is occupying the Belt; that twenty-nine Dreadnoughts are "hanging on to the tail" of the German fleet; that Germany and Austria are already anxious to make peace; with many other exciting and amusing "canards" of a similar breed. The weather has cleared towards sunset, and as we sit on deck, enjoying an after-dinner smoke, the broad, cobble-paved roadway that runs alongside down to the port is thronged and noisy with the tramp of ceaseless streams of reservists, naval and military; rarely, marching to the blaring, lilting strains of a brass band; more generally, trudging along, bundle on back or in hand, in sullen silence; the women-folk, many of them weeping as if their hearts would break, breathlessly struggling to keep pace with husbands, brothers, sons or lovers on either side, as company after company swings past. "For two days past these sturdy sons of the soil have been collecting at their various depôts; some dazedly, ignorant of whys and wherefores, recognizing necessity perforce, and wondering why they should leave their farms so soon before harvest; others have deserted their burnt-up lands with a shrug — in many districts there will be no harvest in any case — and they bear the new caprice of fate with indifference. Shaggy, uncouth peasants, they herd sheepishly into the appointed rendezvous, and are there transformed into genial, swaggering soldiers, a little shy, perhaps, of their trim appearance, easily abashed by personal remarks, but restored to the verge of boastfulness by a hint as to the prowess they will doubtless exhibit against the Germans."

It seems that some gigantic hand
  Behind the veils of sky
Was driving, herding all these men
Like cattle into a cattle-pen;
So few of them can understand,
  So many of them must die.

                              A. Noyes

The swiftness and completeness of this feature of the Russian mobilization is, considering the enormous difficulties of transport, little short of a miracle.

6. BRITAIN'S DESTINY AND DUTY

In the various combatant nations, intellectuals came forward to explain that their particular nation's cause was just. The governments involved were only too happy to have the weight of learning and prestige thrown behind their efforts to stimulate war enthusiasm. *The Times* (of London) published the famous letter that follows, signed by fifty-two British men of letters. The signatories include well-known British literary figures such as J. M. Barrie (author of *Peter Pan*), Arnold Bennett, G. K. Chesterton, Sir Arthur Conan Doyle, John Galsworthy, Thomas Hardy, Rudyard Kipling, and H. G. Wells.

The undersigned writers, comprising amongst them men and women of the most divergent political and social views, some of them having been for years ardent champions of good will towards Germany, and many of them extreme advocates of peace, are nevertheless agreed that Great Britain could not without dishonour have refused to take part in the present war.

No one can read the full diplomatic correspondence published in the White Paper without seeing that the British representatives were throughout labouring wholeheartedly to preserve the peace of Europe, and that their conciliatory efforts were cordially received by both France and Russia.

With these efforts failed, Great Britain had still no direct quarrel with any Power. She was eventually compelled to take up arms because, together with France, Germany, and Austria, she had solemnly pledged herself to maintain the neutrality of Belgium. As soon as danger to that neutrality arose she questioned both France and Germany as to their intentions. France immediately renewed her pledge not to violate Belgian neutrality; Germany refused to answer, and soon made all answer needless by her actions. Without even the pretense of a grievance against Belgium, she made war on the weak and unoffending country she had undertaken to protect, and has since carried out her

From *The Times*, 18 Sept. 1914.

invasion with a calculated and ingenious ferocity which has raised questions other and no less grave than that of the wilful disregard of treaties.

When Belgium in her dire need appealed to Great Britain to carry out her pledge, this country's course was clear. She had either to break faith, letting the sanctity of treaties and the rights of small nations count for nothing before the naked force, or she had to fight. She did not hesitate, and we trust she will not lay down arms till Belgium's integrity is restored and her wrongs redressed.

The treaty with Belgium made our duty clear, but many of us feel that, even if Belgium had not been involved, it would have been impossible for Great Britain to stand aside while France was dragged into war and destroyed. To permit the ruin of France would be a crime against liberty and civilization. Even those of us who question the wisdom of a policy of Continental Ententes or Alliances refuse to see France struck down by a foul blow dealt in violation of a treaty.

We observe that various German apologists, official and semi-official, admit that their country has been false to its pledged word, and dwell almost with pride on the "frightfulness" of the examples by which it has sought to spread terror in Belgium, but they excuse all these proceedings by a strange and novel plea. German culture and civilization are so superior to those of other nations that all steps taken to assert them are more than justified; and the destiny of Germany to be the dominating force in Europe and the world is so manifest that ordinary rules of morality do not hold in her case, but actions are good or bad simply as they help or hinder the accomplishment of that destiny.

These views, inculcated upon the present generation of Germans by many celebrated historians and teachers, seem to us both dangerous and insane. Many of us have dear friends in Germany, many of us regard German culture with the highest respect and gratitude; but we cannot admit that any nation has the right by brute force to impose its culture upon other nations, nor that the iron military bureaucracy of Prussia represents a higher form of human society than the free constitutions of Western Europe.

Whatever the world-destiny of Germany may be, we in Great Britain are ourselves conscious of a destiny and a duty. The destiny and duty, alike for us and for all the English-speaking race, call upon us to uphold the rule of common justice of small nations, and to maintain the free and law abiding ideals of Western Europe against the rule of "Blood and Iron" and the domination of the whole Continent by a military caste.

For these reasons and others the undersigned feel bound to support the cause of the Allies with all their strength, with a full conviction of its righteousness, and with a deep sense of its vital import to the future of the world.

7. MANIFESTO OF GERMAN UNIVERSITY PROFESSORS

The nearly universal condemnation of Germany's violation of Belgian neutrality and widespread allegations of the German army's brutality and atrocities in its invasion prompted Germans to respond to restore their nation's honor. Among the ninety-three professors and scientists who signed the defense that follows of Germany's justifiable behavior were the Nobel Prize–winning chemist Fritz Haber, the prominent physicist Walter Nernst, and the economist Gustav von Schmoller.

To the Civilized World!

As representatives of German Science and Art, we hereby protest to the civilized world, against the lies and calumnies with which our enemies are endeavouring to stain the honour of Germany in her hard struggle for existence — in a struggle which has been forced upon her.

The iron mouth of events has proved the untruth of the fictitious German defeats, consequently misrepresentation and calumny are all the more eagerly at work. As heralds of truth we raise our voices against these.

It is not true that Germany is guilty of having caused this war. Neither the people, the Government, nor the "Kaiser" wanted war. Germany did her utmost to prevent it; for this assertion the world has documentary proof. Often enough during the 26 years of his reign has Wilhelm II shown himself to be the upholder of peace, and often enough has this fact been acknowledged by our opponents. Nay, even the "Kaiser," whom they now dare to call an Attila, has been ridiculed by them for years, because of his steadfast endeavours to maintain universal peace. Not till a numerical superiority which had been lying in wait on the frontiers, assailed us, did the whole nation rise to a man.

It is not true that we trespassed in neutral Belgium. It has been proved that France and England had resolved on such a trespass, and it has likewise been proved that Belgium had agreed to their doing so. It would have been suicide on our part not to have been beforehand.

It is not true that the life and property of a single Belgian citizen was injured by our soldiers without the bitterest self-defense having made it necessary; for again, and again, notwithstanding repeated threats, the citizens lay in ambush, shooting at the troops out of the houses, mutilating the wounded, and murdering in cold blood the medical men while they were doing their Samaritan work. There can be no baser abuse than the suppression of these crimes with the view of letting the Germans appear to be criminals, only for having justly punished these assassins for their wicked deeds.

It is not true that our troops treated Louvain brutally. Furious inhabitants having treacherously fallen upon them in their quarters, our troops with aching hearts, were obliged to fire a part of the town, as a punishment. The greatest part of Louvain has been preserved. The famous Town Hall stands quite intact; for at great self-sacrifice our soldiers saved it from destruction by the flames. Every German would of course greatly regret, if in the course of this terrible war any works of art should already have been destroyed or be destroyed at some future time, but inasmuch as in our love for art we cannot be surpassed by any other nation, in the same degree we must decidedly refuse to buy a German defeat at the cost of saving a work of art.

It is not true that our warfare pays no respect to international laws. It knows no undisciplined cruelty. But in the east, the earth is saturated with the blood of women and children unmercifully butchered by the wild Russian troops, and in the west, dum-dum bullets mutilate the breasts of our soldiers. Those who have allied themselves with Russians and Serbians, and present such a shameful scene to the world as that of inciting Mongolians and Negroes against the white race, have no right whatever to call themselves upholders of civilization.

It is not true that the combat against our so-called militarism is not a combat against our civilization, as our enemies hypocritically pretend it is. Were it not for German militarism, German civilization would long since have been extirpated. For its protection it arose in a land which for centuries had been plagued by bands of robbers, as no other land had been. The German army and the German people are one, and to-day, this consciousness fraternizes 70 millions of Germans, all ranks, positions and parties being one.

We cannot wrest the poisonous weapon — the lie — out of the hands of our enemies. All we can do is to proclaim to all the world, that our enemies are giving false witness against us. You, who know us, who with us have protected the most holy possessions of man, we call to you:

Have faith in us! Believe, that we shall carry on this war to the end as a civilized nation, to whom the legacy of a Goethe, a Beethoven, and a Kant, is just as sacred as its own hearths and homes.

For this we pledge you our names and our honour.

8. GERMAN SOCIALISTS SUPPORT THE WAR

When Kaiser Wilhelm II announced, early in August 1914, that he no longer recognized parties, only Germans, he was responding in part to the Socialist party's* willingness — despite fears and socialist orthodoxy to the contrary — to support the war. The following reading illustrates the German socialists' interpretation of a defensive war. Contrast it with the stance of the Second International — the worldwide socialist forum — reprinted at the end of this section. The symbol of the SPD's readiness to support the war was its acceptance of the financial measures necessary to fund the war effort, the so-called war credits voted by the German legislature.

---

* Known by its German initials as the SPD.

In today's session of the Reichstag the Social-Democratic "Fraktion" voted the war credits demanded by the Government. At the same time it outlined its position as follows:

We are face to face with destiny. The result of the imperialistic policy which introduced an era of competitive preparation for war and roused the antagonistic elements in the different nations is breaking over Europe like a tidal wave. The responsibility for this disaster rests upon the supporters of the imperialistic policy which we reject.

Social-Democracy has always done all in its power to fight this disastrous development, and up to the last moment has worked for the maintenance of peace by strong demonstrations in all countries, especially in close co-operation with our French comrades. Its efforts have been in vain.

Now we face the inexorable fact of war. We are threatened by the horror of hostile invasion. Today it is not for us to decide for or against war but to consider the means necessary for the defense of our country.

We must now think of the millions of fellow-countrymen who are drawn into this disaster without any fault of their own. It is they who suffer most from the horrors of war. Our warmest wishes go with all those, irrespective of party, who have been called to arms.

But we are thinking also of the mothers who must give up their sons, of the women and children who are deprived of the husband and father who supported them. For them the fear for their loved ones is mingled with the dread of need and of actual hunger. And this army of women and children will soon be joined by tens of thousands of wounded and crippled soldiers.

To help all of them, to lighten their lot, to ease their suffering, this we consider our urgent duty.

Everything is at stake for our nation and its development toward liberty in the future if Russian despotism stained with the best blood of its own people should be victorious.

It is our duty to ward off this danger, to protect the civilization *(Kultur)* and independence of our own country. Thus we carry out what we have always emphasized: In the hour of danger we shall not desert the Fatherland. In saying this we feel ourselves in accord with the International which has always recognized the right of every nation to national independence and self-defense, just as we agree with it in condemning any war of aggression or conquest.

We hope that the cruel experience of suffering in this war will awaken in many millions of people the abhorrence of war and will win them for the ideals of socialism and world peace.

We demand that as soon as the aim of security has been achieved and our opponents

Reprinted from *Fall of the German Empire, 1914–1918,* Vol. II, edited by Ralph Haswell Lutz, pp. 6–7, with the permission of the publishers, Stanford University Press. Copyright © 1932 by the Board of Trustees of the Leland Stanford Junior University.

are disposed to make peace this war shall be brought to an end by a treaty of peace which makes friendship possible with our neighbors. We ask this not only in the interest of national solidarity for which we have always contended but also in the interest of the German people.

With these principles in mind we vote the desired war credits.

9. "CHANT OF HATE"

Ernst Lissauer's famous "Chant of Hate," applauded by no less than Kaiser Wilhelm II, is a classic example of the frenzy with which many circles greeted the war. Lissauer, a German Jewish writer, volunteered for service but was rejected on the grounds of health. Eager to contribute in some way, and perhaps to find acceptance too, Lissauer, convinced that England was to blame for the outbreak of war, composed this denunciation of Germany's arch rival.

> French and Russians, they matter not,
> A blow for a blow and a shot for a shot;
> We love them not, we hate them not,
> We hold the Weichsel[1] and Vosges gate.
> We have but one and only hate,
> We love as one, we hate as one,
> We have one foe and one alone.
>
> He is known to you all, he is known to you all.
> He crouches behind the dark gray flood,
> Full of envy, of rage, of craft, of gall,
> Cut off by waves that are thicker than blood.
> Come let us stand at the judgment-place,
> An oath to swear to, face to face,
> An oath of bronze no wind can shake,
> An oath for our sons and their sons to take.
>
> Come, hear the word, repeat the word,
> Throughout the Fatherland make it heard.
> We will never forego our hate,
> We have all but a single hate,
> We love as one, we hate as one,
> We have one foe and one alone —
>   ENGLAND!

"Chant of Hate" by Ernst Lissauer, *The Times*, 14 Nov. 1914.

---

[1] The German name for the Vistula River.

In the captain's mess, in the banquet-hall,
Sat feasting the officers, one and all;
Like a saber-blow, like the wing of a sail,
One seized his glass held high to hail;
Sharp-snapt like the stroke of a rudder's play,
Spoke three words only: "To the Day!"

Whose glass this fate?
They had all but a single hate.
Who was thus known?
They had one foe and one alone —
        ENGLAND!

Take you the folk of the earth in pay,
With bars of gold your ramparts lay,
Bedecked the ocean with bow on bow,
Ye reckon well, but not well enough now.
French and Russian they matter not,
A blow for a blow, a shot for a shot,
We fight the battle with bronze and steel.
And the time that is coming Peace will seal.
You will we hate with a lasting hate,
We will never forego our hate,
Hate by water and hate by land,
Hate of the head and hate of the hand,
Hate of the hammer and hate of the crown,
Hate of seventy millions, choking down.
We love as one, we hate as one.
We have one foe and one alone —
        ENGLAND!

10. "THE BEGINNINGS"

Rudyard Kipling was born in 1865 into a family of Methodist ministers. He rapidly displayed an aptitude for journalism and literature, as well as an abiding interest in the British Empire. Spending considerable time in India, he achieved international prominence with his stories and accounts of the vast subcontinent. When war broke out, he was an ardent supporter of British participation, and he unhesitatingly placed his pen at the disposal of the war effort. His poem "The Beginnings" was a response to Ernst Lissauer's "Chant of Hate."

It was not part of their blood,
It came to them very late
With long arrears to make good,
When the English began to hate.

They were not easily moved,
They were icy willing to wait
Till every count should be proved,
Ere the English began to hate.

Their voices were even and low,
Their eyes were level and straight.
There was neither sign nor show,
When the English began to hate.

It was not preached to the crowd,
It was not taught by the State.
No man spoke it aloud,
When the English began to hate.

It was not suddenly bred,
It will not swiftly abate,
Through the chill years ahead,
When Time shall count from the date
That the English began to hate.

11. COMMON SENSE ABOUT THE WAR

George Bernard Shaw was born in genteel poverty in 1856 in Dublin, Ireland. During his prolific career, he established himself as one of the most brilliant and witty authors of his time. And upon his death in 1950, even Broadway dimmed its lights as a show of respect to the remarkable playwright. The following selection, which demonstrates Shaw's devastating sarcasm and keen insight, was greeted by many contemporaries with dismay.

The time has now come to pluck up courage and begin to talk and write soberly about the war. At first the mere horror of it stunned the more thoughtful of us; and even now only those who are not in actual contact with or bereaved relation to its heartbreaking wreckage can think sanely about it, or endure to hear others discuss it coolly. As to the thoughtless, well, not for a moment dare I suggest that for the first few weeks they were all scared out of their wits; for I know too well that the British civilian does not allow his perfect courage to be questioned: only experienced soldiers and foreigners are al-

(10) "The Beginnings" by Rudyard Kipling, 1914.

(11) From "Common Sense about the War" by George Bernard Shaw, *New York Times,* 15 Nov. 1914.

lowed the infirmity of fear. But they certainly were — shall I say a little upset? They felt in that solemn hour that England was lost if only one single traitor in their midst let slip the truth about anything in the universe. It was a perilous time for me. I do not hold my tongue easily; and my inborn dramatic faculty and professional habit as a playwright prevent me from taking a one-sided view even when the most probable result of taking a many-sided one is prompt lynching. Besides, until Home Rule emerges from its present suspended animation, I shall retain my Irish capacity for criticizing England with something of the detachment of a foreigner, and perhaps with a certain slightly malicious taste for taking the conceit out of her. Lord Kitchener made a mistake the other day in rebuking the Irish volunteers for not rallying faster to the defence of "their country." They do not regard it as their country yet. He should have asked them to come forward as usual and help poor old England through a stiff fight. Then it would have been all right.

Having thus frankly confessed my bias, which you can allow for as a rifleman allows for the wind, I give my views for what they are worth. They will be of some use; because, however blinded I may be by prejudice or perversity, my prejudices in this matter are not those which blind the British patriot, and therefore I am fairly sure to see some things that have not yet struck him.

And first, I do not see this war as one which has welded Governments and peoples into complete and sympathetic solidarity as against the common enemy. I see the people of England united in a fierce detestation and defiance of the views and acts of Prussian Junkerism. And I see the German people stirred to the depths by a similar antipathy to English Junkerism, and anger at the apparent treachery and duplicity of the attack made on them by us in their extremest peril from France and Russia. . . . And I see the Junkers and Militarists of England and Germany jumping at the chance they have longed for in vain for many years of smashing one another and establishing their own oligarchy as the dominant military power in the world. No doubt the heroic remedy for this tragic misunderstanding is that both armies should shoot their officers and go home to gather in their harvests in the villages and make a revolution in the towns; and though this is not at present a practicable solution, it must be frankly mentioned, because it or something like it is always a possibility in a defeated conscript army if its commanders push it beyond human endurance when its eyes are opening to the fact that in murdering its neighbours it is biting off its nose to vex its face, besides riveting the intolerable yoke of Militarism and Junkerism more tightly than ever on its own neck. But there is no chance — or, as our Junkers would put it, no danger — of our soldiers yielding to such an ecstasy of common sense. They have enlisted voluntarily; they are not defeated nor likely to be; their communications are intact and their meals are reasonably punctual; they are as pugnacious as their officers: and in fighting Prussia they are fighting a more deliberate, conscious, tyrannical, personally insolent, and dangerous Militarism than their own. Still, even for a voluntary professional army, that possibility exists, just as for the civilian there is a limit beyond which taxation, bankruptcy, privation, terror, and inconvenience cannot be pushed without revolution or a social dissolution more ruinous than submission to conquest. . . .

But let me test the Militarist theory, not by a hypothetical future, but by the accomplished and irrevocable past. Is it true that nations must conquer or go under, and that military conquest means prosperity and power for the victor and annihilation for the vanquished? I have already alluded in passing to the fact that Austria has been beaten repeatedly: by France, by Italy, by Germany, almost by everybody who has thought it worth while to have a whack at her; and yet she is one of the Great Powers; and her alliance has been sought by invincible Germany. France was beaten by Germany in 1870 with a completeness that seemed impossible; yet France has since enlarged her territory whilst Germany is still pleading in vain for a place in the sun. Russia was beaten by the Japanese in Manchuria on a scale that made an end forever of the old notion that the West is the natural military superior of the East; yet it is the terror of Russia that has driven Germany into her present desperate onslaught on France; and it is the Russian alliance on which France and England are depending for their assurance of ultimate success. We ourselves confess that the military efficiency with which we have so astonished the Germans is the effect, not of Waterloo and Inkerman, but of the drubbing we got from the Boers, who would probably have beaten us if we had been anything like their own size. . . .

In short, Militarism must be classed as one of the most inconsiderately foolish of the bogus "sciences" which the last half century has produced in such profusion, and which have the common characteristic of revolting all sane souls, and being stared out of countenance by the broad facts of human experience. The only rule of thumb that can be hazarded on the strength of actual practice is that wars to maintain or upset the Balance of Power between States, called by inaccurate people Balance of Power wars, and by accurate people Jealousy of Power wars, never establish the desired peaceful and secure equilibrium. They may exercise pugnacity, gratify spite, assuage a wound to national pride; or enhance or dim a military reputation; but that is all. . . .

Now that we begin to see where we really are, what practical morals can we draw?

First, that our autocratic foreign policy, in which the Secretary for Foreign Affairs is always a Junker, and makes war and concludes war without consulting the nation, or confiding in it, or even refraining from deceiving it as to his intentions, leads inevitably to a disastrous combination of war and unpreparedness for war. Wars are planned which require huge expeditionary armies trained and equipped for war. But as such preparation could not be concealed from the public, it is simply deferred until the war is actually declared and begun, at the most frightful risk of such an annihilation of our little peace army as we escaped by the skin of our teeth at Mons and Cambrai. The military experts tell us that it takes four months to make an infantry and six to make a cavalry soldier. And our way of getting an army able to fight the German army is to declare war on Germany just as if we had such an army, and then trust to the appalling resultant peril and disaster to drive us into wholesale enlistment, voluntary or (better still from the Junker point of view) compulsory. It seems to me that a nation which tolerates such insensate methods and outrageous risks must shortly perish from sheer lunacy. And it is all pure superstition: the retaining of the methods of Edward the First in the reign of George the Fifth. I therefore suggest that the first lesson of the war is that the Secretary of State for Foreign Affairs be reduced to the level of a simple Prime Minister, or even of a constitutional monarch, powerless to fire a single shot or sign a treaty without the authority of the House of Commons, all diplomatic business being conducted in a blaze of publicity, and the present regulation which exacts the qualification of a private income of at least £400 a year for a position in the Diplomatic Service replaced by a new regulation that at least half the staff shall consist of persons who have never dined out at the houses of hosts of higher rank than unfashionable solicitors or doctors.

In these recommendations I am not forgetting that an effective check on diplomacy is not easy to devize, and that high personal character and class disinterestedness (the latter at present unattainable) on the part of our diplomatists will be as vital as ever. I well know that diplomacy is carried on at present not only by official correspondence meant for possible publication and subject to an inspection which is in some degree a responsible inspection, but by private letters which the King himself has no right to read. I know that even in the United States, where treaties and declarations of war must be made by Parliament, it is nevertheless possible for the President to bring about a situation in which Congress, like our House of Commons in the present instance, has no alternative but to declare war. But though complete security is impracticable, it does not follow that no precautions should be taken, or that a democratic tradition is no safer than a feudal tradition. A far graver doubt is raised by the susceptibility of the masses to war fever, and the appalling danger of a daily deluge of cheap newspapers written by nameless men and women whose scandalously low payment is a guarantee of their ignorance and their servility to the financial department, controlled by a moneyed class which not only curries favour with the military caste for social reasons, but has large direct interests in war as a method of raising the price of money, the only commodity the moneyed class has to sell. But I am quite unable to see that our Junkers are less susceptible to the influence of the Press than the people educated by public elementary schools. On the contrary, our Democrats are more foolproof than our Plutocrats; and the ravings our Junkers send to the papers for nothing in war time would be dear at a halfpenny a line. Plutocracy makes for war because it offers prizes to Plutocrats: Socialism makes for peace because the interests it serves are international. So, as the Socialist side is the democratic side, we had better democratize our diplomacy if we desire peace.

12. THE SOCIALIST ALTERNATIVE

The Second International — an attempt to provide an organizational basis for cooperation among the various socialist parties throughout Europe — frequently discussed how it might respond to a general European conflict. At its congress in Stuttgart in August 1907, the International adopted the following policy on militarism and international conflict.

Wars between capitalist states, generally, result from their competitive struggle for world markets, for each state strives not only to assure for itself the markets it already possesses,

"On Militarism and International Conflict," pp. 57–59. Reprinted from *The Bolsheviks and the World War: The Origin of the Third International* by Olga Hess Gankin and H. H. Fisher, Stanford University Press, 1940.

but also to conquer new ones; in this the subjugation of foreign peoples and countries comes to play a leading role. Furthermore, these wars are caused by the incessant competition in armaments that characterizes militarism, the chief instrument of bourgeois class rule and of the economic and political subjugation of the working class.

Wars are promoted by national prejudices which are systematically cultivated among civilized peoples in the interest of the ruling classes for the purpose of diverting the proletarian masses from their own class problems as well as from their duties of international class solidarity.

Hence wars are part of the very nature of capitalism; they will cease only when the capitalist economic order is abolished or when the number of sacrifices in men and money, required by the advance in military technique, and the indignation provoked by armaments drive the peoples to abolish this order.

For this reason, the working class, which provides most of the soldiers and makes most of the material sacrifices, is a natural opponent of war, for war contradicts its aim — the creation of an economic order on a socialist basis for the purpose of bringing about the solidarity of all peoples. . . .

If a war threatens to break out, it is the duty of the working class and of its parliamentary representatives in the countries involved, supported by the consolidating activity of the International [Socialist] Bureau, to exert every effort to prevent the outbreak of war by means they consider most effective, which naturally vary according to the accentuation of the class struggle and of the general political situation.

Should war break out none the less, it is their duty to intervene in favor of its speedy termination and to do all in their power to utilize the economic and political crisis caused by the war to rouse the peoples and thereby to hasten the abolition of capitalist class rule.

B. Accommodation to Military Service

1. To Give One's Life
for the Fatherland

Ludwig Frank, born in Baden in 1874, was a Jewish lawyer and member of the German Reichstag for the Social Democratic party. At the age of forty, he enlisted in the army, forgoing his right to an exemption as a member of the Reichstag. Frank's willingness to defend the Fatherland underscores his party's commitment in August 1914 to assist Germany in its war efforts. Frank did not survive the conflict, succumbing to French bullets in early September 1914. The following selection, drawn from one of his letters, provides an example of his personal sense of patriotism.

Mannheim, 23 August 1914

I spend my free Sunday afternoon at the desk of my quarters. I am billeted in the barracks and sleep on my hard camp bed . . . undisturbed from 10 P.M. until 5 A.M. and some mornings until 4 A.M. The bugler wakes me. Effortlessly, I endure the toil of field duty and the marches. I am pleased about that: to give one's life for the Fatherland is not onerous, and is surrounded with romanticism and heroism. It is a far greater sacrifice to sweat under the weight of the knapsack and to renounce . . . cleanliness and comfort, once taken for granted, but which now one recalls like a distant, beautiful land. But the body is really the servant of the soul. Distractions [are avoided] by maintaining a fixed purpose and not losing sight of the larger goal. . . . I serve at the front like everyone else; I am treated by all (enlisted men and officers alike) with great respect (ostentatiously put: with deference). But I doubt if French bullets will also respect my parliamentary immunity. I long passionately to survive the war and then to work toward the rebuilding of the Empire. But for now the only possible place for me is in the line, in the rank and file, and I, like all the others, go happily and certain of victory. . . . When eleven years ago I publicly confessed [my membership in] the Social Democratic party, . . . I surely destroyed the hopes of my good parents — but I had to live my own life, and now more is at stake.

2. WAR LETTER FROM FRANCE

Letter writing served a dual function: placing the serviceman in touch with his own emotions as well as with loved ones at home. Furthermore, it enabled him to escape, if only fleetingly, the ennui of life in the trench or at sea. The following letter, written by a young French recruit at the front during the early campaigns, expresses a broad spectrum of heartfelt emotions and testifies to the high expectations that soldiers held as they entered the war.

The Boches came to visit us, bringing a convoy of wagons to take away the food which we were expected to leave behind us on our retreat; the food that they took away in those same wagons consisted of corpses cut to pieces by our "seventy-fives." A week later to the day we returned their visit. But they failed to duplicate our politeness. They didn't send us back home. Truly their *Kultur* still lacks something in refinement. . . .

   The day before yesterday they did us the honor of sending us an official communication. We had been in a fight, had seen loaded ambulances going to the rear, had

(1) Excerpt from *Kriegsbriefe gefallener deutscher Juden*, trans. by Marilyn Shevin-Coetzee, Bund jüdischer Soldaten, 1935, pp. 20–21.

(2) Excerpt from *War Letters from France*, A. de LaPradelle and Frederic Coudert, eds., B. Appleton, 1916, pp. 18–19.

crossed woods filled with corpses and passed ravaged farms; and we said to each other, "What a battle it has been!" No wonder we were somewhat astonished to read in our official communication, "Situation unchanged in the Lorraine and in the Vosges."

On Thursday the Boches stirred a bit. They came to see what we were doing. We taught them the *pas de quatre* and we played them a pretty tune for it. They learned their lesson quickly. Two hundred of them were left on the field. It was not much and yet the official report simply announced: "The Germans attacked our outposts between Blamont and Baccarate, and their attack was completely stopped." In reality they were thrown violently back on Blamont.

3. GERMAN STUDENTS' WAR LETTERS

These letters are from a collection originally selected and published by Professor Witkop of Freiburg, who culled them from some twenty thousand letters of fallen German soldiers to their relatives and friends. It was Witkop's hope that the letters would remind civilians of the soldiers' sacrifice and reveal the idealistic and ethical concerns of young German recruits, in contrast to their prevailing image abroad as rapacious barbarians and unfeeling automatons.

a. *Franz Blumenfeld*

Student of Law, Freiburg i. Br.
Born September 26th, 1891, at Hamburg.
Killed December 18th, 1914, near Contalmaison.

Freiburg, August 1st, 1914

. . . If there is mobilization now, I must join up, and I would rather do so here, where there would be a chance of going to the Front quite soon, than in Travemünde, Hamburg or Bahrenfeld, where we should probably be used only to defend the Kiel Canal. And I can't think of anything more hateful than to be forced to sit at home doing nothing when there is war and fighting out there.

You must not imagine that I write this in a fit of war-fever; on the contrary, I am quite calm and am absolutely unable to share the enthusiasm with which some people here are longing to go to war. I can't yet believe that that will happen. It seems to me impossible, and I feel sure that things will go no further than mobilization. But if it does start then you will understand that I can't stop anywhere here. I know too that you are

Excerpt from *German Students' War Letters*, A. F. Wedd, ed., Methuen London, 1929, pp. 17–21.

a dear, good, sensible little Mother, and would not wish that your sons should show cowardice in the face of great danger and stay prudently behind.

September 23rd, 1914 (in the train, going north)

. . . At the moment we are sitting in the train. Where we are going we are not told, but we take for granted that it is to Belgium. We are supposed to be in for a thirty hours' journey. Now we are north of Trèves, I think in the Eifel, in most beautiful country. The sun is shining too and everything looks so peaceful. The contrast to the desolation in Lorraine, with all the military activity and the incessant rain, is incredible. But even yet one can't realize the war in earnest, and I keep catching myself simply enjoying all the novel impressions.

You can't imagine the purely artistic, marvellous fascination of this constantly changing, unaccustomed picture. Last night, for instance, the scene round a big table in the living-room of a peasant's house in Lorraine: infantry and artillery all mixed up together in the wildest confusion, one in a helmet, another with his cap on the back of his head or half over his face, all more or less unshaved, smoking, eating, and sleeping. Round the walls one or two more; others sitting on the floor asleep. And in the midst of all this, two old peasant women busy cooking a little soup and making coffee, poor and humble and delighted with the few coppers which they afterwards got from the soldiers for all their trouble. I learn more about the people like this than from all my lectures and touring-companies.

In the train, September 24th, 1914

My dear, good, precious Mother, I certainly believe and hope that I shall come back from the war, but just in case I do not I am going to write you a farewell letter. I want you to know that if I am killed, I give my life gladly and willingly. My life has been so beautiful that I could not wish that anything in it had been different. And its having been so beautiful was thanks above all to you, my dear, good, best of Mothers. And for all your love, for all that you have done for me, for everything, everything, I want to thank you and thank you. Really you can have no idea how keenly I have realized just lately how right you were in your way of bringing me up — I was not entirely convinced of the wisdom of some things before, for instance as regards the importance of physical training — how absolutely right and good.

But not only for the way in which you brought me up do I thank you, but for everything, everything — for the life you gave me, and above all for being just what you are. Oh, but you know, without this letter, and much better than I can write it, how I feel.

Then I want to write to you about something else, which, judging from bits in your letters, you haven't quite understood: why I should have volunteered for the war? Of course it was not from any enthusiasm for war in general, nor because I thought it would be a fine thing to kill a great many people or otherwise distinguish myself. On the contrary, I think that war is a very, very evil thing, and I believe that even in this case it might have been averted by a more skilful diplomacy. But, now that it has been declared, I think it is a matter of course that one should feel oneself so much a member of the nation that one must unite one's fate as closely as possible with that of the whole. And even if I were convinced that I could serve my Fatherland and its people better in peace than in war, I should think it just as perverse and impossible to let any such calculations weigh with me at the present moment as it would be for a man going to the assistance of somebody who was drowning, to stop to consider who the drowning man was and whether his own life were not perhaps the more valuable of the two. For what counts is always the readiness to make a sacrifice, not the object for which the sacrifice is made.

This war seems to me, from all that I have heard, to be something so horrible, inhuman, mad, obsolete, and in every way depraving, that I have firmly resolved, if I do come back, to do everything in my power to prevent such a thing from ever happening again in the future. . . .

October 14th, 1914 (in Northern France)

. . . One thing weighs upon me more from day to day — the fear of getting brutalized. Your wishing you could provide me with a bullet-proof net is very sweet of you, but strange to say I have no fear, none at all, of bullets and shells, but only of this great spiritual loneliness. I am afraid of losing my faith in human nature, in myself, in all that is good in the world! Oh, that is horrible! Much, much harder to bear than being out-of-doors in all weathers, having to get one's own food, sleeping in a hay-loft — I don't mind any of those things. It is much harder for me to endure the incredibly coarse tone that prevails among the men here.

The sight of the slightly and dangerously wounded, the dead men and horses lying about, hurts, of course, but the pain of all that is not nearly so keen or lasting as one imagined it would be. Of course that is partly due to the fact that one knows one can't do anything to prevent it. But may it not at the same time be a beginning of a deplorable callousness, almost barbarity, or how is it possible that it gives me more pain to bear my own loneliness than to witness the sufferings of so many others? Can you understand what I mean? What is the good of escaping all the bullets and shells, if my soul is injured? That is how they would have expressed it in old days. . . .

b. *Herbert Weisser*

Student of Architecture, Charlottesburg
Born May 6th, 1894, at Lissa.
Killed May 25th, 1915, before Ypres.

September 27th, 1914

This longing for productivity after having been for twenty years merely receptive, makes it hard for me to think that my life is no longer my own. Whatever I may do in the war cannot be called production. . . . But, on the other hand, one cannot stand by and see the German people and all that they have created during hundreds of years destroyed by other nations. The only lightning-conductor is burning hatred and contempt for those few men — if they can still possibly be described by that name — who have brought the war about. Those people are lucky who can hold the enemy's whole nation responsible and believe that they are aiming their rifles at the actual culprits. I personally cannot feel any hatred against individual Frenchmen — on the contrary, I regret every young life which will be cut off through my instrumentality. Also I cannot rejoice unreservedly in our victories; but do you know what I do thoroughly and boundlessly rejoice in? In the German character, which now has an opportunity of exhibiting itself in shining splendour; in the faultless functioning of the gigantic machine to which each individual can and does contribute; in the discipline shown by our troops in their treatment of the inhabitants of enemy country; in the eagerness with which each one works for the general good; and in the firm, unshakable sense of justice which is displayed on the German side on every occasion. The great strength of our noble people does not lie in wielding the sword, but in its sense of the high responsibility of making the best use of its gifts, and in its inner worth as the people of culture. Other nations can tear down and destroy in war, but we understand, better than any other, how to build up, and of this I have been certain only since the beginning of the war. Therefore I do not trouble much as to whether the war has a positive or negative end for us.

March 7th, 1915

. . . Soon after our meeting at M. station, you wrote me a postcard in which you said that you tried to remove my "pessimistic view" of the war. At the end you added that you had perhaps misunderstood the reason of my low spirits. And really — I will make an attempt to explain at least one thing: in 1870 the soldiers went into battle saying to themselves: "If we don't get home we get heaven" (I have to express myself briefly). Very few take that view now; a great many don't consider the question at all; others do, and then it depends on what sort of a religion they have worked out for themselves whether it is easier or harder for them to give up their young lives. Many abandon all claim on a future life after death — I am too young for that, and I did hope to survive in what I had created, and above all in the influence which I had exercised on the younger generation, in whom I should see realized all the results of my experience.

Excerpt from *German Students' War Letters*, A. F. Wedd, ed., Methuen London, 1929, pp. 107–110.

Some men say: "I am married and the father of five children, therefore I make a particularly great sacrifice for the Fatherland." In their place I should say: "Thank God that I have a wife who has loved me and whom I have loved, and still more that I have five children who will continue to develop in accordance with my ideas and will justify my existence. Otherwise my position would have been merely receptive and would only have influenced my own and perhaps the previous generation — even the former very imperfectly." That was what depressed me, personally.

Then came the objective view: our nation was, as I believe, on the right road towards self-regeneration from within, though the powers which were to bring about this regeneration were very limited. Now comes the war, tears everything out of the process of being and developing, and deprives us of just what we most needed — the youth of the present generation, who were growing up with progressive ideas.

I also imagined beforehand, what I now find abundantly confirmed: that the notions which our parents, our books and our history lessons had given us of war are either entirely false, or at least incomplete and therefore misleading. We were given to understand that heroic deeds were of the essence and the most frequent result of war. But is that so? How many such actions are in any case simply brought about by the impulse of the moment, perhaps by the bloodthirstiness and unjust hatred which a nation's political views spread among all its members and for which they have to suffer?

4. A British Student in Arms

Donald Hankey, an English author whose collected letters and essays were reprinted after his death under the title *A Student in Arms,* was the son of the highly influential secretary to Britain's War Cabinet, Maurice Hankey. His death in combat was especially mourned as the loss of an unusually sensitive and gifted observer. In the following essay, Hankey probes the meaning of mobilization as an experiment in democracy, as individuals from different social classes join in a spirit of common endeavor.

The unprecedented had occurred. For once a national ideal had proved stronger than class prejudice. In this matter of the war all classes were at one — at one not only in sentiment but in practical resolve. The crowd that surged outside the central recruiting offices in Great Scotland Yard was the proof of it. All classes were there, struggling for the privilege of enlisting in the new citizen Army, conscious of their unity, and determined to give effect to it in the common life of service. It was an extraordinary crowd. Workmen were there in cord breeches and subfusc coats; boys from the East End in the latest fashions from Petticoat Lane; clerks and shop-assistants in sober black; mechanics

Excerpt from *A Student in Arms* by Donald Hankey, Melrose, 1916, pp. 25–29.

in blue serge and bowler hats; travelers in the garments of prosperity; and most conspicuously well dressed of all, gentlemen in their oldest clothes. It was like a section cut out
of the nation.

Men and boys of the working class formed the majority. They were in their element, shouting, singing, cheeking the "coppers" with as much ribald good humor as if
the recruiting office had been a music-hall. But some of the other classes were far less at
their ease. They had been brought up from earliest youth to thank God that they were
not as other men, to set store by the innumerable little marks that distinguished them
from "the lower classes." All these they were now sacrificing to an idea, and they felt
horribly embarrassed. Even the gentleman, who had prided himself on his freedom from
"the snobbishness of the suburbs," felt ill at ease. Of course he had been to workingmen's clubs; but there he had been "Mr. Thingumy." Here he was "mate." He told
himself that he did not mind being "mate," in fact he rather liked it; but he fervently
wished that he looked the part. He felt as self-conscious as if he had arrived at a dinner
party in a Norfolk jacket. A little later on, when he sat, one of four nude men, in a
cubicle awaiting medical inspection, he did feel that for the moment they had all been
reduced to the common denominator of their sheer humanity; but embarrassment returned with his clothes and stayed with him all through the march to the station and the
journey to the depot.

At the depot he fought for the prize of a verminous blanket, and six foot of floor to
lie on. When he awoke the next morning his clothes were creased and dirty, his collar
so filthy that it had to be discarded, and his chin unshaven. He perceived with something of a shock that he was no longer conspicuous. He was no more than the seedy unit
of a seedy crowd. In any other circumstances he would have been disgusted. As it was,
he sought the canteen at the earliest opportunity and toasted the Unity of the Classes in
a pint!

All emerged from the depot clothed exactly alike, and meditated on the symbolism
of clothes. They donned the gray shirt and ready-made khaki of the new era, and de-
posited the emblems of class distinction on a common rag-heap. Even the perfunctory
manner of the Q.M.S. could not rob the occasion of an almost religious solemnity. It
was the formal beginning of a new life, in which men of all classes, starting with something like equality of opportunity, should gain what pre-eminence they might by the
merit of their inherent manhood or the seduction of their native tact. Henceforward all
fared alike. All ate the same food, slept on the same floor in similar blankets, and in their
shirts. Even the pajamas no longer divided them! All took their share in scrubbing floors
and washing dixies; and until the novelty wore off even these menial and dirty jobs
caught a certain glamour from the great ideal which they symbolized. Gradually all
found their level. The plausible were promoted, found wanting, reduced, and replaced
by the men of real grit and force of character. Mechanics joined the machine-gun section, clerks became orderlies, signalers, or telephonists. The dirtiest and most drunken
of the old soldiers were relegated to the cookhouse. Equality of opportunity had been
granted, and the inequality of man had been demonstrated. It was found that the best
formula, after all, was that of St. Paul: "Diversities of gifts, but the same Spirit."

5. WE OF ITALY

Although the conflict had been underway for months when Italy entered the war, there is little in the letters of these fresh Italian recruits to suggest that they were aware of the horrors awaiting them — no doubt because civilians (in any country) had only an imprecise and often heavily censored view of realities of the front. It seems that Italian soldiers manifested the same patriotic surge of anticipation in 1915 that was characteristic of their comrades from other nations the previous summer.

a. Long Live Our Navy

Spezia, 25 May, 1915

Signor Direttore, — At this moment I am recalled to the service of our glorious Navy, and however, in my mistaken past, I have been against the war, to-day I am happy, — proud of my change of conscience, and I feel highly honoured to be allowed to give my arm to our *Patria,* for the redemption of our third Italy.

The enthusiasm among the men who have been recalled is admirable, grand, and sublime, eminently fine in these fathers of families who think of nothing besides being speedily embarked in our glorious squadron.

From this moment begins for me a new life, and I feel superbly proud to transmit by means of your patriotic columns my resignation from the Socialist Party and from the syndicate of the Italian railroad men.

From this moment I can think of nothing but how to be of use to the *Patria* and to the King. The beautiful uniform of the sailor, which I have put on again to-day after seven long years, has awakened sentiments in me of other times, and I feel myself to be another man. My heart is strong, and through your columns I send good wishes for the victory of our Army and Navy.

I hope that my poor words may be an incitement to the few dissenters in this hour of glory, this hour of the redemption of our unredeemed territories.

I salute all the fervent patriots, my dear children and my Cristina. *Viva l'Italia! Viva l'Esercito! Viva la nostra Marina!* [Long live Italy! Long live the Army! Long live our Navy!]

Yours for life and for the *Patria,*

Giuseppe Nob. Sancini,
Corpo Reali Equipaggi, Spezia

Excerpt from *We of Italy* by K. R. Steege, E. P. Dutton, 1917, pp. 18–19.

b. *This War of Liberation*

S. Pietro al Natisone (Udine), May 10th, 1915

I thank you profoundly for the kind and affectionate wishes which you send me. . . .

You as well as I know that each one must meet his own fate in this world. The hour strikes as it has been decreed. If my hour has not yet sounded, then even from the war I shall come forth unharmed. In any case, one thing is sure: that I will do my duty everywhere and always, even to the end. I am proud to be an Italian and especially to be a Bersagliere, and I shall know how to do honour to my nation and to the glorious corps to which I belong. . . .

You know how I have dreamed of this war of liberation, which will make Italy a greater and a more united nation: how for years I have encouraged such a war, and urged it by means of the press. Imagine then with what enthusiasm I shall fight, having the good fortune to be among the first to go, and so to be sent into one of the advanced positions.

If I come out safe and sound from the tremendous conflict I hope to engage in another kind of war, not of blood but of ideals: an ardent struggle for the material and moral uplifting of our country, for its firm fusion and national cohesion against all political abuses and party intrigues, great and small: intrigues which, bound by their own interests and narrow hatreds, tend to overthrow great ideas, undermining our unity of thought and action, and placing the brilliant Latin civilisation in danger from barbaric but disciplined German culture.

May you keep well. I embrace you with great affection, and I send kisses to my nephews.

6. A FRENCH HISTORIAN REMEMBERS

Marc Bloch, whom we have encountered in Part I, Section A, was one of France's greatest historians of medieval Europe. Born in 1886 in Lyon into a Jewish academic family (his father served as professor of Roman history at the Sorbonne), Bloch was one of the most sensitive and acute observers of the First World War. He survived, only to see his country invaded by Germany a second time. Serving in the French resistance during the Second World War, he was captured by the Germans and executed in 1944.

Thus from August 10, 1914, to January 5, 1915, I led a life as different as possible from my ordinary existence: a life at once barbarous, violent, often colorful, also often of a

(b) Excerpt from *We of Italy* by K. R. Steege, E. P. Dutton, 1917, pp. 23–24.

(6) Excerpt from *Memoirs of War, 1914–15* by Marc Bloch, Cornell University Press, 1980, pp. 159, 161–166.

dreary monotony combined with bits of comedy and moments of grim tragedy. In five months in the field, who would not have amassed a rich harvest of experiences?

Like everyone else, I was impressed by the total inadequacy of our material preparation as well as of our military training. In La Gruerie I installed wire without barbs. I have seen my trench showered with bombs to which we could respond only with rifle fire. I have ordered the ground dug with hand tools and intrigued with my colleagues to secure a few good full-size implements for my platoon. I saw — alas, right up to the end — the inadequacy of our telephone lines impede our communication with the artillery. Moreover, only experience taught me — and no doubt most imperfectly — how to dig trenches. Reflecting later on what we did during the first months of war, I realized that the corps of engineers knew little more about that problem than we did. Before Larzicourt, didn't our officers build for our battalion commander a shelter that was cleverly hidden in a cabbage field but totally lacking any direct communication with the front lines? Thus, in the event of an attack, our unhappy major, after having killed off all his quartermaster sergeants by sending them with his orders to the various companies, would have been forced to watch, like a powerless spectator, the combat he should have been directing. I saw progress occur slowly, with difficulty, but surely. By December we had more barbed wire and pointed stakes than we knew what to do with. I heard the noise of our artillery, so weak and intermittent during our first stay in La Gruerie, grow gradually to dominate the uproar of the enemy's cannon.

I was aware, especially at the start of the campaign, of some shocking negligence. When we were holding the trenches near Thonne-la-Long we had absolutely no idea what was in front of us. One day, when we thought we had made contact with the enemy, the French outposts were still in front of us. Our orders to leave Han-les-Juvigny arrived several hours late. At Larzicourt we worked under the supervision of the corps of engineers. On the first day we exerted considerable effort to dig trenches that, being visible from a distance, would have offered the enemy's artillery an invaluable target. The next day the engineers' captain, who was billeted in the village, examined our work, correctly judged it unacceptable, and made us start again; had he come the day before to direct our inexperienced efforts, he could have spared us both the painful fatigue and the discouragement of our wasted efforts. One of my men, a master carpenter from a town in the Ile-de-France, said, "If I were responsible for work like that, I'd soon have to close up shop." Wasn't he right?

I was by no means always satisfied with our officers. Often I found them insufficiently concerned with their men's well-being, too ignorant of their physical condition, and too uninterested to find out. The words "Let them cope" — that sinister phrase which, after 1870, no one should have dared utter again — were still too often on their lips. The officers' and platoon leaders' mess sometimes appropriated too large a share of the supplies. The officers' cooks played too important a role in the company. The quartermaster sergeants should have been kept under closer scrutiny. Obviously there may have been regiments to which my criticisms do not apply. I can only speak of what I have seen, and the range of my experience was necessarily very limited. When in quarters, the company officers did not assemble their men frequently enough. Reservists are no longer children; they always impressed me as eager for news, and its lack discouraged them. It was up to their officers to keep them informed of developments and to comment on them. I had a captain who understood admirably how to communicate with his troops; why didn't he do it more often? In fairness, I should add that at Vienne-le-Château we were forced to avoid meetings, which would be dangerous in a village under constant bombardment.

Our battalion, and then the sixth, were for the time commanded by a captain who was a coarse and contemptible individual. He knew only two ways to make his men perform: either by insulting them or by threatening them with a court-martial. I heard him vilify some men who two days earlier (September 10) had stood without flinching under the devastating cannon and machine gun fire that had covered the German retreat. Once he hit someone; but I believe that incident was hushed up. Our revenge was to watch the terrible fright that his features betrayed at the sound of shellfire. Promoted major, he had himself recalled on the pretext of general exhaustion, which no one believed. But my battalion also served under an officer whom I greatly admired. With a somewhat severe appearance as well as a brusque manner and speech, his thin, almost ascetic face revealed no trace of humor. Yet, though he made not the slightest effort to be popular, he possessed that mysterious quality of personal magnetism which transforms a man into a leader; his soldiers had faith in him and would have followed him anywhere. In my comrade M., a reenlisted noncommissioned officer who rose to second lieutenant, I found the charm of simple courage along with the happy combination of cool self-possession and personal warmth. It was he who produced the heroic reply — so much finer because of its obvious innocence of any literary pretension — when a panic-stricken soldier cried, "The Germans are only thirty meters away from us," "Well, we are only thirty meters away from the Germans."

A company or platoon is not made up of men equally intelligent, attractive, or brave. When I recall the comrades with whom I have lived, men I have commanded, the figures I evoke do not all seem pleasant. By knowing Corporal H., I learned just how far malingering could go (how far in this case would probably have been a court-martial if the lieutenant had not been so kind, perhaps too kind). When I remember the face of Corporal M., I cannot restrain a smile. He was a miner, stocky and rather heavy-footed, with a square face; his nose was adorned with a fine blueish scar of the sort that the carbon dust of the coal pit frequently imprints on workers' bodies. Though an indefatigable walker, he was unaccustomed to shoes, so he traveled the roads of Lorraine and Champagne barefoot. He was so careless and so stupid that it now seems to me I did little during the first six weeks of the campaign but hunt for him from one end of the camp to the other, to transmit orders he never understood. But I should not forget that the last thing I did not succeed in making him understand, on the morning of September 10, was that his place was not at the head of the platoon. When we went into action that day, he fell, whether killed or wounded I do not know.

During the month of August and the first days of September, D. was our joy. A peasant from the region of Baupaume, he had the most beautiful Picard accent. When we saw the first wounded along the route between Grand-Verneuil and Thonne-la-Long, we noticed that many had their arms in slings, leaving their unused coat sleeves dangling. D. thought they were all amputees, and we were never able to convince him that he was mistaken. Very coarse in his own language, he accepted the grossest insults from his comrades without flinching; only one expression infuriated him: "Shut your —— ." He absolutely insisted on having a "mouth." I also muse over our handful of cowards: K., who all but spat at me when I happened on him by chance in his shelter; V., who, miserable at finding himself at war, never referred to himself without saying, "Poor martyr!" But I prefer to remember the good chaps: P., of whose death I have just learned, a Parisian worker with pale complexion, who had the insatiable appetite of a man who has not had all he wanted to eat, who has frequently gone hungry, and who was restless, nervous, and quick both to anger and to rejoice; poor G., secretary of a miners' union, active and talkative, and with a truly generous heart; and T., also a miner, uneducated, as taciturn as G. was loquacious, of dark complexion and gloomy expression, calm in moments of danger and burning with an unquenchable hatred of Germans, whom he never referred to except as "those assassins." Who will ever record the unknown acts of heroism performed in La Gruerie by our dispatch runners? I can still see our first, T., by occupation a manual laborer from Pontoise, small and quick, full of pompous phrases. He trotted through the wood, which was being sprayed with bursts of fire; and when a bullet passed too close, he made with his hand the gesture one uses to chase away a bothersome fly.

Of all my comrades who fell in Champagne or in the Argonne, there is none I mourned more than F., who was the sergeant of my second half platoon. F.'s line of work was not one usually considered important. He ran a shop for a wine merchant near the Bastille. He had scant education and could barely read. Yet no one has done more to make me understand the beauty of a truly noble and sensitive soul. He rarely used coarse language, and I never heard him utter an obscenity. His men adored him for his kindly good nature, which rubbed off on them. His calm courage inspired their confidence because they knew he was prudent as well as brave. Remarkably attentive to the practical details of life, he was one of those of whom it was said he always knew which way was north. I still remember his return from one dangerous patrol he had undertaken with resolute courage, confiding his wallet to me as he left, and which he led with a truly remarkable equanimity. He came back carrying a can of food that he had found in an abandoned sack somewhere between the lines. He devoted himself to making life more agreeable for those of his men he thought were poor, and shared with them those small treats that are beyond price in the field. He had a lofty notion of loyalty among comrades, which he explained by saying, "When I was a recruit, I was in a squad where we got along well together." Unquestionably his main desire and his greatest effort was to ensure that his half platoon should "get along well together." When I lost him, I lost a moral support.

During my months in the field I sometimes saw men show fear. The look of fear I found very ugly. To be sure, I encountered it very seldom. Military courage is certainly widespread. I do not believe it is correct to say, despite occasional opinions to the contrary, that it is easily come by. Not always, to be fair, but often it is the result of effort, an effort that a healthy individual makes without injury to himself and which rapidly becomes instinctive. I have always noticed that by some fortunate reflex, death ceases to appear very terrible the moment it seems close: it is this, ultimately, that explains courage. Most men dread going under fire, and especially returning to it. Once there, however, they no longer tremble. Also, I believe that few soldiers, except the most noble or intelligent, think of their country while conducting themselves bravely; they are much more often guided by a sense of personal honor, which is very strong when it is reinforced by the group. If a unit consisted of a majority of slackers, the point of honor would be to get out of any situation with the least harm possible. Thus I always thought it a good policy to express openly the profound disgust that the few cowards in my platoon inspired in me.

I have finished gathering my memories. T., of whom I have just spoken, wrote me a letter the other day; because it is in pencil, it will no doubt soon fade away. In order not to forget his last sentence, I shall copy it here: "Vive la France, et vivement la victoire!" ("Long live France, and let victory come quickly!").

C. The Realities of War

1. THE ATTACK

The following selection relates many of the features of trench warfare as experienced by a representative participant, in this case H. S. Clapham of the British army. He conveys the excitement of attack, the constant necessity for defensive measures, the relentless shelling, and the persistent reminders of death.

16th June

At 4.15 [A.M.] a whistle blew. The men in the front line went over the top, and we scrambled out and took their places in the front trench. In front of us was a small field, with grass knee-high, split diagonally by an old footpath. On the other side of the field was a belt of trees, known as Y Wood, in which lay the first Hun trench.

In a few moments flags went up there, to show that it had been captured and that the troops were going on. Another whistle, and we ourselves scrambled over the parapet and sprinted across the field. Personally I was so overweighted that I could only amble, and I remember being intensely amused at the sight of a little chap in front of me who seemed in even worse case than myself. Without thinking much about it, I took the diagonal path, as the line of least resistance, and most of my section did the same.

When I dropped into the Hun trench I found it a great place, only three feet wide, and at least eight deep, and beautifully made of white sand-bags, back and front. At that

Excerpt from *Vain Glory*, Guy Chapman, ed., Cassell UK, 1967, pp. 167–173. Reprinted by permission of Peters Fraser & Dunlop Group Ltd.

spot there was no sign of any damage by our shells, but a number of dead Huns lay in the bottom. There was a sniper's post just where I fell in, a comfortable little square hole, fitted with seats and shelves, bottles of beer, tinned meats, and a fine helmet hanging on a hook.

Our first duty was to change the wire, so, after annexing the helmet, I slipped off my pack, and, clambering out again, started to move the wire from what was now the rear, to the new front of the trench. It was rotten stuff, most of it loose coils, and the only knife-rests were not more than a couple of feet high. What there was movable of it, we got across without much difficulty, and we had just finished when we were ordered to move down the trench, as our diagonal advance had brought us too far to the right.

We moved down along the belt of woodland, which was only a few yards broad, to a spot where one of our companies was already hard at work digging a communication trench back to our old front line. Here there was really no trench at all. One or more of our own big shells had burst in the middle, filling it up for a distance of ten yards and practically destroying both parapet and parados. Some of us started building up the parapet with sandbags, and I saw the twins merrily at work hauling out dead Huns at least twice their own size.

There was a hedge along the back of the trench, so I scrambled through a hole in it, piled my pack, rifle, and other things, including the helmet, on the farther side, and started again on the wire. Hereabouts it was much better stuff, and it took us some time to get it across and pegged down. We had just got the last knife-rest across, when I saw a man who was placing sandbags on the parapet from the farther side swivel round, throw his legs into the trench, and collapse in a heap in the bottom. Several others were already lying there, and for the first time I realized that a regular hail of machine-gun bullets was sweeping over the trench.

I made a dive for my pack, but though I found that, my pet helmet had disappeared. Quite a string of wounded and masterless men had passed down the back of the hedge while I was working, and one of them must have thought it a good souvenir to take into hospital. . . .

The attacking battalions had carried several more trenches and we were told that two at least had been held, but our own orders were to consolidate and hold on to the trench we were in at all costs. We could see very little in front. There was a wide field of long grass, stretching gently upward to a low mound of earth several hundred yards away. This was the next line. Away on the right front was Bellewarde Wood and Hooge Château, both above us, but the latter was partly hidden by the corner of Y Wood.

I had just filled a sandbag and placed it on the top of the parapet when I happened to glance down, and saw a slight movement in the earth between my feet. I stooped and scraped away the soil with my fingers and found what seemed like palpitating flesh. It proved to be a man's cheek, and a few minutes' work uncovered his head. I poured a little water down his throat, and two or three of us dug out the rest of him. He was undamaged except for his feet and ankles, which were a mass of pulp, and he recovered consciousness as we worked. The first thing he said was in English: "What Corps are you?" He was a big man, and told us he was forty-five and had only been a soldier for a fortnight.

We dragged him out and laid him under the hedge. There was nothing else we could do for him. He had another drink later, but he must have died in the course of the day. I am afraid we forgot all about him, but nothing could have lived there until evening.

The Captain was the next to go. He insisted on standing on the parados, directing operations, and got a bullet in the lungs. He could walk, and two men were detailed to take him down to the dressing-station. One came back, to be killed later in the day, but the other stopped a bullet en route, and followed the Captain.

When we had got our big Hun out, he left a big hole in the ground, and we found a dead arm and hand projecting from the bottom. We dug about, but did not seem to be able to find the body, and when I seized the sleeve and pulled, the arm came out of the ground by itself. We had to dig deeper for our own sake, but there was nothing else left, except messy earth, which seemed to have been driven into the side of the trench. The man helping me turned sick, for it wasn't pretty work, but I claimed a substitute, and between us we carted out a barrowful in wetter sheets and dumped it under the hedge. After that I had had enough myself.

About 5.30 A.M. the Huns started shelling, and the new communication trench soon became a death-trap. A constant stream of wounded who had come down another trench from the north, passed along the rear. The Huns made a target of the two traverses (unluckily including our own), from which the communication trench opened, and numbers of the wounded were caught just behind us. The trench itself was soon choked with bodies, as it was easier and as safe to pass over the open above it.

The shelling got worse as the day wore on and several more of our men went down. They plastered us with crumps, shrapnel, and whizz-bangs. One of the latter took off a sandbag from the top of the parapet and landed it on my head. It nearly broke my neck and I felt ill for some time after.

It was grillingly hot and the air was full of dust, but although we were parched up, we dared not use much of our water. One never knew how long it must last. I came off better than most in that respect, for I had taken the precaution of carrying two water-bottles knowing that one would never last me.

The worst of it was the inaction. Every minute several shells fell within a few yards and covered us with dust, and the smell of the explosives poisoned my mouth. All I could do was to crouch against the parapet and pant for breath, expecting every moment to be my last. And this went on for hours. I began to long for the shell which would put an end to everything, but in time my nerves became almost numbed, and I lay like a log until roused.

I think it must have been midday when something happened. An alarm was given and we manned the parapet, to see some scores of men retreating at a run from the trench in front. They ran right over us, men of half a dozen battalions, and many dropped on the way. As they passed, something was said of gas, but it appeared that nearly all the officers in the two front trenches had been killed or wounded, someone had raised an alarm of gas, and the men had panicked and run.

A lot of the runaways insisted on gathering by the hedge just behind us, in spite of our warnings not to do so, and I saw at least twenty hit by shrapnel within a few yards of us.

The Brigade-Major arrived, cursing, and called upon some of our own men to advance and reoccupy the trench in front. He led them himself, and they made a very fine dash across. I do not think more than twenty fell, and they reoccupied the trench and, I believe, the third also, before the Huns realized that they were empty.

In connection with this attack a rather amusing incident happened amongst ourselves. As soon as the man next me saw the attack commence, he yelled out: "They're our own men. Come on, we can't let them go alone." He was over the parapet in no time and dragged me half-way with him. As soon as the "gallant lad" was seen, he was ordered back, and the order was repeated by nearly all the men who were manning the parapet. He told me afterwards that it was the funniest of sights as he looked back, a dozen heads projecting over the sandbags, all with their mouths wide open, and all with one accord saying: "Come back, you silly ass!" He came back rather crestfallen.

The interlude was really a welcome one, and useful, too, for we realized then that nearly every rifle was clogged with dirt and entirely useless. We set to work cleaning at once, and this kept us occupied amidst the constant bursting of the shells. Our own guns were practically silent, and we supposed they were reserving ammunition, which was not too plentiful at the best of times.

Soon the runaways began to return. They had been turned back, in some cases, at the point of the revolver, but when their first panic had been overcome, they came back quite willingly, although they must have lost heavily in the process. They crowded into our trench, and there was hardly room to move a limb.

It was scorchingly hot and no one could eat, although I tried to do so. All day long — the longest day I ever spent — we were constantly covered with debris from the shell-bursts. Great pieces fell all about us, and, packed like herrings, we crowded in the bottom of the trench. Hardly anything could be done for the wounded. If their wounds were slight, they generally risked a dash to the rear. Every now and then we stood to in expectation of a counter-attack, but none developed.

About 6.0 P.M. the worst moment of the day came. The Huns started to bombard us with a shell which was quite new to us. It sounded like a gigantic fire-cracker, with two distinct explosions. These shells came over just above the parapet, in a flood, much more quickly than we could count them. After a quarter of an hour of this sort of thing, there was a sudden crash in the trench and ten feet of the parapet, just beyond me, was blown away and everyone around blinded by the dust. With my first glance I saw what looked like half a dozen bodies, mingled with sandbags, and then I smelt gas and realized that these were gas-shells. I had my respirator on in a hurry and most of our own men were as quick. The others were slower and suffered for it. One man was sick all over the sandbags and another was coughing his heart up. We pulled four men out of the debris unharmed. One man was unconscious, and died of gas later. Another was hopelessly smashed up and must have got it full in the chest.

We all thought that this was the end and almost hoped for it, but luckily the gas-shells stopped, and after a quarter of an hour we could take off our respirators. I started in at once to build up the parapet again, for we had been laid open to the world in front, but the gas lingered about the hole for hours, and I had to give up delving in the bottom for a time. As it was it made me feel very sick.

A counter-attack actually commenced as soon as the bombardment ceased, and we had to stand to again. My rifle had been broken in two pieces, but there were plenty of spare ones lying about now. I tried four, however, before I could get one to act at all. All were jammed, and that one was very stiff. As we leaned over the parapet, I saw the body of a Hun lying twenty yards out in front. It commenced to writhe and finally half-sat up. I suppose the gas had caught him. The man standing next me — a corporal in a county battalion — raised his rifle, and before I could stop him, sent a bullet into the body. It was a rotten thing to see, but I suppose it was really a merciful end for the poor chap, better than his own gas, at any rate.

The men in the front trenches had got it as badly as we had, and if the counter-attack was pressed, it did not seem humanly possible, in the condition we were in, to offer a successful defence. One man kept worrying us all by asking what we were to do if the Huns did us in, whether surrender or run! Fortunately, our own guns started and apparently caught the Huns massing. The counter-attack accordingly crumpled up.

In the midst of it all, someone realized that the big gap in the parapet could not be manned, and four of us, including myself, were ordered to lie down behind what was left of the parados and cover the gap with our rifles. It was uncomfortable work, as the gas fumes were still very niffy and the place was a jumble of dead bodies. We could not stand up to clear them away, and in order to get a place at all, I had to lie across the body of a gigantic Hun.

As soon as things quietened down a bit, we had a chance to look around. Since the morning most of the branches of the trees in the wood had gone and many of the trunks had become mere splintered poles. Something else had changed also, and for a time I could not make out what it was. Then it suddenly flashed across my mind that the thick hedge at the back of the trench had entirely disappeared. It was right in the path of the storm of gas-shells and they had carried it away.

We managed to get some sort of parapet erected in the end. It was more or less bullet-proof, at any rate. At dusk some scores of men came back from the front line, wounded or gassed. They had to cross the open at a run or a shamble, but I did not see any hit. Then the Brigade-Major appeared, and cheered us by promising a relief that night. It still rained shells, although not so hard as before dusk, and we did not feel capable of standing much more of it.

2. ENGLISH WAR LETTERS

The three English correspondents that follow express the range of emotions that the war stimulated. Harold Chapin, the first writer, vents his frustration at both the lack of progress and what he believes are the many shirkers at home who stand in the way of military progress. The second soldier, Captain Julian Grenfell, served in a prestigious unit — the Royal Dragoons — and exemplifies the conventional expectations of highly educated men of his social rank. He believed that their duty was to serve without complaint in a masculine, devil-may-care way. The third correspondent, Lieutenant Melville Hastings, was not from a class that thought fox hunting was good preparation for killing Germans. He thus provides a rather more circumspect appreciation of the war's impact.

a. Harold Chapin

[France] May [29th], 1915

[To His Wife]

. . . I wish to God England would come into this war and get it over! I told you I thought November. It won't be November twelve month unless England drops attacking Kitchener, attacking the *Daily Mail,* attacking defenceless Germans in London, striking and all the rest of it, and devotes all its attention to attacking the German Army out here. If you at home could only see and hear the enormous concentration of force necessary to take a mile of German trench; the terrific resistance we have to put up to hold it; the price we have to pay over every little failure — a price paid with no purchase to show for it — if you could only see and realise these things there'd be some hope of you all bucking in and supplying the little extra force — the little added support in resistance — that we need to end this murderous, back and forth business. Every man not engaged in supplying food and warmth and order — bare necessities — to those at home should be directly engaged in supplying strength toward the ending of the war. If he isn't doing so he is contributing by neglect to that killing and maiming of our men out here *which he might be preventing.* I am not exaggerating an iota. This is mere truth which cannot be gainsaid. There can only be one reason for not serving: selfishness. And selfishness at this time is not the commonsense quality it is in ordinary times, since no man is now looking after himself or could look after himself entirely. He is part of the crowd which those of its complement who are serving are looking after, and he could no more look after himself than anyone of the men out here can look after himself, but each can help to look after the crowd and be looked after in return. The Devil of it is that so many have slipped into the crowd and are being looked after in return for nothing. That is the weakness.

Excerpt from *War Letters of Fallen Englishmen,* Laurence Housman, ed., Victor Gollancz UK, 1930, pp. 72–73. All attempts at tracing the copyright holders of these letters were unsuccessful.

b. Julian Grenfell

1st Royal Dragoons
Educated Eton and Balliol College, Oxford. Regular Army.
Died of wounds, France, 26 May, 1915, at the age of 27.

[Flanders] October 24, 1914

[To His Mother]

... I *adore* War. It is like a big picnic without the objectlessness of a picnic. I have never been so well or so happy. Nobody grumbles at one for being dirty. I have only had my boots off once in the last 10 days, and only washed twice. We are up and standing to our rifles by 5 A.M. when doing this infantry work, and saddled up by 4.30 A.M. when with our horses. Our poor horses do not get their saddles off when we are in the trenches.

The wretched inhabitants here have got practically no food left. It is miserable to see them leaving their houses, and tracking away, with great bundles and children in their hands. And the dogs and cats left in the deserted villages are piteous. ...

[Flanders] November 3rd, 1914

[To His Parents]

... I have not washed for a week, or had my boots off for a fortnight. ... It is all *the* best fun. I have never never felt so well, or so happy, or enjoyed anything so much. It just suits my stolid health, and stolid nerves, and barbaric disposition. The fighting-excitement vitalizes everything, every sight and word and action. One loves one's fellow man so much more when one is bent on killing him. And picnic-ing in the open day and night (we never see a roof now) is the real method of existence.

There are loads of straw to bed-down on, and one sleeps like a log, and wakes up with the dew on one's face. ... The Germans shell the trenches with shrapnel all day and all night: and the Reserves and ground in the rear with Jack Johnsons, which at last one gets to love as old friends. You hear them coming for miles, and everyone imitates the noise; then they burst with a plump, and make a great hole in the ground, doing no damage unless they happen to fall into your trench or on to your hat. They burst pretty nearly straight upwards. One landed within ten yards of me the other day, and

Excerpt from *War Letters of Fallen Englishmen*, Laurence Housman, ed., Victor Gollancz UK, 1930, pp. 117–119. All attempts at tracing the copyright holders of these letters were unsuccessful.

only knocked me over and my horse. We both got up and looked at each other and laughed. . . .

We took a German Officer and some men prisoners in a wood the other day. One felt hatred for them as one thought of our dead; and as the Officer came by me, I scowled at him, and the men were cursing him. The Officer looked me in the face and saluted me as he passed; and I have never seen a man look so proud and resolute and smart and confident, in his hour of bitterness. It made me feel terribly ashamed of myself. . . .

[Flanders] November 18th, 1914

[To His Parents]

. . . They had us out again for 48 hours trenches while I was writing the above. About the shells, after a day of them, one's nerves are really absolutely beat down. I can understand now why our infantry have to retreat sometimes; a sight which came as a shock to me at first, after being brought up in the belief that the English infantry cannot retreat.

These last two days we had quite a different kind of trench, in a dripping sodden wood, with the German trench in some places 40 yards ahead. . . . We had been worried by snipers all along, and I had always been asking for leave to go out and have a try myself. Well, on Tuesday the 16th, the day before yesterday, they gave me leave. Only after great difficulty. They told me to take a section with me, and I said I would sooner cut my throat and have done with it. So they let me go alone. Off I crawled through sodden clay and trenches, going about a yard a minute, and listening and looking as I thought it was not possible to look and to listen. I went out to the right of our lines, where the 10th were, and where the Germans were nearest. I took about 30 minutes to do 30 yards; then I saw the Hun trench, and I waited there a long time, but could see or hear nothing. It was about 10 yards from me. Then I heard some Germans talking, and saw one put his head up over some bushes, about 10 yards behind the trench. I could not get a shot at him, I was too low down, and of course I could not get up. So I crawled on again very slowly to the parapet of their trench. I peered through their loop-hole and saw nobody in the trench. Then the German behind me put up his head again. He was laughing and talking. I saw his teeth glistening against my foresight, and I pulled the trigger.

c. *Melville Hastings*

52nd Battalion, Canadian Expeditionary Force
Schoolmaster, Wycliffe College, 1901–1907. Subsequently settled in Canada.
Died of wounds, France, 3 October, 1918, at the age of about 40.

At the Front [France], 1917

[To the Headmaster of Wycliffe College]

I see that many stay-at-homes want to keep the Anglo-German wound raw even after the peace of Berlin, 1917. The returned German prisoners will never second the motion. There are thousands of them round here. They are well fed and well clad and seem as happy as sandboys. Never once yet have I seen any British soldier attempt to ridicule or annoy any prisoner, nay, rather, he shows him all consideration. This is saying much, for we are all sorts and conditions of men, and the German prisoner knows it.

The art of remembering consists largely in discerning what to forget, and to the will belongs the undeniable power to erase the unworthy, and the acid to etch in what is worth retaining. Last night I heard a youngster offer to do another's gas guard rather than awaken him out of a very weary sleep. What I heard has been etched in and preserved with a cover of thick glass. A couple of mornings ago I reached out for my pot of jam. It was jamless. May the sun never shine on his rice garden! No, that is a mistake. I meant I will forget it.

I write this outside a German dug-out wrecked by one of our sixty-pounders. The explosion has thrown five men lifeless down the stairway. Their boy officer, a young Absalom, is suspended head downwards by one of his Bluchers from two viced beams in the roof. Get the harrowing details out of the mind; remember only the faithful service.

It seems to me that so many of our journals urge the remembering of the worthless, the forgetting of the worth remembering. "Remember the *Lusitania,* remember Nurse Cavell." Rather keep them out of the mind. Heaven consists largely in thinking of mothers and wives and children and other things that are thus beautiful. Get the habit. Increase Heaven by thinking of the homely, fat but selfless Frau and the lad who hangs from the ceiling by his foot. Hell consists largely in thinking of our own nastiness. We cannot forget them even when forgiven, and so this Hell survives, but other people's nastiness we can forget quite easily. Forget the *Lusitanias,* the Louvains — there are paid servants of the State who will attend to these.

Kipling has it that "East is East and West is West and never the twain shall meet." Nowadays it is fashionable to put Germany in the place of the East. We are at war and must go on until Justice shall be triumphant. I hope, however, that humanity will not for ever sanction these "Wallace Lines," war-jaundiced and fear-bred. All the world over a boy is a boy and a mother is a mother. One there was Who after thirty years of thinking appealed to *all* mankind, and not in vain.

German food and British food, examine them closely, they are the same. The same in terms of stomach, of ears, of eyes or of the immortal soul. A week since I was lying out in no man's land. A little German dog trotted up and licked my British face. I pulled his German ears and stroked his German back. He wagged his German tail. My little friend abolished no man's land, and so in time can we.

Excerpt from *War Letters of Fallen Englishmen,* Laurence Housman, ed., Victor Gollancz UK, 1930, pp. 122–125. All attempts at tracing the copyright holders of these letters were unsuccessful.

At the Front [France], Autumn, 1917

[To the Same]

Quite frequently, in raids and attacks, British soldiers meet Germans whom they have known before the war. A bird cage facing us in Sanctuary Wood was at regular intervals occupied by an expert sniper who had served with one of our number as a waiter in Broadway, New York. His cage was only about twenty yards away. He killed one or two of us every day. In the intervals he engaged with us in racy conversation. Near Wulvergem I found on a corpse a pay book which showed the man to have been a chemist in Leipzig. On several toilet boxes belonging to my sister, who before the war was a student at Leipzig University, I had often seen this man's name.

It is not to be wondered at that many a Fritz, who has lived amongst us for years, bears us far from bitter feelings. When a very green soldier, I was sent out at Armentieres to cover a party engaged in cutting down a patch of seeding chicory a few yards in front of our own wire. Being ordered to advance a hundred yards Fritzwards, I had paced but eighty odd, when, to my astonishment, I found myself securely entangled in the wire of what was evidently an unlocated listening post. My rifle, wrenched from my hands, evidently collided with a screw stake, and a flare shot up *instanter*. Not fifteen yards away, sticking out from a hole sunk into the turf, were a rifle and the head and shoulders of a man. Of course I "froze" stiff. Seeing, however, no movement of the rifle, I began to think — though such seemed impossible — that I was undiscovered. It was impossible. He had seen me plainly. Perhaps he was a sportsman, and scorned to wing a defenceless man. He laughed heartily, called out "Hallo, Johnny Bull, you silly old —— ," and sank into the earth. Yours truly likewised, plus rifle, but minus half a yard of tunic, and nearly a pair of pants. A very similar experience befell my friend a Captain of Canadian Infantry. Scouting alone in No Man's Land — a most unwise proceeding, by the way — he walked on to the levelled rifle of a sniper. Halting the Captain, the sniper ordered him to hands up and step back five paces. In the couple of minutes of conversation that ensued it appeared that my friend was in the hands of a Saxon, an Oxford graduate, and a man who — despite repeated requests not to be used on the British Front — had been sent against us. My friend was right-abouted and ordered to count fifty. At fifty-one he found himself alone and free. On the Roll of Honour of Oxford University is the name of a German who fell in defence of his fatherland. I have often wondered whether this hero and my friend's captor are different men, or just one and the same.

Behind the lines we use humanity of every hue, from heliotrope to mud and water. Even in the trench regiments colour strains are numerous. Some days ago in Belgium I saw three Chinese walking arm in arm with four French girls, and another carrying a bouncing boy with curls like a Teddy bear and a face which Day, Martin and Co. could not have made more black. The same night I saw two Jamaican negroes win 200 francs from a Canadian sapper, and two Japanese cheat a Russian out of 5 francs at cards. I was myself called "Bo" by a Chink, and offered a cocktail by two Canadian Indians, drunk to the wide, wide world. Whatever are we coming to, when these darned foreigners are allowed all the white man's privileges? In Canada, thank God, we have no black question, and we mean to have no Yellow one, but what about Britain equatorwards? All these blacks and yellows will require hats two sizes larger when they return home.

3. A FRENCH SOLDIER CONFRONTS
THE STALEMATE

The monotony of trench life, the unpredictability of assaults, and the horror of death on the battlefield often numbed those serving on the front lines. The following letter from a French soldier is replete with images of the war, a commentary on the individual under duress, and a testimony to the spirit of survival. Note the epithet "Boche" — a term evoking the image of a lawless and uncontrollable man — used to describe the Germans.

A letter of June 24, 1915, from an artillery man tells how the enemy's trenches are taken:

We are very busy at this moment. My poor captain spent last night (the fifth in succession) out of doors. He has not been at the cantonment since the eighteenth. As for me, it's the same old jig, as we say in military slang. We live a queer kind of life. Take yesterday for example; at six in the morning everybody was sleeping soundly in the safe shelter of the trenches, in spite of the firing nearly all night. At nine o'clock the whistles sounded, everybody was routed out and the firing began, with intervals of three to ten minutes between shots. This irregular fire is harder to conduct, but it is very effective in demoralizing the enemy. The shots now coming close on each other's heels, now separated by several minutes, keep the whole zone demoralized.

The difficulty in this irregular fire lies in the fact that the irregularity is deliberate, and the men pointing the guns have to be ready at any moment to sight the exact spot that the commander of the battery wants to reach. It's tiresome because we are all keyed up from the commander down. The slow firing lasts sometimes for two hours at a stretch.

At half-past eleven it began to rain. We all listened to the patter of it in our shelter. At noon we were eating our soup when all of a sudden the orders came and ninety shells were dispatched into the enemy's lines to paralyze an attack which had already begun. The attack ceased and we went on with our soup.

Then we worked at the screens and the observatory. At three o'clock we were allowed some sleep. At six soup arrived, but with it an order to meet an infantry attack. We fired one hundred and twenty shells at regular intervals. A shot every ten seconds from each battery. The shells fell in the trenches as though dropped from a spoon and tore them badly. Three cannons of Battery 155 were trained on a blockhouse, which

Excerpt from *War Letters from France,* A. de LaPradelle and Frederic Coudert, eds., B. Appleton, 1916, pp. 50–53.

soon disappeared from view in a cyclone of fire and dust. Then we extended the fire and formed a barricade of cannon, under the protection of which the soldiers sprang forward, not one of them falling. One hundred, two hundred, three hundred meters and they were at the Boches' trench and the blockhouse. A bewildering scrimmage, and half the men came back dragging some gray bundles of rags, which we recognized as prisoners. Later we heard that we had taken two trenches and two forts with seventy-five prisoners. The German trenches were filled with corpses, swimming in blood and mud.

The firing was continued until eleven o'clock in the evening in order to prevent a counter-attack, but in order to save ammunition we fired only one shot every three minutes for the whole battery. Everything was calm and we were sleeping when at one o'clock in the morning the counter-attack came. It lasted twenty minutes and the Boches withdrew, leaving a number of corpses on the field as a result of the storm that they had the impudence to draw down on themselves. We went back to bed and slept peacefully until eight o'clock. Finally the relieving party came and we got back to the cantonment for a breathing space.

You can understand that in this kind of life we don't have much time for anything. Firing, working on the intrenchments, eating, sleeping, these are our main occupations, with a little washing and writing on the side. We hardly have time to think, for our whole being is totally fixed on the single end of victory. And it seems as if our end were reached. The Boches are melting away under our fire, for they will be massacred, but will not surrender. Above the aviators are flying incessantly, hindering any rush of the enemy on our position and keeping us informed of his position all the time. We have sometimes six aviators in the air to one German who hovers at a distance, not daring to advance in the face of such superiority. At that there is almost nothing going on in our section. It is on the left that the real action is taking place.

4. German Students at War

Are there significant differences between the experiences related by British and French soldiers and those by German soldiers, which follow? The individual writers range widely in their vocational interests — from theology to electrical engineering — yet these inclinations usually paled in importance before the overriding prevalence of death.

a. Alfons Ankenbrand

Student of Theology, Freiburg i. Baden
Born October 31st, 1893, at Vöhrenbach, Baden.
Killed April 25th, 1915, before Souchez.

Souchez, March 11th, 1915

"So fare you well, for we must now be parting," so run the first lines of a soldier-song which we often sang through the streets of the capital. These words are truer than ever now, and these lines are to bid farewell to you, to all my nearest and dearest, to all who wish me well or ill, and to all that I value and prize.

Our regiment has been transferred to this dangerous spot, Souchez. No end of blood has already flowed down this hill. A week ago the 142nd attacked and took four trenches from the French. It is to hold these trenches that we have been brought here. There is something uncanny about this hill-position. Already, times without number, other battalions of our regiment have been ordered here in support, and each time the company came back with a loss of twenty, thirty or more men. In the days when we had to stick it out here before, we had 22 killed and 27 wounded. Shells roar, bullets whistle; no dug-outs, or very bad ones; mud, clay, filth, shell-holes so deep that one could bathe in them.

This letter has been interrupted no end of times. Shells began to pitch close to us — great English 12-inch ones — and we had to take refuge in a cellar. One such shell struck the next house and buried four men, who were got out from the ruins horribly mutilated. I saw them and it was ghastly!

Everybody must be prepared now for death in some form or other. Two cemeteries have been made up here, the losses have been so great. I ought not to write that to you, but I do so all the same, because the newspapers have probably given you quite a different impression. They tell only of our gains and say nothing about the blood that has been shed, of the cries of agony that never cease. The newspaper doesn't give any description either of *how* the "heroes" are laid to rest, though it talks about "heroes' graves" and writes poems and such-like about them. Certainly in Lens I have attended funeral-parades where a number of dead were buried in one large grave with pomp and circumstance. But up here it is pitiful the way one throws the dead bodies out of the trench and lets them lie there, or scatters dirt over the remains of those which have been torn to pieces by shells.

I look upon death and call upon life. I have not accomplished much in my short life, which has been chiefly occupied with study. I have commended my soul to the Lord God. It bears His seal and is altogether His. Now I am free to dare anything. My future life belongs to God, my present one to the Fatherland, and I myself still possess happiness and strength.

Excerpt from *German Students' War Letters*, A. F. Wedd, ed., Methuen London, 1929, pp. 72–73.

b. *Kurt Peterson*

Student of Philosophy, Berlin
Born February 2nd, 1894, at Magdeburg.
Killed August 3rd, 1915, near Cykow, in Russian Poland.

October 25th, 1914, near Dixmuide

It is Sunday. We are blessed with glorious sunshine. How glad I am to greet it once more after all the horrors! I thought never to see it again! Terrible were the days which now lie behind us. Dixmuide brought us a baptism of fire such as scarcely any troops on active service can have experienced before: out of 180 men, only 110 unwounded; the 9th and 10th Companies had to be reorganized as one; several Captains killed and wounded; one Major dangerously wounded, the other missing; the Colonel wounded. Our Regiment suffered horribly. It was complimented by the Division.

What experiences one goes through during such an attack! It makes one years older! Death roars around one; a hail of machine-gun and rifle bullets; every moment one expects to be hit; one is certain of it. One's memory is in perfect working order; one sees and feels quite clearly. One thinks of one's parents. Then there rise in every man thoughts of defiance and of rage and finally a cry for help: away with war! Away with this vile abortion brought forth by human wickedness! Human-beings are slaughtering thousands of other human-beings whom they neither know, nor hate, nor love. Cursed be those who, while not themselves obliged to face the horrors of war, bring it to pass! May they all be utterly destroyed, for they are brutes and beasts of prey!

How one gossips with the sun after such a night of battle! With what different eyes one looks upon Nature! One becomes once more a loving, sensitive human-being after such soul-racking pain and struggle. One's eyes are opened to the importance of man and his achievements in the realm of culture. To war against war; to fight against it with every possible weapon: that will be the work which I shall undertake with the greatest eagerness if the Almighty grants me a safe and happy return! Here one becomes another man. My parents will receive me as a new-born child, maturer, simpler.

c. *Johannes Haas*

. . . I am alone in the fields. My thoughts keep wandering homewards and dwelling on the past and the future. And what about the present? Oh, at present it is delightful to be alone! I feel just as you do, my dear little brother, shivering out there in Russia with your machine-gun. We agree in that as we do in everything else. I have never been so

(b) Excerpt from *German Students' War Letters*, A. F. Wedd, ed., Methuen London, 1929, pp. 149–150.
(c) Ibid., pp. 199–201.

much alone as I am here, except in Berlin, when I was absolutely by myself, struggling through the crowded corridors of the University to Erich Schmidt's lectures. One feels equally solitary as one marches along with the rank and file, hour after hour, abandoned to one's own thoughts. And I sometimes felt like that in the students' cafés — as if the whole atmosphere were somehow alien to me. If I could only begin my student-days all over again! But I won't let myself think that. After the war everything will be different, and then I *must* begin again, anyhow.

The question is: shall I be a clergyman or not? The old question, the old uncertainty, the old struggle! Here one has time to examine oneself, to prove one's attitude towards God. Many people have found themselves able to make up their minds about such things here, but I find myself more doubtful than ever. I see nothing but question marks. What is the reason of everything? How is that possible? Questions that go round and round in a circle, and find no answer. . . .

It is getting cold outside now. I will go into my tent. I am thinking over the great ethical problem of the war. Preachers in the pulpits at home dismiss the question much more easily; for us here the war remains a most difficult matter for one's conscience to decide about. When one is actually fighting the instinct of self-preservation and the excitement drown every other feeling, but when one is in rest or doing nothing in the trenches, then it is different. One looks with astonishment and horror at the more and more cunningly elaborate means devised for destroying the enemy. One is torn between the natural instinct which says, "Thou shalt do no murder," and the sacred obligation, "This must be done for the sake of the Fatherland." This conflict may be temporarily suspended sometimes, but it always exists. It often occupies my mind after we come in in the evening. The opposition between the two principles is emphasized when one looks out upon such a peaceful valley as this that lies before me. The white-owl, the "bird of death," screeches from the alder-clump, and the thunder of the guns grows louder again. Then all is still. It is night. Slowly I prepare for bed.

April, 1915

The most trying part of this *mole's* war is that one can never have a real straightforward fight. When the first larks soar and, undisturbed by shells and whistling bullets, sing their morning hymn, then the guns begin firing aimlessly into the dawning day. This murdering is so senseless. The one consolation is that one is doing one's duty. I do think that we Germans have, more than any other nation, a stern sense of duty. And we stick to that in this ghastly war. The justification for militarism, which from the ordinary human point of view is detestable, is that it has helped to encourage and strengthen this sense of duty. Of course there are some shirkers here as everywhere else — "it takes all sorts to make a world" — but those who have this sense of duty do not ask: "Is it dangerous? Are the guns firing?" No: one shoots, one stays awake, one is constantly on the watch, burrows in the ground till 12 or 1 o'clock, and is at it again by 5 the next morning, simply because its one's damned duty and obligation. And all that is done just as a matter of course — neither willingly nor unwillingly — naturally, simply, just because it has got to be done. One may be a little braver or a little more skilful than another, but the same cheery tone prevails all through. Everybody does his best, one working for all and all for one.

5. COPSE 125

Some of the most dynamic and intriguing, yet disturbing, accounts of trench warfare were written by Ernst Jünger. Born to middle-class parents in 1895 in the university town of Heidelberg, Jünger enlisted in the German army in 1914 at the age of nineteen, where he served in the 73d Hanoverian Fusiliers for the duration of the war. Jünger fought in some of the bloodiest battles in northern France and Flanders, was wounded seven times, and was decorated for his courage. The spirit of war was etched in his memory. Throughout the conflict, he kept a journal detailing life as a frontline soldier, and in 1920 he shared his innermost thoughts on the subject with the German public when he published *In Stahlgewittern (Storm of Steel)*. The reception of this book was so successful that Jünger became an overnight sensation. The extract that follows is taken from one of his subsequent works, *Copse 125*, which describes the ferocious combat for Rossignol Wood. It had, the author writes, "not the least strategic importance, and yet at that time it had a meaning for all Europe as a local symbol of power where many lines of fate intersected and against which were set in motion a strength in men and machinery that could have reclaimed a whole province."

I generally make some use of this favourite hour of the day, and this morning took a stroll to Copse 125; for it is as well to have a quiet look at the place where at any moment one may be thrown into the battle. Uncertainty of one's ground is a heavy handicap at such moments, and by doing away with it one gains a great advantage over the attack. As it "was shooting" — this expression is a good example of the impersonal way we accept the enemy almost like the weather — and as, too, I had plenty of time, I sat down half-way on a big tussock that had slipped down into the trench and had breakfast and observed the insects. Then I put up my knife that, like a backwoodsman, I find it convenient to carry in a sheath stitched in my breeches, and continued my pilgrimage to the ill-famed copse of which I have already been told so much.

I must say the sight of it is not very cheerful. Shell upon shell has torn up the chalk, over which in any case there was only a thin layer of black humus, and a white powder has settled over what miserable traces of the undergrowth remain, so that they look as pale and sickly as if they had grown in a cellar. Roots and torn-up beeches and severed branches are thrown together in a coil — often hanging over the battered trenches, so that one has to pass by on all fours. The mighty trunks of the timber-trees, if not levelled with the ground, are docked of their tops, stripped of their bark and sapwood; only the hard, battered core remains in an army of bare masts, as though devoured by some

Excerpt from *Copse 125* by Ernst Jünger, Chatto & Windus, 1930, pp. 55–57, 99–100. Reprinted by permission of Random House UK Limited.

horrible cancerous disease. I tried to picture the scene to myself as we may so easily experience it — this petrified wood by night lit by Verey lights, whose white shine turns the bleached undergrowth to a garden of ghostly flora, fixed and fabulous; and among the great bare poles, that every moment throw their shadows at a different angle, flash after flash of a fight with bombs and machine-guns, fought with an insensate desperation that only this stark and epic landscape could inspire.

For here some awful spirit has struck out all redundancy and created a background worthy of a tragedy that far exceeds the pitch of any poet. Hence man has no choice but to become a bit of nature, subjected to its inscrutable decrees and used as a thing of blood and sinew, tooth and claw. To-morrow, perhaps, men of two civilized countries will meet in battle on this strip of land; and the proof that it must happen is that it does. For otherwise we should have stopped it long ago, as we have stopped sacrificing to Wotan, torturing on the rack, burning witches, or grasping red-hot iron to invoke the decision of God. But we have never stopped it and never shall, because war is not the law of one age or civilization, but of eternal nature itself, out of which every civilization proceeds, and into which it must sink again if it is not hard enough to withstand the iron ordeal.

For this reason those who seek to abolish war by civilized means are just as ridiculous as those ascetics who preach against propagation in order to usher in the millennium. They form the belated rearguard of an enlightenment that sought to dispose by the intellect of matters that draw their life from a depth beyond its reach. But they are the real pests of civilization though they have it always on their lips. Wherever they are left undisturbed at their work, there civilization emits the first scent of decay. May they ever be a laughing-stock to the youth of our land. The blood shall circle in it fresh and earthy as the sap of a wood in spring and beat with as manly a pulse as in the veins of our forefathers who made a saint of the Messiah. Rather than be weak and timorous, let us be hard and merciless on ourselves and on others. Because we think in this way that becomes us best we here have made ourselves its living example, and shall so continue till the end of the war and after. As long as we have a youth that stands for all that is strong and manly our future is assured. . . .

. . . We have to employ other means to-day than in the days of Frederick the Great when the officer, with the whole battle on his own shoulders, took in his serried ranks at one glance. A leader of troops today sees very little of his men in the sea of smoke, and cannot compel them to be heroes if they prefer to live for ever in another sense. He must be able to rely on them; and he can only do so if he has trained them to take the initiative rather than to act as puppets who carry out movements at the word of command. They must certainly be schooled in an iron school if they are to be real men, but they must be taught to face death with a higher sense of their own responsibility than in former days.

We have to free ourselves more and more from drill in massed movements; for since the development of mechanical weapons the functions of massed troops devolve more and more upon individuals. The most essential task to-day is to educate the soldier so that he can stand on his own with a machine-gun without losing sight of the engagement as a whole. We shall be able to replace platoons by machine-guns, companies by tanks, cavalry regiments by air-squadrons, and to rely, indeed, entirely on the machine — but only if we can count upon a high grade of specialist. For as Xenophon said when he encouraged his infantry to withstand cavalry, "all that occurs in battle is done by men." It is men who win battles, and only the picked men who know how to wield the best weapons. The materialists — and the supporters of soul-deadening drill are among the worst and the most abandoned of them — must never be allowed to forget it. As soon as ever we can put into battle large bodies of men of the same type as the flying men whom I visited the day before yesterday, resolute, intelligent, bold, and capable of enthusiasm — as I confidently expect from the further development of our people — we shall no longer need what we understand to-day by drill. There will be so much of interest to learn that no time will be left for it. Obedience will, of course, still be the first duty of a soldier, but I must be greatly mistaken if such men are not most disposed of all to be obedient, seeing that they have the best of all foundations of it in their own convictions. A man who feels that an extreme responsibility rests upon him will always strive to do his best.

6. ON THE EASTERN FRONT

The following two selections provide an indication of the conduct of the war by the Russian army. John Morse, an English businessman, found himself in Germany in July 1914, enjoying a vacation in "a scenic and cultivated country." As the outbreak of hostilities increasingly seemed probable, Morse determined to make his way back home by way of Russia but interrupted his journey to experience the adventure of the conflict. Bernard Pares, another Englishman, first visited Russia in 1898 and made its study his life's work. He served as professor of Russian history at the University of Liverpool and as secretary of the Anglo–Russian Committee, which sought to promote better relations between the two nations. From 1914 to 1917 he was attached to the Russian army, and in 1917 to the British ambassador in Petrograd.[*] The extract that follows is drawn from his memoirs of his stay in Russia.

a. *John Morse*

I have not yet mentioned the Bactrian camels which are used in thousands for Russian transport. During the winter the snow was so deep that the usual indications of the

Excerpt from *An Englishman in the Russian Ranks* by John Morse, Duckworth, 1915, pp. 252–256, 262–265.

---

[*] St. Petersburg was renamed Petrograd soon after the outbreak of the war.

roadways were completely buried; and even in the few cases where they could be discerned, it was most difficult to traverse them with either horse-waggons or motor-cars; indeed, the last-mentioned are useless in snow when it lies beyond a certain depth (though much depends on the power of the car); and guns, also, are impeded by the same cause.

Many persons think that the foot of a camel is peculiarly suited to traversing deserts, and is unfitted for progress over other kinds of ground. This may be true of the dromedary, or African one-humped camel; but it is not correct of the Bactrian, or two-humped camel, the species used by the Russians. This animal can keep its footing on the most slippery ground, and travel with facility over the deepest snow without sinking in to an appreciable depth. The Russians say that it will also go with speed over sand, rock and grass land, but founders in bogs and morasses. It carries a weight of 400 to 500 pounds, English; and proved to be very useful throughout the winter, until the thaw came, and three feet of mud succeeded six feet of snow; and then nothing on earth could drag itself through the miserable mire at a greater rate than a funeral pace.

But all the camels in the country were not enough to bring up the necessaries of the army; and the men, though fed and kept supplied with ammunition, were compelled to lack many things that would have increased both their comfort and their efficiency. Boots especially, and other wearing articles, were often badly wanted; and many of the men suffered greatly from frost-bites. My own feet were becoming very tender by the month of March, when the sun sometimes shone with sufficient strength to make the surface of the snow wet: and this added greatly to our troubles. It is essential to the welfare of troops that after marches they should have dry socks and a change of boots; otherwise they are almost sure to suffer from sore feet. It was the habit of the Russian infantry to take their socks off at night and dry them at the camp fires; but when in the presence of the enemy we were often forbidden to make fires; and at other times there was not sufficient fuel obtainable to supply the whole of our vast hosts: nor was there always a full supply of food, though it was the custom of the Russian soldiers to eat those horses and camels which were killed. There is but little difference between horseflesh and beef, and I have eaten it at scores of meals. I have also tasted camel's flesh; and have nothing to say in its favour. It is coarse, tough and flavourless.

The Germans having retired to carefully entrenched positions, from which we found it impossible to force them, a lull ensued; although occasionally attempts were made to surprise and assault some of the enemy's positions.

On the 5th March the Germans squirted liquid fire over one of these surprise parties which had got close up to their entrenchments, and was endeavouring to remove the wire-entanglements. It was the first time such a device had been reported; and there was some mystery concerning its nature. Some thought that boiling pitch had been used; others called it Greek fire. I do not think it was pitch, although I did not actually see it thrown. I examined the clothing of some of the men, who reported that the holes which were burnt smouldered, and were not easily put out. The fire came over them in a shower of sparks, and was not thrown by hand; but squirted out of a tube of some kind. The only actual injury that I could discover it did was in the case of one man who was badly burned about the face and probably blinded. It is astonishing what a number of devilish contrivances these dastardly Germans have invented and used in this war; and it is clear that they would resort to the foullest possible means, if this would give them the victory. . . .

About this time I heard mentioned the poisonous gas which has since become notorious. The Germans, I believe, had not yet resorted to sending the horrid stuff in clouds against a position; but they fired shells which emitted it in considerable quantities, and caused some deaths, and many disablements, amongst the Russian troops. I saw some of the shells burst; and the gas, which gradually expanded to a small cloud with a diameter of about 30 feet, looked like a thick, dirty yellow smoke. The odour of it was horrible and peculiar and very pungent; and it seemed to be a very heavy vapour, for it never rose high above the ground — not more than 20 feet. It dispersed slowly. In my opinion the best way to avoid it would be to rush rapidly through it towards the point from which it had been discharged. Doubtless some of it lurks in the air; but not sufficient, I think, to have deleterious effects. The bulk of it rolls on in a low, dense cloud. That which was shot at us came from *percussion* shells, which do not explode in the air. These projectiles were usually fired at us in salvoes; so as to form a cloud of gas on the ground.

I went to see the bodies of two men who had been killed by one of these poison-shells. They looked as if they had been rolled in flour of sulphur, being completely covered, flesh and clothes, with a yellowish deposit. Some wounded men, and others who had first gone to their assistance, were similarly encrusted. Some of these were insensible; others were gasping for breath, and discharging froth from their mouths. . . .

. . . The Russian soldiers, like soldiers and boys all the world over where snow is to be found, had amused themselves by making snow figures in rear of the trench, mostly those of the Emperors, Saints and Generals. A shot struck one of these and threw the well-beaten, frozen snow to an immense height in the air. The shell did not burst, a circumstance of frequent occurrence, which seemed to show that the fuses were badly made, or fitted badly to the projectile.

When the riflemen at last came out of the trench for a fresh supply of ammunition, they were amazed to find me and my horse standing by their cart. They at first mistook me for an officer and saluted very respectfully; but my awkward replies to their salutations caused them to raise their lantern and examine me more closely. Then I was seized, and an officer began to interrogate me, and I produced my papers; but the officer was not so easily satisfied as my Cossack friends; and I was taken to the trench, and thrust into what the British call a "funk-hole," or small excavated resting-place. My belongings were overhauled, and the supply of food received from the Cossacks at once appropriated by the soldiers, who seemed to be very hungry. They were good enough to give me some of the tallow, and a piece of fat bacon. Fortunately I am as fond of grease as any Russian, and I fortified myself for what might happen by making a plentiful meal: indeed, I ate all they gave me, and drank a full measure of vodka on top of it. Bad things are good things under adverse circumstances.

The men had bales of straw in the trenches, and on them they stretched themselves to sleep — at least those close to me did so; but it was too dark to see much. I obtained some of the straw, and slept very soundly in my "funk-hole," though I had a suspicion that I might have very good cause to funk in the morning.

The soldiers were not unkind, whatever they thought of me. One of them awoke me in the morning by pulling me out of my hole by the legs. I thought this was a preliminary to shooting or hanging, but nothing so drastic happened. I was given a pint of strong tea without sugar and milk, but it was hot, and that was a great deal on a bitterly cold morning. With the tea I received a piece of the dirtiest bread I have ever eaten; and shortly afterwards a gun boomed from the enemy's position, and a shell fell in the advanced trenches. As it caused no commotion I suppose it did no harm. It gave the signal that it was getting light enough for the enemy to see; and our men stood to their arms; and soon afterwards began to "snipe," as the modern phrase has it.

Sometimes I took a peep along the little gutter-like cuts where the men rested their rifles when shooting over the edge of the trench. I did this with impunity so frequently that I grew bold, until a bullet came and knocked the snow and dirt over me. A few minutes later a rifleman was aiming along this very cut when a bullet struck his head and killed him instantly. It entered in the centre of his forehead, and came out behind, carrying away a large piece of the skull and letting his brains out. I was becoming used to such painful sights; and in two moments I had his rifle in hand and his pouch strapped round me, and was watching at the death-cut to avenge his fall.

I had brought my own rifle with me; but this and my cartridges were taken from me the previous night. My revolver was concealed in a pocket, and I thought it wise to keep it there for the present.

I could not see much to shoot at. Some of the enemy's trenches were a long way back; others, salient points, ran up to within fifty yards of our position. Occasionally I saw the spike of a helmet; but it generally disappeared before I could bring the sight of the rifle to bear upon it.

The Germans usually wore their spiked helmets, jocosely called "*Picklehaubes,*" which much betrayed them when aiming from the trenches. Afterwards they became more cunning and wore their muffin-shaped caps when on duty of a dangerous character.

If I could not see the enemy they appeared to see me; for several bullets came unpleasantly close, and another man at my side was struck and badly wounded in the head. Then my chance came. I saw the spike of a helmet and about an inch of the top of it. It remained so still that I concluded the man was taking careful aim, an example which I followed, and fired. I saw the dirt fly up where the bullet struck the parapet, and the spike disappeared. I do not know if the bullet found its billet — probably not; I fired about twenty rounds at similar marks, sometimes seeing just the top of a spike, sometimes nearly the whole helmet; and then, turning rather quickly, I saw the officer who had arrested me the previous night watching me. He nodded approval; and I felt that I had "saved my bacon" if nothing else; and so it proved. I was no longer treated as a prisoner, and had evidently won the respect and goodwill of those who had witnessed my endeavours to trouble the enemy.

b. Bernard Pares

The German method is to mass superior artillery against a point selected and to cover the area in question with a wholesale and continuous cannonade. The big German shells, which the Russian soldiers call the "black death," burst almost simultaneously at about fifty yards from each other, making the intervening spaces practically untenable. The cannonaded area extends well to the rear of the Russian lines, and sometimes it is the rear that is first subjected to a systematic bombardment, the lines themselves being reserved for treatment later. On one of my visits the divisional and regimental staffs were being so shelled that the former had to move at once and one of the latter was half destroyed; but meanwhile there was hardly a shot along the actual front. In this way confusion is created, and reinforcements and supply are made difficult. It is the wholesale character of these cannonades that make their success, for there is nowhere to which the defenders can escape. The whole process is, of course, extremely expensive.

When a considerable part of the Russian front has thus been annihilated, and when the defenders are, therefore, either out of action or in retreat, the enemy's infantry is poured into the empty space and in such masses that it spreads also to left and right, pushing back the neighbouring Russian troops. Thus the whole line is forced to retire, and the same process is repeated on the new positions.

When success in one district has thus been secured, the German impact is withdrawn and again brought forward at some further part of the Russian front. In other words, the German hammer, zigzagging backwards and forwards, travels along our front, striking further and further on at one point or another, until the whole front has been forced back.

The temper of this corps, as of practically all the others, is in no sense the temper of a beaten army. The losses have been severe; but with anything like the artillery equipment of the enemy, both officers and men are confident that they would be going forward. . . .

. . . As large drafts of recruits had come in recently, we halted at the edge of a wood and the General gathered the men round him and made them a very vigorous little speech. He described how Germany and Germans had for several years exploited Russia, especially through the last tariff treaty, which was made when Russia was engaged in the Japanese War, and set up entirely unfair conditions of exchange. He said that the German exploited and bullied everybody; and that was a thing which the peasant could understand, often from personal experience. Then he got talking of the great family of the Slavs, of little Serbia's danger and of the Tsar's championship, of Germany's challenge and of Russia's defiance. Next he spoke of the Allies and of their help. And then he spoke of the regiment, which bears a name associated with the great Suvorov; they were always, he said, sent to the hardest work, often, as now, to repair a reverse; and he spoke plainly and without fear of the recent retreat. Concluding, he told them a story

Excerpt from *Day by Day with the Russian Army, 1914–1915* by Bernard Pares, Constable, 1915, pp. 245–247.

of Gurko: some of his men had said that the enemy would have to pass over their bodies, and Gurko answered, "Much better if you pass over his."

7. THE KEYS OF JERUSALEM

Turkey's entry into the war on the side of Germany and Austria-Hungary ensured that the eastern Mediterranean would figure as another theater of the conflict.[*] Initial Allied efforts to defeat Turkey with an amphibious assault at Gallipoli (at the Dardanelles, near Constantinople) proved a failure. But subsequent campaigns by British and Arab forces in Palestine fared much better. One of the striking scenes of the conflict occurred in December 1917 when British troops under General Edmund Allenby (called the Bull) entered Jerusalem, thus securing the holy city as "a Christmas present for the British people." The campaigns in the Middle East did not decisively speed the overall Allied victory in the war, but they did shape the future course of the region by prompting the British, in the form of the Balfour Declaration of 1917, to declare their sympathy for the establishment of a homeland for the Jewish people in Palestine. In this extract one of Allenby's officers describes the efforts to take symbolic possession of Jerusalem and the powerful sentiments associated with its "liberation."

Towards noon the resistance of the Turks collapsed. They fled east and north, and the advanced troops of the British force on the road from Jaffa pressed forward with an eagerness which was noteworthy. It may have been due to expectation. We had come far, and now the goal was close at hand. The Syrian monk at Enab had told us that El Kubeibeh — the valley where war's intrusion seemed an outrage, so peaceful was the aspect of its sycamores and cypresses and the broad sheet of precious water among those barren hills — once had been called Emmaus, and we knew it was only three-score furlongs distant from the City, a Sunday morning's walk.

After crossing the bottom of a deep ravine, the road skirted its southern edge and climbed in zig-zags to a rocky plateau. The word passed round that this was the last stage; yet even when that long ascent had been accomplished, no city could be seen, and already the short winter day was drawing in. At a bend, where the ravine turned north and the road ran in an easterly direction, were two houses; one was in ruins. Beyond them the ground sloped downwards to another valley into which we could not see. To our right in the south, a storm was brewing: the mountain tops were blotted out by leaden clouds beneath which the landscape seemed convulsed, and from that seething caldron white mists crept along the hidden valley, while wisps of fleecy vapor bore down on the plateau where we stood like riders of the sky.

"The Keys of Jerusalem" by C. B. Thomson, *The Nation,* 17 Mar. 1923.

---

[*] Turkey was also referred to as the Ottoman Empire.

One mountain, rising straight ahead, the storm had not yet reached. We had noted it many times before that day, the two towers on its summit, and a grove of trees surrounding a church with many domes in an enclosure on its side.

"How far off is the top of that hill?" asked a General.

"Just over five thousand yards to the left-hand tower," was the answer.

The hill in question was the Mount of Olives, the enclosure the Garden of Gethsemane, below which the still invisible city lay, not more than one mile off.

"Remember that no one is to go inside the walls. The Bull will be furious if anything of that kind happens." This last injunction given, the General went back in his car to announce to Headquarters and the world that Jerusalem had fallen.

Meanwhile, a small crowd had assembled in and around the ruined house; it consisted of signallers establishing telephonic communication, a German doctor, two Americans, and three Turks. One of the Turks was the Mayor of the Holy City, and he had brought with him the keys as a token of surrender. They were large keys and quite ordinary, except that they were very clean and shone like silver. There were several; no doubt "the keys of all the creeds" were in that bunch. They had been offered to two private soldiers, who had refused to have anything to do with them; their duties as cooks were far too pressing and began only when camp was reached. Dalliance on the road for such as these would have been criminal; others might traffic with key-bearing Mayors; their business was to serve hungry, exacting comrades, and shout out at the earliest moment possible the glad tidings "Dinners Up!"

An Artillery Major had also been approached, but with the same result. He was a solicitor in private life, and the effect of artillery training on his legal mind had been to increase its cautiousness. Those keys were not for him, he felt that instinctively; his ambition was a D.S.O. [Distinguished Service Order]; whereas the keys of Jerusalem were for people who might aspire to a K.C.B. [Knight of the Bath] or even higher. But when he thought of the local Press at home, in Yorkshire, of a whole column devoted to his doughty deeds, headed "A Tyke takes Temple," with a photograph of himself and three heathen Turks inset (one of the Americans had brought a camera), he was sorely tempted.

The keys were still undisposed of when the senior General called up on the telephone. He wanted further details before sending off a telegram; but on being told of what had transpired since he left, his voice became eager, anxious, and imperative.

"The Mayor with the keys? Has he still got them! . . . Keep him till I come; on no account let him go away or give them to anybody else. I will receive them!"

Preparations for the ceremony were made at once: a few women and children had by this time assembled, bringing flowers, and a camera was got into position.

If Robert the Bruce had achieved his heart's desire and been able to fulfil his vow, he might have ridden by that road after lying overnight at Enab. But he would not have stopped one moment by the wayside in his impatience; the keys would have been received by Douglas, the faithful servant of his King. Godfrey of Bouillon, too — "a quiet, pious, hard-fighting knight who was chosen to rule in Jerusalem because he had no dangerous qualities and no obvious defects" — would have left either to Bohemund or Baldwin what to him would have seemed an empty show. But he, of course, was not successful, only the hero of a legend and some songs. The man who actually received the keys was neither King nor Pilgrim, though in some ways a Crusader; his satisfaction was unbounded as he stood, the observed of all observers (and there were at least a dozen present), by the roadside with the ruin as a background. Ruins and conquerors go well together.

Click went the camera, and the General smiled approval; at least there was a record of this historical event with himself the central figure.

In regard to publicity the Solicitor and the General had much in common; but naturally the latter's outlook on affairs was wider. No local Press for him; he aimed at nothing less than the front page of a Sunday illustrated paper — some weekly compendium of sport, vulgarity, follies, crimes, and lies, with an occasional contribution from a Cabinet Minister. This is an age of doubt; people believe little of what they read, but still retain a touching faith in photographs. His niche in the temple of fame and limelight would be secure if a million so-called Sunday readers knew him by sight. And how opportune it was! With any luck the negative would be in London by Christmas week. Thus, suddenly, is a garish glory gained.

A whole series of photographs had in fact been taken; his was the last. The first was of two British Tommies, in shorts, conferring with a Turkish Mayor and two City Councillors, accepting cigarettes and flowers, smiling their gratitude for these gifts. The second was of their backs as they plodded stolidly eastwards, keyless and careless, while three disconsolate City Fathers stared after them, baffled and charmed by their simplicity. The third showed a big, strong man seated squarely on a horse; and looking up at him, appealingly, a frail old Turk holding a bunch of keys. The horseman's face was twitching under the stress of inner conflict between caution and desire. He was neither buying nor selling, but, metaphorically, was looking a gift horse in the mouth. A strange position for a Yorkshireman. "Château qui parle; femme qui écoute." The proverb is incomplete. In all probability, if he, who had neither spoken nor listened to Jerusalem's first Magistrate, had looked at those keys a moment longer he would have yielded. But caution triumphed. The fourth photograph showed a wistful figure, standing apart, watching; the solicitor had lingered, held by some instinct, until the General's car arrived. If to suffer in silence were a military virtue, that solitary spectator earned a D.S.O. during the next five minutes. A Major, of course, should always give way to a General; but this man was only one-third major; he had two other sides which did not wear khaki. Another man, because he was a General, was getting what he, a Yorkshire solicitor, might have got, for nothing. It was enough to make anyone a Bolshevik. He wondered if the smiling recipient of those keys was Irish — quite a quarter of the Generals in the British Army were of that fighting race — and shuddered at the thought.

A few hundred yards further on were the first houses of the western suburb. Neither pomp nor circumstance attended our arrival; we were not entering the walled city, only surrounding it, and marched through squalid streets from a corner near the Jaffa Gate to the main road leading to Damascus. While we passed the storm broke; an icy wind swept up the valley of the Kedron, rain fell in torrents and drenched the tired troops.

We had imagined something very different. In the camp west of Beersheba, life had been strenuous and inevitably ascetic; the soul had been swept and garnished, the vision cleared. Waiting while summer mellowed into autumn, marking the changes of the moon, searching for water in a sandy waste, we had learned the desert's loneliness, tasted the tang of its hot breath, marched through cool, splendid Eastern nights over its trackless surface, watched the sun rise and dissipate the cloudy shimmer of its robe of dew. To some those weeks had been a vigil, the fitting preparation for a high adventure. Even the callous had moments of exaltation, mystical imaginings, mirages of the mind.

Realities are always disappointing; they issue from a gate of horn, not from the ivory gate of dreams.

In our visions we saw a City Beautiful, where once a temple with a golden dome had roused the envy of Samaritans and the cupidity of Vespasian's legions; we found drab, melancholy walls hemmed in on the north and west by a hideous modern suburb. We had surveyed with the mind's eye a green hill without a city wall; but Judgment Place, Calvary, and Sepulchre were huddled *within* the walls, and almost beneath one roof. We had pictured the "Via Dolorosa" as portrayed on stained-glass windows; it was a narrow lane, where ignorance and superstition had been so exploited that there might have been turnstiles at the Stations of the Cross. We had heard of Russian pilgrims paying huge sums to be the first to light their lamps at what was called the "Sacred Fire"; we saw the filament with which the trick was worked. We had conceived an atmosphere compact of memories of an imperishable story, and breathing peace; we entered an arena for all the jarring creeds. Being British, the latest crusaders tried to hide their disappointment, became more taciturn than ever, and registered another lost illusion.

There was no need. We still possessed our dreams, and of their stuff could create cities far more fair than any structure built with hands. Those bright, intangible, dissolving cities, how peaceful and serene, how different from Jerusalem on that day of storm and rain! — no mud, no smells, no noise, no hustling crowds, no simple soldiers hungering for a meal, no envious schemers, no conquerors taking keys, no walls, no secrets, nothing to conceal. They are not rooted to one spot, but come to us wherever we may be, assuming shapes as various as our moods. We are their architects, masters of all, without, within, kings in the kingdoms of our inner selves, whose revelations come and go.

D. The Varieties of War

1. THE FIRST GAS ATTACK

Napoleon Bonaparte argued that the psychological aspects of warfare are ultimately more important than the physical ones. His attention to the morale of his own troops was well founded, and the apparent lessons were not lost on his successors. German scientists hoped to break the morale of Allied troops with the introduction of poison gas, used first on April 22, 1915, at Ypres. The following extract by Brigadier General Sir J. E. Edmonds describes both the debilitating physical effects of that gas attack and its harrowing psychological impact.

The 22nd April was a glorious spring day. Air reconnaissance in the morning had disclosed considerable liveliness behind the German lines and some activity in the Houthulst Forest (2 miles north of Langemarck), where a column was seen on the march, though it tried to evade observation; but there was nothing abnormal in this. In the forenoon there was considerable shelling of Ypres by 17-inch and 8-inch howitzers and lighter guns, and towards midday, of the roads leading into the town; but this gradually ceased and all was quiet again.

Suddenly, at 5 P.M., a new and furious bombardment of Ypres by heavy howitzers was recommenced. The villages in front of Ypres, almost untouched until then, were also heavily shelled, and simultaneously French field-guns to the north-east of Ypres began a somewhat rapid fire, although the German field artillery was silent. At first some officers who heard the firing surmised that the newly arrived Algerian Division was "shooting itself in"; but those who were on points of vantage saw two curious greenish-yellow clouds on the ground on either side of Langemarck in front of the German line. These clouds spread laterally, joined up, and, moving before a light wind, became a bluish-white mist, such as is seen over water meadows on a frosty night. Behind the mist the enemy, by the sound of his rifle fire, was advancing. Soon, even as far off as the V Corps report centre at "Goldfish Chateau" (2,000 yards west of Ypres railway station and five miles from Langemarck) a peculiar smell was noticed, accompanied by smarting of the eyes and tingling of the nose and the throat. It was some little time, however, before it was realized that the yellow clouds were due to the gas about which warnings had been received, and almost simultaneously French coloured troops, without officers, began drifting down the roads through the back areas of the V Corps. Soon afterwards French Territorial troops were seen hurriedly crossing the bridges over the canal north of Ypres. It was impossible to understand what the Africans said, but from the way they coughed and pointed to their throats, it was evident that, if not suffering from the effects of gas, they were thoroughly scared. Teams and wagons of the French field artillery next appeared retiring, and the throng of fugitives soon became thicker and more disordered, some individuals running and continuing to run until they reached Vlamertinghe and beyond. Although the "seventy-fives" were firing regularly, it was obvious that something very serious had happened, and this was emphasized when, about 7 P.M., the French guns suddenly ceased fire.

2. RUSTING AT ANCHOR

By 1915 the soaring spirits with which the German high-seas fleet greeted the outbreak of the war began to plummet. Weeks of inactivity when cautious commanders feared to expose the German surface fleet to the quantitatively superior British fleet had taken their toll. Seaman Richard Stumpf's diary, already cited in Part I, Section A, provides a vivid sense of the growing disenchantment among German sailors.

Excerpt from *Vain Glory,* Guy Chapman, ed., Cassell UK, 1967, pp. 136–137. Reprinted by permission of Peters Fraser & Dunlop Group Ltd.

Today, on [April] 13, the same old thing happened again. Something was going on at sea. Early that morning three or four torpedo boats came into port in a sorry state. One of them was missing her forward mast, her bridge hung crooked and her bowplates were completely smashed in and bent. She had mounted a sail on her starboard side to prevent the water from leaking in. Some bow damage was evident on the other three boats. But all of them came in under their own power.

This incident stirred up a good deal of discussion. We were agreed that the boats must have had a fight with enemy ships. How else could they have lost a mast? We also remembered that a prize crew from our ship which had gone out with the torpedo boats four days ago had not returned. We knew that they had captured and seized as prizes twenty merchant ships. (Today I learned that they were Dutch fishing boats.) The crew included two officers, one reservist steersman, three petty officers, five stokers and six sailors from our ship.

At the ungodly early hour of four in the morning we were wakened to pull in the torpedo nets and to clear the ship for departure. The steam in our engines was set for a speed of 30 kilometers or 16 sea miles per hour. We waited expectantly for something to happen. After breakfast we made preparations which could only point to a battle. All hands were dressed in battle clothes, i.e., their best blue uniforms. The rest of the clothes were packed in the seabags and stowed away. At the same time we stored the tables and benches from the crew's quarters in a safe place. The officers' cabins were emptied and the chests placed in the storage compartment between decks. For a change the men were glad to do this work. The entire squadron was to be ready to sail out at eight o'clock that morning. Gradually we gathered all our ships. [We were surrounded] by heavy and light cruisers and a whole forest of thin tall masts of the torpedo boats. There were five flotillas of eleven ships each. We all sat around waiting for the order to sail out. By eight o'clock, however, we were still at anchor. Then it was announced that we would leave at ten. Only the devil knows why we lay there as though we were paralyzed. By noon we gave up all hope for action. The only thing which made this entire mess bearable was that we did not have to perform our regular duties. Since the sun was smiling down from the sky, we lay down on deck and lazily joked about the navy.

To put it bluntly, I no longer care if we get to fight or not. Once again our principal interest is food, extra rations and shore leave. Nothing has changed. The men often express the hope that there will be no battle. For whom should they allow themselves to be killed? For the wealthy? After the war we will receive the same treatment as in the past and we shall be the ones who have to suffer and pay for it. I ought to add at this point that these statements are caused by our discontent at our inactivity. Should it ever come to a fight, all of us would be eager and raring to go. The adage, "idle hands make the devil's mischief," sums up the situation quite well. One can get used to anything but it is extremely difficult to be kept waiting all the time in the knowledge that our tremendous power is being wasted. The atmosphere is strained and embittered. One can

Daniel Horn, *War, Mutiny and Revolution in the German Navy,* pp. 81–83. Copyright 1967 by Rutgers, the State University. Reprinted by permission of Rutgers University Press.

sense it among the officers and the men. Happy songs and joyful games are no longer in evidence. We are virtually at each other's throats. The happy spirit of camaraderie has vanished and has been supplanted by deep depression. No wonder all of us wish to leave the ship. Whenever there is a call for volunteers for the submarines or for [the naval infantry brigade in] Belgium, everyone steps forward. We are very envious of those few who have already departed. Formerly none of us wanted to leave and we were all afraid lest we be transferred. But now? Some time ago the Chaplain held a sermon on changing values. He could well have cited this as an example.

3. ADVENTURES OF THE **U**-202

Increasingly, the naval weapon that Germany pinned its hopes on was not the battle-ship but the submarine. The submarine's potential for destruction was impressive, and its frequent ability to escape detection could be terrifying, but the early U-boats (from the German for "undersea boat") were still rather primitive vessels; they could not remain submerged for long, and on the surface of the water they were vulnerable. To preserve the element of surprise submarine commanders often attacked without warning; sometimes the victims were civilians. U-boats were eventually nullified by the convoy system, whereby merchant shipping received protection from escorts such as destroyers. Allied naval supremacy on the surface enabled the British to blockade Germany and keep needed supplies from reaching the beleaguered nation. This selection, by a former U-boat commander, illustrates some of the chief features of German submarine warfare.

Noiselessly we slipped closer and closer in our exciting chase. The main thing was that our periscope should not be observed, or the steamer might change her course at the last moment and escape us. Very cautiously, I stuck just the tip of the periscope above the surface at intervals of a few minutes, took the position of the steamer in a second and, like a flash, pulled it down again. That second was sufficient for me to see what I wanted to see. The steamer was to starboard and was heading at a good speed across our bows. To judge from the foaming waves which were cut off from the bow, I calculated that her speed must be about sixteen knots.

The hunter knows how important it is to have a knowledge of the speed at which his prey is moving. He can calculate the speed a little closer when it is a wounded hare than when it is one which in flight rushes past at high speed.

It was only necessary for me, therefore, to calculate the speed of the ship for which a sailor has an experienced eye. I then plotted the exact angle we needed. I measured this by a scale which had been placed above the sights of the periscope. Now I only had to let the steamer come along until it had reached the zero point on the periscope and fire the torpedo, which then must strike its mark.

Excerpt from *The Adventures of the U-202* by Baron Spiegel of Peckelsheim, Century, 1917, pp. 50–57, 172–173.

You see, it is very plain; I estimate the speed of the boat, aim with the periscope and fire at the right moment.

He who wishes to know about this or anything else in this connection should join the navy, or if he is not able to do so, send us his son or brother or nephew.

On the occasion in question everything went as calculated. The steamer could not see our cautious and hardly-shown periscope and continued unconcerned on its course. The diving rudder in the "Centrale" worked well and greatly facilitated my unobserved approach. I could clearly distinguish the various objects on board, and saw the giant steamer at a very short distance — how the captain was walking back and forth on the bridge with a short pipe in his mouth, how the crew was scrubbing the forward deck. I saw with amazement — a shiver went through me — a long line of compartments of wood spread over the entire deck, out of which were sticking black and brown horse heads and necks.

Oh, great Scott! Horses! What a pity! Splendid animals!

"What has that to do with it?" I continually thought. War is war. And every horse less on the western front is to lessen England's defense. I have to admit, however, that the thought which had to come was disgusting, and I wish to make the story about it short.

Only a few degrees were lacking for the desired angle, and soon the steamer would get into the correct focus. It was passing us at the right distance, a few hundred meters.

"Torpedo ready!" I called down into the "Centrale."

It was the longed-for command. Every one on board held his breath. Now the steamer's bow cut the line in the periscope — now the deck, the bridge, the foremast — the funnel.

"Let go!"

A light trembling shook the boat — the torpedo was on its way. Woe, when it was let loose!

There it was speeding, the murderous projectile, with an insane speed straight at its prey. I could accurately follow its path by the light wake it left in the water.

"Twenty seconds," counted the mate whose duty it was, with watch in hand, to calculate the exact time elapsed after the torpedo was fired until it exploded.

"Twenty-two seconds!"

Now it must happen — the terrible thing!

I saw the ship's people on the bridge had discovered the wake which the torpedo was leaving, a slender stripe. How they pointed with their fingers out across the sea in terror; how the captain, covering his face with his hands, resigned himself to what must come. And next there was a terrific shaking so that all aboard the steamer were tossed about and then, like a volcano, arose, majestic but fearful in its beauty, a two-hundred meter high and fifty-meter wide pillar of water toward the sky.

"A full hit behind the second funnel!" I called down into the "Centrale." Then they cut loose down there for joy. They were carried away by ecstasy which welled out of their hearts, a joyous storm that ran through our entire boat and up to me.

And over there?

Landlubber, steel thy heart!

A terrible drama was being enacted on the hard-hit sinking ship. It listed and sank towards us.

From the tower I could observe all the decks. From all the hatches human beings forced their way out, fighting despairingly. Russian firemen, officers, sailors, soldiers, hostlers, the kitchen crew, all were running and calling for the boats. Panic stricken, they thronged about one another down the stairways, fighting for the life-boats, and among all were the rearing, snorting and kicking horses. The boats on the starboard deck could not be put into service, as they could not be swung clear because of the list of the careening steamer. All, therefore, thronged to the boats on the port side, which, in the haste and anguish, were lowered, some half empty; others overcrowded. Those who were left aboard were wringing their hands in despair. They ran from bow to stern and back again from stern to bow in their terror, and then finally threw themselves into the sea in order to attempt to swim to the boats.

Then another explosion resounded, after which a hissing white wave of steam streamed out of all the ports. The hot steam set the horses crazy, and they were beside themselves with terror — I could see a splendid, dapple-gray horse with a long tail make a great leap over the ship's side and land in a lifeboat, already overcrowded — but after that I could not endure the terrible spectacle any longer. Pulling down the periscope, we submerged into the deep.

When, after some time, I came again to the surface there was nothing more to be seen of the great, proud steamer. . . .

"Poor devils," I thought, "I understand how you feel over your beautiful, fine ship, but why didn't you stay at home? Why do you go to sea when you know what threatens? Why do you or your governments force us to destroy your ships wherever we can find them? Do you think we are going to wait until our own women and children starve and let you keep your bread baskets full before we defend ourselves? You have started it. You are responsible for the consequences. If you would discontinue your inhuman way of carrying on the war, then we would let your sailing ships and steamers pass unmolested, when they do not carry contraband. You have wanted war to the knife. Good, we have accepted your challenge."

4. KNIGHTS OF THE SKY

Technological developments pioneered in the First World War, such as the submarine and the tank, would prove far more effective and significant during the Second World War. So it was also with air power. The following selections illustrate the romance, the danger, and, to some extent, the futility of aerial war. It was the Germans who responded with a particular zeal for military aviation in the First World War and a special aptitude for it in the second. The author of the first selection was an officer in the German Jagdstaffel 34, a fighterplane unit stationed on the Western Front; the second, a British airman who warns against regarding aerial combat, at least in its early stages, as a fully modern practice. The final selection is an example of the poetry inspired by the war in the air.

a. *Wings of War*

[March 29, 1918]

Bad weather to-day. Clouds at all heights. A storm. We fly all the same, because the duty machines have to go forward.

Snow at eight hundred metres. We therefore stay quite low and have a scrap with a few English machines. The rain whips against one's goggles; gusts toss the machine up and down; one is so busy trying to manage it that one has no time to look at what is going on below. Through the swirls of mist the earth assumes a spectral appearance as it flits away beneath us.

[March 30, 1918]

The English have dug themselves in. To-day our people are attacking at Hamelet.

Gloomy weather again; getting worse and worse. But what does the weather matter? We just fly.

We start and land on a battle landing-ground close behind the lines. All quiet in front of us — only a few stray shells drone across. The clouds thicken and drop lower; a thin drizzle falls earthward.

At last we can get off. In a trice we are over the lines. And now the artillery fire starts. It rolls and booms; despite the roar of the engine I can hear every explosion. Trails of smoke stream upward everywhere. Groups of infantry work their way towards the enemy's positions, batteries thunder away. Flying quite low, we behold the battle as a huge spectacle.

English observation machines streak off as we approach. As the air is now clear, we take a hand in the battle down below by shooting up nests of snipers and artillery positions. Khaki figures crouch anxiously against the sides of their trenches, pale faces that stare up at us look like distorted-masks. On we go. At one gun the whole crew duck behind the shield, at another they run off into a trench, but one fellow sinks to his knees and throws up his arms to heaven. On we go! Heavy infantry and machine gun fire pelts up at us, and holes begin to appear in our wings. But what does that matter? Carry on!

Now English fighting machines make their appearance. They flit like shadows through the shreds of clouds and try to attack our infantry. They are not going to succeed, because we are there — so they turn about and sheer off.

The rain becomes thicker; it whips against the skin like hail. Goggles are continually getting dimmed, but carry on! A Sopwith hurtles out of a cloud in front of me; he sees me and goes into a turn, but for a moment he stands quite still in the middle of it. I take

Excerpt from *Wings of War: An Airman's Diary of the Last Year of the War* by Rudolf Stark, John Hamilton, 1933, pp. 38–41, 54–55.

aim — shoot — my tracers hiss across to him in long threads and eat their way into his fuselage — a red flame jets out — wing over wing the Englishman goes down in flames — my third! But I have no time to waste thought on him — carry on! Fresh enemies come, vanish and come again, while below us the battle thunders and roars.

[March 31, 1918]

Easter Sunday. The sun has forced his way through. Easter rises in the radiance of a sunny morning. A silvery sheen bedecks the countryside.

I think of home and the mountains. . . .

Far away there lies a fair land. My home land. Now the church bells will be ringing as the peasants go home in their gala dresses. . . .

Our home is the war. We know no other. We are a wheel in a vast mechanism.

We are still young, but our childhood lies far, far behind us. Far away, with our youth, lie our homes and the times of peace.

We have grown old and found a new home — the Jagdstaffel. Our lives, all our thoughts and feelings belong to it.

We have grown lonely. We are only a little group of men who belong to one another. We share the dangers of the front, we are a part of the great battles, but we do not belong to the front.

We are lonely. Generally we are quartered at the base; we enjoy the pleasant life of the base, but we are not part of it.

We are lonely. Everyone of us went forth with some regiment to defend the homeland. We left our country and then we left our regiments, to find loneliness and a new home.

What do the others know of the beauty of loneliness, of the splendour of our new home!

We must be lonely, because we possess the most beautiful of all things — flight and the combat in the air.

All around us lies dead land — ruins that have been thrice levelled to the ground. New shell-holes, with brown pools that reflect the blue of heaven, are born beside the old ones that are choked up and overgrown with grass.

Far and wide there is nothing but dead land — ruins and wreckage.

Here was once a pleasure-garden. . . . Stunted green things are growing amid the burnt debris. . . .

[On his next mission Stark again found himself in combat with an English plane.]

. . . Meanwhile I go on turning with my man, but suddenly the observer stops shooting, and the machine goes down in spirals. This Englishman seems to want to land, but as it may be a trick I follow him down and take care not to let him out of my sights. But he drops deeper; now comes a last turn, the machine flattens out makes a good landing on a field, taxis and comes to a stop.

It sits there on the grass like a big butterfly, with its cockades shining gaily and peacefully.

I send a couple of shots in its direction to make sure that its crew get out quickly and refrain from destroying the machine. But men hasten up from an adjacent camp, and soon the Englishman is surrounded by a crowd of them — the enemy's capture is assured. However I have known our people damage a machine from pure stupidity and therefore land on the same field. I can hardly wait till my machine has stopped taxying, but at last I reach the vanquished foeman.

It is a strange spectacle: a thing that I have been fighting, a thing that was turning its guns on me, a thing I could hardly see at all in the hustle of our turns — and now it stands quite quietly before me.

The pilot, an English lieutenant, is lifted out of his seat; he has a bullet in the upper part of the thigh. The gunner, a sergeant, is unwounded. Both look very unhappy, but their faces brighten up when they catch sight of me. It is rather an unpleasant business to fall into the hands of the troops; they are not very kindly disposed towards enemy airmen, especially if they have just had a few bombs dropped on their huts. And so the two Englishmen are delighted to see a German airman come along.

We greet one another almost like old acquaintances. We bear no malice against one another. We fight each other, but both parties have a chance to win or lose.

In a kind of a way we are one big family, even if we scrap with one another and kill one another. We meet at the front, we get to know the respective badges of Staffel and Squadron and are pleased to meet these old acquaintances in the flesh.

The fight is over, and we are good friends.

b. Aerial Combat

15th April

The first time I ever encountered a German machine in the air, both the pilot (Harvey-Kelly) and myself were completely unarmed. Our machine had not been climbing well, and as I was considered somewhat heavy for an observer, Harvey-Kelly told me to leave behind all unnecessary gear. I therefore left behind my carbine and ammunition. We were taking photographs of the trench system to the north of Neuve Chapelle when I suddenly espied a German two-seater about 100 yards away and just below us. The German observer did not appear to be shooting at us. There was nothing to be done. We waved a hand to the enemy and proceeded with our task. The enemy did likewise. At the time this did not appear to me in any way ridiculous — there is a bond of sympathy between all who fly, even between enemies. But afterwards just for safety's sake I always carried a carbine with me in the air. In the ensuing two or three months I had

Excerpt from *Vain Glory*, Guy Chapman, ed., Cassell UK, 1967, p. 133. Reprinted by permission of Peters Fraser & Dunlop Group Ltd.

an occasional shot at a German machine. But these encounters can hardly be dignified with the name of "fights." If we saw an enemy machine nearby, we would fly over towards it, and fire at it some half a dozen rounds. We scarcely expected to shoot the enemy down; but it was a pleasant break in the monotony of reconnaissance and artillery observation. I remember being surprised one day to hear that an observer of another squadron (his name, Lascelles, sticks in my memory to this day, though I never met him), had shot down a German machine in our lines with a rifle.

c. "A Song of the Plane"

This is the song of the Plane —
The creaking, shrieking plane,
The throbbing, sobbing plane,
   And the moaning, groaning wires: —
The engine — missing again!
One cylinder never fires!
   Hey ho! for the Plane!

This is the song of the Man —
The driving, striving man,
The chosen, frozen man: —
   The pilot, the man-at-the-wheel,
Whose limit is all that he can,
And beyond, if the need is real!
   Hey ho! for the Man!

This is the song of the Gun —
The muttering, stuttering gun,
The maddening, gladdening gun: —
   That chuckles with evil glee
At the last, long dive of the Hun,
With its end in eternity!
   Hey ho! for the Gun!

This is the song of the Air —
The lifting, drifting air,
The eddying, steadying air,
   The wine of its limitless space,
May it nerve us at last to dare
Even death with undaunted face!
   Hey ho! for the Air.
                    Gordon Alchin

From *The Muse in Arms,* E. B. Osborne, ed., John Murray, 1917, pp. 109–110.

5. ZEPPELIN OVER ENGLAND

British civilians found it an unsettling if not terrifying experience to be bombed from the air. But as a former German helmsman relates, the zeppelins were unwieldy and vulnerable, and an arduous bombing run could prove taxing for the crew as well.

On the 19th October the final orders came and we left our shed at half-past eleven. The journey over the sea was cold and misty. We barely sighted some of the other airships off the Frisian coast. There were at least twelve ships under orders to attack England, so I understood Kölle to tell the navigator, and from the radios that were taken on board I think they all must have started. We did not see them all clearly, for it was the custom to fly independently while keeping a general direction. Once started the radio gave us little news. Once or twice we thought we saw another ship; L 54 we recognized by the setting of her cars; L 47 we distinguished through the glasses. Then I heard Kölle identify L 50, so it seemed to him, and he passed some disparaging remark about her commander, for he despised his skill as an airman no less than he suspected his determination. L 49 we thought we recognized, or so the navigator said, by her little flag that she flew from her forward car. But it was a dreary, windy crossing and owing to the cold and height many of us were feeling numbed and slack by the time we made the English coast at about 8 P.M. We could not be sure of our landfall as it was dark and our navigation was undoubtedly at fault. We should, so I believe, have crossed the Lincoln coast; but from an argument we had with the officers our navigating warrant officer, Hashagen, expressed grave doubts as to the landfall. I felt sure we were a long way south of that. Kölle, however, though looking anxious would not give way. I looked at my comrades in the car to see if I could read their thoughts, but only cold and anxiety were there. The wind must have freshened from the north for even then, like the lightning, some searchlights cut the air; all I could see by their warm beams was the leeway that we were making. Kölle swore and jumped at the ballast control cords. The ship rose rapidly. "5,800!" [i.e., metres, 19,000 ft.] read Hashagen off the altimeter; the height and the cold made him look ghastly in the pale searchlight beam as he leant on the glass panels. I shall never forget his face. I felt, too, that I would get little sympathy from him, if I dropped out, for the height and anxiety were telling on him already. Guns opened on us too, but that did not trouble us.

For nearly two hours more we struggled to keep our westward course but the wind blew ever stronger and I could tell that our navigation was getting more and more uncertain. We dropped a few bombs at some faint lights but providence alone knows where they went. I scarcely believe that Lieutenant Schütz, our second-in-command even troubled to set the bombing sight.

Excerpt from *Vain Glory,* Guy Chapman, ed., Cassell UK, 1967, pp. 472–478. Reprinted by permission of Peters Fraser & Dunlop Group Ltd.

By this time it was bitterly cold. Hashagen once read the thermometer aloud and gave over 30 degrees of frost [C. about 60° of frost F.]. I heard him mention Birmingham as our target, but he did not believe we had reached that locality. We climbed still higher as the weight of the bombs and petrol grew smaller and it grew still colder. Hahndorf, an engineer, now came in to report to Kölle that the men were feeling the cold. The sailmaker, in particular, who was attending to the valves of the gas-bags, complained of his feet. Well he might do so, for he could not wear his felt boots when climbing about the ship. He said he could not go on much longer. Two engineers, so Hahndorf said, were sleepy; while the petrol rating was grumbling and fumbling over his work.

Something must be done. The wind was rendering our progress westwards laborious. It was clear to us who had no say in the matter, that we ought to turn back, yet Kölle would not give in. The navigator and director began to express misgivings. Finally, Hahndorf re-appeared and gave it as his opinion that his engineers could not be trusted to go on much longer under such conditions. Reluctantly Kölle gave the order to turn; it was now about 11 o'clock. Hurriedly he gave his instructions for the return overland over Belgium. This was a bad sign, for it was not a step that our airship commanders would do unless the weather or other conditions were threatening. I could tell by the compass that we were now steering south-eastwards. The wind must have increased in violence and the cold was the worst I have ever experienced; I could scarcely continue, in spite of all felt boots and quilted clothing, it was terrible. It grew too cold to pull out the food to eat; the meat that one man pulled out was hard as stone. Kölle clearly not knowing where he was let out more ballast; we must have touched 6,500 metres or more.

At about 11.30 we began to see lights below and as the lights continued so it suddenly dawned upon us that it could only be the city of London that we were crossing in the air. Even Kölle looked amazed at the dim lights as Schütz suddenly shouted "London!" It was then that we first realized the fury of the savage tempest that had been driving us out of our course. But Kölle clearly had but one thought — that was higher. So he released more ballast and the bombs — first two sighting shots and then the rest. Over London! We had achieved what no other German airship had done since Mathy had bombed that proud city over a year ago! And his last trip across the city had proved his undoing. Fortunately for us we were unseen; not a searchlight was unmasked; not a shot was fired; not an aeroplane was seen. If the gale had driven us out of our course, it had also defeated the flying defences of the city! It was misty or so it seemed, for we were above a thin veil of cloud. The Thames we just dimly saw from the outline of the lights; two great railway stations, I thought I saw, but the speed of the ship running almost before the gale was such that we could not distinguish much. We were half frozen, too, and the excitement was great. It was all over in a flash. The last big bomb was gone, and we were once more over the darkness and rushing onwards.

It was then that our misfortunes began. Hahndorf reported to Kölle that the engine of the port wing car was scarcely working — he thought owing to the sooting of the plugs. The plugs were cleaned by the engineers but alas! their hands were so cold and they themselves so clumsy with lassitude and fatigue owing to the height that, by the time the plugs were cleaned and replaced, the engine had ceased to function — the cooling water had frozen; the radiator had split and there was no means in our power to get the engine into action again.

From this moment our journey became one long story of misery and pain. The cold grew intense and we all began to feel dejected at the consciousness that our real attack on England must have failed. The jubilation at having flown over the enemy's capital gave way to anxiety. At the helm of the ship we began to feel that the gale was driving us away, still further out of our course. We were so high that the earth was scarcely visible. Clouds were obviously being driven beneath us until we could not distinguish the sea. It was somewhere after midnight that Hahndorf came to report to the commander that the sailmaker could scarcely go on with his duties; his feet were frostbitten and the poor fellow was now lying in his hammock unable to do more. The petrol rating was complaining of weariness and sickness, leaning up against his tanks. Two engineers were suffering from height: one of these had been relieved by the man from the port wing car. Kölle became visibly perturbed! Even Schütz, usually so cheerful, looked pale and anxious. So we went on in gloomy silence.

For some two or three hours — we hardly knew how the time went by — we drove on, but, as events showed later, our course was now pure guess work. When and where we crossed the sea we could not tell. Hashagen argued we were now steering over Belgium, but somehow his voice lacked conviction. Kölle uttered not a word. We well knew that he was more than uneasy. The want of our port propeller told on the steering and I myself feared that this would endanger our safe return to Germany.

The hours dragged on. The petrol rating was now really ill. Both ratings from the port wing car were now relieving other sufferers. Hahndorf was growing anxious about his fuel supply and said so. Kölle stormed at him. But the man's worn, pale face and his frozen black moustache and beard deserved only pity. He was gallantly struggling against sickness.

At last dawn began to light up the sky. One, and then another, airship were barely distinguished against the eastern light. They could only be German, but we dared not use our radio, and that in itself was proof that we might be over the enemy's air defences. Kölle rapped out a bitter exclamation as this suspicion grew into certainty; flashes on the ground showed hostile gun-fire to be at work; whether shooting at us or not we could not tell. We saw no bursts. Still more, to our intense relief, we never sighted an aeroplane! Schütz assumed a reassuring tone, but this was abruptly checked when we felt the forward engine behind us slowing down and finally stop! Hahndorf came in; he was almost breaking down. The petrol supply for the forward engine had given out and the radiator, as the engine ceased running, had frozen solid.

With this accident our hopes of reaching home decreased greatly. Yet somehow we could not realize it or else Kölle had succeeded in making us believe that things were better than they were. This failure of the engine, directly occasioned by the illness of the petrol rating, was the outcome of a bad leakage in a union of the feed pipe. It had occasioned the entire loss of two tanks of fuel before Hahndorf could discover the mishap. Worse still, the forward engine actuated the radio dynamo and this was now useless. The telegraphist had only a small accumulator to work with.

We tried to steer eastwards; but, with two engines and two propellers gone, we began to make worse leeway. We could see the land below and it was becoming clear to me at least that this could not be Germany. The north wind was not abating and the struggle to fly eastwards became desperate. The telegraphist soon reported that his apparatus could no longer transmit. In the last attempt to fly eastward, Kölle determined to come down so as to avoid the tearing wind that was driving us more south than was safe for us. But there was little need to come down very far. In spite of the bombs, ballast and fuel that had gone, it seemed to me that we could scarcely have kept our extreme height, for we had lost much gas.

Shortly afterwards another misfortune overtook us: a third engine failed! This time it was in the after car, where the men had been refilling one of the radiators that had all been steaming heavily owing to the height of our flight. The water-inlet cover had been clumsily replaced, the water had been jolted out or steamed away until the engine grew so hot that the exhaust side was red. In vain they struggled to rectify the damage — it was all to no purpose, and the pistons seized before it could be remedied.

It was, if I remember, at this same time while at a height of some 4,000 metres or rather less that we flew over a large town in the early morning. What it was I do not know. A voice in the car exclaimed "Dijon!" That caused me to think. If that indeed was Dijon then we must fly over Switzerland to reach our own country. We still struggled on, but it was now obvious to me that we should never bring the ship home to our country. Before nine o'clock Hahndorf came to report that the petrol supply was failing and that his men were nearly exhausted.

Kölle turned to his charts once more, but could find none to help him, for they did not extend so far south. So he brought the ship down nearer the ground to look where he might be.

By this time we thought we were over Switzerland and it appeared as if internment in a neutral country would be the only method of putting an end to our sufferings and of avoiding a total wreck of the ship with evil consequences to ourselves. Kölle was doing the right thing, so I felt. Two of the others, as we were coming down, exclaimed "Switzerland! See the snow mountains!" People could now be seen streaming out of their houses to look at the ship, which was now only 1,500 metres up. That fact alone made us feel sure that we had not reached Germany, for at home the population would never be seen rushing out to look at a Zeppelin airship like this. Before we could land we were to have further unpleasant experiences.

Between 8 A.M. and 9 A.M. we sighted a curious little town in a gorge, such as might be expected in central Switzerland. But the country was growing rocky and Kölle turned north again to look for level ground for a landing. The valley here grew broad and level — a good place for an emergency descent and we might still save the ship — who could tell? But we were to have a rude shock. Suddenly we saw a large tract of ground all cultivated with vegetables. On this there were working some gangs of coloured men — so we could see from their heads and bare arms — all dressed in blue.

"Black men! French soldiers!" rang out a cry. Kölle stamped his foot and hurriedly ordered full speed on an eastward course again. But Hahndorf came in and talked rapidly. His men were exhausted; and the petrol supply was nearly running out: he could not go on with only two engines out of five and two propellers out of four in action. It was risky and he pointed to the mountains eastwards. A forced landing would be the only means of saving the crew.

Kölle bowed to the inevitable and manœuvred as though descending at Ahlhorn in Germany itself. He calmly ordered the emergency land flags to be flown and manœuvred the valves for the landing. We could not but admire our commander in this moment for his conduct was well worthy of what a German naval officer's should be. But ill-luck was to pursue him to the bitter end. In this mountainous valley where we now found ourselves, the north wind was no longer blowing as it had done high overhead, but sharp little squalls were felt at times. As we were touching the ground, one of these eddies came swirling across the water to our ship. She heeled over to port and the wing car was torn off as it scraped the ground. Two men from the car jumped clear to land. Then lightened of this weight the whole ship seemed to pivot on her nose and was again caught by the wind. Swaying and jolting, we were tossed across the stream until the whole craft came hard against the eastern side of the valley where she stuck fast entangled in the bushes and wedged among the stones. It was almost with a sense of gratitude that we clambered or jumped out of the cars. The long ordeal was over, but at what cost! No sooner were we on the ground than Kölle ordered us to fall into line by the ship. All the ship's charts and papers, all our private papers, he and Schütz collected from us. They were stacked into the forward car. The tools were distributed to us and with them we proceeded to break all the instruments and batter the forward car. Hahndorf drew out the emergency pistol, and fired a blazing charge into the central gas-bags, which were still more than partly inflated. With beating hearts we watched the fire take hold of our fine airship. Some of us who were not too exhausted felt as though our last link with the Fatherland was snapped and that the future mattered nothing. We were brought to our senses as the last few tanks of petrol exploded and we had to run from the blazing gas and spirit. Some were almost too exhausted to move and were helped away to safety. Kölle was splendid in this trying moment. We then gave a last salute to the ship and the ensign as it was vanishing in the flames. But with a hoarse shout as though in pain Kölle made us fall in and marched us up a narrow track out of the valley. The sailmaker had to be carried for his feet were frozen stiff, while two others were almost too ill to walk. So our little party of thirteen struggled on to the neighbouring farm where we found a German sergeant in charge of a party of prisoners! What a strange meeting in the enemy's country. This man called his party to him and they helped us to the farm where we surrendered, weak, exhausted and dejected, but still proud of our ship, our commander, and the great flight that we had just completed. Few men could boast as we might do, that they had accomplished such a journey and thrown bombs at the enemy's great capital! But we were too exhausted to do more or go further.

6. The New Heroes

The following selection, with its penetrating view of the role of technology, was written by Ernst Jünger. He applauds the talents and bravery of airmen. We first encountered Jünger in Part I, Section C.

I must mention the airmen once more, for a school friend whose existence I had half forgotten and who now belongs to a celebrated scout squadron, heard I was in his neighbourhood and invited me to a little festival yesterday evening.

I was taken by car from Achiet and driven to a château where the aerodrome is. The dinner was given by the squadron commander to celebrate his twentieth victorious combat. I was given a very cordial reception in spite of the characteristic rivalry that has developed between the infantry and the Air Force, owing to the claim each makes to having the more dangerous job. We got on remarkably well. I was only once pulled up when I spoke of "going to Paris," for these fellows do not "go." They know nothing but "flying" — a vaunt that I find very proper. For the rest I was surprised to find there was an *esprit de corps* and a spontaneous comradeship amongst them such as one would expect only from an old tradition. The spirit that animates them must be a very strong one to have achieved so marked an expression in so short a time. A spirit like that has its own future within it, and I feel sure this type of man, once called into activity by the war, is capable of playing a leading part in the Europe of to-morrow whether in peace or war. Something new is going forward here that is easier to imagine than describe; or rather something new and predestined finds here a starting-point from which it will proceed and develop. And I would even say that it will achieve a development that will make the political, social, and moral ideas of the latter half of last century appear strange and perhaps barbarous.

I am not speaking of these men themselves, of whom scarcely one will survive the war, but of a new manifestation of mankind which I, in the grip perhaps of a fixed idea, believe that I have encountered more and more frequently precisely in the last year or two. Just because I know that a man does not as a rule survive his enrolment with it for more than half a year, and so has only a brief acquaintance with his kindred spirits, I was all the more surprised by its homogeneous form and the strength of the spirit that must be its shaping force.

Who, then, are these men? It is clear that they are less conscious than any one of their own significance. Otherwise their protagonists would not write the stuff they do, in stock phrases only fit to be cooked up again by war correspondents. That is just the best of them. They cannot write and do not need to. Enough will soon be written of them. Their life is blood not ink, deeds not reflections. Their part is to make history, not literature. And later, perhaps, when after the war the current of life flows in other channels, the saying of Nietzsche will be borne out by one or other of them: "Write with blood and you will find that blood is spirit."

Excerpt from *Copse 125* by Ernst Jünger, Chatto & Windus, 1930, pp. 86–90, 129–130. Reprinted by permission of Random House UK Limited.

They are like flame kindled from the mighty army that lies before them under continual fire. They are a band picked out by the impulse towards ever bolder and more exciting forms of war. There are cavalrymen among them, hard-riding fellows whose blasé features stare in goggles. They got tired of waiting in villages and country houses behind the line for the advance to begin again. One can see in them that they belong to a race that has had mounted warfare in its blood for centuries, and that they look down upon all this business of motor transport and automatic guns as something not in their line. But there are others, too, who have been reared in the centres of modern industry and are true representatives of the new century. Young fellows of twenty whose faces have the imprint of hard fact. The ardour of speed, the tempo of the manufactory, the poetry of steel and reinforced concrete have been the natural surroundings of their childhood. Wealthy, proud young fellows brought up to work by their fathers and sent in the holidays to Bavaria to shoot, or to Kiel to yacht. Technical science is a joke to them. They have their aeroplanes under control as a bushman his boomerang. They are thoroughly accustomed to the enhancement of life by the machine.

Yet all are bound together by the high tension of action, by that fighting spirit which has perhaps its strongest expression in those little communities. The game of life and death is a sport to them and the players are esteemed according to their coolness. Battle is not only their duty, but the keystone of a particular kind of life which they strive to embody in its extremest form and for which they have been prepared by an upbringing in feudal, national and military circles. The inevitable climax is a decadence, or, rather, a dandyishness that is in strange contrast with the frightful strength it masks. When they sit together in light open coats and the white collars and bow-ties that they habitually wear, in spite of the annoyance they cause in the army, they discuss the prospect of life and death with the same frivolity as the chevaliers of the *ancien régime* discussed love. This recklessness, so often indulged in words that only the simplest expressions of it escape being ridiculous, is sharpened into paradox and pointed by cynicism just as happens in the case of every great and long-enjoyed passion.

Yes, battle is their great passion, the joy of challenging fate and of being fate themselves. They feel this when, after taking off, they cast themselves into the unknown as a whirring flight of eagles. When they soar to a height from which the front appears as a thin network beneath them, and they themselves are visible in the trenches only as a succession of dots, they are filled with the sense of hitherto unimagined daring and of invading entirely new territories of feeling. It is their fortune to try their strength against the picked manhood of the whole world in a new dimension, in unbounded space and amid the ever-shifting scenery of the clouds. They know that only one of two possibilities awaits them; and hence every encounter is inspired by the fury of desperate animals. And yet there is more than a blind pugnacity in these circlings, these sprays and jets of tracer bullets, in these banks, in the pursuits prolonged almost to the very earth, these steep dives, loops, and spins. The crisis of the battle cannot find its vent in the muscular system. It has to be transmitted to a delicate machinery in cool blood. This calls for a race with brains of steel above hearts of fire. To this is due the triumph with which they soar above the enemy machine when, in flames and dismembered by the rush of air, it falls headlong to the earth — a feeling of incomparable intensity. This sense of power is what urges all who know it to go up again into the clouds.

Another thing that makes the contrast more emphatic is the attractive shape in which death appears to them. They have no week-long marches, no grubbing about in mud and putrefaction and blood. They know nothing of battle by night and in mist, and of limbs shot away. They throw away their cigarettes, climb into the cockpit with clean uniform and snow-white linen and carefully tended hands, and in one hour they are back again.

It is a matter of good form when talking after a flight to stick to the purely technical details of the adventure without embarking upon feelings like a servant girl who has seen a ghost. When some one says that he lost control at two thousand feet and only flattened out just above the ground, every one knows what that means. It is always pleasant to live among people with whom there is no need to explain one's feelings.

It often happens that one of them does not get back. That is arranged for after the fashion of soldiers. It is a custom to leave a sum as a deposit for one's own obsequies. This was the way of our ancestors. A good carousal is the best celebration of the dead. What matter if the fallen man is not in the circle where change alone is invariable?

We to-day are not such materialists to make anxious talk of it. We leave that to those who tremble for their lives, because they feel in themselves nothing but mortality. Yet, every time that a flying-man falls as a burning brand to earth, a nobler issue is answered than that of being or not being.

What this war emphasizes again and again as the new and decisive factor is the entry of the machine into battle and the corresponding retirement of purely manual work. Of our three main arms, to which aviation was added as a fourth, two, infantry and cavalry, if we except the machine-gun companies of the infantry, were wholly occupied in what I call manual work in distinction from machine work. Of these two, the cavalry will soon disappear altogether from the field of battle; indeed it has disappeared already, even though one cannot accept trench warfare as the normal state of affairs — one that, on the other hand, has given a preponderance to artillery still far short of what is due to it, great as it is already. Perhaps if we had had enough horses the cavalry might in those few hours — when strategic communications between the English and the French were broken through in the great offensive — have taken leave of the battlefield with a last brilliant and historic achievement. As for the future, at any rate, their part is over, even though their mounted artillery and machine-gun companies might be strengthened.

The infantry will, perhaps, hold out longer; but it, too, is threatened by a process of disintegration that has begun already. The time will come when the single unprotected rifleman will be ground between the millstones of machinery. At present, owing again to the influence of trench warfare, this process gives the impression of deterioration. The infantry is burdened with a profusion of weapons by which its weight of fire is increased at the cost of weakening its impetus. Its power of cohesion, too, already endangered by the immense extension of the battlefield, seems to be called in question by the variety of arms. Hence we shall have to break away from the idea of the massed attack in its old form — so inherent particularly in the German blood — that launched the living force of the bayonet by an impulse of its own upon the enemy. It is a question no longer of launching men in mass, but machines — that is to say, death in a concentrated form that only yesterday put at our disposal.

7. Humor and Morale

Amid the tensions and horrors of war, soldiers found release in humor and satire. The *Wipers' Times*, its name drawn from the British army's derisive name for the hotly contested Belgian city of Ypres, was probably the best known of a wide variety of so-called trench newspapers produced by frontline soldiers in the various armies. Produced beginning in February 1916 by a former printer, the newspaper was notorious for its irreverent attitude toward authority, with frequent caricatures of senior officers and government officials.

a. "War"

Take a wilderness of ruin,
Spread with mud quite six feet deep;
In this mud now cut some channels,
Then you have the line we keep.

Now you get some wire that's spiky,
Throw it round outside your line,
Get some pickets, drive in tightly,
And round these your wire entwine.

Get a lot of Huns and plant them,
In a ditch across the way;
Now you have war in the making,
As waged here from day to day.

Early morn the same old "stand to"
Daylight, sniping in full swing;
Forenoon, just the merry whizz-bang,
Mid-day off a truce doth bring.

Afternoon repeats the morning,
Evening falls then work begins;
Each works in his muddy furrow,
Set with boards to catch your shins.

"War," *Wipers' Times,* 25 Dec. 1916.

Choc a block with working parties,
Or with rations coming up;
Four hours scramble, then to dug-out,
Mud-encased, yet keen to sup.

Oft we're told "Remember Belgium,"
In the years that are to be;
Crosses set by all her ditches,
Are our pledge of memory.

b. *"Ten German Pioneers"*

Ten German Pioneers went to lay a
mine,
One dropped his cigarette, and then
there were nine.
Nine German Pioneers singing Hymns
of Hate,
One stopped a whizz-bang, and then
there were eight.
Eight German Pioneers dreaming hard
of Heaven,
One caught a Flying Pig, and then
there were seven.
Seven German Pioneers working hard
with picks,
One picked his neighbour off, and then
there were six.
Six German Pioneers, glad to be alive,
One was sent to Verdun, and then there
were five.
Five German Pioneers, didn't like the
war,
One shouted "Kamarad," and then
there were four.
Four German Pioneers tried to fell a
tree,
One felled himself instead, and then
there were three.

"Ten German Pioneers," *The B. E. F. Times,* 10 Apr. 1917.

Three German Pioneers, prospects very
blue,
One tried to stop a tank and then there
were two.
Two German Pioneers walked into a
gun,
The gunner pulled the lanyard, and then
there was one.
One German Pioneer couldn't see the
fun
Of being shot at any more, and so the
war was done.

c. "Rats"

I want to write a poem, yet I find I have
no theme,
"Rats" are no subject for an elegy,
Yet they fill my waking moments, and
when star-shells softly gleam,
'Tis the rats who spend the midnight
hours with me.

On my table in the evening they will
form "Battalion mass,"
They will open tins of bully with their
teeth,
And should a cake be sent me by some
friend at home, alas!
They will extricate it from its cardboard
sheath.

They are bloated, fat and cunning, and
they're marvels as to size,
And their teeth can penetrate a sniping
plate,
I could tell you tales unnumbered, but
you'd think I'm telling lies,
Of one old, grey whiskered buck-rat and
his mate.

"Rats," *The B. E. F. Times,* 10 Apr. 1917.

Just to show you, on my table lay a tin
of sardines — sealed —
With the implement to open hanging
near,
The old buck-rat espied them, to his
missis loudly squealed,
"Bring quickly that tin-opener, Stinky
dear!"

She fondly trotted up the pole, and
brought him his desire,
He proceeded then with all his might
and main,
He opened up that tin, and then — 'tis
here you'll dub me "Liar!" —
He closed it down, and sealed it up again.

These Women Are Doing Their Bit *by Septimus E. Scott, c. 1917 (Great Britain)*
(Hoover Institution Archives)

Part II

Society Under Stress

Fear of internal strife haunted many European politicians and military planners as they contemplated the prospect of major conflict. The persistent labor unrest of the pre-war years, the growth of social democratic or labor parties, the fervent articulation of syndicalism and anarchism — all hinted at the potentially disruptive forces percolating in each of the combatant nations. In addition, leaders worried that national, ethnic, and religious minorities would prove untrustworthy in a time of crisis. Hoping to emphasize cohesiveness, Europe's elites made strident appeals to patriotism and invoked the ideals of religion and national unity.

Such politicians also sought to use the forces of nationalism to their advantage. A century before the Great War, nationalism was primarily associated with progressive political loyalties; as such, those in charge had sought to contain and repress it. By 1914, however, European leaders realized that nationalist sentiments, with their unifying power, could serve as an important new weapon in the war. But nationalism's appeal had limited breadth and depth, and there was no guarantee that it would sustain the governments that chose to emphasize it. As one example, a majority of Italians advocated that nation's neutrality in 1914, despite fiery prowar rhetoric from the Right. When the conservative government finally committed Italy's troops to combat in 1915, it did so without support from either the Italian parliament or the majority of its citizens.

Nevertheless, ultranationalist organizations had become a pervasive presence in all the major European nations on the eve of the war. Their shrill clamor for increased military spending and their support from a patriotic citizenry mobilized against internal and external foes only aggravated the bellicose tenor of the period. Still, they could not attract and retain a broad, committed following, and they often alienated potential members by disparaging government policy.

Religious passions contributed to the tension, too. Churchmen who might have been expected to press for international cooperation in the Christian spirit of brotherhood instead delivered incendiary sermons extolling Christ's sacrifice and the necessity of bloodshed to do His work against the nation's enemies. Some British clergy denounced the Germans as heathens from whom all of civilized Christendom needed saving; others equated German militarism with the devil incarnate. Prelates such as Belgium's Cardinal Mercier became articulate critics of the German campaigns, especially Germany's destruction of the library of Louvain and other atrocities reportedly committed against the Belgian population.

All combatants waged their war of scripture with equal vehemence. Respected German theologians issued the *Appeal to Evangelical Churches Abroad* in September 1914, claiming that Germany had to defend itself from the Russian barbarians, not the other way around. The British response, *To the Christian Scholars of Europe and America,* backed by the archbishop of Canterbury, pointed to Louvain as proof of Germany's un-Christian mentality. Similar images of the Germans emerged from the sermons of French priests. Neither Protestant nor Catholic clergy could resist this sort of exaggeration. Only Pope Benedict XV steadfastly refused to bless one side's military campaigns at the expense of the other, even if his strict neutrality infuriated some. Already before 1914, the German Right had argued that war possessed a purifying and redemptive quality; therefore, most European nations viewed combat as a struggle against evil and as a striving for ultimate salvation.

Not surprisingly, clergy who served in the field and who witnessed the carnage emerged with sobered outlook and moderated rhetoric. The soldiers, for their part, had various reactions to the horror. Some drew closer to religion; others questioned the very existence of God. Superstition abounded; some soldiers carried trinkets and charms — shark's teeth, horseshoes, rabbit's feet, and dolls — into battle for protection.

Appealing to religious prescriptions offered one way to cultivate a united front. Fear of internal disintegration through espionage prompted some European nations to take extraordinary measures against their ethnic and religious minorities as well. In several cases, legislation such as Great Britain's Defence of the Realm Act (DORA), passed soon after the outbreak of hostilities and later revised, regulated the movement and actions of aliens living in the United Kingdom. Germans and Austro-Hungarians were required by the law to register their names, often at the nearest police station; some German-born naturalized citizens so dreaded being accused of spying for Germany and drawing reprisals from fellow Englishmen that they Anglicized their names. Even the ruling English monarchy, with its German ancestry (House of Saxe-Coburg), officially changed its name to the House of Windsor in July 1917.

The Austro-Hungarian monarchy, comprising a multitude of ethnic and religious minorities, stood to lose the most from internal dissension. Germans and Magyars represented approximately 43 percent of the total population (in 1910); other significant groups were Czechs and Slovaks (16 percent), Poles (10 percent), Ukrainians (8 percent), Croats and Serbs (8.5 percent), Romanians (6 percent), Slovenes (2 percent), and Italians (1.5 percent). Initially the citizens of the Dual Monarchy obeyed mobilization orders, but the army's poor showing in the early campaigns left many shaken. Some minority soldiers defected in entire battalions. Others, interned in Russian and Serbian camps following capture, agreed to serve as soldiers for the enemy and took up arms to free their fellow ethnic and religious minorities from the Austro-Hungarian yoke. Indeed, the disparity between the composition of the rank and file and the officer corps, whereby a German-speaking minority dominated influential positions, paralleled the internal problems plaguing the empire.

In Germany, too, religious and ethnic minorities became suspects. Before 1914 Germany's extreme right-wing parties and extraparliamentary associations demanded that the government tighten the laws against alleged spies. Early in the conflict, wild rumors abounded in Germany and other countries of spies on the loose, some hiding in coffins, others riding in trains disguised. Thus patriotic fervor and appeals to unity heightened ethnic tensions. The German government forever suspected the intentions of Poles and Alsatians even before the war and closely scrutinized their activities.

Although many German Jews at first supported their nation's entry into the war they often deplored the "unhealthy chauvinism" that it unleashed. The Jewish poet Ernst Lissauer's florid "Chant of Hate," for example, so praised by the kaiser, repulsed German Jews with its xenophobic excesses. Nonetheless, like their Christian brethren, 85,000 Jews served their country with distinction. Ten thousand of them died in the war. Rabbis such as Göppingen's Dr. Aron Tänzer and Berlin's Leo Baeck ministered to their comrades in uniform at the front.

Yet antisemitism still flourished, especially among the extreme Right, as associations such as the Pan-German League excoriated Jews as disloyal citizens and profiteers. In October 1916, the German High Command and the Prussian war minister issued the *Judenzählung,* or Jewish Census, to all German commanding officers. The order demanded statistical information on the numbers and activities of Jewish soldiers, officers, and administrative personnel serving under these officers' command, presumably to document whether the Jewish population had come forward for service in adequate numbers, and perhaps to expose draft evaders. Austro-Hungarian antisemites also charged the Dual Monarchy's Jewish population with shirking their duty at the front and engaging in profiteering. Three hundred thousand Austro-Hungarian Jews, however, served in the army, 25,000 of them as officers.

French Jews also rallied around their nation's flag. Forty-six thousand of France's and Algeria's Jews were mobilized, one-third of them voluntarily, and 6,500 perished in battle. In the early days of the conflict, even notorious antisemites such as Maurice Barrès accepted Jews into the *union sacrée.* As the war dragged on, however, antisemitism would again creep into French society.

In Russia, where Jews made up 4 percent of the population, they represented over 5 percent of the soldiers in the Russian army. While some Jews expressed patriotic sentiment and joined the ranks to defend the Russian motherland, most were forced into the army by a law that imposed stiff penalties for noncompliance or desertion.

In Britain, Parliament had shown signs of xenophobia and antisemitism even before 1914, with the reemergence of protectionism, condemnation of cosmopolitan finance, and immigration restriction in 1905 (the Aliens Act). The war would only aggravate such sentiments. Moreover, the paranoid British Right often linked antisemitism and Germanophobia. Journalists and respectable members of the medical profession railed against resident aliens and German-born naturalized citizens and accused them of spying for the kaiser. One right-wing newspaper even charged England's Jews with using German money to buy prostitutes, who in turn spread venereal disease and thereby undermined the nation's war-making powers.

Legal persecution of religious minorities was bad enough; physical violence and attempts at genocide, as in the decimation of the Armenians at the hands of the Turks, represented xenophobia at its most virulent. In the spring of 1915, the Turkish government secretly ordered the deportation of Christian Armenians, who had sought to regain the independence from Turkey that their people had lost some thirteen centuries earlier. Although tensions had long simmered between Turks and Armenians, Turkey's poor performance in the war and the Armenians' efforts to reclaim their autonomy prompted the Turkish government to crack down on this religious minority. Between May and October 1914, police forcibly removed most of Turkey's Armenians from their homes, seized their property, and either deported or massacred them or left them to die of starvation and exposure. (Even today, no one knows with certainty how many perished; the modern Turkish government's refusal to admit its complicity in the attacks further complicates matters.) Some figures estimate that half a million Armenians were killed and an equivalent number deported.

Aside from suppressing religious minorities and launching programs of what is now called "ethnic cleansing," the Entente and Allies alike stoked certain groups' desires for independence in an effort to destabilize vulnerable enemy regions. In Germany one notorious figure on the extreme Right urged a "holy war" against the British and French colonialists. In a plan spearheaded by Sir Roger Casement, German extremists and Irish nationalists sought unsuccessfully to overthrow British authority in Ireland in April 1916. Despite the failure of the so-called Easter Uprising, several died in the melee, and the nationalists controlled sections of Dublin for five days. The German occupying government in Belgium also cultivated Flemish nationalism, in part because it resembled Germanic culture. More generally, however, the government hoped to divide Belgium by earning Flemish gratitude over the devaluation of rival Walloon, Francophilic influence. Likewise, Germany and its Turkish ally sought to disrupt the British war effort in India and the Middle East by stirring up anti-British sentiment. For their part, the British devised subversive plots of their own, especially in the Middle East, where T. E. Lawrence and General Edmund Allenby cooperated with Arab nationalists to dislodge the Turks from the region.

Racial hatred heated up during the first total war. Even before 1914, dire warnings had proliferated about the "yellow peril," and European leaders widely interpreted Russia's defeat at the hands of the Japanese in 1905 as a blow to European "superiority" over Asiatic peoples. During the war itself, France's and Britain's use of black colonial troops and manual laborers excited particular comment. The radical Right in Germany condemned this violation of the supposed customary conduct of war and accused France of promoting racial mixing and catalyzing the degeneration of pure Aryanism. When the United States joined the fray using its own black soldiers, all of western Europe feared for its racial purity despite the persistence of racism and segregation in the ranks.

This exaggerated concern over race betrayed a deeper fear of the breakdown of the larger social order. In particular, combatant nations faced the dilemma of spurring industrial production while nurturing the population base so crucial to the war effort.

Nevertheless, poor planning and resource management led inexorably to food shortages and eventually rationing in Germany, France, and England. Italy fared no better; by the end of 1916, food shortages had become a way of life, and between 1917 and 1918, the government resorted to rationing.

Although intended to provide a basic minimum caloric intake for citizens, rationing in fact did not solve the problem of food shortages. Those who needed food the most, such as working-class children and pensioners on fixed incomes, still found sustenance difficult to obtain, for the government allocated the best food to male workers. Britain and France seem to have suffered the least privation, compared with Russia, Austria-Hungary, and blockaded Germany. In Austria, the number of hunger strikes climbed from 40 percent of all strikes in 1916 to 70 percent the following year. Beginning in the spring of 1915, Russian women agitated against shortages and skyrocketing prices. In Italy in 1917, severe bread shortages sparked protests in Milan and Turin.

Food prices throughout Europe had begun rising before the war, but individuals increasingly turned to paying black-market prices for basic necessities. Government subsidies to soldiers' families failed to stem burgeoning infant mortality and disease and the declining birthrate. In desperation, politicians began preaching frugality and thrift, not to mention ingenuity, as the best way to endure home-front hardships. Small "war gardens" were planted, and cookbooks instructing working-class wives on the principles of nutrition and stretching the family food budget proliferated.

For women, the war became a mixed blessing. Whether employed in the industrial or agricultural sectors or engaged in domestic service, women still bore principal responsibility in the traditional female sphere and on the home front. They endured the burdens of domestic life, such as standing in seemingly interminable lines for scarce food, especially meat, eggs, and sugar. And although the conflict offered them avenues into the workplace, European women remained disfranchised and earned inferior wages. During the first few months of the war, unemployment actually rose for women in industries such as textiles and clothing that supplied civilian markets.

But as the war ground on and casualties mounted, industrialists and governments realized the potential pool of labor that women represented and began to train them for skilled positions left vacant by male employees now serving in the military. Beginning in 1915, women received access to occupations from which society had formerly excluded them. In 1916, the French government adopted a policy by which women, many of whom had never worked before or who had labored in more traditional areas (such as textiles), replaced male workers called to the front. French women, lured by the chance to earn crucial extra income, accounted for one-quarter of personnel in war factories; their numbers had quadrupled to some 1.6 million. The

German government also sought to offset loss of male labor by recruiting women for positions in war industries in 1917, offering them special incentives such as higher pay and factory housing. Because government supplements for soldiers' families were meager and housing extremely expensive and difficult to come by, such incentives had instant appeal. German women worked in engineering, metallurgy, and chemical production in numbers six times greater than on the eve of the war, and British women flocked to munitions factories. Russian women assumed prominence in the transport and utility industries, and in Vienna, women constituted 54 percent of the city's streetcar workers by 1918.

Many women who worked in the factories did so out of necessity, to provide for themselves or, their husbands at the front, for their families. Financial incentives, however, masked the realities of the industrial workshop. On the factory floor, women encountered discrimination by men who envied their ability to learn difficult skills rapidly and who feared that they would take jobs from their brethren at the front. Some men, especially French munitions workers, went so far as to accuse women of indirectly contributing to the bloodbath at the front by freeing up males for military service. Even clothing provoked clashes: the overalls that many women wore to protect themselves from the dirt and dangers of the workplace drew ridicule from men who resented the "masculine" attire.

The blurring of gender lines in the workplace and at the front, with the service of female nurses and ambulance drivers, underscores the turmoil of the war years. Yet in other respects, the war actually reimposed traditional values. In Great Britain, for example, some historians have argued that organized feminism lost much of its prewar momentum and returned to the notion of innate differences between men and women. Some suffragettes such as Millicent Fawcett and her organization, the National Union of Women's Suffrage Societies, relinquished the idea of pacifism, supported Britain's entry into the war, and implored women to take up their traditional duties of caring for children and destitute women so as to maintain domestic order. Feminists in France, too, embraced the war effort but with the expectation that after the war, the government would reward French women with suffrage and employment opportunities. In Germany, the Federation of German Women's Associations (Bund deutscher Frauenverein), an umbrella organization comprising a broad spectrum of women's groups led from 1910 until 1919 by Gertrud Bäumer, was swept up in the initial frenzy of the war and eagerly volunteered its members' assistance for the Fatherland. Likewise, Russian feminists called on women to do their patriotic duty for Mother Russia and extracted educational and employment opportunities for them from the tsarist government.

Male domination persisted, however, in the inequities of women's legal status. In France, Germany, and Italy, the Civil Codes reinforced the *paterfamilias:* men continued to maintain custody of their children and, to a large extent, fiscal control over their wives. Germany became an exception: wives could administer any money that they themselves earned.

The fiscal, psychological, and social impact of the war on widows proved equally unsettling. For the first time in their lives, many women found themselves required to manage their own affairs and those of their children. The loss of their husband's income, coupled with paltry widows' pensions, wreaked havoc on their already shattered lives. In Germany, for example, widows of privates, corporals, and sergeants received a meager allowance of approximately 33 to 50 marks (roughly $8 to $12) monthly, plus 9 marks per child. In Italy, widows of low-ranking soldiers received between 630 and 1,900 liras per year, depending on the number and age of their children.

Destitute, distraught, and dismayed, Europe's widows sought to comprehend why their male-dominated governments abandoned them after they had urged their husbands and companions into battle, where their men had died for the cause. Although in some cases a widow might reclaim rights denied to her in marriage, such as property and child custody, by and large she remained a social outcast, no longer part of the traditional family hierarchy. Some nations subjected widows to yet other traumas. Italian law, for example, imposed a strict ten-month mourning period on all widows; failure to comply suggested disrespect for the deceased spouse and resulted in the forfeiture of the woman's dowry or inheritance from her deceased husband.

While women demonstrated their skill, dexterity, and physical strength in the factories, pronatalist movements throughout Europe, less impressed by women's functions in the public sphere, reminded them of their first duty as mothers and patriots: procreation. Declining birthrates before the war, coupled with the loss of men in combat, renewed fears about the shrinking of future generations. Demands for the strengthening of familial bonds revived. For example, when in 1915 and 1916 the French birthrate fell to a record low, the government promoted romantic liaisons through suggestive postcards that appealed to both sexes. One postcard, captioned "Frenchmen, this is what you are defending," featured a wife and grandparents seated around a small infant in a crib, with a map of France in the background. The card portrayed traditional images of men as fathers and warriors and women as procreators and protectors of hearth and home. Another postcard applauded the sexual escapades of soldiers and the biological function of women. Entitled "A good thrust," the card depicted three male babies dangling swaddled from a bayonet, with a soldier's cap and leave card nestled in the lower corner.

Germany had also long fretted over its declining birthrate and, like France, promoted domesticity for women, but through legal means. The German government intended to deny women the right to use contraceptives, although condoms for men remained permissible. Germany also sought to outlaw abortion unless a woman's life or health depended on the procedure. The government would have implemented these measures had the November revolution of 1918 not intervened. Even in Britain, pronatalist sentiments surfaced as couples continued to produce fewer children and as married women constituted a large share (about 40 percent) of the wartime work force. The fear that gender roles would fall into a permanent muddle and that female babies would continue to outnumber males led to calls, especially by extremist groups, for women to produce offspring rather than machine guns.

In assessing the impact of the war on women, some scholars have suggested that by permitting access to paid employment and occupational choice, the war proved a liberating experience for women. Women supposedly gained satisfaction from their contribution to the war effort, while men were forced to concede, however grudgingly, that female workers in fact could perform many tasks once segregated by gender. Yet the war merely accelerated a trend of women's entering the workplace that actually began before the conflict, although it did redistribute women into new work classifications. In fact, the upsurge in female employment in war-related industries proved transitory. After the war, women workers were displaced as economies readjusted to peacetime and soldiers returned home to resume their jobs.

One could also point to the concession of female suffrage during the war by Denmark (1915) and the Netherlands (1917) and in Britain (1918) and Germany (1919) as proof that the position of women improved. But women's right to vote was often subject to special restrictions. In Britain, the government granted woman suffrage in conjunction with introducing universal manhood suffrage, but only to women over thirty. Men could vote at age twenty-one. Under the Weimar Constitution, German women obtained sexual equality, although the document left the civil rights and duties of both men and women ambiguous. French women, on the other hand, were denied the vote until after the Second World War.

The confusion of gender lines and the pent-up frustration, even anger, leveled at women also had roots in the combat neuroses suffered by soldiers. Whereas the term *hysteria* had once described only women who challenged the definitions of late nineteenth-century femininity, it now applied to men as well. Medical practitioners, however, reluctant to use the phrase "male hysteria" because of its connotations, preferred the term *shell shock*. The constant bombardment of shells and ammunition, the graphic horrors of dead and dying comrades, the despair of isolation and helplessness, and the lingering effects of gas warfare all took their toll. Some memoirs recounted stories of once-brave soldiers lying wounded in hospitals, sobbing uncontrollably in nurses' arms. Still other men, shaken by what they had witnessed, faked injury or inflicted minor wounds on themselves to escape duty on the front. The war, some claimed, had effeminized men by lowering their tolerance for pain and sapping their self-confidence. Indeed, the Great War unleashed a "crisis of masculinity" evidenced by a rise in cases of male hysteria and in conscientious objection and suicides. In Great Britain, soldiers diagnosed as suffering from shell shock were shunted off to lunatic asylums, mental institutions, and spas, so as to quarantine them from "masculine" soldiers. All these assaults on the ideal of masculinity pushed many men to vent their resentments at women.

Nationalism and the restriction of minorities, religion and the invocation of God's assistance in a righteous cause, racial tensions, the reassertion of familiar gender roles, the idea of shell shock — all of these developments reflected the undeniable strain of mobilizing for total war and nations' efforts to sustain the widespread support essential for survival. As the conflict wore on, however, social fissures widened and presented severe challenges to the authority of the state.

A. Religion, Nationalism, and Nationalities

1. THE SACRED UNION AND FRENCH CATHOLICISM

In France, the legacy of church-state relations complicated the efforts of politicians, military leaders, and publicists to provide moral justification for the war and to promote a sense of shared commitment by defining participation as a sacred duty. Since its establishment in 1870, the Third Republic had witnessed a strong strain of anticlericalism. For example, the government attempted to reduce the role of the Catholic church in public education and to substitute instruction in republican citizenship for religious teaching. Accordingly, during the war, the church sought to reclaim influence it had lost during the preceding decades. But as the following selection demonstrates, not everyone was persuaded that deepened republican patriotism and renewed religious faith were wholly compatible. The author, Jean-Jacques Becker, is one of France's most prominent historians and its preeminent student of the war's impact on that country.

Was it only coincidence that, with war hardly having been declared, a religious vocabulary should have sprung to the lips of the Republic: Union *sacrée;* patriotic *faith* . . . ? Clearly it was felt that French steadfastness in wartime would depend to some extent on the attitude of the Churches, and on that of the Catholic Church in particular.

In fact, all Churches vied with one another in patriotic ardour, even though the Catholic hierarchy, when calling for national unity and cooperation with the government of the Republic, might have felt some reservations as they remembered the persecutions to which they believed their Church had been subjected during the recent past. This may explain why some Catholics contended that the sufferings brought by the war were a much-needed expiation for France. . . .

Nevertheless, it seems that most Catholics saw no need to search for such justifications and that they broadly agreed with Barrès's . . . dictum: "We have ceased dividing ourselves into Catholics, Protestants, Socialists and Jews. Suddenly something more basic has emerged, something all of us share: we are Frenchmen." . . .

. . . [A]ttempts by the clergy and their flock to underpin patriotism knew no bounds. . . .

. . . [F]requent attendance at communion was "a patriotic duty to the Church and to France." Public prayer meetings were held, because as *La Croix* wrote: "In this hour, patriotism makes it incumbent on every citizen to contribute everything he can for our country's defence and for victory. Now, prayer is a large part of that contribution."

Excerpt from *The Great War and the French People* by Jean-Jacques Becker, pp. 178–191. Copyright © 1985, reprinted by permission of Berg Publishers, Oxford, UK.

That the authorities should have persistently refused to associate themselves with these prayer meetings, and even with those invoking Joan of Arc, caused the organisers both sorrow and indignation. Joan of Arc was also the subject of innumerable sermons and devotional prints. St. Denis and St. Geneviève were also called upon. The cult of the Sacred Heart, "one of the hallmarks of nineteenth-century spirituality," became infused with nationalist sentiment.

A Catholic Committee for Propaganda Abroad, founded by the future Cardinal Baudrillart, set itself the task of aligning Catholic opinion in other countries against Germany. Protestants and Jews, moreover, did not lag far behind and founded similar propaganda committees. French Protestants, in particular, tried to prove that they had nothing in common with their German co-religionists. In 1917, André Spire wrote *Les Juifs et la Guerre* [The Jews and the War], a book in which he explained that anti-Semitism was essentially a German phenomenon and that all Jews must therefore side with France. An appeal from "French Israelites to neutral Israelites" declared: "The French Revolution freed the Jews in the West, the victory of the Allies will free the Jews in the rest of Europe. . . ."

Nor did the churches spare any effort in their support of war charities, subscriptions and loans. In *De l'or pour la Patrie* ("Gold for the Country"), a tract published by the Christian schools, we read: "Each piece of gold handed in for the National Defence is one tear less shed by mothers. What will we not do for our country especially when that country is called France? Give your gold joyously; God loves a joyous gift." . . .

The patriotic exertions of the Catholic Church were the more intense as French Catholics felt the war to be an occasion for reuniting the nation and restoring the Church to its rightful place, from which it had been displaced, as the result of anti-clerical struggles.

This objective seemed perfectly legitimate to the Church, which had not concealed its intention of pursuing it from the moment war was declared. In August 1914, in an article entitled "Pour le Christ et pour la France" ("For Christ and for France"), *La Semaine religieuse de Paris* declared: "In becoming completely French once again, the soul of the nation will discover that it is Catholic. The transformation will take place in individuals: the political effects will follow." . . .

The Bishop of Auch rubbed it in. He reminded his priests: "You are priest-soldiers and not merely soldier-priests. What I mean is that God enlisted you before your country did." The Church often pursued its political objectives so blatantly that it earned stiff reprimands, and not only from journals on the left. In September 1914, *Le Temps* set about "politicians of the faith," and sparked off a lively debate with *La Croix*.

The *Renseignements généraux* followed this aspect of Catholic activity very closely, and on several occasions drew the attention of the authorities to it: They reported in 1916:

Those Catholics who propose to win over public opinion for the purpose of changing the country's internal policies are preparing the ground on which they hope to build after the war. As the objectives and real aspirations of the Catholic world gradually become clearer, we discover that they reflect an impatient hope to see the war bring to the hierarchy and religious institutions of the Church official recognition by the Republic.

And in 1917 they reported that "all the major orders are preparing to make great play of the services rendered to the national defence effort by their mobilised members. . . . Members of religious orders appear avid for medals and rank, obviously following instructions from their superiors whose ulterior motive seems undeniable."

No one denied the patriotic fervour of the Church, even if the mass distribution of devotional medals to soldiers and the wounded irritated some and certainly provoked among many a hostile reaction to what they considered undue pressure on impressionable minds. We are, in any case, entitled to ask whether, in pursuing objectives not uniquely "patriotic," above all in the eyes of those who did not believe that the temporal and spiritual spheres were necessarily connected, the Church in fact jeopardised its influence and hence weakened its role in sustaining French morale.

This question is the more justified as the Church was forced, throughout the war, to combine its attempt to capture souls with efforts to refute the charges of its detractors.

Catholics referred to these accusations as an "infamous rumour," but they had two distinct aspects. The Church was accused first of being responsible in part for the war, and secondly, of hoping for the defeat of France — this last being based on the attitude of the papacy.

One can understand how the first rumour came about. From the idea of an expiatory war, those who were hostile to the Church — and they were many in a country where the fight for secularism had been so fierce — found it easy enough to come to the conclusion that the priests had wanted the war in order to chastise France, a chastisement which would be even more fitting if France were beaten. This assumption about Catholic motives is well documented. In Brittany, for example, the chairman of a regional tribunal reported that the headmistress of a private Catholic school had come to him in tears, claiming that people were saying she had made her pupils pray for the Kaiser and for the Kaiser's victory.

> This was obviously false [our witness declared]. But the source of the "calumny" was easy to discover: the headmistress in fact admitted that she had said, like so many of the priests she came into contact with, that the war was France's punishment. From that remark it was only a short step to crediting her with the belief that the defeat of France would be an even fitter punishment, that the Kaiser was the instrument of God and that Catholics should pray for the Kaiser's victory.

While it is difficult to tell what precise impact the "infamous rumour" had, we know that it was ubiquitous. Monseigneur Raymond, Bishop of Mans, did not, for one, think it could be ignored: "Our priests are accused of being friends of Germany, of praying for a German victory, of sending money to Prussia." . . .

The issue was really quite staightforward: on purely doctrinal grounds, the papacy could not approve of the war, and on political grounds it could not support one side against the other, because there were Catholics on both. . . .

The Holy See could not therefore be anything but neutral, working for the restoration of peace, or at least calling for peace. During the early days of the war, Pius X, followed by Benedict XV, his successor, never deviated from this path, a stand many Frenchmen found incomprehensible. Believing that right was on their side and that they had been the victims of aggression, they could not understand how anyone could place the two warring sides on a par. . . . Benedict XV never ceased calling for a return to peace in his letters, his prayers, his messages addressed to governments, to the Catholic hierarchy, to the entire world. Since from the beginning to the end of the war the "map of war" favoured the Central Powers, a mere return to peace would inevitably have been to their advantage: so could a victorious Germany, if she accepted a compromise peace, really be expected to return Alsace-Lorraine to France?

Benedict XV was therefore accused of being pro-German. In 1915, Clemenceau mocked him with: "It would be a Boche's peace, O Pontiff of the Holy Empire!" Moreover, Austria-Hungary was said to have the ear of the Vatican, if only because, unlike France, she had diplomatic relations with the Holy See. . . .

From the beginning of the war, the French Catholic hierarchy was torn between duty to their country and obedience to the pope. . . .

For some time this difficult balancing act did not cause too many problems, but feelings ran high on 22 June 1915, when Louis Latapie published an interview with the pope in *La Liberté,* a paper reputed to be sympathetic to the Church. Asked about the sinking of the *Lusitania,* Benedict XV had allegedly replied: "I know of no more heinous crime, I have the broken heart of a bereaved father. But do you think that the blockade which is throttling two empires, which condemns millions of innocent people to starvation, reflects any more decent human feelings?"

The French press reacted virulently: "So there is no difference between aggressor and victim?" asked *L'Humanité.* Public opinion too was taken aback. As Louis Debidour wrote from the front: "The pope has made a most serious blunder with his pro-German declaration. His Jesuitical arguments, his evasions, have aroused violent fury in Italy and have been very badly received in all the Allied countries. The Holy See will end up having to pick up the pieces. So much the worse for it." . . .

Though *L'Osservatore Romano,* the mouthpiece of the Vatican, published a partial repudiation of the interview, quoting several errors, French public opinion remained convinced — and rightly so — that the position of the Holy See was not one of unqualified support for France.

On 1 August 1917, Benedict XV launched an "appeal for peace to the heads of the belligerent nations" in which he reaffirmed his desire for peace and put forward ideas for attaining it, among them the freedom of the seas and the waiving of reparations. However, he made no reference to Alsace-Lorraine. . . . In most dioceses, the reactions were mixed, if not critical. They reflected "two imperious and contradictory preoccupations of the French episcopate," namely, not to deviate from the general line adopted by the French government and not to fail in obedience to the Holy See — a difficult tightrope act indeed.

The letters intercepted by the postal censorship boards are a good barometer of French public opinion, Catholic and otherwise. From 15 August to 15 September, to take just one period as an example, the board sitting in Bordeaux listed twenty-one letters referring to the pontifical note.

Two of these letters approved the pontifical initiative and deplored the hostile re- actions of the press. . . .

All the other correspondents believed that the affair had political undertones, and that Austria was behind the pope's intervention. "I wonder if the Holy See might not have launched this note as a sort of bridge across which Austria can advance," wrote one. Others argued that, even if there had been no direct intervention by Austria, the pope's own pro-German feelings needed no prompting. . . .

The least one can say is that the pope's desire to remain neutral was not understood in France, by Catholics any more than by non-believers.

Was papal neutrality likely to undermine the influence of Catholics on French opinion and hence their patriotic message? . . .

As far as quantity is concerned there is no doubt: the onset of war brought an unquestionable "return to the altar." . . .

As far as the quality of the faith was concerned, the impression is less clear. One full account came from the parish priest of Job, near Ambert:

> There was a religious revival the moment mobilisation was announced, at least as far as prayers were concerned. There was more fervent praying in families, for the diocese, for France and for our soldiers. . . . People prayed more fervently and more frequently in church; particularly when there were services connected with the war, the parishioners would attend more often than usual. However, when it came to living the true Chris- tian life, to the strict observance of the commandments of God and of the Church, the religious revival was not nearly so noticeable. . . .

Must we then take it that the religious revival was a purely superficial response? Was it, in fact, religious at all? To a schoolmaster from Cantal it seemed to be rather a sign of the solidarity of war. "In rural areas, the church alone holds collective rites for the dead, so much so that people with no religious affiliation are obliged to participate in church services if they wish to pay their last respects to those who have died for their country."

Of the two objectives of the Church — working towards the strengthening of pa- triotism and working towards the strengthening of religious faith — the second was not attained, at least not in any substantial way. Indeed the Church's wish to harness patri- otic fervour to the good of the faith rebounded on her. Moreover, it was clear to one and all that the faithful had no more of a monopoly on patriotism than did unbelievers, Catholics no more than Protestants or Jews, priests no more than teachers. . . .

By contrast the Church undoubtedly attained its first objective: neither the "infa- mous rumour," however distasteful, nor the pope's ambiguous attitude, seemed to have appreciably weakened the appeal of the Church's patriotic message. Was Catholicism then "the backbone of French patriotism"? It certainly helped to ensure that patriotism did not disintegrate when put to the test.

2. A BRITISH CLERGYMAN
AT THE FRONT

The selection below represents a reflective and introspective response by a clergy-man during the war. The Reverend Oswin Creighton, who served as a British Army chaplain, shrank from the jingoistic declarations of the "glorious cause." The atten-tive reader will note his lack of hatred for the enemy and his conviction that the omni-presence of death itself was no more distressing than the pervasive ignorance of true spiritual habits. Creighton was killed in 1918 in France at the age of thirty-five during an aerial bombardment.

[France, early 1917]

. . . On Tuesday (27th) I was up at the batteries for a burial. The trench mortar working party was out and a shell fell among them, killing two men and wounding six. . . . The whole battery turned out, and we escorted the bodies to the grave. I talked a little about the meaning of death. But I never quite know if it helps people to realise the meaning of life and its persistence. There are few people who definitely wish to deny it. But men generally take up such an extreme agnostic position with regard to it, largely as an escape from the sloppy sentimentalism of hymns and Christmas cards, that they stand by the grave of their friends and merely shrug their shoulders. I think it is rather a splendid attitude. As Gibbon, I believe, said, the Turks fought with the fanaticism born of an overwhelming conviction of the joys of Paradise, and the Christians fought equally courageously though they had no such certainty. I suppose the finest character springs from those who see nothing beyond the present. And yet the future seems so increas-ingly clear and certain to me. Death is absolutely nothing to me now, except rather a violent shock, which one's peaceful and timid nature shrinks from. The gloomy articles in *The Nation,* for instance, which see nothing but the horror of Europe soaked in blood, and all the flower of youth being cut off, say very little to me. The horror of war is the light it throws on all the evil, ignorance, materialism, bigotry, and sectional inter-ests in human nature. Surely death is not the horror of war, but the causes which con-tribute to war. The Cross is beautiful — the forces which lead up to it are damnable. It really does not in the least matter how many people are killed, who wins, whether we starve or anything else of a transitory nature, provided that in the process human nature is transformed in some way or another. I am not nearly so much depressed by death, or even by the thought of the success of the U-boat campaign or a revolution in Ireland, as by the absolute stone walls of ignorance, prejudice and apathy one finds oneself face to face with everywhere. . . .

Curiously enough, another incident happened immediately after the funeral. I was

Excerpt from *War Letters of Fallen Englishmen,* Laurence Housman, ed., Victor Gollancz UK, 1930, pp. 77–79. All attempts at tracing the copyright holders of these letters were unsuccessful.

in the mess, taking down particulars, when we heard the sound of machine-gun fire. We rushed out and found an aeroplane battle on. Some Boche planes had come right over the town and were swooping down on our observer. No anti-aircraft guns were firing at them. The Hun planes are tremendously fast. A plane just above us caught fire and dropped a flaming mass to the ground just behind the convent. Instinctively we all rushed round. I thought possibly one might be able to do something. There lay a smouldering mass of wreckage. They dragged it away, and there lay two charred, black, smouldering lumps, which a few minutes before had been active, fearless men. It was not a pleasant sight to one's refined and delicate feelings. I felt rather staggered, and it loomed before me all day and night. But after all what did it signify? — the utter futility of violence and force. Ignorance again.

The Colonel wanted a canteen started, and that same day I found a place for one behind the guns. It was the house belonging to a doctor, an eye specialist, sumptuously built, heated with hot water, with a nice garden at the back. We soon got the canteen going there. The men patronise it all the time. It is really extraordinary the part played by the stomach in life. It simply rules the world, and affects all our outlook on life. We are paralysed, absorbed, hypnotised by it. The chief topic of conversation is rations with the men, and food and wine with the officers. Men pour into my canteens and buy everything up. For four Sundays I have been up to Arras to hold evening service. Twice I arranged it at the canteen. The men filed out when it began, and were back again for cocoa when it was over. (I have just stopped writing this to eat a piece of cake.) I felt rather furious last time. What is the use of feeding men if they deliberately set themselves against any attempt to teach or help them see the truth? I preached at all services one Sunday on "Man shall not live by bread alone," and said that while that was the first truth laid down by Christ, it was the last that man could understand. We have no need to worry about the U-boat campaign, but we must worry over the absolute famine of words proceeding from the mouth of God. What is Government doing now, but hurling invective and living in suppressed strife? How can there be a united nation without the passion for truth above all else? We are hypnotised by an unscrupulous press. We are always being taught to hate the Germans, and to refuse to think or speak of peace. We are told about our glorious cause till it simply stinks in the nostrils of the average man. We all know we have got to fight as long as we wear the uniform, and have thereby committed ourselves to slaughter as many Germans as possible. But I, for one, and I tell the men exactly the same, utterly refuse to hate the Kaiser or any of them or to believe that I am fighting for a glorious cause, or anything that the papers tell me. But if man learns to live a little more on the words coming out of God's, and not Northcliffe's, ecclesiastics', politicians', or any one else's mouths — the war does not really matter.

3. ITALIAN CLERGY GREET THE WAR

Italy entered the war in 1915 without the insistence of the general population. Nonetheless, with the nation's honor and interests at stake, some Italians expressed their readiness to serve in terms similar to those adopted by other Europeans in August

1914. From a religious viewpoint, Italian Catholics sometimes drew on the imagery of Christ's sacrifice while Italian Jews often prayed for victory and the relief of their brethren from oppression. The first prayer that follows is by Don Donatelli, military chaplain to an Italian cavalry division; the second is by Dr. Guiseppe Levi, the chief rabbi of the synagogue of Casale Monferrato.

a. *Military Chaplain Donatelli*

June 1915

Officers and soldiers! —
   I feel profoundly moved at this moment, when I have for the first time in my life celebrated the Divine Sacrifice of the Holy Mass at this little field altar: and I am very glad, thanks to the kind permission of my superiors, to add a few words on faith and Christian strength.
   Here, where the land marked the extreme limits of our *Patria,* here where the echo brings the uneasy roar of the cannon which accompanies our march of triumph, it is beautiful and divine to lift up our mind and our heart to God, asking that he will favour the work which we have well begun. . . .
   . . . But we also have one idea; that which to-day unites all hearts and all hopes; which draws us together under the banner of our beloved Italy for the triumph of her rights, of her civilisation, and of her greatness. For this great and sweet idea our parents, the fathers, the mothers, the wives, the sons, the sisters have for us to-day, from the hundred cities of Italy to the last village, a growing and silently enthusiastic admiration. For this pure and sacred flame from one end to the other of our peninsula blooms miraculously the flower of sacrifice, straight on its stalk, under the shadow of tempest; for this high sentiment our battalions, not unworthy of the conquering legions of Rome, cross the boundary to-day with the fateful cry of *"Savoia!"* Oh, happy those who in this magnificent age, in which Italy sings "with the round mouth of cannon," shall write a refulgent page of story! To-day the *Patria* wants the testimony of blood; and so from the first soldier to the last she expects the grand sacrifice.
   Before this altar upon which was offered the prayer to the Son of Man, to Him who died for all humanity but with the one country in His heart, we remember as brothers all those who have bravely fallen. Let us give a thought to the heroes of the Independence who first marked out the way of our redemption: to the brave sons of the army and navy who in Asia and in the Dark Continent made beautiful the tricolour and great the name of Italy, especially there where the Italian mothers go even to-day with remembrance but with dry eyes, to gather the petals of Italian flowers which a traitor wind of the desert once scattered on the African sands: let us turn our gaze confidently and serenely to the first of the dead on this land of our fathers restored to liberty; and in the

Excerpt from *We of Italy* by K. R. Steege, E. P. Dutton, 1917, pp. 25–27.

face of such examples and such glory let us repeat the cry of the brave — We follow you!

May the Lord bless our August Sovereigns, their Majesties, the King and the Queen; bless the brave leaders of the army, the officers all, and the soldiers of the army and the navy; bless in a special manner this division of which we are proud to form a part, and grant by Thy mercy that from the shining steel of the bayonet, the lance and the cannon shall soon sound together for our Italy the hymn of peace and the song of victory.

b. Rabbi Levi

Our God is the God of victory.

God great and omnipotent, God of pity and of justice! Hearken, we pray, with mercy to the prayer which we raise to Thee! Thou who from Thy throne lookest down to judge the world and the people with equity, Thou who hast always loved justice and hated arrogance and oppression, look, we pray, with an eye of love upon this our land, Italy!

Taught by the holy law in the sublime words of Thy Prophets, we Hebrews of Italy, in these days sacred to the *Patria,* feel our hearts burn and palpitate for the cause of Italy, for the fate of Italy, and for the victory of Italy. We feel to-day more living, more strong, more ardent our love for this our *Patria,* which permits us always to follow Thy Divine Word, and which loves us like sons: and to her, with fervent longing, we give our hearts and our sons!

Oh Lord of the universe! Be Thou with us! May Thy right arm weaken the enemy and be a shield and defence to the Italian armies; make them strong and vigorous by Thy mighty power — with Thy extended arm bless them, save them from the murderous wiles of the enemy, since from Thee alone can come help and salvation; make the just cause to prosper, Thou who hast always loved justice!

Our Father! Gather, we pray, into Thy celestial kingdom the souls of our brothers fallen for the glory of Italy, receive them in Thine arms, and grant them eternal reward, eternal peace!

Comfort and support the suffering wounded and mutilated, be Thou the Father of the orphan, sustain and protect the forsaken mothers and the unhappy widows.

May all the oppressed be released, and come to us, the brothers whom tradition, history, and language consecrate as Italians.

Make cruelty and oppression to cease everywhere and may liberty be given in all parts of the earth to our brothers in Israel.

Oh Lord of the universe! Take away evil from the world, hasten the day of justice and of love, of truth and of peace. Make to cease the horrors, the wars, the fierce passions, to give place to universal brotherhood and to Thy eternal Kingdom.

Excerpt from *We of Italy* by K. R. Steege, E. P. Dutton, 1917, pp. 27–28.

Bend the bow and break the spear in sunder, we pray Thee, and make wars to cease even to the uttermost parts of the earth. Amen.

4. A GERMAN RABBI IN THE FIELD

Leo Baeck, born in Germany's eastern province of Posen in 1873, was one of Judaism's leading figures of the twentieth century. A prolific scholar and tireless advocate of Germany's Jewish community, Baeck served as rabbi in Berlin from 1912 until 1942 and as president of the Reich Representation of German Jews (Reichsvertretung der deutschen Juden) from 1933 until 1943. Baeck's position as chief spokesman for German Jewry during the Third Reich led to his arrest and ultimate internment in the concentration camp of Theresienstadt. Upon his liberation in 1945, he immigrated to London, where he presided over the Council for Jews from Germany and devoted himself to teaching in Britain and the United States. The following excerpt conveys Baeck's initial experiences as a field chaplain during the Jewish High Holidays in the autumn of 1914.

Noyon, 15 October 1914

. . . On the 28th day of September I moved from Allemant to Chauncy in order to celebrate Yom Kippur, the Day of Atonement.[1] Thanks to the commanding officer, a specific section of the Church of Notre Dame was set aside for it, since all other large rooms in the city were reserved for the military hospital and soldiers' barracks, while every free space was occupied by heavy goods' vehicles. I delivered my sermon twice, on Tuesday, the 29th of September at 5:30 P.M. and on Wednesday at 9:00 A.M. At the behest of those gathered I also offered a Neeila Service with a sermon at 4:30 P.M.

All three services were attended in the same way by approximately 35–40 men from Chauncy, soldiers of varying ranks and doctors. The middle part of the church at our disposal, away from the altar and the other sacraments, lit by candles, made for an impressive sight. I presented the prayers and the sermon . . . from the lower pulpit; the seats for those gathered were placed in front of it. To my delight there were several members of our community among the small group. . . . I and all of the others were deeply stirred by the lines of Avinu Malkeinu [Our Father, Our King] repeated aloud. . . . I would also like to mention that before the concluding service the curé of the church, who is familiar with Germans, asked me [to be allowed] to attend the service, and requested a prayerbook in commemoration.

Excerpt from *Kriegsbriefe deutscher und österreichischer Juden*, Eugen Tannenbaum, ed., trans. by Marilyn Shevin-Coetzee, Neuer Verlag, 1915, pp. 82–88.

---

[1] On Yom Kippur, the holiest and most solemn day in the Jewish calendar, Jews fast for twenty-four hours, praying for forgiveness from God for all their transgressions and broken promises.

I stayed a week in Chauncy in order to visit the numerous field hospitals there as well as in its environs. Chauncy . . . is a central dispensary for the wounded. The way to the neighborhoods was facilitated for me by a wagon placed at my disposal for several days. These visits to the military hospitals prove to be an essential part of my duties. "A little piece of home" is brought to the wounded and their spirits are raised; they feel, as I have often noted, comforted that a chaplain attends to them [as he does] to those of other faiths. Next to this, the wounded are able to receive mail regularly. On some days I have quite voluminous amounts of mail to distribute.

In many cases I unfortunately have also had to send news about the death of a member. I have presided over the burial, at which the dead are mostly interned in a mass grave, along with the Protestant and Catholic clergymen. . . . I have always informed the relatives about the place and time of burial and other particulars about the deceased.

From Chauncy I embarked upon a longer journey, which would take me to the individual divisions. In order to get closer to the troops, it became apparent to me that I would have to join the individual divisions and brigades. I dedicated the entire past week to this task and spent time with two divisions every three days. I held two small field services in the open and where Jewish soldiers are distributed only sporadically among a unit, I seek them out. Besides that I inquired about Jewish wounded in field hospitals and canteens. [Searching for them] in all places was often difficult and tiresome. Some villages in which I quartered at night were almost entirely destroyed by grenades, and the few houses that still had a roof and a few windows were understandably always reserved for the unit beforehand. But all of these problems were eased by the consideration of the unit leader, especially the General and the other high-ranking officers. . . .

I still have not been able to ascertain how my colleagues, who were called up as field clergymen, manage their duties. I have been able so far to meet only one. At the suggestion of the commandant, this fellow has taken a permanent position at headquarters. . . . Despite all the troubles, it is by all means necessary to visit all sections of the army. Only in so doing is it possible that perhaps not everyone, but at least many, will . . . [know] . . . that a rabbi is available to them. It is very important that Jewish soldiers are aware of this, but equally so that individuals of other religions know as well. This is of immense importance for the recognition of Judaism and . . . every acknowledgment of the Jews is first and foremost dependent upon the recognition of Judaism. It is also important for the position of the Jewish soldier that his religion is visible among the others.

5. FAITH IN THE MIDST OF DEATH

Did the indescribable horror of the trenches, the prospect of imminent death, and the daily injunctions to kill harden men spiritually or encourage them to embrace religion more strongly? The following selections provide different answers. Members of the British working class, sympathetically observed by Donald Hankey in the first selection, were already inclined to reject formal institutional religious observance. Nonetheless, their commitment to a more generalized Christian ethos of neighborliness and respectability, rather than association with a formalized church, may have been strengthened. In the second extract, a French cavalry officer, Marcel Bechu (who wrote under the pseudonym Marcel Dupont), comments on the apparent devotion and simplicity of religious observance in stark contrast to the harsh surroundings. Finally, the prominent Belgian socialist theorist Hendrik de Man suggests that the idealism and humility central to spiritual observance are incompatible with success in warfare.

a. The Religion of the Inarticulate

I have said that the life of the barrack-room is dull and rather petty. In point of fact, it bears somewhat the same relation to ordinary working-class life as salt-water baths do to the sea. We used to read that Brill's Baths were "salt as the sea but safer." Well, barrack life is narrow and rather sordid, like the life of all workingmen, and it lacks the spice of risk. There is no risk of losing your job and starving. Your bread-and-margarine are safe whatever happens. As a result the more heroic qualities are not called into action. The virtues of the barrack-room are unselfishness in small things, and its vices are meanness and selfishness in small things. A few of the men were frankly bestial, obsessed by two ideas — beer and women. But for the most part they were good fellows. They were intensely loyal to their comrades, very ready to share whatever they had with a chum, extraordinarily generous and chivalrous if anyone was in trouble, and that quite apart from his desserts. At any rate, it was easy to see that they believed whole-heartedly in unselfishness and in charity to the unfortunate, even if they did not always live up to their beliefs. It was the same sort of quality, too, that they admired in other people. They liked an officer who was free with his money, took trouble to understand them if they were in difficulties, and considered their welfare. They were extremely quick to see through anyone who pretended to be better than he was. This they disliked more than anything else. The man they admired most was the man who, though obviously a gentleman, did not trade on it. That, surely, is the trait which in the Gospel is called humility. They certainly did believe in unselfishness, generosity, charity, and humility. But it was doubtful whether they ever connected these qualities with the profession and practice of Christianity.

It was when we had got out to Flanders, and were on the eve of our first visit to the trenches, that I heard the first definite attempt to discuss religion, and then it was only two or three who took part. The remainder just listened. It was bedtime, and we were all lying close together on the floor of a hut. We were to go into the trenches for the first time the next day. I think that everyone was feeling a little awed. Unfortunately we had just been to an open-air service, where the chaplain had made desperate efforts to frighten us. The result was just what might have been expected. We were all rather indignant. We might be a little bit frightened inside; but we were not going to admit it.

Excerpt from *A Student in Arms* by Donald Hankey, Melrose, 1916, pp. 104–111.

Above all, we were not going to turn religious at the last minute because we were afraid. So one man began to scoff at the Old Testament, David and Bathsheba, Jonah and the whale, and so forth. Another capped him by laughing at the feeding of the five thousand. A third said that in his opinion anyone who pretended to be a Christian in the Army must be a humbug. The sergeant-major was fatuously apologetic and shocked, and applied the closure by putting out the light and ordering silence.

It was not much, but enough to convince me that the soldier, and in this case the soldier means the workingman, does not in the least connect the things that he really believes in with Christianity. He thinks that Christianity consists in believing the Bible and setting up to be better than your neighbors. By believing the Bible he means believing that Jonah was swallowed by the whale. By setting up to be better than your neighbors he means not drinking, not swearing, and preferably not smoking, being close-fisted with your money, avoiding the companionship of doubtful characters, and refusing to acknowledge that such have any claim upon you.

This is surely nothing short of tragedy. Here were men who believed absolutely in the Christian virtues of unselfishness, generosity, charity, and humility, without ever connecting them in their minds with Christ; and at the same time what they did associate with Christianity was just on a par with the formalism and smug self-righteousness which Christ spent His whole life in trying to destroy.

The chaplains as a rule failed to realize this. They saw the inarticulateness, and assumed a lack of any religion. They remonstrated with their hearers for not saying their prayers, and not coming to Communion, and not being afraid to die without making their peace with God. They did not grasp that the men really had deep-seated beliefs in goodness, and that the only reason why they did not pray and go to Communion was that they never connected the goodness in which they believed with the God in Whom the chaplains said they ought to believe. If they had connected Christianity with unselfishness and the rest, they would have been prepared to look at Christ as their Master and their Saviour. As a matter of fact, I believe that in a vague way lots of men do regard Christ as on their side. They have a dim sort of idea that He is misrepresented by Christianity, and that when it comes to the test He will not judge them so hardly as the chaplains do. They have heard that He was the Friend of sinners, and severe on those who set up to be religious. But however that may be, I am certain that if the chaplain wants to be understood and to win their sympathy he must begin by showing them that Christianity is the explanation and the justification and the triumph of all that they do now really believe in. He must start by making their religion articulate in a way which they will recognize. He must make them see that his creeds and prayers and worship are the symbols of all that they admire most, and most want to be.

In doing this perhaps he will find a stronger faith his own. It is certainly arguable that we educated Christians are in our way almost as inarticulate as the uneducated whom we always want to instruct. If we apply this test of actions and objects of admiration to our own beliefs, we shall often find that our professed creeds have very little bearing on them. In the hour of danger and wounds and death many a man has realized with a shock that the articles of his creed about which he was most contentious mattered very, very little, and that he had somewhat overlooked the articles that proved to be vital. If the workingman's religion is often wholly inarticulate, the real religion of the educated man is often quite wrongly articulated.

b. Mass and Benediction in the Field

I knelt down humbly, almost timidly, in the shadow of one of the great pillars near the altar.

Then I could distinguish my fellow-worshippers better. A priest was saying mass. He was young and tall, and his gestures as he officiated were slow and dignified. He did not know that some one was present watching him closely; so it could not be supposed that he was speaking and acting to impress a congregation, and yet he had a way of kneeling, of stretching out his arms and of looking up to the humble gilded cross in front of him, that revealed all the ardour of fervent prayers. Occasionally he turned towards the back of the church to pronounce the ritual words. His face was serious and kindly, framed in a youthful beard — the face of an apostle, with the glow of faith in his eyes. And I was surprised to see underneath his priest's vestments the hems of a pair of red trousers, and feet shod in large muddy military boots.

The kneeling figure at the bottom of the steps now stood out more distinctly. The man was wearing on his shabby infantry coat the white armlet with the red cross. He must have been a priest, for I could distinguish some traces of a neglected tonsure among his brown hair.

The two repeated, in a low tone by turns, words of prayer, comfort, repentance, or supplication, harmonious Latin phrases, which sounded to me like exquisite music. And as an accompaniment in the distance, in the direction of Saint Thierry and Berry-au-Bac, the deep voice of the guns muttered ceaselessly.

For the first time in the campaign I felt a kind of poignant melancholy. For the first time I felt small and miserable, almost a useless thing, compared with those two fine priestly figures who were praying in the solitude of this country church for those who had fallen and were falling yonder under shot and shell.

How I despised and upbraided myself at such moments! What a profound disgust I felt for the follies of my garrison life, its gross pleasures and silly excesses! I was ashamed of myself when I reflected that death brushed by me every day, and that I might disappear to-day or to-morrow, after so many ill-spent and unprofitable days.

Without any effort, and almost in spite of myself, pious words came back to my lips — those words that my dear mother used to teach me on her knee years and years ago. And I felt a quiet delight in the almost forgotten words that came back to me:

"Forgive us our trespasses. . . . Pray for us, poor sinners. . . ."

It seemed to me that I should presently go away a better man and a more valiant soldier. And, as though to encourage and bless me, a faint ray of sunshine came through the window.

Excerpt from *In the Field* by Marcel Dupont, W. Heinemann, 1916, pp. 160–163.

"*Ite, missa est*. . . ." The priest turned round; and this time I thought his eyes rested upon me, and that the look was a benediction and an absolution.

But suddenly I heard in the alley close by a great noise of people running and horses stamping, and a voice crying:

"Mount horses! . . . Mount horses!"

I was sorry to leave the little church of Péry; I should so much have liked to wait until those two priests came out, to speak to them, and talk about other things than war, massacres and pillage. But duty called me to my men, my horses, and to battle.

c. *Spiritual Consciousness*

I have been asked many a time by clergymen, especially in America, whether I thought that the war had deepened the spiritual consciousness of most of the soldiers and made them more religious. I would myself call this question the supreme test of the psychological influence of the war on combatants, provided that religion be taken in such a broad sense that it becomes almost synonymous with idealism. But then the problem becomes so vast that I dare not answer by yea or nay. There are so many contradictory influences involved, and their relative importance varies so much according to the individuals or groups concerned, that I confess myself unable to discern what the ultimate balance will be. I would however dissuade people from overestimating the favourable effect of constant danger to life on the spiritual attitude of soldiers.

It is a popular notion, in Europe at any rate, that people whose occupation constantly confronts them with a danger that makes them seem like toys in the hands of a supernatural and eternal power, thereby become particularly religious. Sailors and deep-sea fishermen are the classical instances. It is often inferred that this must especially apply to combatant soldiers. I doubt very much, however, whether it is not merely superstition that in these cases is commonly assumed to be religion. From my experience with Flemish and French deep-sea fishermen, I would say that their attachment to the symbols of ancestral cult, their idolatry of innumerable saints, and the omnipotence of their local clergy are less in favour of their religious turn of mind than the general level of their morality is against it. I fail to see why the case of the soldiers should be different.

On the whole, I am inclined to believe that whilst the spiritual life of a minority who were truly religious from the outset may have been deepened by their experience of war, the great majority have not had enough native idealism to counteract the brutalising influence of the circumstances they have to live in. This majority have reacted to the hardships and the uncertainty of life by seeking solace in an essentially materialistic fatalism, accompanied by an inordinate desire for coarse physical enjoyment whenever the slightest opportunity occurred. When going on short leave from the front, for instance, the general disposition of mind was to "have a good time" at any

Excerpt from *The Remaking of a Mind: A Soldier's Thoughts on War and Reconstruction* by Hendrik de Man, Scribner's, 1919, pp. 206–211.

cost; and so-called pleasures, which under ordinary circumstances would have disgusted a man by their vulgarity or immorality, were then excused with the argument that perhaps it was the "last chance, anyway." . . .

. . . Anybody with some experience of the front will understand that the natural reaction to months and years of danger, hardships, sexual continence, and privation of practically any sort of entertainment, is anything but an inducement to spiritual self-communing. I am afraid that the exceptions to this rule are few. In spite of the pains I took not to miss the intellectual and spiritual benefit of my experiences, I would not even unreservedly claim the favor of this exception on my own behalf. Life at the front has made me superstitious to the extent that even now I find it hard not to ascribe my good luck to some "mascot" or other talisman in which I confess to have believed. I have often caught myself, just before passing a peculiarly dangerous spot, in the act of straightening my deportment, fingering the buttons of my uniform to make sure that they were all right, and reflecting whether I had shaved recently enough to meet death as a smart soldier; but at such moments I gave no thought to my conscience. I remember how, being on leave in Paris once after a particularly severe spell at the front, I felt tempted by the programme of a classical concert that was to be given that afternoon by a renowned symphonic orchestra. I thought it would do me good, for I had not heard any music but soldiers' songs and ragtime improvisations for more than two years. So I went there and listened for a couple of hours to Bach, Beethoven, and Mozart. I could have wept for delight in feeling like a human being again. It was as though I had suddenly been relieved of the armour which had become identified with myself for two long years. But after it was over it seemed to me that all my strength had been taken away from me together with my armour, and that it would hurt me beyond expression to put it on again. I never felt so womanish and altogether so miserable in my life. Then I realised that it did not do a trench mortar officer a bit of good to cultivate "soft spots" by worshipping musical beauty. All he had to do was to win the war by killing "Boches." The less he was a human being, the better he would be suited for his job — and there was no other job worth doing until the war was won. So I concluded that next time, rather than concert-going, I would spend my money on a good dinner with a big bottle of wine, to make up for four months of poor meals and gather strength for another four months (perhaps — "touch wood!") to come.

I am perfectly aware that this will seem supremely silly to many people. But then perhaps they do not care for good music as much as I do — or else they have never fired a trench mortar. Under these circumstances it has cost me some very hard fighting with myself not to lose my religion, or shall I say my idealism if the former term seems inappropriate to describe the spiritual attitude of a man haughty enough to think his religion too big for the size of any church or chapel. I doubt indeed whether the war has not made me lose some of the human modesty that is the fundamental attitude of mind required by any Church. I can still feel modest when I look up to a starlit sky, or for that matter, when I lie down in the grass and stare at the flowers and the insects — but I find it very hard to bow my head to any living human being or to any of their works. This kind of modesty has been *shelled* out of me. I am quite prepared to admit that this is probably a moral loss; but then this is no boast, but a confession. I merely think it necessary to make it, because I know that the same thing has happened to many men of a similar turn of mind who have been through the same experience.

6. RUSSIAN JEWS DEMAND AN END TO DISCRIMINATION

In Russia, where half of the world's Jewish population resided in 1914, antisemitism was nurtured by discriminatory laws and promoted by pogroms. The Russian government forced six million Jews to live within designated geographic regions — Russian Poland and parts of western and southwestern Russia — known as the Pale. Not only were their movements restricted, but they also were subjected to special taxes, educational quotas, and occupational and property constraints. When the war broke out, Jews, who were not subject to military service, found themselves in an increasingly hostile environment. Russian authorities often accused Jews in the Polish districts occupied by German troops of spying for or collaborating with the enemy. Caught in the midst of battle, Russia's Jews continued to suffer religious discrimination and deprivation during the war. Reprinted below is the speech of the Jewish deputy Friedman in August 1915 to the Duma, or Russian parliament, in which he demanded an end to the injustices experienced by his co-religionists.

In spite of their oppressed condition, in spite of their status of outlawry, the Jews have risen to the exalted mood of the nation and in the course of the last year have participated in the war in a noteworthy manner. They fell short of the others in no respect. They mobilized their entire enrollment, but, indeed, with this difference, that they have also sent their only sons into the war. The newspapers at the beginning of the war had a remarkable number of Jewish volunteers to record. Gentlemen, those were volunteers who were entitled through their educational qualifications to the rank of officers. They knew that they would not receive this rank; and nevertheless they entered the war.

The Jewish youth, which, as a result of the restrictions as to admission to the high schools of the country, had been forced to study abroad, returned home when war was declared, or entered the armies of the allied nations. A large number of Jewish students fell at the defense of Liege and also at other points on the western front.

The Zionist youths, when they were confronted with the dilemma of accepting Turkish sovereignty or being compelled to emigrate from Palestine, preferred to go to Alexandria and there to join the English army.

The Jews built hospitals, contributed money, and participated in the war in every respect just as did the other citizens. Many Jews received marks of distinction for their conduct at the front.

Before me lies the letter of a Jew who returned from the United States of America:

"I risked my life," he writes, "and if, nevertheless, I came as far as Archangel, it was only because I loved my fatherland more than my life or that American freedom which

Excerpt from *The Jews in the Eastern War Zone,* American Jewish Committee, 1916, pp. 111–117.

I was permitted to enjoy. I became a soldier, and lost my left arm almost to the shoulder. I was brought into the governmental district of Courland. Scarcely had I reached Riga when I met at the station my mother and my relatives, who had just arrived there, and who on that same day were compelled to leave their hearth and home at the order of the military authorities. Tell the gentlemen who sit on the benches of the Right that I do not mourn my lost arm, but that I do mourn deeply the self-respect that was not denied to me in alien lands but is now lost to me."

Such was the sentiment of the Jews that found expression in numerous appeals and manifestations in the press, and finally also in this House. Surely these sentiments should have been taken into account. One should have a right to assume that the Government would adopt measures for the amelioration of the fate of the Jews who found themselves in the very centre of the war-like occurrences. Likewise, one should have taken into account the sentiments of hundreds of thousands of Jews who shed their blood on the field of battle.

Instead of that, however, we see that from the beginning of the war the measures of reprisals against the Jewish populace were not only not weakened but, on the contrary, made much stronger. Banished were Jewish men and women whose husbands, children, and brothers, were shedding their blood for the fatherland. . . .

In a long war lucky events alternate with unlucky ones, and in any case it is naturally useful to have scapegoats in reserve. For this purpose there exists the old firm; the Jew. Scarcely has the enemy reached our frontiers when the rumor is spread that Jewish gold is flowing over to the Germans, and that, too, in aeroplanes, in coffins, and — in the entrails of geese!

Scarcely had the enemy pressed further, than there appeared again beyond dispute the eternal Jew "on the white horse," perhaps the same one who once rode on the white horse through the city in order to provoke a pogrom. The Jews have set up telephones, have destroyed the telegraph lines. The legend grew, and with the eager support of the powers of Government and the agitation in official circles, assumed ever greater proportions. A series of unprecedented, unheard of, cruel measures was adopted against the Jews. These measures, which were carried out before the eyes of the entire population, suggested to the people and to the army the recognition of the fact that the Jews were treated as enemies by the Government, and that the Jewish population was outside the law.

In the first place these measures consisted of the complete transplanting of the Jewish population from many districts, to the very last man. These compulsory migrations took place in the Kingdom of Poland and in many other territories. All told, about a half million persons have been doomed to a state of beggary and vagabondage. Anyone who has seen with his own eyes how these expulsions take place, will never forget them as long as he lives. The exiling took place within twenty-four hours, sometimes within two days. Women, old men, and children, and sometimes invalids, were banished. Even the feebleminded were taken from the lunatic asylums and the Jews were forced to take these with them. . . .

I saw also the refugees of the Government of Kovno. Persons who only yesterday were still accounted wealthy were beggars the next day. Among the refugees I met

Jewish women and girls, who had worked together with Russian women, had sewed garments with them and collected contributions with them, and who were now forced to encamp on the railway embankment. I saw families of reservists. I saw among the exiles wounded soldiers wearing the Cross of St. George. It is said that Jewish soldiers in marching through the Polish cities were forced to witness the expulsion of their wives and children. The Jews were loaded in freight cars like cattle. The bills of lading were worded as follows: "Four hundred and fifty Jews, en route to ———."

There were cases in which the Governors refused outright to take in the Jews at all. I myself was in Vilna at the very time when a whole trainload of Jews was stalled for four days in Novo-Wilejsk station. Those were Jews who had been sent from the Government of Kovno to the Government of Poltawa, but the Governor there would not receive them and sent them back to Kovno, whence they were again reshipped to Poltawa. Imagine, at a time when every railway car is needed for the transportation of munitions, when from all sides are heard complaints about the lack of means of transportation, the Government permits itself to do such a thing! At one station there stood 110 freight cars containing Jewish exiles.

Another measure which likewise is unprecedented in the entire history of the civilized world, is the introduction of the so-called system of "Hostages," and, indeed, hostages were taken not from the enemy, but from the country's own subjects, its own citizens. Hostages were taken in Radom, Kieltse, Lomscha, Kovno, Riga, Lublin, etc. The hostages were held under the most rigorous régime, and at present there are still under arrest in Poltava Jewish hostages from the Governments of Kieltse and Radom.

Some time ago, in commenting upon the procedure against the Jews, the leader of the Opposition, even before the outbreak of the war, used the expression that we were approaching the times of Ferdinand and Isabella. I now assert that we have already surpassed that era. No Jewish blood was shed in defence of Spain, but ours flowed the moment the Jews helped defend the Fatherland.

Yes, we are beyond the pale of the laws, we are oppressed, we have a hard life, but we know the source of that evil; it comes from those benches (pointing to the boxes of the Ministers). We are being oppressed by the Russian Government, not by the Russian people. Why, then, is it surprising if we wish to unite our destinies, not with that of the Russian Government, but with that of the Russian people? . . . We likewise hope that the time is not distant when we can be citizens of the Russian State with full equality of privileges with the free Russian people.

Before the face of the entire country, before the entire civilized world, I declare that the calumnies against the Jews are the most repulsive lies and chimeras of persons who will have to be responsible for their crimes. [Applause on Left.]

It depends upon you, gentlemen of the Imperial Duma, to speak the word of encouragement, to perform the action that can deliver the Jewish people from the terrible plight in which it is at present, and that can lead them back into the ranks of the Russian citizens who are defending their Fatherland. [Cries of "Right."]

I do not know if the Imperial Duma will so act, but if it does so act it will be fulfilling an obligation of honor and an act of wise statesmanship that is necessary for the profit and for the greatness of the Fatherland. [Applause on the Left.]

7. Ethnic Minorities in the Austro-Hungarian Empire

A fragile patchwork of competing and often antagonistic nationalities, the Austro-Hungarian empire was forced to wage two battles: one against the external foes, the other, equally pressing, against internal nationalist movements. The Hungarian government proved more hostile than its Austrian counterpart to the calls for autonomy or even independence from Slovaks, Serbs, Croats, and Ukrainians, among others. T. G. Masaryk, the leader of the Czech nationalist movement, fled Hungary to London, from where he led the battle against the Dual Monarchy with the ultimate goal of a Czechoslovak homeland. The Hungarians were particularly concerned about the Serbian population, with its cultural and emotional ties to Russia, and thus took extraordinary measures to thwart their aspirations. The selection that follows deals with the complicated issue of nationality within Hungary during the First World War.

After the outbreak of the war, and even more so after the defeats suffered from the Serb and Russian armies, the Serb and Ukrainian minorities living in the Monarchy were greatly oppressed. The greatest part of the Hungarian territories inhabited by Serbs and Ukrainians also belonged to the military zone, which was under the management of the supreme command. The Hungarian government, exercising its special powers, also took some harsh measures.

In November 1912, a secret codicil marked "Cs–1" had been added to the service regulation of the gendarmerie. This codicil summed up the duties of the gendarmerie concerning the prevention of espionage. Article 11 ordained that "persons under acute suspicion of espionage should be detained on the day of mobilization." "Suspicion of espionage" was used in such a wide sense that it could be applied to almost any person belonging to the nationalities living near the border.

The arrests started on July 25. In a few days, they reached such enormous proportions that on August 2 the minister of the interior modified Article 11 of the secret regulation by a circular: only those persons were to be arrested who "really had a harmful influence on our preparations for the mobilization," while those under suspicion were to be reported to the police of the municipal authorities, but were not to be detained. Mass arrests went on, however, on various other pretexts. Thus e.g. people suspected of being members of the Narodna Odbrana[1] were arrested without any other reason. Many of them were not set free even later. Internment also attained mass proportions.

Excerpt from *Hungary and the First World War* by Josef Galantai, Akademiai Kiado, 1989, pp. 95–102. Reprinted with permission.

---

[1] The National Defense Association sought to create a Greater Serbia at the expense of both Austria and Turkey.

The measures taken against the Serb population of the southern regions were in some cases just local atrocities, mostly, however, they were based on central directives. On the day after the rupture of diplomatic relations with Serbia, the prime minister instructed the lord lieutenants: "I call your attention with particular emphasis to the attitude to be taken towards the non-Hungarian population . . . We must show them our strength." In his letter of September 5 to the government commissioner of the territories inhabited by Serbs, Tisza advised moderation in connection with local excesses, demanding at the same time "relentless severity against the criminals," and actions to be taken "without much ado."

The emergency measures were in force in Croatia too, where they were mostly used against the Serb population. The authorities turned first of all against the Serb Sokol associations functioning in Croatia. Even before the outbreak of the war, on July 14, the Minister of Defence Krobatin had informed Tisza that in Croatia-Slavonia "the Serb Sokol associations and popes were the main agitators of the Great Serb revolutionary movement." When the war broke out, the members and leaders of the Sokol were arrested. Not even the immunity of MPs was respected. Krobatin had already mentioned in his letter that "some of the MPs are positively agitators and promoters of revolutionary propaganda." Now several Croatian Serb MPs were arrested on various pretexts. E.g. Srdjan Budisavljević, a member of the Zagreb provincial diet and as its delegate, a Hungarian MP, was detained on the pretext that he was the president of the Krajiska district center of the Sokol associations. Later Tisza intervened for him because "he is being calumniated for a trifle," he wrote.

Before the war, the Hungarian government had not been very interested in the domestic situation in Bosnia and Herzegovina. Now, however, Tisza attached great importance to the fact that the Serb population of Hungary and Croatia was closely attached to the Bosnian Serb population. One of the basic principles of Tisza's policy was that the annexation of Serbia and the union of the Serb population living in the Monarchy were out of the question. Therefore not only the links of the Serbs of Hungary, Croatia and Bosnia with Serbia demanded a counter-action, but also their aspirations at unity within the Monarchy. At the beginning of the war Tisza wanted the expected gains of the Monarchy to be distributed according to the dualist principle. He even included in his plans Bosnia and Herzegovina, which were treated as separate provinces. If Austria gained some Polish regions, Bosnia and Herzegovina could become Hungarian crown provinces. This idea was one of the reasons why the Hungarian government paid special attention to Bosnia during the war.

Even in the state of emergency, the Serbs of Hungary, Croatia, and Bosnia found ways to express their sympathy with the war waged by Serbia. The minister of the interior, as we have seen, made mention of this fact at the cabinet meeting held in late August 1914. Another proof was furnished by the documents captured later, at the occupation of Serbia, especially by the Belgrade archives of the Narodna Odbrana. These show that many of the Austro-Hungarian soldiers of Serb nationality captured by the Serbian troops asked to be admitted to the Serbian army. 21 Hungarian Serb soldiers figured in the lists. Many young men who had not been enlisted yet fled to Serbia . . . and joined the Serbian army as volunteers. . . .

The measures taken against the Serb civil population also gave rise to some disagreements between the Hungarian government and the commanders of the common army units stationed in southern Hungary. As we have already seen, the Austrian emergency law invested the military authorities with far-reaching rights against the civil population, while the Hungarian one extended the rights of the government agencies, but did not invest the military authorities with governmental rights. The commanding officers of the common units stationed in Hungary, especially in the territories qualified as "military zones," often behaved as if they were in Austria, i.e. according to the Austrian emergency measures. This provoked protests from the Hungarian authorities. Already in late August Tisza sent a telegram to Burián, in Vienna, saying: "Excesses committed by military commanders disregarding government and authorities are increasing . . . Please do everything possible by all means to stop this madness . . . I shall be obliged to see His Majesty and make this a matter of principle." In these frictions the government was trying to preserve its sovereignty; at the same time it was obvious, however, that the military proceedings were more serious even than the special civil proceedings permitted by the emergency law.

A characteristic example of such a friction took place at Zombor. In early September 1914 soldiers and civilians demanded in a chauvinistic demonstration the removal of Cyrillic notices from shops. One Serb shopkeeper refused to do so, and, fleeing the insults of the mob, ran into his house and shot at the demonstrators. The civil authorities arrested him. The joint military command of Zombor demanded his extradition, threatening the public prosecutor and the police commissioner with arrest. At this, the latter gave in. Tisza heard about the matter from the mayor's report, and wanted to ask for a severe inquiry against the Zombor military command. They, however, had acted quickly: the shopkeeper had been sentenced to death by court martial and the sentence had been carried out straight away. In addition, the court martial designated twelve hostages among the Serb intellectuals and landowners of Zombor, saying that "if the population revolted against the military proceedings and hampered the functioning of the militia with its treacherous behaviour, the hostages will be arrested and immediately executed by the military authorities." On September 15 Tisza addressed a lengthy memorandum concerning this and other similar matters to the commander in chief, Archduke Frederick himself. He wrote that in the question of competence "the situation had really become intolerable" between the military authorities and the Hungarian government agencies. He was therefore asking for vigorous action. A few days later Tisza thanked the archduke for the quick action. . . .

With the Slovaks and Croats, if only for military reasons, the government tried to avoid any actions that could give rise to agitation. At the beginning of the war they counted on the Croatian regiments and Slovak soldiers as reliable troops.

In the first weeks of the war the Hungarian prime minister was trying to restrain the chauvinistic tone of the Hungarian papers of Upper Hungary. In late August he gave a satisfactory answer to the complaints lodged by Slovak politician Matus Dula, and on September 10 he spoke in support of allowing the banned daily *Slovenský Dennik* to appear again. But in this area as well, the liberal tone was to change soon.

Following the autumn defeats of the Monarchy a Czechoslovak movement began to take shape among the emigrés. The Hungarian government showed concern not so much for Masaryk's camp as for the movement of the Slovak emigrés in Russia. It was even more disquieting for the government that as a result of the defeats the idea of Czechoslovak unity within the Monarchy was gaining ground among the Slovaks. The Hungarian government had already considered this problem a year before the war. At that time it had received several indications that this trend was gaining strength among the Slovak population. In his report of June 26, 1913, addressed to the prime minister and marked "Confidential! Into his own hands!", the lord lieutenant of Trencsén county had also warned that this movement was supported from Bohemia by economic means: "The small banks and savings banks fed by Czech money . . . give credit to the people even at a time when money is lacking all over the world." In November 1913 the government drew up a 23-page memorandum for domestic use entitled "The Problems Concerning the Slovak Nationality Living in Hungary." The summary characterized all Slovak trends. . . : "The Slovak national movement has hardly any favor which is not backed by Bohemian-Moravian agitation, culture, and money. Movements founded purely upon the racial strength of the Slovaks themselves can hardly be encountered today, which is certainly the result of long years of steady work done by the Czechs . . . Owing to the strong Czech influence the idea of the racial separatism of the Slovaks is being completely relegated to the background."

Following the military defeats suffered by the Monarchy, the Czechoslovak tendency grew stronger among the Slovaks. Now Tisza was urging the authorities and the local forces to act with more determination. In February 1915 he intervened over the minister of justice, because he considered the steps taken too lenient. However, he could not prevent the Slovak national movement from gaining ground. The editorial in the July 31, 1915 issue of *Národnie Noviny,* the paper of the Slovak National Party . . . , raised, cautiously but explicitly, the issue of dismissing the idea of the Hungarian national state. The Hungarian government attached great importance to this. . . : "The Slovaks constitute, at present, an element faithful to the dynasty and the state," but the ideas of a Czechoslovak union had "spread among the Slovaks too," and the war conditions were highly suitable for the government to take "the necessary preventive measures." . . .

In Croatia, in the first few months of the war the government was occupied with the reprisals and preventive measures taken against the Serbs. Quite soon, however, difficulties arose in connection with the Croats as well. Among the Croats, the Great Croat tendency was gaining more and more ground. The ban of Croatia, Baron Ivan Sherlecz, who adjusted himself to the policy of the Hungarian government, was constantly signalling this fact from late 1914 on. The Hungarian prime minister also gave account of the size of the movement. "Quite a lot of Croatians," he wrote . . . , "have trialist Great Croat delusions."

The idea of a South Slav union led by the Croats within the Monarchy, which would at the same time entail the transformation of the Dual Monarchy into a trialist one, was not a new idea. It was after the outbreak of the war, however, that it became widespread in Croatia. At first the strengthening of this trend did not effect the military efficiency of Croatia, on the contrary, precisely because of this "austrophil" and at the same time Croat nationalist tendency, the morale of the Croatian regiments was among the best. The commander of the Zagreb Army Corps for this reason even supported the movement. This led to serious disagreements between the ban of Croatia, who followed the policy of the Hungarian government, and the Zagreb military commander. In February 1915 this infuriated Tisza so much that he wrote . . . : "I shall be obliged to ask for the removal of the Zagreb military commander and for his successor to be categorically forbidden any contact with the opposition."

There were other factors, too, which favoured the strengthening of the Great Croat movement after the outbreak of the war. Before the war, the provincial government of the ban relied on the Croatian-Serb coalition, forcing Frank's Croatian Party of Rights into opposition. Owing to the highly restricted franchise and the electoral system, the Croatian-Serb coalition got the majority in the provincial diet. However, this governmental basis had become highly unstable already during the Balkan wars, since the Serb wing of the coalition could not be relied on. Károly Khuen-Héderváry, whom Tisza regarded as a specialist in Croatian affairs, wrote to the prime minister on August 7, 1913 regarding Croatia, the Balkan events had "dispelled many an illusion. The traditional disagreement between Croats and Serbs is being revived." After the beginning of the war against Serbia, and especially after the atrocities committed against the Serb population, the government could no more rely on the Croatian Serb politicians who had, until then, supported the provincial regime. But the Croats, who supported the ban, were only in majority in coalition with the Serbs. Because of this the former basis of the regime was upset. Frank's opposition party with its trialist aspirations came increasingly to the foreground and became ever stronger. On the other hand, the Hungarian government, i.e. the ban, no longer had a reliable political basis in Croatia. In these circumstances the ban tried to gain some support by making minor concessions. Thus in the summer of 1915, he supported the Croatian idea that on the occasion of the large-scale manifestation of homage planned for September 2, a separate Croatian delegation should be sent to Vienna. Tisza, however, for fear that this might favour the Great Croat tendency, insisted on sending a joint delegation. He succeeded in having his way, and rebuked the ban, who was one of his men of confidence, in a fulminatory letter: "It will come to no good if you try at every moment to assert here the worries of a few Croatians about your attitudes instead of settling them of your own authority, by persuasion and reassurance if possible, or, if not, with determination. You yourself must have the leading and directing role, and not let yourself be pushed." In his later letters, too, he often reproached the ban for similar cases of indulgence and urged him to adopt a harsher attitude.

The increasing severity of the Hungarian government's Croatian policy was also due to a certain extent to fear of the influence of the Croatian emigrés. The Croatian movement which demanded separation from Austria-Hungary found its first supporters among the Croats living in the United States. Already on July 4, 1914, the Pittsburgh Croatian paper *Hrvatski Glasnik* had outlined, in connection with the assassination of Archduke Francis Ferdinand, a program based on the idea of the death of the Monarchy and the creation of an independent Croatian kingdom. Later, the center of the movement shifted to Italy, where the leading role was played by the members of the Croatian diet who had left the country, Fran Supilo and Hinko Hinković, and the former mayor of Spalato (Split), Ante Trumbić. The Hungarian authorities made extensive investigations of Supilo in order to isolate him from those inside the country. Reprisal against the Croatian emigrés was one of the main reasons for the enactment of the law "On the Financial Responsibility of Traitors to the Country" (Article XVIII of the Act of 1915).

8. RACE AND RELIGION

Edwyn Bevan, born in London in 1870, was a scholar whose interests included religion and philosophy, especially of the ancient world; his most influential work dealt with the Hellenistic age. When war broke out, he turned his attention to contemporary events and placed his talents at the service of the Foreign Office's political intelligence department. The following extract, which was written privately rather than under official auspices, probes the likely impact of the war in terms of race and appraises the positive role to be played by Christianity in mitigating racial conflict in the postwar era.

The war which we are witnessing marks an epoch, not only in the history of England or of Europe, but in the history of mankind. If there were any spectator who, through the unnumbered ages, had followed the course of the creature called Man upon this planet, he would have seen naked cave-men, thousands of years ago, drive each other in pursuit and flight over the hill-sides with stones and clubs; he would have seen, later on, the mail-clad armies of Assyria and Rome move over wide regions, sacking and slaying; and in recent time he would have seen the still larger armies of Europeans fight with weapons that mowed men down at long range. But he would never have seen a war which engaged so large a part of the men upon earth, which affected, directly or indirectly, the whole world, as this war does. And the reason is that this war has come at the end of an epoch wherein a certain process, which our supposed spectator would be able to follow, has gone forward at a rate such as he would not have observed at any earlier time. That process is the formation in the human family of ever larger groups with common purposes, common interests and tasks. What made the process possible was a development by spasmodic steps forward, over the course of the centuries, in the means of communication. Intercourse of man with man among the cave-men had to depend upon speech and gesture; the great States of antiquity had writing, and the speed of horses for traffic, and wind-wafted ships; but in the last few generations the process has made a leap forward, with steam, electricity, petrol. The whole world has been bound together as never before. It has got, as it were, a single nervous system. The agitation in one part is communicated almost directly to other parts far away. . . . A war of the great nations, supervening upon such a state of the world, inevitably means a

Excerpt from *Brothers All: The War and the Race Question* by Edwyn Bevan, Papers for Wartime #4, Oxford University Press, 1914, pp. 3–16.

more widespread convulsion than any former war. Larger masses of men come into action, and can be handled organically: a battle has a front extending two hundred miles, and may require weeks to be fought out. Men of all races, in all continents, feel in their private lives the disturbance in the vast system of international business.

Now, before the war had come, this process of the drawing of the world together, this diminishing of distances, equivalent, in some of its effects, to a shrinkage of the surface of the globe, had brought up great problems for the new generation: and that because the human species thus drawn into closer contiguity was not all of one kind. The contact, as men then were, between alien races, was not altogether happy and comfortable. Masses of men were brought together before either side was ready for the encounter. What is called "the Colour Question" had become acute in certain regions. Already, before the discovery of steam-power, advance in the art of navigation had made it possible for the white men of Europe to go to the lands inhabited by brown and black men in sufficient numbers to win a predominant position in far-off countries, and one may believe that even then the dark man was conscious that the intruder belonged to a widely different breed from himself. But the introduction of steam accentuated the difference; for as the journey became shorter, and the communication of the white man with his home became easier, he retained his European character and European interests with less adaptation to the new environment than his predecessors had done. It is said that the Englishmen in India before the Mutiny had a human relation with the people of the land such as the official of to-day, less high-handed indeed but more distant, is seldom able to establish. The new conditions at the same time made it easier for the peoples of Asia to go to countries occupied by Europeans, so that the contact of races took place, not only where the white man was the stranger, but where the brown or yellow man was the latest comer. Contact in either sphere brought its special variety of friction. We had not only unrest in India and anti-foreign feeling in China, but the thorny Indian question in South Africa and Canada, and the agitation against the yellow man in the United States.

THE CO-OPERATION OF THE EAST

And now we have suddenly ceased to talk of these questions. Instead, we find brown men and yellow men and black men joined with ourselves in one colossal struggle, pouring out their treasure, pouring out their blood, for the common cause — Japanese and English and Russians carrying on war as allies on the shores of the Pacific, Hindus and Mohammedans from India coming to fight in European armies on the old historic battlefields of Europe, side by side with Mohammedans from Algiers and black men from Senegal. We had often spoken of the wonderful drawing together of the world in our days, but we never knew that it was to be represented in such strange and splendid and terrible bodily guise.

To our enemies the disregard of the "colour bar" in the combination against them is a matter for reproach. We know already that they charge us with disloyalty to the cause of European culture, and we must be prepared to hear the charge flung against us with still greater passion when the war is over, and echoed in German books for generations to come. It has not yet appeared that they consider the employment of Indian and African troops a disloyalty: in the book, so often referred to, by General Bernhardi, the employment of "coloured" troops by France and England is spoken of as something to be expected, with no note of blame; it is our alliance with Japan that arouses their indignation. The difference is, no doubt, that Indian and African troops seem to be used merely as instruments for the purposes of the European Powers, whereas the European has entered into alliance with Japan as with an independent Power of equal standing; that is the abominable thing!

The distinction here indicated may show an imperfect apprehension of the facts on the German side. The idea involved in the distinction, however, may help us to see the real significance of what is before our eyes. As a matter of fact, there is nothing very new or strange in the employment by a civilized Power of alien troops, as a weapon. It does not involve the admission of the aliens to any footing of equality. There is no question of co-operation in the real sense. They are used, just as horses are, as the instruments of a purpose not their own. The French had already used black troops against the Germans in the war of forty-four years ago. If we were merely using Indian troops in the same way, without any will of their own, there would be nothing so very remarkable in it. The mere fact, taken by itself, that Indians are fighting side by side with British soldiers is not the point. In India they fought side by side with the British for one hundred and fifty years. What gives the moment its significance is that the presence of these Indian troops does not represent solely the purpose of England. It represents in some degree the will of India. However the complex of feelings which we describe as "loyalty" in India is to be analysed — and a true analysis would probably differ largely in the cases, say, of a Rajput prince, a Parsi merchant, and a Bengali journalist — behind the Indian troops there is the general voluntary adherence of the leading classes in India, the fighting chiefs and the educated community, to the cause for which England stands. We may speak truly of co-operation in the case of India, as in the case of Japan.

It is the promptitude, the eagerness and the unanimity of this voluntary adherence which has seemed to England almost too good to be true. Some one present when Mr. Charles Roberts read to the House of Commons the message from India has reported that he had never before known the House so moved. After all, whatever the shortcomings of the British rule in India, there has been a great mass of good intention concerned in it; and we had been told so often that it was absurd to expect any recognition of good intentions from the mass of the Indian people. When, at the test, the recognition comes in such generous volume, we are almost taken aback, perhaps a little ashamed of what may seem a want of generosity in our own previous attitude; we are conscious of a new glow of friendliness not unmixed with compunction. The atmosphere is changed in temperature, and some of the barriers which seemed so dead-hard in the old days show a tendency to melt. Indian students moving about in London feel that the eyes which rest upon them are kindly and welcoming, and no longer hostile or suspicious. Almost in a moment the atmosphere has been changed, and that alone is a great thing. One cannot say what may come of it; but things that seemed impossible before seem so no longer in the new day.

It was such a change in our temper as this that Christianity might have brought about, if it had been effectual. It is somewhat humiliating to think that it has been brought about, not by Christianity, but by participation in a war. The reason, one supposes, is that the British public generally has risen to the level represented by, "Love those who love you," but not yet to the Christian level of loving in advance. It could not show any warmth of goodwill to the oriental stranger while he was still a dark mystery and his goodwill problematic; the war has given occasion for him to prove his goodwill, and we hold him out the hand.

However true it may be that war is the outcome of sin, and productive of sin, we must recognize here too how good things are in strange wise brought out of evil by the divine art running through history. It looks as if the human family would really have made a step towards the ideal of brotherhood by waging war together, as if the cynic had some truth on his side, who said: "There is no bond like a common enmity." Each people will soon feel of all other peoples but one that they are brothers in arms; we cannot imagine ourselves without a kindliness for many years to come towards French and Russians and Belgians. No doubt the fact that one has to make an exception in a brotherhood so conditioned — "to all other peoples but one" — shows it imperfect from the Christian point of view, shows something fatally defective in its basis. Yet here meanwhile is the new glow of friendliness, and we cannot do otherwise than recognize it as a good. It seems obvious wisdom to take it for all it is worth, and to work from it to something more. The "colour bar," against which Christianity had beaten itself, largely in vain, has been weakened by another force. The other force has to that extent made the task of Christianity in the future easier. There is no reason why Christians should not be thankful for that.

SHOULD THE "COLOUR BAR" BE MAINTAINED?

But one must remember that the German people as represented, not only by its military caste, but by its thinkers and spiritual leaders — the persons, for instance, who signed the *Appeal to Evangelical Christians Abroad* — points to this very disregard of the "colour bar" as an evil. It is probable that there are many amongst ourselves who sympathize with that view. Just at the present moment, while applause of India fills the press and the Japanese are being so obviously useful to us on the Pacific, such persons may not give utterance to their feelings, or their utterance may be drowned. But that many Englishmen shared all the colour prejudice of the Germans last July is certain, and it would be miraculous if in these few weeks all that inveterate prejudice had ceased to exist. When the applause dies down, the voices of these men will be heard again. We cannot afford to overlook their objection.

So far as the mere fact of a difference in complexion, taken by itself, is urged as a barrier which we should not try to transcend, the prejudice appears in a form so crude that it would perhaps be vain to argue with it. The antipathy of men of different complexions to each other, we are sometimes told, is something deep-lying and essential in human nature. . . .

Where the objection to our close association with Indians and Japanese takes a more reasonable form it might perhaps be stated as follows: "It is not the difference in complexion in itself" (so the objector might say) "that matters; it is the fact that in the present state of the world a brown complexion and a yellow complexion go with a religion and culture and social tradition different from the tradition of Christendom. The white races represent a higher culture — or at any rate a culture that ought to be kept uncontaminated by alien elements. For this reason it is important that the material power of the white races, taken as a whole, should not be diminished as against the power of the non-European peoples. If the white races fight amongst themselves, their power as a whole is not necessarily decreased; it may be merely shifted from one European nation to another. If, on the other hand, Asiatic peoples are allowed to take part in the struggle, Europe parts with some of its power to non-Europeans. The power of Europeans in the world," the objector might continue, "is not entirely due to superior material force. It is largely a matter of prestige, of suggestion; the imagination of the other races must be held captive. In all conflicts, *morale* is a prime factor. It would be fatal for the predominance of Europeans if non-Europeans in large numbers lost the sense of the white man's superiority. If they face a European enemy and take part in his defeat, awe of the white man, as such, is gone."

THE GREAT OPPORTUNITY

One surely cannot deny that this reasoning has something in it. It is true that we Christians believe the culture of Europe — permeated, however imperfectly so far, with Christianity — to have in it something of special value for the world. It is true that the position of Europeans as rulers, outside Europe, has in the past been secured largely by their impressing the imagination of the peoples they governed. It is further true that if this prestige, this control by suggestion, were taken away, and no better relation substituted for it, the result might be worse than the present state of things — a lapse of the East into chaos.

"And no better relation substituted for it" — that is the great issue of the present crisis. We have been forced by events into a position where safety is to be found only by going forward. We are being called to new things; the fatal thing is to stand still. While we are rightly glad and proud at the cordial advance of India, while the air is full of congratulation and applause, quiet reflection may recognize that the entry of India upon the scene has its dangers. It is big with possibilities of evil. For one thing, it means inevitably a disturbance of the situation in India. Yes, but it is big too with possibilities of good, because that disturbance of the situation may open the way to something much better. It would be a mistake to suppose that in the loyalty of India at the present moment we had attained everything; we have really attained little, except an immense opportunity. It depends how we use it. We shall be less able after the war than before to take our stand in India on some supposed superiority of the white man, as such. We have given way on that ground. And to any one who would tell us that our sacrifice of the white man's prestige is rash and foolish, we can answer that in any case, even apart from the

war, circumstances were forcing us from that ground. As European education spread in India, as India awoke more and more to the modern world, that ground would have become increasingly untenable. Sooner or later, if India remained a member of the British Empire, it would be because India chose the association voluntarily, intelligently, with head held high. By admitting India to cooperation in a European war, we have accelerated the disappearance of the old imaginative awe. But the war has given us an opportunity we could never have forecast of substituting for the old relation a new relation built on the consciousness of great dangers faced and great things done together, feelings of mutual friendship and respect and trust. In the kindled atmosphere of the present moment, when hearts are warm and quickly stirred, things may take a new shape which time will so solidify that the attachment of the British and Indian peoples to each other in the future will be stronger than any bond which conquests of the old style could fashion. It all depends, as has been said, how we use the opportunity.

The cry that a Christian Power which in any circumstances enters into co-operation and alliance with a non-Christian Power against Christians commits an act of treachery seems to spring from a deeper loyalty to Christianity. But, to be honest, is the motive behind the declamatory protest after all not just the old bad feeling of race prejudice, the pride of the white colour, which is the very antithesis of real Christianity? What is really the source of the cry is the refusal to acknowledge that the whole human race is all potentially one in Christ. It departs from the fundamental principles of Christianity — the principle of truth and the principle of charity. It departs from the principle of truth, because it goes by names and appearances and labels, instead of by realities. The nations of Europe have become Christian only to a very imperfect degree. When the action of a so-called Christian State is determined by the very anti-Christian principles of national egoism and "will to power" it is untrue to regard it as a Christian State, even if one can point to a nucleus of real Christianity among its people. Supposing we wished to present a false appearance to the non-Christian world, to cover up the truth for fear of scandal, it would be in vain. The sooner the non-Christian world realizes that Christendom is not yet Christian, the better for the prospects of Christianity. And whilst one has to admit a great mass of paganism, still unleavened, in Christendom, one ought to recognize in all that is morally sound in the non-Christian civilizations something germane to Christianity, something due to the same Spirit who is fully manifested in Christ.

Even apart from the direct action of Christianity upon these races in recent times, that would be true. But we know, as a matter of fact, that just as in England and France and Germany there has been a nucleus of real Christianity for many centuries, influencing in various degrees the national life as a whole, so there is now in India and China and Japan a nucleus of real Christianity, whose influence is already making itself felt far outside the limits of the organized Church. In the case of the individual, it is a part of Christian charity to recognize, even when the Christian name is not assumed, the fruit of the Christian spirit: in the same way, to label the Asiatic peoples of today in that absolute way as non-Christians, to shut them out from co-operation in the work of establishing righteousness in the world, where they are prepared to act on righteous principles, is not only a disloyalty to truth but a breach of Christian charity. And that is not the way to win Asia for the Universal Church.

Of one thing we may be sure: neither Europe nor Asia will be left by the war the same as before. It is too soon to affirm that they will be made better by it. A harvest of good will not come automatically out of this convulsion. Its outcome, for good or evil, will be determined largely by the action of England, by the action of the Christian Church, at this crucial time. It may be that neither England, nor the Christian Church, will ever be given such an opportunity again.

9. GERMAN SUBVERSION IN LONDON

Anti-alien sentiments in England increased as the war wore on. The extreme Right accused naturalized German-born British citizens of maintaining their allegiance to the kaiser; as former Admiral Lord Charles Beresford put it, "Once a German, always a German." On August 5, 1914, Parliament passed the Aliens Restriction Order, which provided for the internment of aliens (with the exception of women, children, and non–military age men) suspected of collaboration with the enemy. Over the course of the war anti-German hysteria, heightened by reports of German atrocities in Belgium, the sinking of the *Lusitania,* and the introduction of gas and submarine warfare, led to the destruction of German-owned property, boycotts of their businesses, and violent riots. In May 1915, Lord Beresford and William Joynson-Hicks — a Conservative member of Parliament who had risen to prominence by his victory over the liberal candidate for Manchester, Winston Churchill — presented a petition with over 250,000 signatures to the House of Commons, calling on the government to intern all aliens of military age and to remove both alien men and women "to a distance of at least 30 miles from the sea coast." The issue continued to surface in political debate. In the selection that follows, from June 1916, Joynson-Hicks returned to the question of subversion and espionage on home soil. His arguments were countered by Home Secretary Herbert Samuel on behalf of the government.

[Mr. Joynson–Hicks:]
Now let me give the facts: In August or, September, 1915, a young Czech friend of my own, a young man about whom I made the most careful and adequate inquiries, about whom I have consulted one of the most eminent Czech members of the Austrian Parliament, who is now over here, and upon whose head a penalty has been put by the Austrian Government — it is well known that Czechs are fighting for Russia when they can, and that they are only too anxious to fight for us against the tyranny of Austria — and I find that reports with regard to this restaurant made by this young man were taken down to the police day after day in September of last year, more than seven months before the right hon. Gentleman spoke in the May of this year.

It is rather interesting that we should see what goes on in London in the heart of the Empire seven months before the police swoop down on this place, and I will read some of the reports. On the 9th of September, the day after a Zeppelin raid, my young

Excerpt from *House of Commons Parliamentary Debates,* June 29, 1916, pp. 1055–1059, 1079–1080.

friend reported: "V. had for dinner on the menu Zeppelin Soup" — that was actually on the menu: —

> They told me they knew beforehand about last night's raid and were waiting for it at V., as this place was out of the danger zone. There was general rejoicing in the restaurant. One said "it was the happiest day of his life." Another one had a complete list of all the places where damage was done. He knew every house and mentioned the factories, warehouses and offices by their names. I seldom saw such a crowd of happy people. They were mocking the English, who, as they said, fled in panic at the Zeppelin raids.

Sir George Makgill, secretary of the British Empire Union, took that report down to Scotland Yard on the following day. On the 11th of September this young man went again. He called again in the evening at 8.45. He says:

> They are expecting the Zeppelins this night as they have information of their arrival. About 11 P.M. there are still about fifteen customers there. Voigt is called to the telephone. He comes back from the telephone cabin, exclaiming, "They are here. In an hour they will be in London." The others shout, "Long live Germany!" and are mad with joy.

They came here that night. They were on the East Coast. I am not dealing with unknown raids or raids that were kept secret. This was made public. They were on the East Coast about that time. Fortunately they did not come to London. On the 12th of September he was there again. He met some Hungarians. They were more anti-English than the Germans. One of them, an old man, perhaps fifty-five years of age, said to someone who disapproved of their German sentiments, "Just wait! When the Germans come to London I will denounce you, and you will be one of the first to be shot as a traitor." That was reported to the police.

I will not weary the Committee with all these reports, but I will give a concluding episode. I have seen the young man and talked to him again and again. On the 21st of September he was there again, and the young son in our Army was back on furlough, and he was speaking in this restaurant, and he said — fortunately we know now these things to be right — that there was great unrest amongst the English troops, and that there were complaints by the soldiers, and that they are all sick of this War. Then he makes remarks about the Canadians, which I will not read. One of the Germans said, "It is a shame that you have to be side by side with niggers and Indians. It is a disgrace to Britain." My young friend could not stand this any longer, as he was a loyal friend of the Allies, and he said something about German atrocities. They asked him what he meant, and he replied, "Read Lord Bryce's Report." This German said, "Lord Bryce's report! Lord Bryce is a blank, blank liar! Wait until the Germans come to London, and then you will see that we do not commit atrocities." The proprietor called out, "People like you will be hanged for this. We will take good care. You dare to insult the German Army! You are a Czech; get out of this!" After some more language my young friend got outside. I should like to know whether the son is still in our Army. It may perhaps be said that those are very excited statements of my young friend. I do not think they are. At all events those statements were sent to Scotland Yard, and seven months afterwards their general accuracy was admitted in the Home Secretary's statement that he had discovered a public-house kept by a naturalized German which might become a most dangerous centre, and that he had interned practically the whole lot of them. Suppose that the case of that naturalised German had been considered by one of these remissions committees. Suppose that his position had been considered, or that Scotland Yard had been keeping an eye on these naturalised Germans who keep German restaurants, which are naturally German centres.

There are — my right hon. Friend has had a list of them — a dozen German restaurants in London to-day which are just as much German as if they were in Berlin itself where alien enemies congregate, naturalised or unnaturalised, where, if you are not a Scotland Yard detective looking British all over, wearing British boots, and if you are a man who can pass himself off as a German, you can go and hear most instructive statements. Here is a bill of fare for one of those German restaurants in London for the day before yesterday. It is written in German. I am not a good German scholar, and I do not understand everything here, but there are such things as gries suppe, wiener rostbraten, rindfleisch, wirsing kohl, kartoffeln, gurken salat, and pfankuchen. If you go into that German restaurant you will see notices on the wall in German, you will see that the waiters are German, and if you ask for an English bill of fare you will not get it. It does not exist. It is a German restaurant and might be in Berlin. There are a dozen of them in London to-day in the very heart of the Empire while we are fighting for our lives. In order that this might be confirmed I asked a great personal friend of my own to go to this restaurant yesterday. Two ladies went to lunch, and into this German restaurant for lunch yesterday an English soldier in uniform was brought in by German friends. There is no question about that. I will tell the right hon. Gentleman who the ladies were. It was in Kleinschmarger's Restaurant. We do not want our soldiers to be taken into lunch by people speaking German. I do not say that it was a trap or that they were spies; I only say that we do not want the existence of Germans in the shops where our soldiers are brought in. We ought to be protected from it. There is only one remedy — sweep the whole lot of them away and then it will not exist. Night after night in these restaurants you will find German women of bad character congregating. One knows for what purpose — to worm things out of English soldiers. All the gossip of the German camps goes there. Men who come out go where they will get German food and meet fellow Germans, and all the gossip and news of the camp flies from mouth to mouth in these same restaurants. Another instance was brought to my notice only last week. In Manchester a man was arrested, whose name was William Sauter; he was not a naturalised German at all; he was a German pure and simple, for he had served fourteen and a half years in the German army as lieutenant, and when the police raided his lodgings they found a German ordnance map of France and letters from Germans hostile to this country. The magistrate very rightly sentenced him to six months' imprisonment, and directed that he was to be interned as soon as he came out. If the police had received orders to intern all Germans, that man would not have been at large. . . .

I have only given a few examples, and it must not be supposed for a moment that I know all the cases; but if we have these samples you may be perfectly certain that there are other cases. But the most important point is that these men are really the outposts of

German trade after the War is over. I should like to see all the alien enemies of military age and alien women repatriated. We have now some 40,000 or 50,000 interned, and at the end of the War these men will come out. In the meantime their businesses have been carried on by their wives or by managers, as far as they possibly can, as going concerns; they will be more bitter than ever against this country when they do come out, and they will go on with their businesses as the outposts of German trade. I want to call attention to a very wise observation made by the French Minister of Commerce when he said that:

> Germany is preparing for a trade war against us. She is getting ready to swamp the
> world's markets with damned goods the moment the War is ended. The Allies must
> beware against employing Germans in any capacity in commerce and industry.

I believe I am right in saying that while Russia has sequestrated a very large number of German establishments, France at once sequestrated every German business entirely. They know how to deal with this subject, and we might take a lesson from our Allies in this respect. At the end of the War these interned Germans will come out, and what reason is there for this feeling of kindness and tenderness to the German enemies in our midst. There is a very strong idea throughout the country — I do not want to make accusations, of course, against any member of the Government — that the Government do not really appreciate the determination of the people to stop this German menace in our midst, and, after the War is over, to see that England shall be for the English. We do not want these Germans; we do not want to be friends with men and women who are the relations of those who have so cruelly treated our men at Ruhleben and other camps in Germany. We do not want to encourage relations with men and women, cousins and uncles, and so forth, of the men who have treated Belgium and France as we know the Germans have treated those countries. We want to get rid of them. We want to see that the existing power with regard to internment is carried out much more stringently, and above all, that the power of repatriation shall be exercised in the case of every German man and German woman, where it can possibly be done without cruelty. We want to see them sent back to their own country, where they will receive a warmer welcome than they get here. . . .

[Mr. H. Samuel:]
The next instance I will give is from a newspaper with a vast circulation — one of the largest in the country. It printed a letter not long ago from a correspondent stating that "Germans are being encouraged to leave the Isle of Man to work in hotels," and this imaginative person, like a true artist, in order that his work should be as complete as possible, gave all the details of the employment these men would get, and the terms of payment. They were to receive 15s. a week, and everything found, the only restriction being that they were to be indoors by 7 P.M. I have looked through the records, and find that in the last six months during which I have been at the Home Office, not a single waiter has been released from the internment camps, and no one has contemplated for a moment the release of any men for that purpose. At a meeting of the hop trade recently, a member of that business declared that the taxi-cab driver who had driven him

to the gathering was, he had discovered, an alien enemy, an Austrian, and his statement was received with every sign of disapproval by his audience. That seemed to me very odd, because, as a matter of fact, all licences were withdrawn from alien enemy taxi-cab drivers at the beginning of the War. But the police, having received a letter the same day to the same effect, they made inquiries, and they found that the taxi-cab driver in question was a natural-born British subject of British parents, but that he had an impediment in his speech and a broad Yorkshire accent. The following statements were made in Scotland by a councillor and a justice of the peace:

> Our War Office seems to be under German influence.

> An Hon. Member: He was made a J.P.
> Mr. Samuel: Not on account of this.

> There are in Edinburgh German pork butchers, barbers, hotel-keepers, caterers, etc., dominating Edinburgh, and I am in possession of information which if known would stagger the country. I know for a fact that on the Saturday night previous to the raid on Edinburgh a considerable number of Germans left this city and went to country towns and returned again on the Monday after the raid was over. I have absolute proof that telegraph wires were cut and telephone wires were cut also.

This gentleman, having been challenged by the military authority under the Defence of the Realm Act to produce his evidence, signed the following statement:

> I regret that I have made these statements as they are not statements of facts.

B. Standards of Living

1. A BREMEN FAMILY'S SUFFERING

The following excerpt points to the problems associated with Germany's faulty system of food distribution. The paucity of essential foods, coupled with inadequate methods of distributing them, led to both malnutrition (especially among the nation's youngest and oldest citizens) and widespread discontent. Black marketeering and appropriation of foods by Germans who could still afford to pay for hard-to-get items produced an angry backlash by working-class women, who resented having to stand in long lines for small handouts and to account for every pfennig (the German currency) they could muster. The letters of Anna Pöhland, a working-class wife from the northern port city of Bremen, to her soldier husband, Robert, underscore the inequities of food distribution. With her husband at the front, Anna was left to fend for herself and their children amid increasing food shortages. Far from being helpless, Pöhland, as her letters reveal, was a resourceful, intelligent, and sensitive woman who was active in the local Social Democratic party. Anna's letters testify to the persistence of class tension and the demise of the *Burgfrieden* (harmony within a "Fortress Under Siege").

27 April 1916

My beloved, darling Robert,

. . . The days are so warm now that the children are scampering about as if it was the height of summer. I need to lengthen the summer clothes for our little ones. . . .

It is really a shame that you, my loving Robert, cannot watch the children develop. Don't be angry that I haven't answered every letter, but I have had so much sewing that there never was enough time. Tomorrow I am preparing you another package, and I'll include a spoon. . . .

When I was asked by [a worker for the Red Cross] whether we have had enough potatoes until now, . . . I responded: mornings, potatoes, afternoons and evenings potatoes.

Yes, she said she had more than enough coupons for bread, but she had eight people for Easter and only one-quarter pound of butter. To that I responded that when one has a succulent joint or something similarly tasty . . . , then one hardly needs butter. But we have never once had enough money to be able to buy bones for soup, and additional butter — . . . we weren't even able to consume during peacetime because of a lack of money.

Yes, she replied, the old shopkeepers are at fault. No, I retorted. The government did not fulfill its obligation. Suggestions were made by our side [presumably a reference to the local branch of the Social Democratic party]. My suggestion was for a city kitchen so that the rich wouldn't be able to get anything [better to eat] than the poor. We always had lectures about [the importance of] economizing; instead the rich lived better. . . .

Your Anna

22 May 1916

My beloved, darling husband,

. . . You mean, dear Robert, we should take some excursions. You should understand, though, that one has to have sturdy shoes for that, and all our money goes toward food. Eggs cost three marks per dozen; financial support [from the government for wives of soldiers] remains unchanged. Meat is so expensive!

We are drinking more milk, however, at times three liters. We get two liters daily from our milkman. Frau H. can only get half a liter. . . . When will things improve? . . .

Anna

Excerpt from *Die Pöhlands im Krieg* by Anna Pöhland, trans. by Marilyn Shevin-Coetzee, Pahl-Rugenstein, 1982, pp. 105–106, 113.

2. No Meat in Berlin

Before the outbreak of the First World War, the German Social Democratic party (SPD) had complained about the exorbitant price and poor quality of food for the working classes. Long lines at the butcher shop and shortages of necessities during the war renewed the socialist critique of the inequities of capitalist distribution and the grievous failure of the German government to make adequate preparations for the protection of living standards. The following selection contains the speech of an SPD parliamentary deputy, Emanuel Wurm (1857–1920), who subsequently defected to the Independent Socialist party (USPD), and the response to criticisms of governmental food policy by a municipal councillor from Berlin.

Speech of Emanuel Wurm

Gentlemen, the question on the agenda, though of Socialist origin, has also been indorsed by the other parties. It is a common question of all the city aldermen to the Municipal Council. It reads: What measures does the Municipal Council intend to adopt for procuring and regulating the supply of meat for the Berlin population?

Only a few weeks ago we had to call attention from this very platform to the unsatisfactory supply of provisions for Berlin and especially for the poorer classes. At that time it was the lack of potatoes and the failure to take measures to insure the necessary amount of potatoes for the market. At present the only alteration to be recorded is that of a scarcity of fat; butter and meat have supervened on a scarcity of potatoes. You all know to what tumults, rushes, and collisions people are exposed in order to procure those few provisions accessible to them. For hours they have to wait in front of the stores only in the end to face the well-known "Sold out!" It scarcely needs mentioning that these hardships fall chiefly upon the working population. How can willing and capable women, employed on war work, find time to stand before the shops and actually beg the necessary food for their families? At the same time these faulty arrangements entail a waste of productive power and a danger to health in the weather we had last week. And yet the proper authorities who alone can afford effective relief fail to take the necessary steps.

When today we put this question of relief measures to the Municipal Council, we do so in the first place because we demand of this body, as the official government of Berlin, that it definitely inform the responsible imperial and state departments that this mismanagement cannot be any longer tolerated. . . .

The ridiculous anxiety as to what foreigners may think and say — anxiety which causes the suppression of every unpleasant utterance — is merely a shield against criticism. [*"Quite right!"*] If the safety of the Reich is really dependent on what foreigners

Reprinted from *Fall of the German Empire, 1914–1918,* Vol. II, edited by Ralph Haswell Lutz, pp. 166–169, with the permission of the publishers, Stanford University Press. Copyright © 1932 by the Board of Trustees of the Leland Stanford Junior University.

know about us it would be in a precarious state, for a glance into the foreign press will convince one that it is often better informed about German affairs than we Germans.

The renowned German organization is more and more being revealed as a mere dodge to protect the farmers against the towns. . . . The root of the evil lies in the fact that in our whole arrangement we have no uniform regulation for the entire Reich and that consequently the individual districts have to compete with each other in their attempts to supply the necessary provisions. . . .

We approve, further, the adoption of the recommendation of the Municipal Congress that there should be, after the autumn of this year, a strict regulation of the distribution and price of potatoes, so that Germany's supply for the ensuing year may be amply secured. . . .

The arrangements for supplying butter, too, are very paltry. The butter card is a barrier card; it limits upward but not downward. You know the lamentable situation. Well-to-do people order butter by telephone and it is being kept for them, whereas the poor people have to wait for hours to get a small pat or else none at all. . . . Recently the papers stated officially that Berlin had received 125 grams of butter a head, . . . consequently there should be no shortage of butter. The fact is that the Central Depot has never delivered this quantity allocated to the city. . . . This is an intolerable situation and the executive must really take energetic steps to bring relief. It seems to us that Berlin is being treated as a stepchild. . . . The supply brought by post must be subjected to control. . . . In addition to scarcity of potatoes and butter, Berlin has now to face a scarcity of meat. . . . According to a contract with a Pomeranian company, 2,000 pigs should be delivered in Berlin every week. . . . The recent weekly deliveries of that company have been 500, 1,000, and 1,500, respectively. . . . For some weeks Berlin has had a system of delivering fat cows, and the number of meat cards has been increased to 500,000. But the old pressure of crowds at the meat shops continues, . . . although the number of selling depots has been increased to 500. Even this number is insufficient. . . .

A second source of meat supply is the Cattle Syndicate. . . . This combine includes no representatives of urban interests. . . . It is in close touch with the farmers, and does not send forward supplies even in fulfillment of contracts. This is another cause of the evil plight of Berlin. The city should have weekly deliveries from the syndicate of 2,125 full-grown horned cattle, 2,185 calves, 4,500 sheep, and 14,000 pigs. But in the first three weeks of April there was a shortage of 2,831 cattle and 8,278 sheep, and a surplus of 3,889 calves; and instead of 42,348 pigs, only 2,000 were delivered — a shortage of 40,000! If contracts are to be fulfilled in this manner, the city, of course, is powerless. ["Quite right!"]. . . .

Now it has been argued that it would be an agricultural crime to slaughter lean beasts, and therefore they are being kept on the pastures to be fattened. . . . That would be quite right if people were living in times of peace and had enough to eat. But now Berlin must demand that cattle should be brought to market even though they be not quite fat. . . . In conclusion, we must demand an organization that would be truly a central department, to be headed by a man who will be fairer to the cities than has been the case hitherto. We need a central organization, an imperial department which has the right to attach and confiscate provisions and to deliver them to the municipal unions.

Such a department has been advocated by my comrades for some time. . . . There has been enough talk. . . . Consumers must no longer be sacrificed for experimental purposes. . . . There is no sense in issuing meat cards, unless the system is being extended uniformly throughout the Reich. . . . Such a regulation must take place, for the present situation is unbearable. . . .

Speech of Berndt, Councillor

Gentlemen, the council fully shares the anxieties of the previous speaker. . . . The regulation of the meat distribution is based upon the Federal Order of March 27 last, two regulations of which must here be emphasized: (1) the procuring of meat, and (2) its distribution. The first task is assigned to the Cattle Trade Association, the second to the Municipal Council. This order, therefore, has wrought a complete change in the state of affairs. What formerly was done by free trades is now assigned to the city. . . . As regards the distribution of meat, the Municipal Council was obliged to employ the services of an existing organization, the Berlin Cattle Commissioners, whom it is paying a commission of one per cent. . . . The reason for this arrangement is that the council has no available staffs of suitable persons for taking up the new duties. . . . The difficulties besetting the supply of meat are almost insurmountable. . . . The council has done everything possible to overcome them. . . . In the last three or four weeks we have done everything within human capacity, but of what use are any measures whatsoever if no meat can be obtained? This is the crux of the question; but it is just at this point that the council is powerless. The supplies contracted for are not delivered. From one combine, instead of 16,000 pigs we got only 96. [*"Hear, hear!"*]

What is the cause of this defective supply? In my opinion it is not due to lack of cattle, for conditions are so much better in other cities and other federal states. The trouble is due entirely to defective organization, the poor functioning of the existing Cattle Trade Associations, and the insufficient regulation of financing. . . . The introduction of a meat–card system for Greater Berlin at present is impracticable. . . . In view of the scarcity of the present supplies in Berlin the daily ration can be only 50 grams, and to fix such a slender ration by a formal document would be inimical to the interest of the Fatherland because of the effect of the bad impression that such a measure would have abroad. . . . However, as soon as it is possible to fix the daily ration at 500 grams the council will not hesitate to introduce the meat–card system.

3. DIET AND NUTRITION IN WARTIME

Given the partial disruption of food imports by German naval action, the diversion of essential resources such as fats and oils to munitions production, and the rising cost of foodstuffs, there were serious questions about whether prewar living standards might be maintained during the pressure of war. One effort to investigate the cost of living and its impact on wartime diets was undertaken by the physiology department of the University of Glasgow. It studied forty working-class families in Glasgow during

1915–1916 and compared the results with those from a similar investigation four years earlier. To appraise the war's long-term impact, investigators chose families with young children. But after visiting over 600 families in all, they insisted that the forty they eventually studied were representative. The first selection summarizes that study's conclusions. The second reading, by Nellie De Lissa, a cooking instructor to the Middlesex County Council, and the third, by Mae Byron, are from typical wartime cookbooks. Cookbooks of the war years paid particular attention to compensating for scarce ingredients, especially meat and sugar, and attempted to extract maximum caloric value from unfamiliar sources.

a. *Workers' Diets*

The following study of the diet of labouring class families in Glasgow was made as part of an investigation upon the etiology of rickets at present being carried out in the Physiological Department of the University of Glasgow. But the information gathered by Miss Lindsay in her study of the diet of the same class in 1911–1912 makes possible a very interesting comparison between the conditions of living then and under the present war conditions, and the fact that these studies extended over three periods — (1) Summer of 1915, (2) Winter of 1915, (3) Spring of 1916 — enables some idea of the progressive effects of war conditions to be obtained.

Forty families have been studied. . . .

This table [at right] is very interesting as showing the fluctuation of the values of the main articles of diet. The tendency of prices is upward, with a slight fall in one or two of the commonest articles in Autumn 1915.

At pre-war prices oatmeal was the most economical source of both energy and protein; peas following for protein, and wheat flour for energy.

A year later (June 1915) beans were our cheapest source of protein, and rice of energy. Next came peas for protein, and flour as a source of energy.

In November 1915 oatmeal had almost recovered its position, being the most economical source of energy, and taking the second place as a source of protein. Beans were still the cheapest protein obtainable, and rice followed oatmeal as the cheapest source of energy.

In June 1916 (1) lentils and (2) oatmeal were the cheapest sources of protein, and (1) oatmeal and (2) flour the cheapest sources of energy.

Sugar and potatoes have undergone the greatest changes in value. At pre-war prices sugar was the most economical source of energy, following oatmeal and flour. Being restricted in import, sugar has been more subject to the causes which brought about the rise in prices than many other foodstuffs. Potatoes being mostly home grown did not rise immediately on the outbreak of war; indeed for a short time in the Autumn of 1915

Excerpt from "The Family Budgets and Dietaries of Forty Labouring Class Families in Glasgow in Wartime" by M. Ferguson, *Proceedings of the Royal Society of Edinburgh* 37 (1916–17), pp. 117, 126–127, 130–131.

Food Values Obtainable for 1d., according to Retail Prices in Glasgow at various Periods (calculated from Cooper & Co.'s Glasgow Price List)

	Immediately pre-War			June 1915			November 1915			June 1916		
	Price per lb. in Pence	Protein in Grams	Calories	Price per lb. in Pence	Protein in Grams	Calories	Price per lb. in Pence	Protein in Grams	Calories	Price per lb. in Pence	Protein in Grams	Calories
Beef (stewing)	9	9.6	132	12	7.2	98.75	12	7.2	98.75	13	6.6	91
suet	10.5	1.9	337	10.5	1.9	337	10.5	1.9	337	11.5	1.7	308
corned	12	10	107	17	7	76	17	7	76	18	6.6	71
Mutton (cheaper parts)	8	6.8	132	12	4.5	88	12	4.5	88	12	4.5	88
Bacon	10.5	3.9	256	13.25	3.1	203	14.25	2.7	189	15	2.7	179
Cheese (Canadian)	8.5	15.5	241	12	11	171	10.5	12	195	13.5	9.8	152
Margarine	5.5	1	659	6	.9	587	6	.9	587	7	.8	504
Herring (fresh)	4	12.7	92	4	12.7	92	4	12.7	92	6	8.5	62
(smoked)	4	22.7	187	4	22.7	187	4	22.7	187	—	—	—
Sugar	2	—	930	3.5	—	—	3.75	—	—	5	—	372
Potatoes	.57	14.3	542	.57	14.3	542	.43	19.1	723	1.17	7.1	271
Oatmeal	1.23	59	1512	2.47	25.4	753	2.14	34	869	2.29	21.7	814
Wheat flour	1.43	36.26	1155	2.14	24.2	770	2.07	25	798	2.29	22.7	722
Bread	1.5	27.9	810	2	20.9	607	2	20.9	607	2.125	19.7	572
Lentils	2.5	47.2	648	3.5	33.7	463	7.5	16	216	3.5	33.7	463
Peas	2	56.8	827	3	37.9	552	4	28.4	414	5	22.7	331
Beans	2.5	41.8	640	2.5	41.8	640	3	34.8	533	3.5	24.1	457
Barley	2	19.3	825	2.5	15.4	660	3	12.9	550	3.5	11	471
Rice (Rangoon)	2	18.1	815	2	18.1	815	2	18.1	815	2.5	14.5	652

they were selling at 5d. a stone, and formed the cheapest food at the time. An early frost in the Autumn of 1915, however, wasted part of the crop, and potatoes have become very dear. For a short period in June 1916 they were selling at 2s. 6d. a stone, a prohibitive price for the working-class housekeeper.

Animal foods are expensive at all times. At pre-war prices protein could be obtained from flour, lentils, peas, and oatmeal at about one-sixth of its cost when got from beef and mutton.

In June 1916, although meat had not risen in price to the same extent as the vegetable foodstuffs, it was still five times as dear as a source of protein, and over seven times as expensive as a source of energy. . . .

CHANGE IN COST OF LIVING

These investigations enable some answer to be given to the question of whether real wages have risen or fallen since the outbreak of war.

The percentage of unemployment has fallen from 3 per cent. in 1911 to 0.5 per cent. in June 1916. Thus under pre-war conditions unemployment represented a loss of 2.5 per cent. more of the weekly wage than in June 1916.

The weighted cost of food, calculated from the relative values purchased per penny in the family budgets studied at the two periods, has risen about 50 per cent. since 1911–12. In the families studied about two-thirds of income was spent on food, so that a rise of $\frac{2}{3} \times 50$ per cent. = $33\frac{1}{3}$ per cent. of income would be necessary to compensate for the advance in the price of food. Adding to this the 6 per cent. rise from other expenditure, and subtracting 2.5 per cent., the difference in the loss of wages due to unemployment at the two periods, a rise in wages of 36.8 per cent. would be required to keep the standard of well–being constant.

In the recently published interim report of the Committee appointed by the Board of Trade to investigate the principal causes which have led to the increase of prices of commodities since the beginning of the war, the rise in the weighted cost of food is estimated at 65 per cent., which is equivalent to a rise of 45 per cent. in the cost of living among the working classes. These figures are calculated from June 1914 to September 1916.

According to figures supplied by the Board of Trade Department of Labour Statistics to the above Committee, the weighted cost of food has risen by 6 per cent. since June, when the last group of the present dietary studies was carried out. This is equivalent to a further advance of 4 per cent. in the cost of living, or an increase of 41 per cent. since the outbreak of war, according to the present calculations. The difference between this figure and that estimated by the Board of Trade Committee may be due to the following causes: —

1. That the character and quantity of the commodities purchased by the housekeeper has altered somewhat in the direction of economy. The use of less meat in some families, the substitution of cheap for the dear cuts of meat in others, and the increased consumption of margarine are instances of this.

2. That the "weighting" from which the Board of Trade figures are calculated does not exactly correspond with the proportionate use made of the various commodities by the labouring classes in Glasgow. As above stated, an average of 40 per cent. of the total energy in the food of the forty families studied came from bread, which had only advanced from 3d. to 4¼d. for the 2 lb. loaf (or 42 per cent.) by June 1916.

CONCLUSIONS

If the results of these studies can be applied to the labouring classes in industrial centres generally, they show to June 1916 —

1. That on an average the food supply was not less adequate than in pre-war times, although there was a tendency to a decreased consumption of protein in meat and an increased consumption of fat.
2. That the cost of energy in food had risen about 50 per cent.
3. That the total cost of living had probably increased by 37 per cent.
4. That the increase in the cost of living, resulting in a diminished supply of the necessaries of life, is being chiefly felt by the families of labouring men with a fixed wage, say from 20s. to 30s. weekly. Among the men who were irregularly employed before the war, or are now doing Government work, or are otherwise having a good deal of overtime work, the surplus of income over the necessary expenditure has materially increased.

In conclusion, I should like to express my indebtedness to the housemothers for their kindly consent and co-operation, without which the studies could not have been made.

b. *Wartime Cookery*

In most kitchens to-day and for a long time to come the great question will be, not what to provide, but *how* to provide good meals for all, not which materials to choose, but which to do without, to meet the reduction in purse and the increased cost of living. The list of articles in common use, nay, lavish even to extravagant use, in the average kitchen in pre-war times would feed an army, and the waste or over-provision would feed their wives and children. Every one knows that economy is now imperative, but many do not know how to arrive at its consummation without too severely curtailing the daily meals, and yet at the same time to maintain a pleasing variety, nor do they know what ingredients may be used as valuable and suitable substitutes for many that will now show prohibitive prices to moderate and restricted housekeeping allowances.

Excerpt from *War-Time Cookery* by Nellie De Lissa, Simpkin and Marshall, 1915, pp. 5–7.

This little book is intended as an aid to housewives to whom existence under the new conditions is a problem, and also to their more fortunate sisters who have the means and the will, and perhaps not the practical knowledge, as to how they may economize and thus indirectly make things easier for others less generously provided with the needful.

Particularly is it devised with a view to the proper nourishment of children, and to help those who fancy that meat is the only nourishing food. There are so many nice and nourishing things commonly neglected in the dietary, really as the result of a more than sufficient choice, and also in a measure due to the indifference to careful and detailed cooking that is only too prevalent in this country, that a varied, appetizing and satisfying repast may be furnished as often as required each day, and every day of the week, without danger of repetition of monotony.

All that is required in following out the recipes given is great pains in cooking slowly and thoroughly in good flavouring and attractive serving. The correct balance of the food-values in the meals in sample menus described, and the attentive study of the relative nourishment of various foodstuffs so accessible nowadays, will do the rest for the receptive and open mind. All prejudice against so-called "messes" must be put on one side in the general interest, for this book does not deal with cookery for the rich, nor does it speak of big joints of meat and "flesh-pots." It is simply a practical attempt to help my sisters in the hard winter months which we must all face cheerfully, and to assure to them the "contented mind" which a well-lined stomach never fails to give. Shakespeare spoke of the judges with "fair round bellies in good capon lined," and they were more likely to have a bright outlook on mankind and things in general than Cassius, of whom it was said, "I like him not, he hath a lean and hungry look." Evidently thin men are not so amiable as fat men, and we know that. *Punch*'s advice to the young wife must not be forgotten, namely, "Feed the Brute." Sound advice. So I invite one and all to come and feed, and to do so well and cheaply.

NOURISHING SOUPS

I will begin at once with a very delicious and popular form of food, good for all ages and accessible at all times, which provides both drink and light digestible nourishment, acceptable alike to young and old, delicate and robust, and especially welcome at night to tired workers unable to digest heavier foods, and easily prepared in the day and warmed up without loss of goodness at nighttime.

First among these come the fleshmaking soups, to take the place of bone and meat stocks, namely, those soups whose foundation is the valuable and savoury lentil, pea and haricot. These are perfect foods in themselves and do quite completely take the place of meat, with less waste in the process of assimilation and with the additional advantage of giving warmth to the blood, and having a tonic effect on the stomach; and last, but not least, they are extremely cheap and easy to procure and to make into attractive food form.

c. Practicing Strict Economy

At the present juncture it is obvious that we have all got to practise strict economy at every conceivable point. Not only is this advisable; it is absolutely necessary. And economy, like charity, begins at home.

It is more than merely economy in food which we have to consider. We must try to combine at least five methods of saving:

1. Economy in Fuel.
2. Economy in Labour.
3. Economy in Time.
4. Economy in Health.
5. Economy in Food.

The first and the last are, to most people, those of chief importance.

Economy in fuel is a matter to be studied at every turn. Wood and coal are both likely to be greatly enhanced in price as time goes on; gas will rise coincidentally; oil is not, to most people, an acceptable substitute for the above. In days when we each and all are desirous to "do our bit" towards the national good, when many of us are perforce working at a rate and to an amount which we never attempted before, and when such a number of women are obliged to fit in bread-winning with housework, the care of labour and time are vitally important. Unfortunately, as every woman who can cook is aware, it takes a vast amount of time and trouble to "make-up" small tasty dishes, and to do so cheaply. Economy, plus palatability, means so much grating, chopping, mincing, pounding, frying, whisking, etc., etc., that the person who achieves some little culinary triumph is often much too tired even to wish to taste it. And she has, therefore, carried out her economy more or less at the expense of her health. Economy in health is a much more vital point than usually strikes one in connection with cooking. Most of us are feeling the wear and tear of hard and anxious times; few women are quite as "fit" as they were before the war. Worries react upon the digestion, and it is no use setting food before people which will disagree with them. In almost every household there is somebody who can't digest certain viands — whether farinaceous foods, sweet dishes, cheese, pulse foods, uncooked vegetables, root vegetables, pork, etc., etc., etc. — and although it is impossible to cater for that one person separately, it is no use concocting meals of which he or she cannot partake.

It is extremely difficult to reconcile these five methods of thrift in matters of cookery for a household.

Cold dishes in general save fuel, and to a great extent time and labour (even though they entail a certain amount of preliminary cooking), but they are not so wholesome or digestible as hot ones.

Hot dishes, especially those which use up odds and ends, are more palatable and

Excerpt from *Mae Byron's How-to-Save Cookery,* Hodder and Stoughton, 1915, pp. 1–5.

digestible than others, and one can save in food and money by them; but they entail more expenditure in labour, time, and fuel. . . .

To begin with the actual material. It is increasingly difficult to say how one best may live cheaply in the matter of food. (1) Fish is at almost a prohibitive price; for this reason I have only dealt with the cheapest fish, and tinned fish such as salmon and sardines. (2) Eggs are dearer and dearer; therefore, so far as possible, I have omitted all dishes requiring more than one egg, and have regarded eggs according to their definite dietetic value — not to be squandered lightly. I recommend the use of egg-powder and custard-powder for puddings and cakes. (3) Cheese is abnormally expensive; so, instead of treating it as a little extra luxury, I have strictly considered it as a very valuable article of food. (4) Meat is rising sky-high in price; it was therefore necessary only to include the cheaper cuts, and methods of utilising cold meat where a joint might once-in-a-way be bought. All dishes of veal and lamb have been entirely omitted. Dripping and "stock" are such indispensable articles to the cook, that she may think the above omissions increase her difficulties. But dripping can be bought, as it is wanted, by the pound; so can bones, for breaking up and boiling down towards stock and gravy. And this is a much cheaper way of procuring them than when they are purchased as part of a joint, and at the same high price as solid meat. (5) Bacon and ham, which are already beyond most people's purses, are barely mentioned in this book. . . . (6) Vegetables are none too cheap for the town-dweller; the more fortunate countrywoman can here secure many opportunities for thrift. In any case, however, they are less expensive than the more highly concentrated forms of nutriment — meat, cheese, eggs, etc. . . . (7) Sugar is dear; but as an article of food it is so invaluable, combined with farinaceous or fruitarian diet, that a large amount of space has been given to simple family puddings and wholesome cakes. (8) Flour is "up"; but the advantages of home-made bread are beyond question, and probably the greatest saving of all, from a health point of view, can be effected here.

In conclusion, a number of topical hints and suggestions have been inserted, for the help of the harassed housewife, to whom, with most sincere sympathy, I commend this little book.

4. THE EXPERIENCE OF CHILDREN

Prior to 1914 the European Right, worried about declining birthrates, moral decay, and physical deterioration of their youth, promoted for young people larger families, abstinence from smoking and drinking, and military training. Europe's young recruits who survived suffered from the mental as well as physical scars of war; children too young to understand the meaning of the war also suffered from malnutrition and — all too often — the loss of a father. Initially the frequent absence of parental supervision or the isolation from the bonds of authority may have seemed liberating, as in the reminiscences of two Belgian refugees (the first two selections), but the long-term consequences of the disruption of familiar family life proved serious and often devastating, as the third extract shows. Crippled men, widowed mothers, and orphaned children were inescapable reminders of the human cost of the conflict.

a. Marie Lacante

(Born 1904, in Ypres)

Barely an hour after we had left Ypres our house was shelled and burned out. Surely we would have been killed. We fled on foot to Vlamertinge, where we boarded an old train taking refugees to France. For fourteen days we did everything on that train: we slept there, ate, and sat. I cannot remember all the places we passed on our way through the Pas-de-Calais into Normandy. They told us that we were going "to the country," and we thought they meant the ends of the earth.

We were "unloaded" in Normandy and brought to a market square . . . where people looked us over as though we were for sale. My father and mother were taken away to work on a farm. My father was told to drive the horses though he had never handled a horse in his life. I was twelve and a half years old and my sister was ten[1]. We had to work in a bakery, two small children alone in a foreign country, not knowing any French! After two days we ran away.

We finally ended up in Paris. Many Belgians went there, and so we did too. We lived on the fifth floor. We slept by the stove. . . . Paris is a dirty city, if you ask me. . . . The Soldiers, especially the English, would go out around North Station. It is only natural, on leave from the front. Away for months, and all those women at the station to welcome them. There were plenty of bars and whorehouses. All those women had to have a red card and were examined weekly. If they were caught without the necessary stamp they were arrested. The authorities wanted to keep disease under control.

We did not stay in Paris. We found a house in Villeneuve, a suburb. My sister and I worked together in the city: we would take the train into the city, to the Place Saint-Michel, then the subway and bus to Montmartre. We worked in a factory making batteries. Every day we did the commute, alone. I do not know how we survived it.

b. André Houwen

Born in 1904, in Reningelst, near Ypres

We children had a wonderful time while the English were in Reningelst. We almost never went to school. The English had their canteen across the street from our house. . . . When the soldiers came out they gave us oranges and chewing gum. The gum was much better than it is now: it kept its taste until you'd spit it out, nowadays the taste is gone after half a minute. They also gave us chocolate. What more could a child want?

(a) Excerpt from *Van den Grooten Oorlog*, Jan Hardeman and Marieka Demeester, eds., trans. by Walter Simons, Malogijs, 1978, pp. 51–53.

(b) Ibid., pp. 82–85.

---

[1] This must be an error: at the time of their flight — probably in the spring of 1915 — the girls were only ten and a half and eight years old.

They had also converted a barn to a cinema. Every Thursday afternoon we got to go to the movies, from two until four. The general was there too. All the children were given an orange, a chocolate bar, chewing gum, and sometimes a banana. That alone would have been enough to get us there. We saw many films with Charlie Chaplin. Charlie in the trenches, Charlie the fireman. We had a great time, but we still went there chiefly for the oranges. . . .

We got used to the gunfire and shelling. If we heard a shell, we would see it explode two hundred meters away from us. Those shells no longer frightened us. You won't hear the shell that kills you, it moves faster than sound.

Of course we children would spend the entire day with the soldiers. Two railroad tracks ran right through the park and manor of Reningelst, carrying small ammunition trains to Dikkebus and Wijtschate. One day we saw a wagon standing there, with a brake. We just had to get that one for us, never mind what the English would say! They could keep the other wagons. . . . Soon we were on our way with the wagon. At Klijte or Dikkebus we were often stopped by English M.P. and sent back. They asked what we were doing there, it was much too dangerous for us, with all those shells. We said we would play a bit further away, out of reach of the shells. They didn't scare us at all.

The things we did! I wouldn't dare to do them now. We cut a crate of ammunition open with a pick-axe. We would put a shell on the tracks to extract the gun powder. Or we lined the bullets up on the ground and smashed them with the pick-axe. Or we'd set fire to a bag of gun powder and then hurl it away from us. Like a mountain of fire. One second late and you would be burned to death. I can't understand we never got killed.

c. Orphans

Most war orphans were infants when their fathers were killed, and the impact of the war on them can only be inferred. Central institutions in the child's life were shattered by the war. The family was disrupted not only by the prolonged absence of the father and older brothers, but also by the chronic worry and illness of the mother. Not infrequently, the mother too was forced to leave the children temporarily while she sought employment. Schools were also disrupted when male teachers went into the army. Together with this social dislocation was the ever worsening health problem.

One surprise was that the infant mortality rate did not increase during the war. Possibly, since the overall birth rate dropped, more resources were devoted to the smaller number of infants. Or perhaps the very extremity of living conditions encouraged adults to be especially careful of babies. The war did, however kill slightly older children in significant numbers.

Reprinted from Robert Weldon Whalen, *Bitter Wounds: German Victims of the Great War, 1914–1939,* pp. 77–80. Copyright © 1984 by Cornell University. Used by permission of the publisher, Cornell University Press.

Children's death rate (1913 = 100)

		1914	1915	1916	1917	1918
Boys,	5–10	106.4	142.9	129.3	150.3	189.2
	10–15	107	121.7	128.5	154.2	215
Girls,	5–10	101.4	142.2	133	143.8	207.3
	10–15	104.1	128.3	131	152.9	239.2

Not only did girls generally have a higher death rate than boys of comparable ages, but the increase in the death rate was higher for girls than for boys. Why? Without further evidence, one can only guess. It may be that boys and girls endured the same hardships, but that girls proved more vulnerable. Or, it may be that boys and girls did not endure the same hardships, that in the distribution of scarce resources, little girls received less.

Children's physical deterioration during the war was obvious. They were underweight by as much as 8 to 12 percent. They did not grow normally; average height by age declined by 3 to 4 percent. Rickets, a disease associated with malnutrition, was common, and polio increased among teenagers. Ordinary childhood diseases did not increase significantly, but stomach disorders, such as vomiting and cramps, were common, and there was an increase in tuberculosis. Nervous disorders were frequent; for example, an "enormous increase" in bed-wetting was reported among school children. . . .

Before the age of 10 or 11, boys and girls showed little difference in their perceptions. Their drawings were of genderless stick-figures, their poems and essays tended not to distinguish between war and non-war. Poems to "O Hindenburg, O Hindenburg," quickly drifted into the more familiar rhythmic pattern of "O Tannenbaum, O Tannenbaum." To one 11-year old girl, the most important part of a victory celebration was that it involved a school holiday.

After the age of 10 or 11, however, a marked break appeared in the perceptions of the girls and boys. Boys demonstrated a passion for, and an amazing mastery of, military minutiae. Their drawings emphasized violent action, with abundant gore. Their identification with their soldier-fathers and brothers was intense. Of course, boys played at being soldiers, but they also collected maps, military photos, and pictures of war heroes, such as Baron von Richthofen. . . .

Girls seemed to experience the war in a totally different way. Their poems, drawings, and essays in the Breslau collection are melancholy and introspective. They concentrate on death and suffering. The war's "ruthless attack on the love-relationship of the family filled their souls. . . . Again and again, appears the same theme: death of the soldier and the grief of his loved ones, but in always new, extraordinarily diverse manifestations . . . many poems concern the soldier's grave — a theme which frequently appears in the girls' sketches." While sons tried to be heroic like their fathers and brothers, daughters mirrored the worry, grief, and passivity of their mothers.

C. Gender and Feminism

1. A NEW SPIRIT AT WORK

The following selection, written in 1916, is an attempt to take stock of the impact of the war on women in Britain. Edited by Lady Randolph Churchill, it presents an optimistic view of the situation, emphasizing that women had put aside prewar frivolity and discovered new sources of inner strength.

Many and drastic as are the changes war has brought to our land, there is none more striking than the subtle change which has crept over the British home. This is a change marked less plainly in material reductions, perhaps, than in the spirit of the people concerned. Over cottage and mansion alike, in the heart of London or the most remote country farm, has spread a new atmosphere and a strangely different attitude towards life.

This change takes many concrete forms, according to the particular circumstances of the home in question, but there is no question that to-day it is one of the most powerful factors in our domestic life. The housewives of 1914 — for it is with women at all times, and more especially now, that home life rests — had their foes to face as well as the men. And with a high courage, that in many cases is little short of heroic, they buckled on their armour, and wore it as uncomplainingly as they would a silk gown.

The shadow of war, terrible as it is, acted as a scavenger of innumerable home littlenesses. Probably no other event could have done it in the same wholesale fashion, for it is doubtful if anything else could have touched all classes and districts to the same keen, personal depths. This war is a calamity that every home in the land has felt, and will feel still more in the months to come.

In this limited sense perhaps "calamity" is hardly the word to use. Few will deny that, on the whole, the home life and outlook of England have gained far more than they have lost, in this sharp contact with the realities of war. There may be gnawing anxiety for the men-folk away in the firing line, the pinch of unemployment, and often, alas, the many hardships that are born of actual privation, yet side by side with these ills are the new brave spirit that astonishes possessor as much as onlooker, and the patient uncomplaining endurance of burdens. They form the home contributions to the spiritual side of life in war.

The face of daily existence has altered in many directions. Prices are higher. Wages or salaries are often greatly reduced. The country has many extra mouths to feed. Altogether, apart from the emotional side of things, life is infinitely harder to-day than it was eighteen months ago. Yet never has the standard of courage and cheerfulness been so high.

The universal motto, "Business as usual," covers very much more than its matter-

Excerpt from *Women's War Work* by Lady Randolph Churchill, Pierson, 1915, pp. 144–153.

of-fact tone implies, simply because, with the world at sixes and sevens in an altogether unparalleled degree, the running of the home on ordinary lines has become, in most cases, a strenuous task. It is a great cause for thankfulness, and not a little for legitimate pride, that that wholesome business precept is as general as we know it to be. New conditions of feeding, lodging, and clothing are met with sharpened wits and more patient contriving; the gospel of doing without has made enormous strides since August 4th, 1914. . . .

In the home, as in the nation's chambers of legislation, the bigger cost is quietly taken as inevitable. The household expenditure is patiently rearranged on any new basis the times demand. Mother and grandfather and children accept the pinch without complaint — often with thanks to the fates that so far they have always been able to spare enough for the weekly parcel of sweets or food that is sent away to firing line or camp. There is a fine determination that our soldiers shall have such comforts as are possible, even if it means stinting and scraping at home. The girl who exacted of her fiancé more expensive theatre tickets, flowers, and bonbons than he could afford, is ungrudging now in the amount she spends on her air-tight tins of chocolate and cigarettes. In the new war spirit, self-sacrifice is a liberal ingredient.

For many women, perhaps, especially for the younger ones, it is harder to dress shabbily than to forgo little luxuries of diet. Yet in the department of dress, "do without it" is again the prevailing motto. Of late years many serious-minded people have censured the growing love of fine raiment among our women, but war has proved a more effective deterrent than all their diatribes.

Months ago, when the strife was yet new, and summer was just fading into autumn, I saw a young girl of seventeen or eighteen gazing eagerly and intently into a milliner's window, which displayed a dazzling assortment of autumn hats. The girl was respectably but none too well dressed — she looked like a maidservant or a worker in a small shop. On her head was a decidedly battered black straw hat, and in the window a charming blue felt, on which her heart was very obviously set. A great, clumsy five-shilling piece peeped from between her clenched fingers.

Next door a little crowd had gathered round the bulletin board hung out by a newsagent, and here and there someone furtively dropped a coin into the National Relief Fund money-box, which hung just beneath. The girl I was watching glanced from the hat to the box, and clutched her money more tightly than ever. It was rather pitiful to see the struggle in her face. Finally, she stepped over to the box, dropped in her crown, set the battered hat straighter on her head, and hurried very quickly away.

Truly, where dress is concerned, the change of feeling is immense. It is difficult to realize that the pretty business girl, who, seated in train or tube, steadily knits her way to town in the morning and back again at night, is the gay butterfly who less than two years ago was contemptuously reported to "put all her salary on her back." Or take the older woman who frivolled away her time in every sort of social gaiety before war came with its awakening force, and wore gowns that were the envy of every feminine acquaintance. Now she is clad in a costume that evidently dates from previous years, and will tell you that with a reduced income and two Belgians to feed and clothe, the amount of money spent on dress must needs be rigorously curtailed. . . .

One has only to glance through a recent issue of any fashion paper, to see how large a part such economies as renovations play in its contents. Editors have been quick to give the new spirit concrete form, and they are helping women to maintain the gospel of "making do" that has often been gibed at in the past, but which really covers a multitude of little braveries and self-denials. The clothes which one looks for and finds, both in the women's press and in the shop-windows, are the simple, useful garments that everyone must have.

Gay, flimsy fripperies are quite second in importance, and even then often appear only as inexpensive renovations. The seamstress who suffers least by the war is she who for the expenditure of a few shillings can give an up-to-date appearance to an old gown, and so lengthen its life by a few months. Makers of new clothes only have been among the heaviest financial sufferers, and it is noticeable that many modistes who formerly disdained "making over," have now added the word "Renovations" to their signs and advertisements.

The decline of the dressmaking trade is partly accounted for, not merely by the fact that women are having fewer new clothes than formerly, but also because a larger proportion are boldly tackling the feat of making their own wardrobes. This war will leave not a few with a more abiding knowledge of plain needlework than they could have acquired through any other cause.

The influence of uniform has also had its effect in reducing the number and extravagance of clothes. Many a pretty maid who formerly spent half her waking hours in thoughts of new frocks, is to be seen day in and day out in the plain navy outfit of the Red Cross, or the more picturesque equipment of a hospital probationer. These uniforms are badges of honour which may carry their wearer to any and every function, and among those who possess them, it has become positively bad form to wear ordinary clothes. Then too, even in the case of others who have no such distinctive mark, the day's occupations are now of so much more serious a nature, that flimsy attire is largely out of place. With first-aid classes to attend, clubs for soldiers' wives to run, and often the greater part of the household work to do as well, the cooking apron and the dustcap have become far more essential than teagowns.

It is doubtful if, even when peace is restored, the old extravagant ways will more than partially return. Women will have learnt to regulate dress to its comparatively unimportant niche, and the taste for simplicity acquired during these dark days, is likely never wholly to leave them.

Of the unmaterial aspects of the new spirit, it is far more difficult to speak, because they are so intensely individual and personal. The quiet, steady courage that readjusts old ideas of household expenditure and dress, does not falter in the harder task of altering old ideals and realizing new ones. The pangs of separation and bereavement are borne heroically by many women, who in times of peace were small-minded enough. Little meannesses, little tricks of sharp speaking, evil thinking and impatience, have been washed away in the flood-tide of national perils and necessities.

Self-control is now a universal instead of an occasional trait, and has been shown strikingly in different enemy air-raids and naval disasters. Even children are learning to hush their own griefs to comfort those whose troubles are heavier. The mere playing at mimic warfare has taught them that soldiers bear their mishaps bravely, that they do not cry out when things go wrong. Instilling these precepts into her little ones, many a mother is learning these lessons anew herself, to her own upholding when the heavy blow falls. . . .

. . . The new home spirit reaches the highest in every one, touches chords that in many cases have never been touched before, and brings out unsuspected melodies of patience and courage and charity.

The charity of to-day is a thing to be very thankful for. Only in a great crisis could people give as they are continually giving now, pardon as we see them pardoning every day of our lives. . . .

In little as well as great things the new spirit is rife. The small grumblings that used so often to overshadow a day, how conspicuously are they absent now! Train services are disorganized, the goods one needs can no longer be procured, the streets are yawning caverns of gloom after dark. Every inconvenience is accepted with the stoic resignation that knows such things are necessary and inevitable, with the same resigned calm that attends the loss of a battle or the sinking of a ship at sea. In the plainer vision which calamity has given, small deceits no longer appear worth while, and little grumbles are seen in all their ugliness.

The men of the Empire are abroad, lending their strong right arms to the crusade against tyranny and "frightfulness." And the women, in millions of homes up and down the land, are winning day by day nearer to the new era. With charity and courage and patience, they are making way for the clearer light that shall dawn with the coming of peace.

2. LOSS AND GAIN

Also dating from 1916, this selection differs from the previous one. While not ignoring the new spirit at work, it nonetheless points to the pain and misfortune inherent in the sacrifices for the war effort extolled by less pessimistic observers. The author, the countess of Warwick, was just one of many privileged women who, by promoting recruitment, organizing charitable drives, and so forth, threw themselves wholeheartedly into a conflict that promised liberation, not just from Prussian militarism but implicitly from patriarchical subordination as well.

The long-drawn-out agony of strife is now two years old and, as each day adds its tale of slaughter to the incalculable total, we women may pause in our war work for a moment and endeavour to estimate our own position. . . . We women did nothing to cause our own misfortune; on the contrary, we strove in our little way to promote peace, and to that end, above many others, we sought a hearing in the councils of the nations.

Excerpt from *A Woman and the War* by the Countess of Warwick, G. H. Doran, 1916, pp. 49–55.

But it was not to be. Our claims were ridiculed or ignored, and now man-made war has swept over Europe like a blight, and we are left to aid our country through the day and to mourn, when the long day's work is done, for our fathers and brothers, our husbands and sons. . . .

After all, this claim to national service is no more than was advanced in the old days when access to the heads of the Government was barred and the hooligans of a great city were allowed to give full rein to their impulses. Then our rulers thought they could dispense with women, to-day we are recognised as indispensable. That is all, but it is very much, and it sets me the question that is the title of this brief paper — What has woman lost and what has woman gained?

She has lost much that was dearest to her, much that life is powerless to replace. All the springs of her being have nourished the love that she has given to her dear ones, to the man who was her choice, to the son who fed upon her life. In many cases she has lived almost entirely in her children, for the ties that bind her to the active pleasures of life grow weak in conflict with the powers of maternity. She has forgotten the brief years in which she lived for herself and savoured all the sweets of existence, she has lived in her children, happy chiefly in their happiness, ambitious only for their future and concerned with the struggle for the freedom of her sex less on account of her own generation than on account of that which is to follow. It is woman's *rôle* to give, it is man's *rôle* to take, and custom has staled for him the infinite variety of his taking. And now he has taken so much that made life worth living that she seeks an anodyne for her grief in giving him all that is left to give, the labour of her hands.

This is not only true of the women of England, it applies equally to the women of every belligerent country, friend and foe alike, and it may be said that between the women of the world there is a common sacrifice and a common sympathy. All have suffered, all must continue to suffer, on a scale that this old world of ours, with all its crimes and tragedies beyond number and beyond belief, cannot parallel. It is this truth that steadies our nerves and strengthens our hearts and sets us looking, past the ultimate sacrifice, to what may lie beyond, not for ourselves but for others.

All that we have has been taken or is being demanded of us. Is there in all the world something to which we may look forward with confidence, something that may justify hope? I think there is. Without any sense of pride we may claim that woman has at least vindicated the claims she advanced in those peaceful days that seemingly lie so far behind us. She claimed that she was worthy to play her part in the conduct of national life, that she was in very truth indispensable to it; she was told, by brutal word or brutal deed, that her ambitions outran her capacities. One year of war has given the lie to this assertion. Woman, even before the coming of compulsion, encouraged her dearest to go, if needs be, to their death, in a war for which she has no shadow of responsibility before God or man. Conventions, agreements, treaties, alliances, in all these things she has no share, but as soon as they materialise in war she must pay the heaviest price.

The excitement and glory of a struggle in which the fighter feels that he has surrendered his life to high causes is not for her, she must be content with the pale reflex or with the tragedy. In her heart she may know that man incurs the penalties of his ambitions or bad diplomacy or unpreparedness for upheaval; but those penalties press heavier on women than on men, for, even granting that the love of husband for wife and wife for husband be equal, yet the passion of a mother for her child and her grief when he is snatched from life in the hours when life is unfolding all its possibilities, is something beyond the strength of man to grasp.

But woman has not failed on account of her griefs, she has strangled them — or she has tried to with all the strength that has been given to her — and she has gone out into the market-place and said, "What more do you require of me? Ask and I will give, direct and I will obey." . . .

She realises that man is at last beginning to understand and even to acknowledge her place in the world, that the future cannot repeat the errors of the past, that the day-dawn of her emancipation is visible. This war, reconciling so many differences, rebuking so much pride and bringing so many men and women face to face for the first time in their life with life's actualities, has united all workers, irrespective of class or sex. It is seen now that woman has a part to play in the conduct of the State, and that there are spheres of activity in which women might and must work for the common good. She and man together must build up a new civilisation out of the wrecks of the old one, not only here but throughout the strife-stricken world. Old barriers, time-worn prejudices, a blind conservatism — what part have these in the mental attitude of nations freed from over-whelming peril?

The soul of my sex would be as desolate to-day as the ruined cities of Belgium, Poland, and Servia, were it not for the certain knowledge that our sacrifice has not been made in vain. We have the right to hope that our share in the work of the world is to be acknowledged at last, and that the spheres of our activity are to be widened. In this way, and only thus, we shall be able, in years that have yet to be, to influence thought and to influence action, to bring a humanizing note into the great chord of life. We shall strive through the sisterhood of women towards the brotherhood of man, and we shall be working among those who will be able to see for themselves what one-sided rule and one-sided domination have done for progress and civilisation after their slow ascent to a position that at best left so much to be desired.

The women of my generation will sow where they may not hope to reap, but there is nothing new for woman in this experience. It is her mission in this world to sacrifice herself, from the hour when she accepts motherhood until the end. Her happiness is derived from the contemplation of the happiness of others, she lives in the new lives with which she renews the world. She will leave contentedly to others the prizes for which she laboured in years of peace and suffered through the season of war. It will be sufficient for her dimly to foresee the time when those who have replaced her will give birth to sons with no more pangs than Nature demands, and give birth to daughters in the belief that they will not be widowed or fatherless or childless through catastrophes of man's own making.

So it seems to me, looking back at the cruel record of two years, that woman, for all her losses, has gained, that what she has lost is matter for her private sorrow, and what she has gained is matter for universal joy. She has found the uses of adversity, she has accepted self-sacrifice for the sake of those who will be the better able to enjoy the rich fruits of life. In this knowledge she will labour, for the sake of this truth she will persevere with a confidence in the future that no shifting tides of chance can shake. And her watchword in the coming year is, Hope.

3. A New Role for Women?

Helena Swanwick was born in Germany in 1864, the only daughter among the six children of her Danish artist father and her British mother, the illegitimate offspring of a Cambridge don. Against the wishes of both her mother and father, who would have preferred her to pursue a more sedentary life at home, she studied economics at Girton College. Inspired by John Stuart Mill's *The Subjection of Women,* she worked tirelessly for women's political and economic rights and served from 1909 until 1912 as editor of *Common Cause,* the journal of the National Union of Women's Suffrage Societies (NUWSS), headed by Millicent Fawcett. When the NUWSS declared its support for the conflict, she resigned in protest at this violation of her own pacifist inclinations. Swanwick joined several organizations devoted to achieving a peaceful settlement to the war and later was an advocate of the League of Nations. The selection that follows is an effort to take stock of the war's specific impact on women of all social classes, but within a framework by gender.

How has the war affected women? How will it affect them? Women, as half the human race, are compelled to take their share of evil and good with men, the other half. The destruction of property, the increase of taxation, the rise of prices, the devastation of beautiful things in nature and art — these are felt by men as well as by women. Some losses doubtless appeal to one or the other sex with peculiar poignancy, but it would be difficult to say whose sufferings are the greater, though there can be no doubt at all that men get an exhilaration out of war which is denied to most women. When they see pictures of soldiers encamped in the ruins of what was once a home, amidst the dead bodies of gentle milch cows, most women would be thinking too insistently of the babies who must die for need of milk to entertain the exhilaration which no doubt may be felt at "the good work of our guns." When they read of miles upon miles of kindly earth made barren, the hearts of men may be wrung to think of wasted toil, but to women the thought suggests a simile full of an even deeper pathos; they will think of the millions of young lives destroyed, each one having cost the travail and care of a mother, and of the millions of young bodies made barren by the premature death of those who should have been their mates. The millions of widowed maidens in the coming generation will have to turn their thoughts away from one particular joy and fulfilment of life. While men in war give what is, at the present stage of the world's development, the peculiar service of men, let them not forget that in rendering that very service they are depriving a corresponding number of women of the opportunity of rendering what must, at all stages of the world's development, be the peculiar service of

Excerpt from "The War in its Effect upon Women" by Helena Swanwick, 1916, pp. 3–11, 13, 23–25.

women. After the war, men will go on doing what has been regarded as men's work; women, deprived of their own, will also have to do much of what has been regarded as men's work. These things are going to affect women profoundly, and one hopes that the reconstruction of society is going to be met by the whole people — men and women — with a sympathetic understanding of each other's circumstances. When what are known as men's questions are discussed, it is generally assumed that the settlement of them depends upon men only; when what are known as women's questions are discussed, there is never any suggestion that they can be settled by women independently of men. Of course they cannot. But, then, neither can "men's questions" be rightly settled so. In fact, life would be far more truly envisaged if we dropped the silly phrases "men's and women's questions"; for, indeed, there are no such matters, and all human questions affect all humanity.

Now, for the right consideration of human questions, it is necessary for humans to understand each other. This catastrophic war will do one good thing if it opens our eyes to real live women as they are, as we know them in workaday life, but as the politician and the journalist seem not to have known them. When war broke out, a Labour newspaper, in the midst of the news of men's activities, found space to say that women would feel the pinch, because their supply of attar of roses would be curtailed. It struck some women like a blow in the face. When a great naval engagement took place, the front page of a progressive daily was taken up with portraits of the officers and men who had won distinction, and the back page with portraits of simpering mannequins in extravagantly fashionable hats; not frank advertisement, mind you, but exploitation of women under the guise of news supposed to be peculiarly interesting to the feeble-minded creatures. When a snapshot was published of the first women ticket collectors in England, the legend underneath the picture ran "Superwomen"! It took the life and death of Edith Cavell to open the eyes of the Prime Minister to the fact that there were thousands of women giving life and service to their country. "A year ago we did not know it," he said, in the House of Commons. Is that indeed so? Surely in our private capacities as ordinary citizens, we knew not only of the women whose portraits are in the picture papers (mostly pretty ladies of the music hall or of society), but also of the toiling millions upon whose courage and ability and endurance and goodness of heart the great human family rests. Only the politicians did not know, because their thoughts were too much engrossed with faction fights to think humanly; only the journalists would not write of them, because there was more money in writing the columns which are demanded by the advertisers of feminine luxuries. Anyone who has conducted a woman's paper knows the steady commercial pressure for that sort of "copy."

The other kind of women are, through the war, becoming good "copy." But women have not suddenly become patriotic, or capable, or self-sacrificing; the great masses of women have always shown these qualities in their humble daily life. Now that their services are asked for in unfamiliar directions, attention is being attracted to them, and many more people are realising that, with extended training and opportunity, women's capacity for beneficent work would be extended. . . .

. . . The problem of the readjustment of men's and women's work after the war is going to be so difficult and so great that we want none of this frivolous sentimentality in dealing with it. We want facts. We want a sober judgment. We want an alert mind, which will meet the problems with no dead obstructive prejudices, but with the single intention to make the very best use of the men and women who will emerge from this ghastly catastrophe. To condemn any section of the people to inaction, to restrict or cramp their powers of production and of healing, is going to cripple the nation and be the most unpatriotic course conceivable.

THE NEED FOR PRODUCTION

It is often forgotten that for full prosperity a country needs to be producing as much wealth as possible, consistently with the health, freedom, and happiness of its people. To arrive at this desired result, it is quite clear that as many people as possible should be employed productively, and it is one of the unhappy results of our economic anarchy that employers have found it profitable to have a large reserve class of unemployed and that wage-earners have been driven to try and diminish their own numbers and to restrict their own output. To keep women out of the "labour market" (by artificial restrictions, such as the refusal to work with them, or the refusal to allow them to be trained, or the refusal to adapt conditions to their health requirements) is in truth anti-social. But it is easy to see how such anti-social restrictions have been forced upon the workers, and it is futile to blame them. A way must be found out of industrial war before we can hope that industry will be carried on thriftily. Men and women must take counsel together and let the experience of the war teach them how to solve economic problems by co-operation rather than conflict. Women have been increasingly conscious of the satisfaction to be got from economic independence, of the sweetness of earned bread, of the dreary depression of subjection. They have felt the bitterness of being "kept out"; they are feeling the exhilaration of being "brought in." They are ripe for instruction and organisation in working for the good of the whole. The desperate need of war blows away many obstructions, and we see now that the good of the country requires the hearty work of all, and anything which discourages or diminishes that work damages our chances of success in the war. We may hope that, with the aid of awakened women, we shall at last see that it damages our chance of success in peace also. Reactionary or repressive laws and regulations; the sweating and over-driving of the workers; the starvation and subjection of the mothers; the limitation of the child's right to education; the monstrous growth of luxury; the denial of the right use of the land, for the nourishment and refreshment of the whole people; the neglect to provide decent houses; all these lower vitality and limit output. But beyond any other cause for the limitation of output is the horrible waste caused by unemployment and the lack of incentive to the whole people to do their best.

> *Work without hope draws nectar in a sieve,*
> *And hope without an object cannot live.*

Under a profiteering system the worker has no hope. What is needed is a hopeful and trustful policy, constructive and vital, not coercive and timid.

READJUSTMENT OF EMPLOYMENT

Most people were astonished in 1914 at the rapidity with which industry and social conditions adapted themselves to the state of war, and there are those who argue that, because the fears of very widespread and continued misery at the outbreak of the war were not justified, we need not have any anxiety about any widespread and continued misery at the establishment of peace. Certainly depression or panic are worse than useless, and a serene and cheerful heart will help to carry the nation beyond difficulties. But comfortable people must beware of seeming to bear the sorrows of others with cheerfulness, and a lack of preparation for easily foreseen contingencies will not be forgiven by those who suffer from carelessness or procrastination. We know quite well what some, at least, of our problems are going to be, and the fool's paradise would lead straight to revolution.

It would be wise to remember that the dislocation of industry at the outbreak of the war was easily met; first, because the people thrown out by the cessation of one sort of work were easily absorbed by the increase of another sort; second, because there was ample capital and credit in hand; third, because the State was prepared to shoulder many risks and to guarantee stability; fourth, because there was an untapped reservoir of women's labour to take the place of men's. The problems after the war will be different, greater, and more lasting; much will depend upon whether the people see to it that a progressive and intelligent Government shall be in power to deal with vital issues with courage and in a living and constructive spirit, unhampered by precedent and unafraid of vested interests, or whether they will tolerate an unintelligent and timid Government which meets difficulties with inertia and the consequent unrest with coercion. Capital will have been destroyed, literally blown to pieces on a vast scale; yet there will be great need of the production of the necessaries of life. Unless the Government will boldly take the risks of the operations of peace on a scale as vast as the operations of war, at any rate for a time, there will be huge waste of life, of health, and of labour out of employment, and therefore degenerating, as all unused force does degenerate, with consequent misery and disorder. The return of millions of men to civil life and work will tax the goodwill and organising capacity of the whole nation. The change from war production to peace production will possibly be even greater. The readjustments required must necessarily be slow and difficult, and unless there can be co-operation between employers and employed, and between all sections of employed, there will be friction to the raw and many disastrous mistakes.

Because it will obviously be impossible for all to find work quickly (not to speak of the right kind of work), there is almost certain to be an outcry for the restriction of work in various directions, and one of the first cries (if we may judge from the past) will be to women: "Back to the Home!" This cry will be raised whether the women have a home or not. . . . We must understand the unimpeachable right of the man who has lost his work and risked his life for his country, to find decent employment, decent wages and conditions, on his return to civil life. We must also understand the enlargement and enhancement of life which women feel when they are able to live by their own productive work, and we must realise that to deprive women of the right to live by their work is to send them back to a moral imprisonment (to say nothing of physical and intellectual starvation), of which they have become now for the first time fully conscious. And we must realise the exceeding danger that conscienceless employers may regard women's labour as preferable, owing to its cheapness and its docility, and that women, if unsympathetically treated by their male relatives and fellow workers, may be tempted to continue to be cheap and docile in the hands of those who have no desire except that of exploiting them and the community. The kind of man who likes "to keep women in their place" may find he has made slaves who will be used by his enemies against him. Men need have no fear of free women; it is the slaves and the parasites who are a deadly danger.

The demand for equal wage for equal work has been hotly pressed by men since the war began, and it is all to the good so far as it goes. But most men are still far from realising the solidarity of their interests with those of women in all departments of life, and are still too placidly accepting the fact that women are sweated over work which is not the same as that of men. They don't realise yet that starved womanhood means starved manhood, and they don't enough appreciate the rousing and infectious character of a generous attitude on the part of men, who, in fighting the women's battles unselfishly and from a love of right, would stimulate the women to corresponding generosity. There are no comrades more staunch and loyal than women, where men have engaged their truth and courage. But men must treat them as comrades; they must no longer think only of how they can "eliminate female labour"; they must take the women into their trade unions and other organisations, and they must understand that the complexities of a woman's life are not of her invention or choosing, but are due to her function as mother of men.

The sexual side of a woman's life gravely affects the economic side, and we can never afford to overlook this. As mothers and home-makers women are doing work of the highest national importance and economic value, but this value is one which returns to the nation as a whole and only in small and very uncertain part to the women themselves. The fact that a woman is a wife and mother diminishes her value in the "labour market," and even the fact that she is liable to become a wife and mother has done so in the past. Unless men are prepared to socialise the responsibilities of parenthood, one does not see how women's labour is ever to be organized for the welfare of the whole, nor does one see how women are to perform their priceless functions of motherhood as well as possible if they are to be penalised for them in the future as they have been in the past. . . . It does not at all follow that the best homes will be made by all women doing all the manual work of their own homes themselves. The mere waste of physical effort by the doing of work individually which might be done co-operatively is only one side of the waste. The work of motherhood is often very seriously crippled by the need for exhausting and unremitting toil on the part of the mother, and if the need to earn a wage in money is added the whole of the woman's work suffers. Organisation and rational development are urgent in the life of the working housewife. . . .

It has been dinned into the ears of women for ages past that "a woman's place is the home," and that her first duty is a private and individual one. Now, suddenly, women are told that they must come out of the home and that their country has first claim upon them, as upon men. Appeal is made even to mothers with husbands at the front to leave their children and go out to work.

EQUAL WAGE FOR EQUAL WORK

While the women were responding to these appeals as best they could, hampered by conflicting duties and insufficient training, they were met by another perplexing problem. Whereas a few women had of late years made persistent claim to equal pay for equal work and had been generally met with the reply that this was a ridiculous demand — unjust in view of women's smaller responsibilities, injurious to the women themselves, since it would drive them altogether out of the market — and whereas the great mass of women had, from custom and ignorance and docility, acquiesced in this lower status, they were suddenly assured that they must ask the same wage as the men they were displacing, otherwise the men would suffer when they returned to industry. . . .

. . . [W]hen people talk of a "living wage" they must define who and how many are supposed to live upon this wage. Is it to be the single person, man or woman? That would be comparatively simple. Is it to be the person, man or woman, plus his or her "dependents"? That is very complex, because the number of dependents varies, not only between different people for the same period, but between different periods for the same people. Thus, on the whole, men have more dependents than women, and this has led to a general opinion that men ought to have higher wages than women. But a great many women have dependents, and some have as many as men. It frequently happens, also, that the women with most dependents (such as widows) are less capable of earning just at the time when the dependents are thrown upon them, or that (as in the case of unmarried women) the dependents are such as will never become independent (such as the old, the cripples, the wastrels). . . .

. . . Important as the economic side of the question is, we must not forget, however, that there are other factors of ever-growing importance to be found in the change in the position of women and of their thoughts and ideals of motherhood. Even if motherhood were endowed by the State, and the individual parents relieved of personal anxiety about the upkeep of the children, we should have to take these thoughts and ideals into consideration. Those who deplore a falling birth-rate never seem to see any other remedy than for the already married women to have larger families. But a much better remedy would be that more women should be married. Before the war there were about two-and-a-half millions of marriageable bachelors. If it had been made possible for these young men to marry and have two or three children, it would have been better than that the mothers of four or five children should be required to have two or three more, regardless of whether they want them. The preponderance of women over men is a bad thing in itself, and the largely artificial restriction of marriage accentuates the evil.

Married women have changed their outlook during the past century, and the birth-rate must be treated as the product of a partnership in which the mother is nominated by nature as the predominant partner. If motherhood is woman's supreme function, it is important that it should be denied to as few as possible, and to women should belong its supreme direction. The racial instinct of women is of tremendous importance to the welfare of the race, and it is encouraging to note how scientific knowledge is coming to reinforce much of what is instinctive in the mother. She feels the value of temperance, soberness, and chastity; she feels the need to rest and recuperate; she feels the outrage of unwilling motherhood. In addition to this, the modern woman feels urgently the need to be a complete person, to develop herself, to be a comrade to her husband and children and friends, and to take part in the wider world outside the home. She cannot live this complete life if she is to spend all her best years in incessant child-bearing, from which she will emerge stupefied and worn out. She looks round on the world and sees many women pining for children and many others overdone with them, and she sees little girls turned into little mothers before their time, docked of their education and their play, because their mothers require help with their intolerable burden. A modern woman expressed a woman's thoughts with mordant wit when she wrote of human beings as "the only animal alive that lives upon its young."

ENFRANCHISEMENT AND EMANCIPATION

The course and conduct of the war, throwing upon women greater and greater responsibilities, bringing home to them how intimately their own lives and all they hold dear and sacred are affected by the government of the country, will tend greatly to strengthen and enlarge their claim for a share in the government. The growth of what was known as "militancy," in the last few years of the British suffrage movement, was the disastrous result of the long denial of justice, the acrid fruit of government which had become coercion, because it was no longer by consent. Now that, for two years past, the women of Great Britain have made common cause with their men in this time of stress, the heat of the internal conflict has died down, and one hears on all sides that prominent anti-suffragists have become ardent suffragists, while others have declared their resolve at any rate never again to *oppose* the enfranchisement of women. The battle of argument was won long ago, but we are not, as a people, much given to theory; custom has a very strong hold over us. The shock of war has loosened that hold, and now almost every one who used to oppose, when asked whether women should be given votes, would reply: "Why not? They have earned them!" I cannot admit that representation is a thing that people should be called upon to "earn," nor that, if essential contribution to the nation is to count as "earning," the women have not earned the vote for just as long as the men. . . .

What the war has put in a fresh light, so that even the dullest can see, is that if the State may claim women's lives and those of their sons and husbands and lovers, if it may absorb all private and individual life, as at present, then indeed the condition of those who have no voice in the State is a condition of slavery, and Englishmen don't feel quite happy at the thought that their women are still slaves, while their Government is saying they are waging a war of liberation. Many women had long ago become acutely aware of their ignominious position, but the jolt of the war has made many more aware of it.

4. DOES WOMEN'S SERVICE ENTITLE THEM TO THE VOTE?

The issue of women's suffrage, prominent in political debate in Britain before the war, acquired urgency in the wake of the undeniable female contribution to the war effort in the public sphere. It remained a thorny question, however, because a party truce adopted at the outset of the conflict could be cited as a reason for delaying consideration of so controversial a matter (it might further divide the parties), and because its resolution inevitably depended on the concurrent — and also controversial — extension of the franchise to all adult males. Throughout the debates, the liberal journal *The Nation* could always be counted on for a clear, reasoned, balanced exposition of the progressive case. The following editorial was published in mid-1916, when franchise reform could no longer be indefinitely delayed.

When our politicians agreed to a party truce, some of us imagined that the questions which divide us could be kept in cold storage for the duration of the war. There is no process by which the life of the mind can be sterilized, nor do nations pass through a period of hibernation. Nothing will emerge unchanged from this war, and we shall discover that the country has been doing its thinking none the less actively because it has not been led or regimented. Among the questions which have by common consent matured, we must reckon the enfranchisement of women. There is something like a general agreement that women have by their magnificent service to their country in its need added immeasurably to the proofs (already ample enough) that they are a reserve, as yet but half-utilized, which the nation neglects to its cost. Until this perception came to the nation as a whole, enfranchisement would not have brought with it its full potential benefit. After it has come it would be a meanness and a waste to impose on women a further period of agitation and delay. We stand in need of all their humane intuitions and constructive enthusiasm and we shall display a peculiarly callous folly if we drive them again to plead and argue for their rights, and to squander on this superfluous process the energies which they would prefer to spend for the common good. While this change has come to public opinion, the war itself has accidentally made an emergency which will compel Parliament to deal with the franchise. Some means must be devised by which the soldiers and munition workers, who have lost their electoral qualifications by their services to their country, may be enabled to vote at the next general election. That might conceivably be done by some *ad hoc* measure conferring a vote for this single occasion on every man who had served away from his own home, and possibly the problem of enabling soldiers to vote who are still abroad may have to be faced. The better plan is to use the emergency to simplify the franchise itself. Make residence for some brief period the standard qualification, and the soldier (like everyone else) will be enabled to vote, as soon as need be, after his return from the front. It is

From *The Nation,* 27 May 1916.

natural and proper that the Unionists, if they are asked to give their consent to what will be virtually manhood suffrage, should make their own terms, and they ask for a redistribution of seats to correspond with changes of population. That is a measure which ought never to have been regarded through party spectacles, and it will be conceded with the best of goodwill. It is unthinkable that we should go so far as this towards electoral reform, without at the same time meeting the demands of women.

This is a point which really argues itself. Only a small mind would contend that such considerable measures as these are not "franchise reforms." One may call them an *"ad hoc"* adaptation of the register to an emergency. But they will certainly be permanent. If we establish a three months' qualification at the next election, we shall never go back to the old twelve months' period. They will also bring upon the register, not merely men who had a vote when they enlisted, but large numbers who never possessed a vote at all. Their effect, in short, will be, not merely to prevent a possible wrong to a specially deserving class of men, but also to enlarge the male electorate. They would, therefore, enhance the grievance of women, if they stood alone, by making their disability more invidious and more exceptional. That is not the whole of the case. The main point is that registration reforms or Reform Bills (call them what you please) cannot be a standing item in our politics. When once this subject is dealt with, no one wishes to touch it again for several years at least. That means that any postponement now is necessarily a long postponement. If we mean within any measurable period to enfranchise women, the only handsome way to do it, and, indeed, the only way compatible with entire sincerity, is to do it in time to enable them to vote at the next election. A failure to do it now will mean that all our politics will be confused for the next five years by a distracting agitation, and women, when they do come in, will enter, not in a mood of good comradeship and patriotic unity, but after the embitterment of a needlessly protracted struggle. These arguments are so strong that we need hardly clinch them by reference to the too numerous Ministerial pledges which promise to women their opportunity of sharing in the next instalment of Parliamentary reform. Those pledges have never yet been fulfilled, and we feel sure that the disposition of those who gave them will be to take the first opportunity of redeeming them, without considering too nicely whether an emergency Registration Bill (which will in effect set up manhood suffrage) might plausibly be distinguished from an organic Reform Bill.

The objection might conceivably be raised that a Coalition Government cannot during a party truce handle a question so contentious as Woman Suffrage. Contentious it certainly was. It is less so to-day, but at the worst the Contention never followed party lines. A truce is, indeed, the appropriate moment, and it was during the brief truce which followed King Edward's death that the Conciliation Committee was formed, and the whole question brought vastly nearer to settlement than it had ever been before. The Coalition Cabinet, to be sure, is divided on this issue, but not more seriously than either a Liberal or a Conservative Cabinet would be. Mrs. Fawcett, in her able letter to the Prime Minister, has asked for an "agreed" Bill. We hear so much of the conversion of prominent opponents, that women need not despair of inducing this Government itself to introduce the Bill. It is certainly not more sharply divided on this issue than it was on compulsory service, and if individual convictions could give way in that instance there may be room for some self-abnegation in this. We should hope ourselves for a large and final settlement, which could confer the franchise on a short residential quali- fication on men and women, single and married alike; but we should not reject any reasonable compromise, if compromise were necessary, to ensure a prompt settlement. The Cabinet might, if it required a mandate, first of all submit the principle in the form of a resolution to the House. If a free vote showed a majority, it ought then to proceed with its united authority.

Mr. Asquith has encouraged hope by the brief letter to Mrs. Fawcett, in which he promised, not merely that her claim should be considered, but "impartially weighed without any prejudgment from the controversies of the past." We hope we may deduce from that phrase that Mr. Asquith has himself begun to see the question in a new light, and that his opposition is no longer the fatal obstacle to progress which it was in the past. He wrote of the "magnificent contribution" of women to our "country's cause." It has surprised only those who failed to measure at its real worth the contribution which they always brought in the calm years of peace. The doctors, the nurses, the relief workers, and the great army which hastened to replace male labor in field and factory did not suddenly develop their endurance, their unselfishness, their quick, adaptable intelli- gence. These qualities they have always had, since a broad and humane education eman- cipated them from a tradition of subjection and effacement. The war brought its oppor- tunity, and no class has risen more splendidly to seize it. The qualities hidden and diffused in time of peace, have suddenly been concentrated and illuminated by our hour of need. Those who lacked the occasion or the insight to recognize them before, have been surprised into generous homage. We would not speak of the vote as a reward for all this service. We prefer to say that the nation has seen that it impoverishes its own life by a refusal to give full scope to all this ability and public spirit. We cannot afford to face the future with one-half of the nation's brains in shackles, with one of its hands still reaching vainly for its tool. The only theoretical argument which stood in the way was the doctrine that the State is based on physical force. We call that argument "Prussian- ism" to-day. Nor is this all. The transformation of industry by the mobilization of women which has taken place during the war is in some degree permanent, and it must confront us at the peace with intricate questions of readjustment — questions of wages, of combination, and of the division of labor. Unless we summon women to share in the solution of these problems, which must govern their future and ours, we risk a one- sided settlement. The vote has become more than ever an urgent domestic question, while to the nation has come the will to solve it generously and promptly.

5. THE WOMAN WORKER AFTER THE WAR

Elizabeth Leigh Hutchins (1858–1935), the author of the next selection, devoted her life to protecting the rights of working-class women. She studied at the London School of Economics and later served as an executive member of the Fabian Society, founding its Women's Group. In her numerous publications on the conditions of working women in the factories (especially in textiles), Hutchins argued for increased state intervention to protect female workers, greater awareness among women about their position in society, and for efforts toward their economic independence.

We have a constantly falling birth-rate and an infant death-rate which, though greatly reduced, still moves near 10 per cent., and has lately increased. We have also to face a terrible depletion of young men of the present generation. No problem can be more vital to us than the saving of infancy and young life. The lower birth-rate of our Ally, France, and of ourselves from many points of view is no doubt a mark of a higher civilisation and a finer type of humanity, but the power of rapid recuperation will be relatively less with us than with the enemy, and it will be necessary to put our best thought into the preservation of the children who are born. Increased thought and care for children has been a notable feature of the present century. The child has become recognised as an object of importance to the community, and by some vague, half-understood process of conversion society has begun to feel that it owes a duty to the future, or, in other words, that it owes its own future existence to the child and the unborn. The growth of institutions such as municipal health visiting, school and infant clinics, infant consultations, and so forth means the formation of a body of opinion which becomes more and more articulate against child neglect. Besides the women teachers, we now have a large number of women who follow professions and occupations such as those of the school doctors, sanitary inspectors for a large part of their time, health visitors, doctors, and nurses who specialise in children in clinic work, &c., Care Committee organisers, and others with less well-defined posts, including a good many volunteers who give a large part of their time to the care of children. It may be said, it *is* said by some, that these officials and voluntary workers are doing the work the children's mothers should themselves do, but this objection seems to have little justification. In point of fact, social work on behalf of children is not an effort to replace the parent; it is much more a new effort to do work that was previously not done at all. It does not supply the place of parental interest, but serves to supplement and guide that interest, give it a better definition, even perhaps in some cases to awake an interest that was previously dormant through ignorance and lack of stimulus. The medical adviser of school or clinic, as a matter of course, calls for the mother's attendance, and will not be satisfied unless someone is responsible to give the necessary attention to Tommy's ears or Polly's chest, knowing well that otherwise the little invalids will not profit much either by advise or medicine.

The recruiting of women for industry will no doubt go on briskly, but it will have to be limited by the needs of the rising generation, and improved care of children means more work; it means more women taking up the subject as a life's work and

Excerpt from "The Position of the Woman Worker after the War" by B. Leigh Hutchins, *The Economic Journal* 26 (June 1916), pp. 186–188, 190–191.

profession; it will probably mean the introduction of new forms of municipal service, "home helps," and so forth, to lessen the burden of housework on women at the times of having infants, and it will probably mean some kind of social provision to enable mothers of young children to give up their industrial work for a time, so that the child should have proper care and attention. The system of granting allowances to soldiers' wives relative to the number of children is one which may perhaps be followed in the case of widows and wives of men who are not physically capable of work, and all these forms of care for the child tend to lessen the economic pressure which is the main cause of married women's employment. Solicitude for children will be emphasised from two directions, by those who regard life as sacred *per se* and look to see the development of humanitarian ideals in the future and the growth of nobler and finer forms of society than those which are at present engaged in the struggle for mutual destruction; and also by those who sincerely believe in militarism and desire the growth of population to feed the great armies they hope will be maintained in the future. The childless wife and widow, when of suitable age, can be drawn on, but the main source from which female labour power will be recruited in the near future will thus probably be the young single woman; a source which will be augmented by restriction in the prospect of marriage. That she will retain her place in commercial work and in certain posts in transport work (such as booking clerks) there can be little doubt. Her place in industry will be opposed more warmly, and may occasion some of the most arduous battles of the future. . . .

The experience of the months of war shows that it is not difficult to get working girls to endure considerable strain and make a tremendous effort at a time of national emergency. But the imperative needs of the present should not blind us to the equally exigent needs of the future. To use up the vitality of the young girl in factory and workshop is a suicidal policy. Factory rules and regulations have been largely suspended for the duration of the war, but it is to be hoped will be re-enforced at the earliest possible moment. The close economic relation between welfare of workers and efficiency in production has long been realised by the best employers, but a stimulus is needed for its general recognition and acceptance. Organisation of women workers and steady unremitting pressure by the inspecting authorities are vitally necessary to protect our young women at their work. They must be better paid and better nourished. The war has, however, certainly stimulated thought and care for the welfare of employees. The need of good food for industrial workers, for instance, has obtained fuller recognition in these later months of war than ever before, partly no doubt from a perception of the possible consequences of neglect.

Another important consideration that emerges at the present time is the need for opening higher posts to women and giving them positions of greater responsibility. The appeal to the patriotism of women should not be coupled with the old customary policy of restricting them to the hard, dull, monotonous work that men do not want to do. They must be given a chance of rising to the more dignified occupations and the posts of greater amenity and responsibility. Women are needed in the direction of industry. To such questions as those indicated above, the industrial employment of married women of short shifts, the dilution of labour, or the substitution of women for men, working women would bring a grasp of detail and a perception of the facts in their reaction on the family and the household which men, however able, do not always possess. In the factory, in the trade union, in the office, it will become more and more apparent that if women are to do their share of work to the best advantage they must also take their share in the planning, arrangement, and co-ordination of means to ends.

6. Women's National Service in Germany

Helene Lange (1848–1930), a teacher and advocate of women's education, in 1890 founded the General German Association of Women Teachers (Allgemeiner Deutscher Lehrerinnenverein), the largest professional association for women in Germany. Only three years earlier she had published the Yellow Pamphlet, criticizing the Prussian Ministry of Education's perception and administration of young women's education. Lange nevertheless believed in sexual differentiation; she argued that women would achieve emancipation not by conforming to male standards but by accepting and refining their natural role as mothers and preservers of the stable family. The excerpt that follows suggests the importance of women's compulsory war service as a contribution complementary to that of men's recruitment into uniform. The second selection, by Magda Trott, affiliated with Germany's National Liberal party (Nationalliberale Partei), points to some of the difficulties associated with women's entry into areas of the workplace that had been jealously guarded as male preserves.

a. Helene Lange

The national service of men reaches its ultimate destiny only in times of war, while the national service of women is essentially destined for constant duties throughout times of peace. The efforts of women in war are basically the same as their efforts in peace. These efforts consist of nursing and all sorts of organized welfare work. Thus we see that women need no special preparation for war. Peace offers them duties of service in all areas of social work. Through the introduction of a female service duty with preparation and training, we would gain forces for voluntary social service who would be truly qualified.

Female national service consists of voluntary management of social services, of

Excerpt from "Speech before the Congress of the Union of German Women Teachers" by Helene Lange, 1915.

boards of guardians, of care of the poor, of orphans, of youth services, etc. This civic duty should be delegated to women in the same way as it is delegated to men. Women should only be excused from carrying out these duties for the same reasons that apply also to men. With the exception of women with small children, or domestic conditions that allow them no free time for voluntary activities, this also applies to gainfully employed housewives.

Nursing the wounded is a particular service duty for women in wartime. This should be done as far as possible by professional nurses. However, volunteers must be used as aides in military hospitals. These volunteers must serve as part of their official female service duty.

The educational basis for all forms of female service duty is the capacity to manage a simple household. This must therefore be a prerequisite for further training, or it must form the content of the female service or training period.

Physical training must also be a major part of the female service year, since it has proved to be a considerable advantage in men's training.

Based upon these different prerequisites, it is clear that a different type of education is required for girls who will graduate from elementary schools and those who will graduate from secondary schools. These different types of education are analogous to different types of service duties for men.

(a)   Girls who have graduated from elementary schools ought to receive one year of free education between their 17th and 20th years. This year should offer them a thorough grounding in home economics, with heavy emphasis on the national economic responsibilities of housewives: health-care, infant care, and a knowledge of civic affairs. Only with such an arrangement would the service year achieve its goal completely.

(b)   A general introduction of such a service duty is not feasible for private and for national economic reasons at this time. However, a beginning in this direction could be attempted as follows: (1) a general extension of one-half year of the education of girls, devoted entirely to the practice of household management; (2) introduction of academic institutions modeled on Danish high schools, which offer older girls with an elementary education the opportunity to have a year's free service-education in the format suggested under (a) above; (3) an increase in the establishment of agricultural schools for household management.

Like voluntary soldiers who are doing their year of service, girls who have graduated from secondary schools must pay the costs of their own training. Before entering the service duty they must present proof of the household management training they have received either at home or in a designated institution of household management. Their service training time — between the ages of 17 and 20 — will be taken up with training for some social service. This could be a specialized training for infant care, care of the poor, nursing, etc.

By developing the women's schools we can prepare for compulsory introduction of the female service duty for this class of women.

b. *Magda Trott*

With the outbreak of war men were drawn away from the management of numerous organizations and, gradually, the lack of experienced personnel made itself felt. Women working in offices were therefore urged not to waste the opportunities offered them by the war, and to continue their education so that they would be prepared to take on the position once held by a male colleague, should the occasion arise.

Such occasions have indeed arisen much sooner than anticipated. The demand for educated women has risen phenomenally during the six months since the war began. Women have been employed in banks, in large commercial businesses, in urban offices — everywhere, in fact, where up till now only men had been employed. They are to be tested in order to see whether they can perform with equal success.

All those who were certain that women would be completely successful substitutes for men were painfully disappointed to discover that many women who had worked for years in a firm and were invited to step up to a higher level, now that the men were absent, suddenly handed in their resignations. An enquiry revealed that, especially in recent days, these notices were coming with great frequency and, strange as it may seem, applied mostly to women who had been working in the same company from four to seven years and had now been offered a better and even better-paid job. They said "no" and since there was no possibility for them to remain in their old jobs, they resigned.

The enemies of women's employment were delighted. Here was their proof that women are incapable of holding down responsible positions. Female workers were quite successful as clerks, stenographers, and typists, in fact, in all those positions that require no independent activity — but as soon as more serious duties were demanded of them, they failed.

Naturally, we enquired of these women why they had given up so quickly, and then the truth of the matter became plain. All women were quite ready, if with some trepidation, to accept the new positions, particularly since the boss made it clear that one of the gentlemen would carefully explain the new assignments to them. Certainly the work was almost entirely new to the young ladies since till now they had only been concerned with their stenography, their books, and so forth. However, they entered their new duties with enthusiasm.

But even on the first day it was noticeable that not everything would proceed as had been supposed. Male colleagues looked askance at the "intruder" who dared to usurp the position and bread of a colleague now fighting for the Fatherland, and who would, it was fervently hoped, return in good health. Moreover, the lady who came as a sub-

Excerpt from "Frauenarbeit, ein Ersatz für Männerarbeit?" by Magda Trott, 1915.

stitute received exactly half of the salary of the gentleman colleague who had previously occupied the same position. A dangerous implication, since if the lady made good, the boss might continue to draw on female personnel; the saving on salaries would clearly be substantial. It became essential to use all means to show the boss that female help was no substitute for men's work, and a united male front was organized.

It was hardly surprising that all the lady's questions were answered quite vaguely. If she asked again or even a third time, irritated remarks were passed concerning her inadequacy in comprehension, and very soon the male teacher lost patience. Naturally, most of his colleagues supported him and the lady found it difficult, if not impossible, to receive any instruction and was finally forced to resign.

This is what happened in most known cases. We must, however, also admit that occasionally the fault does lie with the lady, who simply did not have sufficient preparation to fill a difficult position. There may be male colleagues who would gladly share information with women; however, these women are unable to understand, because they have too little business experience. In order to prevent this sort of thing, we would counsel all women who are seeking a position in which they hope to advance, to educate themselves as much as possible. All those women who were forced to leave their jobs of long standing might not have been obliged to do so, had they been more concerned in previous years with understanding the overall nature of the business in which they were employed. Their colleagues would surely and generously have answered their questions and given them valuable advice, which would have offered them an overview and thereby avoided the total ignorance with which they entered these advanced positions when they were offered. At least they would have had an inkling and saved themselves the questions that betrayed their great ignorance to their colleagues. They might even have found their way through all the confusion and succeeded in the new position.

Therefore, once again: all you women who want to advance yourselves and create an independent existence, use this time of war as a learning experience and keep your eyes open.

7. A WOMAN IN THE SERVICE OF THE TSAR

European women served as nurses, relief workers, and even ambulance drivers, but only in Russia did they enlist for active duty. Largely from humble origins, these women were often forced to disguise themselves as men in order to become soldiers. The two most famous Russian female participants were Anna Krasilnikova, the first female soldier, and Maria Botchkareva, whose adventures in the army are detailed in the following selection. Put to work at the age of eight, seduced in her early teens, and forced into prostitution, Botchkareva, at the age of twenty-five, chose to join the colors. She was decorated for her bravery under fire.

The news from the front was exciting. Great battles were raging. Our soldiers were retreating in some places and advancing in others. I wished for wings to fly to their succor. My heart yearned and ached.

"Do you know what war is?" I asked myself. "It's no woman's job. You must make sure before starting out, Marusia, that you won't disgrace yourself. Are you strong enough in spirit to face all the trials and dangers of this colossal war? Are you strong enough in body to shed blood and endure the privations of war? Are you firm enough at heart to withstand the temptations that will come to you, living among men? Search your soul for an answer of truth and courage."

And I found strength enough in me to answer "yes" to all these questions. I suppressed the hidden longing for Yasha in the depths of my being, and made the fateful decision. I would go to war and fight till death, or, if God preserved me, till the coming of peace. I would defend my country and help those unfortunates on the field of slaughter who had already made their sacrifices for the country.

It was November, 1914. With my heart steeled in the decision I had made, I resolutely approached the headquarters of the Twenty-Fifth Reserve Battalion, stationed in Tomsk. Upon entering, a clerk asked me what I wanted.

"To see the Commander," I replied.

"What for?" he inquired.

"I want to enlist," I said.

The man looked at me for a moment and burst out laughing. He called to the other clerks. "Here is a *baba* who wants to enlist!" he announced jokingly, pointing at me. There followed a general uproar. "Ha! ha! ha!" they chorused, forgetting their work for the moment. When the merriment subsided a little I repeated my request to see the Commander, and his adjutant came out. He must have been told that a woman had come to enlist, for he addressed me gaily:

"What is your wish?"

"I want to enlist in the army, your Excellency," I answered.

"To enlist, eh? But you are a *baba*," he laughed. "The regulations do not permit us to enlist women. It is against the law."

I insisted that I wanted to fight, and begged to see the Commander. The adjutant reported me to the Commander, who asked to have me shown in.

With the adjutant laughing behind me, I blushed and became confused when brought before the Commander. He rebuked the adjutant and inquired what he could do for me. I repeated that I wanted to enlist and fight for the country.

"It is very noble of you to have such a desire. But women are not allowed in the army," he said. "They are too weak. What could you, for instance, do in the front line? Women are not made for war."

"Your Excellency," I insisted, "God has given me strength, and I can defend my country as well as a man. I have asked myself before coming here whether I could

Excerpt from *Yashka. My Life as Peasant, Officer and Exile* by Maria Botchkareva, Frederick A. Stokes, 1919, pp. 72–81.

endure the life of a soldier and found that I could. Can't you place me in your regiment?"

"*Golubushka* [little dove]," the Commander declared gently, "how can I help you? It is against the law. I have no authority to enlist a woman even if I wanted to. You can go to the rear, enlist as a Red Cross nurse or in some other auxiliary of the service."

I rejected his proposal. I had heard so many rumors about the women in the rear that I had come to despise them. I therefore reiterated my determination to go to the front as a regular soldier. The Commander was deeply impressed by my obstinacy, and wanted to help me. He suggested that I send a telegram to the Tsar, telling him of my desire to defend the country, of my moral purpose, and pray that he grant me the special right to enlist.

The Commander promised to draw up the telegram himself, with a recommendation of his own, and have it sent from his office. He warned me, however, to consider the matter again, to think of the hardships I would have to bear, of the soldiers' attitude toward me, and the universal ridicule that I would provoke. I did not change my mind, though. The telegram was sent at my expense, costing eight rubles, which I obtained from my mother.

When I disclosed to my folks the nature of my visit to the Commander of the Twenty-Fifth Battalion they burst into tears. My poor mother cried that her Maria must have gone insane, that it was an unheard-of, impossible thing. Who ever knew of a *baba* going to war? She would allow herself to be buried alive before letting me enlist. My father sustained her. I was their only hope now, they said. They would be forced to starve and go begging, without my help. And the house was filled with sobs and wails, the two younger sisters and some neighbors joining in.

My heart was rent in twain. It was a cruel, painful choice that I was called upon to make, a choice between my mother and my country. It cost me so much to steel myself for that new life, and now, when I was seemingly near the goal, my long-suffering mother called upon me to give up this ideal that possessed me, for her sake. I was tormented and agonized by doubt. I realized that I must make a decision quickly and, with a supreme effort and the help of God, I resolved that the call of my country took precedence over the call of my mother.

Some time later a soldier came to the house.

"Is Maria Botchkareva here?" he questioned.

He came from headquarters with the news that a telegram had arrived from the Tsar, authorizing the Commander to enlist me as a soldier, and that the Commander wanted to see me.

My mother did not expect such an answer. She grew frantic. She cursed the Tsar with all her might, although she had always revered him as the Little Father. "What kind of Tsar is he?" she cried, "if he takes women to war? He must have lost his senses. Who ever heard of a Tsar calling women to arms? Hasn't he enough men? Goodness knows, there are myriads of them in Mother-Russia."

She seized the Tsar's portrait on the wall, before which she had crossed herself every morning, and tore it to bits, stamping them on the floor, with imprecations and anathema on her lips. Never again would she pray for him, she declared. "No, never!"

The soldier's message had an opposite effect on me, and I was thrown into high spirits. Dressing in my holiday costume, I went to see the Commander. Everybody at headquarters seemed to know of the Tsar's telegram, smiles greeting me everywhere. The Commander congratulated me and read its text in a solemn voice, explaining that it was an extraordinary honor which the August Emperor had conferred on me, and that I make myself worthy of it. I was so happy, so joyous, so transported. It was the most blissful moment of my life.

The Commander called his orderly in and instructed him to obtain a full soldier's outfit for me. I received two complete undergarments made of coarse linen, two pairs of foot-rags, a laundry bag, a pair of boots, one pair of trousers, a belt, a regulation blouse, a pair of epaulets, a cap with the insignia on it, two cartridge pockets and a rifle. My hair was clipped off.

There was an outburst of laughter when I appeared in full military attire, as a regular soldier of the Fourth Company, Fifth Regiment. I was confused and somewhat bewildered, hardly being able to recognize myself. The news of a woman recruit had preceded me at the barracks, and my arrival there precipitated a riot of fun. I was surrounded on all sides by green recruits who stared at me incredulously, but some were not satisfied with mere staring, so rare a novelty was I to them. They wanted to make sure that their eyes were not deceived, so they proceeded to pinch me, jostle me and brush against me.

"Get out, she ain't no *baba*," remarked one of them.

"Sure, she is," said another, pinching me.

"She'll run like the devil at the first German shot," joked a third, provoking an uproar.

"We'll make it so hot for her that she'll run before even getting to the front," threatened a fourth.

Here the Commander of my company interfered, and the boys dispersed. I was granted permission to take my things home before settling permanently at the barracks, and asked to be shown how to salute. On the way home I saluted every uniform in the same manner. Opening the door of the house, I stopped on the threshold. My mother did not recognize me.

"Maria Leontievna Botchkareva here?" I asked sharply, in military fashion. Mother took me for some messenger from headquarters, and answered, "No."

I threw myself on her neck. "Holy Mother, save me!" she exclaimed. There were cries and tears which brought my father and little sister to the scene. My mother became hysterical. For the first time I saw my father weep, and again I was urged to come back to my senses and give up this crazy notion to serve in the army. The proprietress of the house and old Nastasia Leontievna were called in to help dissuade me from my purpose.

"Think what the men will do to a lone woman in their midst," they argued. "Why, they'll make a prostitute of you. They will kill you secretly, and nobody will ever find a trace of you. Only the other day they found the body of a woman along the railroad track, thrown out of a troop-train. You always have been such a level-headed girl. What has come over you? And what will become of your parents? They are old and weak, and you are their only hope. They often said that when Marusia came back they would end their lives in peace. Now you are but shortening their days, dragging them to their graves in sorrow."

For a short space of time I vacillated again. The fierce struggle in my bosom between the two elements was resurrected. But I stuck by my decision, remaining deaf to all pleas. Then my mother grew angry and, crying out at the top of her voice, she shouted:

"You are no longer my daughter! You have forfeited your mother's love."

With a heavy heart I left the house for the barracks. The Commander of the Company did not expect me, and I had to explain to him why I could not pass that night at home. He assigned me to a place in the general bunk, ordering the men not to molest me. On my right and on my left were soldiers, and that first night in the company of men will ever stand out in my memory. I did not close my eyes once during the night.

The men were, naturally, unaccustomed to such a phenomenon as myself and took me for a loose-moraled woman who had made her way into the ranks for the sake of carrying on her illicit trade. I was, therefore, compelled constantly to fight off intrusions from all sides. As soon as I made an effort to shut my eyes I would discover the arm of my neighbor on the left around my neck, and would restore it to its owner with a crash. Watchful of his movements, I offered an opportunity for my neighbor on the right to get too near to me, and I would savagely kick him in the side. All night long my nerves were taut and my fists busy. Toward dawn I was so exhausted that I nearly fell asleep, when I discovered a hand on my chest, and before the man realized my intention, I banged him in the face. I continued to rain blows till the bell rang at five o'clock, the rising-hour.

Ten minutes were given us to dress and wash, tardiness being punished by a rebuke. At the end of the ten minutes the ranks formed and every soldier's hands, ears and foot-rags were inspected. I was in such haste to be on time that I put my trousers on inside out, provoking a veritable storm of hilarity and paroxysms of laughter.

The day began with a prayer for the Tsar and country, following which every one of us received the daily allowance of two-and-a-half pounds of bread and a few cubes of sugar from our respective squad commanders. There were four squads to a company. Our breakfast consisted of bread and tea and lasted half an hour.

At the mess I had an opportunity to get acquainted with some of the more sympathetic soldiers. There were ten volunteers in my company, and they were all students. After eating, there was roll-call. When the officer reached my name he read: "Botchkareva," to which I answered, "Aye." We were then taken out for instruction, since the entire regiment had been formed only three days previous. The first rule that the training officer tried to impress upon us was to pay attention, watch his movements and actions. Not all the recruits could do it easily. I prayed to God to enlighten me in the study of a soldier's duties.

It was slow work to establish proper relations with the men. The first few days I was such a nuisance to the Company Commander that he wished me to ask for dismissal. He hinted as much on a couple of occasions, but I continued to mind my own business and never reported the annoyances I endured from the men. Gradually I won their respect and confidence. The small group of volunteers always defended me. As the Russian soldiers call each other by nick-names, one of the first questions put to me by my friends was what I would like to be called.

"Call me Yashka," I said, and that name stuck to me ever after, saving my life on more than one occasion. There is so much in a name, and "Yashka" was the sort of a name that appealed to the soldiers and always worked in my favor. In time it became the pet name of the regiment, but not before I had been tested by many additional trials and found to be a comrade, and not a woman, by the men.

I was an apt student and learned almost to anticipate the orders of the instructor. When the day's labors would be completed and the soldiers gathered into knots to while away an hour or two in games or story-telling, I was always sought after to participate. I came to like the soldiers, who were good-natured boys, and to enjoy their sports. The group which Yashka joined would usually prove the most popular in the barrack, and it was sufficient to secure my cooperation in some enterprise to make it a success.

There wasn't much time for relaxation, though, as we went through an intensive training course of only three months before we were sent to the front. Once a week, every Sunday, I would leave the barracks and spend the day at home, my mother having reconciled herself to my soldiering. On holidays I would be visited by friends or relatives. On one such occasion my sister and her husband called. I had been detailed for guard duty in the barrack that day. While on such duty a soldier is forbidden to sit down or to engage in conversation. I was entertaining my visitors when the Company Commander passed.

"Do you know the rules, Botchkareva?" he asked.

"Yes, your Excellency," I answered.

"What are they?"

"A soldier on guard duty is not allowed to sit down or engage in conversation," I replied. He ordered me to stand for two hours at attention, at the completion of my guard duty, which took twenty-four hours. Standing at attention, in full military equipment, for two hours is a severe task, as one has to remain absolutely motionless under the eyes of a guard, and yet it was a common punishment.

During my training I was punished in this manner three times. The second time it was really not my fault. One night I recognized my squad commander in a soldier who annoyed me, and I dealt him as hard a blow as I would have given to any other man. In the morning he placed me at attention for two hours, claiming that he had accidentally brushed against me.

At first there was some difficulty in arranging for my bathing. The bath-house was used by the men, and so I was allowed one day to visit a public bath-house. I found it a splendid opportunity for some fun. I came into the women's room, fully dressed, and there was a tremendous outbreak as soon as I appeared. I was taken for a man. However, the fun did not last long. In an instant I was under a bombardment from every corner, and only narrowly escaped serious injury by crying out that I was a woman.

In the last month of our training we engaged in almost continuous rifle practice. I applied myself zealously to the acquisition of skill in handling a rifle and won a mention of excellence for good marksmanship. This considerably enhanced my standing with the soldiers and strengthened our relations of camaraderie.

D. A Crisis of Masculinity

1. A SCANDALOUS TRIAL

In May and June 1918 England was enthralled by one of the most remarkable trials in its long legal history. Pemberton Billing was an eccentric and rabidly right-wing member of Parliament who had made a public crusade of revealing corruption in high places. In the spring of 1918, as publisher of a journal largely devoted to that task, the *Vigilante,* he was sued for libel by a dancer, Maud Allan, who, the *Vigilante* implied, was a lesbian involved in a scandalous production of *Salome.* (This work's dubious morality made it thoroughly unsuitable, the *Vigilante* thought, for British audiences.) During the trial Billing conducted his own defense and, owing to the weak handling of the case by the presiding judge, Justice Darling, succeeded in turning the proceedings into a forum for denouncing the deleterious impact of German influence. Billing was persuaded that German agents had compiled a "Black Book" listing 47,000 Englishmen whose sexual perversions and other moral failings rendered them vulnerable to enemy blackmail. The following extracts from the full account of the trial in *The Times* detail Billing's examination of a sympathetic witness about the existence of the supposed "Black Book" and his concluding summation. He was acquitted, though the verdict is of less interest than the ways in which respectable masculine behavior, "unnatural vice," and anti-alienism were all drawn into the debate about why Britain had failed to secure victory by mid-1918. It confirms the importance of gender roles to fears about the durability of the social order under duress.

The witness said that Mr Neil Primrose explained to her that the people mentioned in the book were persons who were under German influence.

For various reasons? — Yes.

Traitors? — Yes.

And one of them the Prime Minister of England? — Yes.

Were other people in public life referred to? Privy Councillors? — What do you call Privy Councillors? I am not well up on the law.

Peers, members of the House of Commons and men holding high positions of trust? — Yes, quite a lot.

In fact, the majority of persons in public life? — No, not quite the majority.

All traitors? — I conclude they were traitors because their names were in that book.

Mr JUSTICE DARLING — That assumes the strict truthfulness on the part of the Germans for which I have never before heard them given credit.

From *The Times*, 4–5 June 1918.

The witness, answering the JUDGE, said that she did not ask Mr Primrose where he got the book from.

Were you not interested? — I did not ask questions because he asked me not to ask them. . . .

Are you prepared to tell the Court how many names you can swear on oath that you saw? — I can remember only eight or ten now.

Are they mainly people holding important positions in England? — Yes.

Was it only for sex perversion that names were put in the book or were there other reasons? — There were other reasons.

Tell us some? — There were so many.

How was the book drawn up? — First there was a list of German agents in England, then came the names of the 47,000, and then paragraphs giving information about the 47,000.

Were there any instructions to agents in the book? — Yes. . . .

Mr Billing then addressed the jury. In accepting responsibility for the paragraph in the *Vigilante,* he said, he had accepted responsibility for something that he had not written, and that he knew nothing of it until nine hours after it had been published because he deemed it to be in the public interest to do so. After three and a half years of war, it was time that the things to which he had referred should see the light of day. . . . If they were true how much more necessary it was that the influence, the mysterious influence which seemed to have dogged our steps through the whole conduct of the war, which, after three and a half years of war, kept German banks open in England, which left Germans still uninterned in that Court at that moment, which had paralyzed the Air Services of this country and had prevented our raiding Germany, should be removed. . . . He hoped that the jury would not disagree as to all that had been said about the mysterious influences which were sterilizing our Empire. "I expect there are people," Mr Billing exclaimed, "in this country today who think I am mad. I am mad on one subject. I am obsessed with it, and that is the bringing of this country out of the war a little cleaner than when it went into it. I plead guilty to that."

2. SHELL SHOCK

An increase in the number of cases of men who, while not wounded, were rendered physically or mentally incapacitated as a result of military service, fueled fears among the more conservative elements of European society that the war was not accentuating the ideals of masculinity but rather having the opposite effect, of effeminizing its participants. Disease and moral decay had been prominent themes in the medical literature and social commentary before 1914, so physicians, officers, and politicians were challenged to diagnose the inability of many men to return to the front. In some cases, that inability was interpreted as behavior verging on cowardice and defined as malingering. The response was harsh discipline, for many military physicians believed that malingering was more prevalent in units with poor morale and lax discipline. The alternative was to diagnose the problem as a physical result of the noise and concus-

sions of modern combat, hence the term *shell shock*. The following selections describe some of the reported symptoms and attempted cures of battle-induced hysterical behavior — which in such later conflicts as the Vietnam War would be more sympathetically known as combat stress syndrome.

a. Nature and Causes

Case 225

(Meige, February, 1916)

One of Meige's victims of shell-shock tremors was an artist. He stood the hardest sort of
trench life for many months without disorder. Under particularly sharp fire, "the machine went off the track," as the artist said, and he began to tremble. Both arms and head
trembled, but especially the head, which was subject to small sidewise oscillations, vari-
able in degree, and almost permanent, — a sort of vibration which the patient could
diminish somewhat by stiffening his neck muscles. His manual tremor was not exaggerated by voluntary movements. Superficially he resembled a Parkinsonian case. He presented a curious appearance of combined vibrations and stiffness.

There was no doubt that this tremor had an emotional origin. In fact, the psycho-
pathic status of the patient was described by the artist himself. "My nervous state, which
I thought ought to last not more than a fortnight, still persists more than three, or almost
four, months after being evacuated, although the trembling is a little less. I am calmer
and palpitate less, and my hands perspire less when I am emotional or making an effort.
At first, the slightest shock immediately ran through me, followed by an uncontrollable
trembling. Now there is an appreciable delay between the shock and the trembling; I
can control it for a few seconds but not longer. The subway gate noises, a flaring light,
a locomotive whistle, the barking of a dog, or some boyish prank is enough to set off
the trembling; going to the theater, listening to music, reading a poem, or being present
at a religious ceremony, acts the same way. Recently when a flag was being raised at the
Invalides, I thought at first that I was going to be cured by so moving a spectacle, but
then I suddenly began to tremble so violently that I had to cry out, and I had to sit
down, weeping like a child. Sometimes the trembling comes on suddenly without any
cause. I went to a novelty shop to do some errands with my wife. The crowd, the lights,
the rustling of the silk, the colors of the goods — everything was a delight to me to look
upon, — a contrast to our trench misery. I was happy and chatted merrily, like a school-

Excerpt from *Shell-Shock and Other Neuropsychiatric Problems* by E. E. Southard, W. Leonard, 1919, pp.
310–311.

boy on a vacation. All of a sudden I felt that my strength was leaving me. I stopped talking; I felt a bad sensation in my back; I felt my cheeks hollowing in. I began to stare, and the trembling came on again, together with a great feeling of discomfort. If I can lean against something, sit down, or better, lie down, the trembling gets better and pretty soon stops. There are three conditions in which I feel well: first, upon waking after 11 or 12 hours' sleep; next, after a meal, especially if it is a good one; and lastly, and above all, when I get the electric douche. Then, as if by magic, my ideas get clear, cheerful, and regain color; I feel myself again. That lasts for an hour or so; then I relapse into my sad state."

As to the tremophobia, this patient says "In the tramway or in the subway, I perceive that people are looking at me, and that gives me a terrible feeling. I feel that I am inspiring pity. Some excellent woman offers me her seat. I am deeply touched; but if they look at me and say nothing, what are they thinking of me? This anxiety makes me suffer a good deal. If I am able to speak it is less painful to me, for then it is obvious that, despite my trembling, I am not a coward. What a sad situation this is!"

Meige remarks that therapeutics is not especially successful in these cases of tremor. Sedative drugs . . . do not last long and should be used cautiously. Static electricity works well in some cases. Rest isolation, and calm.

As for the military prognosis, a period of observation of some three to four months may be necessary to learn the nature of the tremor. If the tremor then fails to alter, a convalescent leave for one or two months may be given.

b. Malingering

He was taken into the electrical room, where a strong faradic current was applied by means of a wire brush to the bend of the elbow. Standing with my back to him and holding the arm firmly, I told him that I was going to spend four hours with him, during which time the current would be from time to time increased. When I applied the current I further assured him that his condition was most interesting, it being obvious that he felt the current. In less than one minute he made an effort to draw his arm away. I removed the electrode, at the same time asking him if he felt the current. He answered that he did not feel it. Taking another firm hold of his right arm and increasing the strength of the current to the full, he almost instantly shouted out, "You have beaten me; you have beaten me; I'll give in to you," as he began to use the hand normally. He admitted that he had been shamming.

Malingering may be seen in soldiers who have been in the Army for some time, and who attempt to evade further military service on the pretext of some wound, which is sometimes self-inflicted. Such cases are rarely met with, but the following illustration of a private, 22 years of age, who enlisted in February, 1915, will serve as an example.

Excerpt from *Hysterical Disorders of Warfare* by Lewis Yealland, Macmillan, 1918, pp. 242–244.

The man was sent to France in the following December. A few months later he was sent to Salonika. In January, 1916, both feet, he said, were frost-bitten. He had a faint recollection of a bullet wound in the right ankle, but no scar could be found to establish this claim. The patient was taken to a hospital in Salonika, and the lower limbs became paralysed on his arrival there. He was transferred to Malta, and remained in a hospital there for three months. Then he was transferred to England and treated in hospitals at Portsmouth and Bournemouth. In the latter place he underwent an operation for appendicitis early in January, 1917.

The patient was carried into the National Hospital on a stretcher in the middle of February, and when put to bed looked very ill, and had to be assisted when turning in bed. The appendix scar was healed, and there were no signs of organic or functional disease. Movements of the legs were very slightly performed, and there was no accompanying contraction of antagonistic groups of muscles.

I made no comment to the man, but when the examination was finished I took him unawares by seizing his arms quickly, and, hurrying him to the floor, I ran along the ward with him. Before he had realised what I was doing he had taken a dozen or more steps. Then he became very resistive, and made an attempt to fall, but I cautioned him against this, reminding him that he had already walked a dozen steps, and that it was too late to carry on with his old method. After that he walked quite normally round the ward. He was soon discharged from the hospital. The man later paid a visit to the hospital, but only came to see me, and avoided returning to his ward. Although I had not mentioned malingering to him, or indicated what I thought of his condition except as stated above, he reproached me with the fact that I considered him to be a malingerer, and attempted to assure me that he was not shamming. Further, he said that it would do him a great deal of harm if anybody were informed that such was suspected of him. I had nothing whatever to say to him.

Hysteria sometimes predisposes to malingering, particularly when the hysterical disorder has extended over a long period of time.

3. THE DISABLED SOLDIER

One of the central areas in which the state would have to assume new responsibilities was the provision of pensions for men crippled by the war. Inevitably, discussion on the subject was informed by conceptions of masculine dignity and earning potential on the one hand, and on the other hand of the state's inability to finance enormous additional expenditure at a moment's notice. Accordingly, despite the universal agreement on the necessity of doing justice to the injured soldiers' sacrifices, the actual provision and dispensation of pensions proved a protracted matter. The documents that follow illustrate typical responses to the question of the disabled. The first is a portion of a British leaflet produced by the War Office to explain official thinking on the subject; the second, by C. W. Hutt, the deputy medical officer for Brighton, outlines some measures of rehabilitation undertaken by other countries which he thought might serve as examples for similar action in Britain.

a. *What the Disabled Soldier Wants to Know*

(Regular, Special Reserve, Territorial, or New Army)

If discharged for *disability caused by the present War*, what Pension will he get?

(*a*) Every European soldier discharged as totally incapable of earning a livelihood owing to wounds or injuries or sunstroke, received in action or in the performance of military duty, or on account of blindness caused by military service, or of disease due directly and wholly to war service, gets a pension of 25s. a week, under the Royal Warrant of 21st May 1915.

(*b*) If partially capable of earning a livelihood he may be granted such pension as will, with the wages he may be deemed capable of earning, bring his total income up to 25s. a week.

(*c*) To this total of 25s. an addition is made, according to rank, as follows: Corporal, 2s. a week; Sergeant, 4s.; Colour-Sergeant, 6s.; Quarter-Master-Sergeant or Warrant Officer, Class II., 8s.; Warrant Officer, Class I., 15s.

(*d*) A soldier totally incapacitated will, in addition, during the period of total incapacity, draw an allowance of 2s. 6d. a week for each of his children up to the age of 16.

(*e*) If partially incapacitated he may be granted an allowance, in addition to his pension, not exceeding 2s. 6d. for each child, ceasing at the age of 16.

(*f*) If a partially disabled soldier is able to earn so much that he gets very little benefit under the New Pension Warrant (even with the allowances for children) he may be pensioned under the 1914 Warrant if more favourable to him. This Warrant carries no children's allowances.

b. *Training the Disabled*

When the War produced war-cripples, owing to their previous experience of the problem of disabled men the Belgian Government were prompt in making suitable provision; within a few months of the beginning of the War a large school for disabled soldiers was started at Rouen.

In December 1914 a home for discharged soldiers was instituted at Havre which has gradually merged into a school for vocational re-education.

(a) Excerpt from *The Ex-Soldier by Himself* by W. G. Clifford, A. & C. Black, 1916, pp. 54–55.

(b) Excerpt from *The Future of the Disabled Soldier* by Cecil William Hutt, John Bale, Sons and Danielsson, 1917, pp. 15–18, 63–67.

L'Hospital Anglo-Belge was opened later in December for about fifty men more or less convalescent, in some rooms in one of the military barracks. It has gradually grown and now comprises about 250 beds with two dependent establishments providing an additional 700 beds. Gradually into this hospital, all the aids of medical science were introduced, mechanotherapy, thermotherapy, radiology, electrotherapy, medical gymnastics and gymnastics. In addition artificial limbs were made and fitted at the hospital, enabling the stumps to be educated to their maximal mobility and function.

The accommodation for training these men in useful work . . . opened in August, 1915. . . . The land provided was part of a forest; a saw mill was erected, the trees scientifically thinned out, the timber not used for building the huts was sold. The smaller wood was made into pickets and stakes for the use of the Belgian Army. The cost of the buildings 450,000 francs (£18,000) was repaid out of profits on the lumber; the cost of the equipment and plant for the workshops (£12,000) has been repaid out of the profits of the different workshops, which have sold their output at a cheap rate to the Belgian War Office thus effecting a double economy to the Government. A large farm forms part of the establishment; on it horses wounded in the War are cared for and made useful again.

There is at present accommodation for 800 patients; in addition attached to the Institute is a staff of 350 quasi-civilians unfit for military duty on account of age or on medical grounds; they serve as teachers, overseers, manual instructors or as workmen.

The fact that the entire population of Belgium is mobilized for military duty enables Captain Haccour, the director of the technical work, to requisition the services of the very best craftsmen in the different trades for the teaching staff who receive the ordinary pay of a soldier.

The cost per day to the Belgian Government for each man is just over 2 francs; the feeding and clothing cost 1 franc, 54 centimes, the daily pay is 43 centimes, the cost of lighting and heating is 8 centimes per man per day.

Forty-three different trades are taught including almost every imaginable occupation. The workshops provide for instruction in book-keeping, shorthand, typewriting, telegraphy, moulding in clay, wood carving, drawing and designing of all descriptions, wall paper designing and painting, the manufacture of motor vehicles, and electrical machinery of all descriptions, tinsmithing and plumbing, tailoring, bootmaking, basketmaking, poultry farming, and rabbit farming to which fur curing, dyeing and trimming are added.

The Institute makes all the tools used by the workmen besides a large number for the Army. All the printing and photographic work required is done on the premises in addition to much work for the Government. The men are paid in addition to their Army pay from 5 to 20 centimes an hour, according to the work they do; the surplus profits are now being funded for the benefit of the men.

The underlying principle of the whole establishment is constant work; no man is permitted to be idle. In part of the buildings is a small hospital for men who become ill or are temporarily suffering from their old wounds. Unless these men are absolutely helpless they are required to do some sort of work in bed, the hospital orderlies being efficient instructors of such work as net-making or light basket-work. . . .

GERMANY

Germany was fortunate in being able to utilize the organization already in existence for some ten years for dealing with cripples. In 1914, fifty-four institutions had already been established for cripples providing 221 workshops for training in all trades of every description, some fifty-one trades being taught. Full use is being made of these institutions; after treatment at hospital schools, the disabled man is transferred to the Orthopædic Institution nearest his home for continuation of his medical treatment and vocational training. The men are kept under military discipline, the institution being placed under the command of an officer detailed as military director.

Special institutions have been created for the one-armed at Berlin and Heidelberg. Employment is obtained through the local labour bureau for the province; in some bureaux special departments have been formed to deal with disabled men.

The State will find work for its own disabled employees; in Germany the State is relatively a larger employer than in England, many enterprises such as railways which are with us under private control are under the State in Germany. A proposal widely advocated is that the State when placing orders with private companies or firms shall impose the condition that a proportion of the labour employed should consist of disabled men.

Many municipalities have inserted a clause to this effect in the regulations relating to municipal contracts.

No effort is spared to impress upon the wounded soldier and the public the fact that even severely disabled men can be taught to work and earn their living. The measures utilized include continuous propaganda by the Press, both lay and medical, lectures illustrated by lantern slides, visits to institutions for cripples, the distribution of pamphlets to soldiers and the visiting of the wounded men in hospital to advise and persuade them to take up training where necessary.

The mass of expert opinion is opposed to the establishment of large colonies of disabled men, although in some instances colonies of forty to fifty families provided with workshops have been formed near towns. Wherever possible, it is considered that the man should return to his own home and resume his former work and employment and become an ordinary member of the community.

Stress is laid on the need for providing the disabled with skilled advice as to future employment. The general tenour of the advice given is that disabled men should when possible return to their pre-war occupations. . . .

In Prussia, local authorities are required to exercise caution in granting licences as pedlars to disabled men. . . .

. . . At Mannheim, a Military Orthopædic Hospital (for non-amputation cases) was opened in April, 1915, with a school attached to provide instruction, both practical and theoretical, of an elementary nature during medical treatment. Stress is laid on the value of theoretical training to increase the patient's knowledge of his former occupation.

The subjects taught are: —

THEORETICAL. — Writing and arithmetic, shorthand and typing, English and French. Special lectures are given on building trades, metal work including electrical work, commercial subjects.

PRACTICAL. — Carpentering, bootmaking, locksmith's work, metal work including electrical work, wheelwright's work, bookbinding.

During the first seven months over 700 patients attended the various courses, about 300 at any one time receiving instruction. . . .

Munich has arranged for training in almost every branch of manual work. The men taught are still under medical care, the institution being both a convalescent home and school.

SOLDIERS ALL.

"TOMMY" (home from the Front, to disaffected Workman). "WHAT 'LD YOU THINK O' ME, MATE, IF I STRUCK FOR EXTRA PAY IN THE MIDDLE OF AN ACTION? WELL, THAT'S WHAT YOU 'VE BEEN DOING."

Soldiers All *from title page of* Punch *magazine, March 10, 1915 (Great Britain)* (Boston Athenaeum)

Part III

State and Society in Crisis

The war decisively altered the relationship between state and society, public and private spheres, and authority and compliance. Given the unprecedented demands of total war, European leaders felt justified in using government regulation and intervention to impose on, to an unprecedented degree, their citizens' rights and liberties. The synchronous necessities of cultivating national unity and curtailing dissent, of ensuring an adequate flow of men and material to the front and of laborers into the workplace, and of preserving standards of living while minimizing industrial conflict all contributed to the state's pervasive intrusion into society. These wartime exigencies aggravated existing social tensions and brought many of the combatant nations to the brink of crisis by the war's latter stages.

Misguided assumptions that the war would be brief and that it would have a minimal impact on citizens' daily life were responsible in part for the hesitation by Europe's governments to create special administrative agencies for smoothing the transition from peacetime to wartime. In some cases, as in Germany, the far Right had unsuccessfully broached the idea of economic mobilization to the government just before the war's outbreak. Individual initiatives were often as critical a factor in the establishment of such agencies as were official state directives. For example, the German Jewish industrialist Walter Rathenau pressed the German government to establish a War Raw Materials Section, known as the *Kriegsrohstoffabteilung* (KRA), to oversee the distribution of raw materials to crucial war-related industries and to prevent shortages of them. In Italy public opposition to the war and economic disorganization led the government to impose military discipline in the factories and to allow the country's industrialists considerable leeway in matters of production. Meanwhile, in Russia, critical munitions shortages, a disorganized transportation network, and competing and overburdened administrative agencies forced the government to adopt a policy of industrial mobilization by the spring of 1915.

The British government, however, aware that war would interrupt the natural flow of the economy, took only a handful of immediate measures, among them the control of the nation's railway network, to ensure the distribution of food and manpower, and thus to avoid economic chaos. Britain made the first step toward a total war economy in August 1914 with the passage of the Defense of the Realm Act (DORA), which initially protected the public safety but subsequently covered food policy and other areas. Until 1915–1916, in short, the British pursued "business as usual." With rising food prices in 1915, the implementation of conscription in 1916, and the concomitant departure of men from the labor force, the government under David Lloyd George was forced to review its voluntarist policies.

Reluctant to erect additional bureaucratic structures, the French government relied largely on prevailing market forces as well as on the cooperation of French businessmen. Once industrial mobilization was officially instituted in September 1914, the French pursued a policy of "organized economy" under which capitalist ideals (profit, private production) were combined with elements of collectivist organization.

Whether economic mobilization was prompted by individual or by state initiative, the ways in which it was implemented directly affected both domestic and military morale. The change most visibly affected the shop floor. All European governments imposed special measures to ensure the uninterrupted flow of industrial goods. In establishing the Industrial Mobilization (MI), the Italian government sought to prevent dissension within Italy's work force by making strikes illegal, reducing workers' job mobility, and enforcing strict factory discipline, even among women and children. To dissuade workers from going against the grain, the Italian military also maintained a physical presence on the factory floor.

While Italian labor relations were particularly harsh, restrictions also squeezed the German work force. With the support of most of its Socialist representatives, the German parliament approved the passage of the *Hilfsdienstgesetz,* or Auxiliary Service Law, in early December 1916. The law may be seen as a compromise between the interest of Germany's industrialists, who feared declining profits and potential ammunition shortages, and those of the trade unions. The law satisfied the demands of the industrialists by providing for industrial conscription for all males between the ages of seventeen and sixty and by restricting workers' right to change employment (other than for higher wages); but so as to forestall industrial unrest and general war weariness, the law strengthened the hand of Germany's trade unions by legitimizing them as arbitrators of the working classes.

In Britain, in an effort to maximize labor power and to hold down industrial wages, the government negotiated the so-called Treasury Agreement (which lacked legal sanction) with a number of Britain's trade union leaders in March 1915. Under this agreement workers in war industries agreed not to strike and to submit all industrial disputes to arbitration; in return, the government would safeguard wage standards. Not long after the agreement, the government sought to legalize it with the passage of the Munitions of War Bill.

Relations among government, factory owners, and industrial employees generally deteriorated as the war progressed and as skyrocketing food prices and rents cut into real wages. Throughout Europe, workers flouted laws barring them from striking, and by 1917 strike activity peaked. Although British workers did not want for food as their counterparts on the Continent did, their wages could not keep pace with higher food prices and rents, and they deplored the widespread profiteering, especially in the coal-mining and shipbuilding industries. In July 1915, 200,000 coal miners in South Wales went on strike. Instead of jailing them, the government, fearful of provoking further industrial unrest, granted them wage concessions. In other work stoppages the government responded in a less conciliatory fashion, banishing some of the strike leaders to various parts of the country, but by 1917, after an increase in the number of strikes, Parliament had conceded to workers the right to occupational choice. The trade unions, rather than being subdued by government legislation, benefited in the short run. Union membership spurted from 4 million in 1914 to 6 million by the armistice and 8.3 million in 1920.

In Germany the Allied blockade brought a scarcity of foodstuffs, high food prices, longer working hours, poor working conditions, and a restlessness with the length of the war. German workers responded with strikes, sporadically in 1915 and more intensively in 1917 and 1918. Although industrial wages in fact increased, they were offset by inflation; indeed, the cost of living was reportedly 200 percent higher than in 1914. The Ruhr and Upper Silesian districts (with their concentration of heavy industry and coal) were flashpoints of strike activity in the summer of 1917. More than 50,000 workers took industrial action during each month of 1917, and approximately 100,000 struck during 1918. As in Britain, Germany's trade unions, whose membership had fallen initially, increased in 1917–1918.

In Italy the women who had entered the labor force in large numbers in 1916 led the initial labor unrest. Dissatisfied with their treatment on the factory floor and with the strict control imposed by a military presence, women struck for better conditions. By 1917 they were joined by their male counterparts, despite men's vulnerability to prosecution for striking under Italy's laws. Perhaps the most vociferous strike action occurred in Turin in August 1917, when workers erected barricades in their districts and staved off the Italian army for three days.

French industries too saw a jump in strike activity during 1917. Most of the labor unrest in 1916–1917 stemmed from disputes over wages, which could not keep pace with rapidly rising food prices. As in Italy, French women workers in war industries composed a high proportion of the militant strikers. They complained about insufficient wages, overwork, and rude foremen. If the 1917 strikes concerned economic benefits, those in 1918 took a political turn, advocating an immediate peaceful settlement to the war. France's trade union, the *Confédération général du travail* (CGT), grew during the war from 355,000 members in 1913 to a record 600,000 by 1918, following patterns in Germany and England.

By far the most intensive strike activity occurred in Russia. Labor unrest had been a part of the Russian worker's daily existence before 1914. In the last two prewar years, nearly 75 percent of the industrial work force took part in strikes, and work stoppages continued for at least the first seven months of the war. In 1916 their intensity and frequency increased substantially as a result of higher food prices (which had doubled since 1913), a rise in factory accident rates and illness (especially among children and women), greater demands on workers (including longer working hours), and the presence of government factory inspectors who acted as informants to deter unrest among workers. As Russian workers' real wages steadily declined and as food prices climbed, some laborers, even in higher-paying metalworking jobs, were forced to spend a minimum of 75 percent of their income on food and clothing. The strike movement that had been gaining momentum throughout 1916 exploded in January and February 1917 and continued until the autumn of 1917, encompassing the overthrow of the tsarist regime and the subsequent Provisional Government.

As the war ground on, growing unrest in the workplace was a symptom of broader-based dissent on the home front and the battle front. Early in the war, active, vocal dissent was confined to a relatively small number of individuals and organizations. Some French syndicalists spoke out against the war in the periodical *La Vie Ouvrièr,* and Charles Merrheim was one of the first figures openly to oppose France's entry into the war. Marx, of course, had argued earlier that workers in different countries owed their ultimate allegiance not to their respective national governments but to the idea of international proletarian solidarity. Many nationalists had feared that when war did break out, the constituent member parties of the Second International would reject entry into the conflict as participation in a war that would promote the interests of capitalism and hinder those of working people. In fact, most of Europe's Socialist parties had supported their respective nations' decision to enter the war, believing that doing so was a defensive response.

Nonetheless, the elevation of transnational class solidarities over national and patriotic loyalties was one strand feeding into pacifist opposition to the conflict. So, too, was a genuine horror at the human and financial cost of war, as well as the influence of moral inhibitions against the taking of human lives. Organizations such as Britain's Union of Democratic Control, which advocated a negotiated peace and open, democratic conduct of foreign policy, were small in numbers but rich in talent. Prominent opponents of the war included Bertrand Russell, the famous philosopher, and Ramsay MacDonald, chairman of the Labour party and a future prime minister.

The debate surrounding conscientious objection to military service in Britain provides perhaps the clearest illustration of the moral dilemmas posed by the war. That nation had entered the conflict with a long-standing, deeply entrenched tradition of hostility to standing armies, and so for the first two years of war Britain relied on volunteers. By 1916, however, the notion that compelling men to serve by means of a draft was an unwarranted intrusion by the state on individual liberty had fallen victim to the army's continuing need for soldiers, and conscription was introduced. Now legal sanctions reinforced moral pressure to "join up," yet some 15,000 men refused to do so. Individuals who would not accept conscription were then afforded the opportunity to plead their case before a tribunal of civilian and military representatives. Men citing religious scruples might be exempted (Quakers, for example, almost always were), but the tribunals were highly suspicious of, and frequently insulting toward, objectors who lacked clear denominational ties or who appealed to their freedom of conscience. Tribunals often asked objectors whether they would not take up arms to protect a sister's chastity; if they admitted that in some circumstances they might resort to force, their objections were denied. Perhaps a third of conscientious objectors were imprisoned for their failure to serve, but many more found themselves the targets of virulent abuse. In York, for example, a town with a prominent Quaker community, advocates of conscription complained bitterly that "this crowd of physical and mental degenerates are left behind to produce, in conjunction with the unparticular women who would be satisfied to mate with weaklings like these, a race that would, like their sires, sell our land to the unspeakable Hun, and all for a purely imaginary conscience."

These sorts of ravings had originally inclined some socialists to be skeptical of the appeals to patriotic unity, but initially most accepted the idea of participation as a legitimate defensive measure. By 1917 several ideological rifts were undermining that original position. Only the Italian Socialist party (*Partito socialista italiano*, or PSI) initially opposed the war, but it later was forced into adopting a neutral position. In 1917 Germany's Social Democratic party (SPD) split into three factions: the majority Socialists (those who supported the war and who remained within the original SPD organization), the Independent Social Democratic party (*Unabhängige Sozialdemokratische Partei Deutschlands)*, and the Spartacists, the latter two of which were smaller groups opposed to the war's continuation and contained the more radical left-wing elements of the former SPD. In France, too, dissenting voices were heard within the *Section française de l'International ouvrière* (SFIO) by the autumn of 1916. A minority of Socialists on the extreme Left under the leadership of Fernand Loriot eventually formed the nucleus of the French Communist party (*Parti communiste français*, or PCF) in the 1920s. Thus, although a majority of Europe's trade unionists and Socialists supported their countries' initial involvement in the war, by 1917 even the most diehard patriot had come to cherish a relatively swift, peaceful settlement.

Impatience with victory, dissatisfaction with incompetent or inefficient military authority, and an unwillingness to be sacrificed for the sake of a few hundred meters of land led to mutiny in the French army in the spring of 1917, while inaction and a suicidal final mission prompted rebellion in the German navy in the autumn of 1918. Eager to reverse the debacle at the Somme, and convinced that the Allies must seize the offensive against the German forces before they were shifted from the Eastern to the Western Front following the Russian Revolution, French general Robert Georges Nivelle, the victor of Verdun, ordered French soldiers into battle once again in April 1917. His ill-conceived plan, about which the Germans had knowledge, resulted in the massacre of 40,000 Frenchmen on the first day of the offensive at Chemin de Dames. Nivelle's dismissal did nothing to relieve the overwhelming feeling among the *poilus* (French soldiers) that they had been sacrificial lambs. Tens of thousands of rank-and-file troops openly rebelled against their superiors following the failed offensive. General Henri Philippe Pétain, who replaced the detested Nivelle, conceded in May to the demand that the French army adopt a more defensive posture that would not squander more lives. Some mutineers were incarcerated and brought to trial for their disobedience; although hundreds of the most serious offenders were condemned to death by French courts, the sentences were imposed on less than 10 percent of those involved.

The mutiny in November 1918 at the German port of Kiel on the Baltic Sea differed in immediate impact from its French counterpart. The rebellion ignited revolutionary action throughout Germany. On the other hand, the sailors' decision openly to defy their superiors' orders to set sail out of Kiel to attack the British navy also constituted a rebellion against military authority. Worried that the impending armistice would require the German navy to surrender to the British fleet, high-ranking naval officials had sought a final encounter with their bitter rivals. But the attack would not occur. Years of dissatisfaction with shipboard working conditions, poor relations with their officers, refusal to be sacrificed for the sake of naval pride, and frustration over Kaiser Wilhelm II's reluctance to abdicate his throne and submit to constitutional reform prompted the sailors' mutinous action.

Popular defiance of military and civilian authorities exploded in revolutions in three of the combatant countries: Russia, Austria-Hungary, and Germany.

In Russia the stark consequences of military defeat had already been apparent a decade earlier, when Russia's dismal performance in a war against Japan had prompted revolution in 1905. In that case, the tsar had retained power only through substantial concessions, most notably the creation of constitutional government and a parliamentary legislature, the Duma. The Bolshevik leader V. I. Lenin believed that "Nicky" would never repeat the blunder of involving Russia in a disastrous war, and he despaired of ever seeing revolution achieved during his lifetime. But the strain of total war aggravated a number of persistent sources of discontent: the peculiar concentration of Russian heavy industry and the harsh discipline prevailing in that sector; the indebtedness and minimal living standards of the peasants, who, despite formal emancipation in 1861, had never developed into the conservative class of owner-occupiers characteristic of Napoleon III's France; and the dissatisfaction of the intelligentsia, who perceived Nicholas and his bureaucrats as unwilling to accept representative government as a legitimate legislative partner and unable to administer the war effort effectively (witness the excessive influence of the mad monk Rasputin).

In the spring of 1917, these pressures grew too great to contain. Strikes, food riots, and political demonstrations signaled a challenge to the tsar's authority, and, because the military was tied up at the front (and its ultimate loyalty no longer unquestioned), the full repressive arsenal of the state could not be mobilized to preserve domestic order. With no victory in sight and with mounting casualties and lengthening bread lines, Nicholas II abdicated in March 1917 (February by the old Russian calendar). A Provisional Government emerged, with responsibility to oversee the war effort until elections could be held, a constitution written, and a more representative political system introduced.

What resulted, however, was a system of dual power, whereby the constitutionalist Provisional Government found itself forced to share authority with the rapidly emerging representative councils (the so-called soviets) elected by military units, factories, and the like. Ultimately, dual power proved unworkable, for the various soviet workers' and soldiers' councils (especially the most prominent, in Petrograd) disagreed fundamentally with the Provisional Government over the war's future course. The soviets insisted on an eventual peace settlement without annexations and on a relaxation of discipline and working hours in the factories, while the Provisional Government (headed by Aleksandr Kerensky and others) was committed to victory with territorial gains and insisted that increased production, longer hours, and more stringent discipline were the only means to secure the expulsion of German soldiers from Russian soil. During the summer of 1917, a major Russian military offensive failed (with further horrendous losses), as did an attempted right-wing coup led by General Lavr Kornilov. With the revolution seemingly in danger and with victory as elusive as ever under the Provisional Government, the Bolshevik platform of peace, land, and bread attracted growing support and illustrated Kerensky's vulnerability. Finally, in November 1917 (October in the older calendar), the Bolsheviks ended the system of dual power, dissolving the Provisional Government and substituting authority in the name of the soviets, although, as Lenin had indicated, a dictatorship of the proletariat would be justified to preserve a socialist revolution in its vulnerable early stages.

The unfolding of events in Russia and the growing momentum of strikes and food riots placed Europe's governments on the defensive. In Austria-Hungary and Germany, however, impending defeat, food shortages, mounting casualties, war weariness, and the slow response by their monarchs toward reform aggravated already explosive domestic situations. Another significant factor in the Dual Monarchy's collapse was the nationality problem. In the autumn of 1918, Czech nationalists controlled Bohemia, while Serbs, Croats, and Slovenes created a Yugoslav council. Distressed by the attempts at secession from the empire, Emperor Charles, who succeeded Franz Joseph on his death in November 1916, proclaimed in October self-government for all nationalities within Austria — but not within Hungary. Military defeat at the hands of the Italian army, however, eliminated what shreds of authority he still possessed; by the end of the month, republics had been proclaimed in the major components of the now defunct Hapsburg dynasty — Austria, Czechoslovakia, Hungary, and Yugoslavia.

In Germany the revolution of 1918 did not lead to the dictatorship of the masses as in Russia or to the establishment of individual nations as in Austria-Hungary. The Kiel naval mutiny inspired unrest throughout other parts of Germany. In early November sailors' councils assumed control of Wilhelmshaven, Germany's largest naval base, and sailors and soldiers in Hamburg demanded control of food distribution and of the dissemination of communications. From northern Germany revolutionary activities spread to the Rhineland and then to Bavaria, where, in its capital of Munich, left-wing Socialist Kurt Eisner and his supporters seized power and announced the formation of the Bavarian Republic. Convinced that the events in Bavaria foreshadowed the dissolution of the German empire, Prince Max of Baden, who assumed the position of chancellor in September 1918, announced the resignation of his government and the intention of both the Kaiser and the crown prince to relinquish their rights to the throne. The leader of the Majority Socialist party, Friedrich Ebert, became the new chancellor, and on November 9 Wilhelm II fled to Holland, leaving Ebert to quell further revolutionary unrest, to deal with the provisions of the armistice of November 11, and to form the new Weimar Republic in January 1919.

Industrial unrest, political dissent, and revolution suggested, however, that the restrictions placed by the various European states on their citizens' civil and moral liberties were permeable, that they did as much to generate new energies as to stifle them, and that they promoted both constructive and destructive tendencies. Indeed, in their artwork and writing, European artists and literary figures reflected both the triumphant mood and the uneasiness of their countrymen, proving that neither the war itself nor the government interference it stimulated could dampen the creative forces of the human spirit.

A. The Expansion of the State

1. THE WAR AND BRITISH LIBERTIES

In 1914 many British observers believed that the war was justified, even ennobled, as a struggle to eliminate the specter of "Prussianism" that was menacing free, civilized Europe. But as the conflict dragged on, necessitating an increasing degree of governmental compulsion, liberal theorists worried that the end — victory over Germany — no longer justified every possible means. The excerpt below, by John A. Hobson, reflects this reappraisal. Hobson was a prominent exponent of the New Liberalism in England and best known for his scathing critique of colonial expansion, *Imperialism: A Study* (1902). Consider what Hobson implies by use of the term *Prussianism,* and note how he links wartime developments with the apparent willingness of British conservatives before the war to renounce constitutional procedures.

Liberty as a True War Economy

Even if the defence of the British democratic State, founded on the maintenance of the free moral personality of its citizens, were adjudged unsound, the attempt suddenly to transform our worse policy into the better German policy for the purposes of war, would be exceedingly unwise. The addition of, at the most, a few hundred thousand unwilling men to the fighting forces of the nation is a poor compensation for the moral and intellectual shock of a sudden reversal of the forces which have moulded the entire course of British history. And when I call it a poor compensation, I do not mean merely in the long run, I mean also for the immediate practical work which Britain has in hand,

From *The Nation,* 29 July 1916.

the winning of the war and the attainment of some settlement which afterwards will give a prospect of security. For though the full havoc of this intrusion of the spirit of Prussianism into our British life is not realized at once, the culmination of the long series of attacks on personal liberty in this striking and widespread example will do more to undermine the confidence in the Government and the moral support given to the purposes and conduct of the war than any other action that could have been taken. For that confidence and moral support have been evoked and sustained by the appeal to the judgment, will, determination, and voluntary co-operation of men's minds. They have responded lavishly with their work, their money, and their lives, because they were trusted. Conscription has been a rude formal withdrawal of this faith. It says, in effect, "You have sent out your sons, husbands, and brothers in millions to toil in the trenches and to risk and lose their lives: you think you have been liberal in your patriotic sacrifice of those near and dear to you. But, after all, you are unprofitable servants, you have not done nearly as much as you ought to have done. So, having drained you dry of all your voluntary services, we will extort the rest by force." The effect is to damp the ardor and depress the spirit of the people. They feel it to be a cruel and an unjust accusation. It begins to stir a spirit of criticism in those who hitherto had cheerfully accepted the statements of their rulers as to the national needs of life and money for the conduct of the war. Suspicions begin to spread, questionings as to the necessity of these new enlargements of our forces, the wisdom of their wide dispersal over many fields of precarious and unsuccessful action, doubts regarding the solidarity of the Government, and the discretion and disinterestedness of the ruling classes who are so dissatisfied with the extent of the people's voluntary sacrifices. I am not at all concerned with the validity of such doubts and suspicions. I merely cite them as examples of the sort of moral damages which in such a country as ours are the natural and necessary result of the sudden introduction of the Prussian method. Our militarists may reply that they care nothing, provided that they get the men, the munitions, and the money. But this is a foolish and short-sighted reckoning. History shows that the consent and the moral support of the people are essential to the successful conduct of a war, and that what the men and women at home are thinking, feeling, and suffering does act with direct and great force upon the *moral* of every army.

In other words, the collective strength of the nation, wielded by the State for the defence of its existence, is not enhanced but diminished by a sudden abandonment of normal liberty and a reversion to the distinctly lower principle of physical coercion. For what it gains in the sum of physical resources, the number of formal fighting men, is lost, and more than lost, by the weakening of that very factor of moral consent and spiritual conviction which constitutes the will to win.

It has been admitted that some losses of civil liberty are necessary in a State at war. It may not be easy, or possible, to draw any exact lines as to the particular encroachments upon normal liberty that are justified and those that are not. But when the determination of the limits of such interference is removed from all effective control either of the legislature or the civil courts, to be exercised by the arbitrary will of the military authority or by special tribunals relieved from the ordinary rules and safeguards of civil procedure, all sorts of excesses are to be expected. . . .

The real peril of these encroachments upon civil rights is not recognized by those who look upon them as mere war emergencies, and fondly imagine that when the war comes to a close they will automatically pass into oblivion. Those who have watched with growing anxiety the course of political events in the years immediately preceding the war will recognize that the forces of political reaction were gathering strength before, and have found in this national emergency their opportunity. The premature attempt to "rush" Protection in 1903 and the following years was the first open evidence of this reaction. It was followed by the offensive-defensive action of the House of Lords against the control of finance by the representative House. The crushing defeats sustained in these attempts, followed by popular attacks in Parliament and the country upon the landlord interests and other fortresses of social economic privilege, stirred to their depths the fighting instincts of the Conservative classes. Finding their enemies too strongly entrenched under the shelter of the constitutional rights of Parliament and a free electorate, they were preparing, in the last resort, to throw over the Constitution and to work their will by a political-military *coup d'état* in which the revival of the Royal prerogative was to be supported by the sympathetic action or inaction of the Army. The resistance to the Home Rule Act in Ireland and in Great Britain was to be the great occasion of this revolutionary movement. In this connection it is worth while to remind ourselves that several of the pledged leaders of this conspiracy against the Constitution and the Law are the members of the present Government who have been the most active agents in fastening Conscription on the nation.

Our habit of refusing to envisage the political situation as a whole, and of confining our attention to its separate measures and movements, prevented most of us from realizing the full significance of the threatened defiance of the Home Rule Act by leaders of Conservative opinion in Great Britain. Similarly we are slow to appreciate the profound significance of the militarist rule set up in the country, as we imagine only for the duration of the war. In Germany and in other countries, militarism and conscription have not been merely the instruments of an offensive or defensive foreign policy. They have also been developed and utilized by the possessing and ruling classes for the protection and furtherance of their political and economic privileges, and for defence against popular movements threatening their power. It is not merely the possession of armed force for the maintenance of civil order, and in particular for the suppression of industrial disturbances, that is sought. It is the belief that military service will instil into the masses of the people habits of discipline and obedience to those placed in authority over them, thus rendering innocuous the popular franchise, representative Parliaments, and other instruments of democracy.

2. THE STATE AS THE SUPREME GOD?

Introspection about the unintended consequences of total mobilization was not confined to intellectuals such as Hobson. In this document, Captain John Crombie of the Gordon Highlanders, an ordinary soldier from one of the army's best units, reflects in a letter to his mother on the state's growing authority.

[France] March 2nd, 1917

. . . The Union of Democratic Control was the only sensible Socialist organisation before the war, and a very good one. I don't know what its Peace ideas are, but as a matter of fact I am quite in agreement with Snowden and that lot. Their trouble to my mind is, that they have such an irritating way of putting their opinions, not that the opinions are wrong in themselves. Anyhow when you think of it, the moral situation is damnable — we can only beat Germany by assuming her mentality, by recognising the State as the Supreme God whose behests as to military efficiency must be obeyed, whether or no they run counter to Christianity and morality. We call their use of gas inhuman, but we have to adopt it ourselves; we think their policy of organising the individual life contrary to the precepts of freedom, but we have to adopt it ourselves; we profess to shudder at the Zabern incidents, but what of our treatment of conscientious objectors? Oh! There are stacks of incidents, and the only hope is that we can drop it after the war. I agree I can't suggest an alternative, but I also agree with Ramsay Macdonald, that it shows that the way to defeat German militarism was not by fighting it — not the best way at least. And I don't believe we shall stamp out German Militarism at the end of it; you can't change a nation's morality by military conquest, I am sure. But of course one must admit that if we had not fought them, what else were we to do? I suppose at this stage of the world's history one could not expect anything else. It is an interesting question.

3. GERMANY'S GOVERNMENT AT WAR

Albrecht Mendelssohn-Bartholdy boasted an eminent heritage, counting among his ancestors the philosopher Moses Mendelssohn and the composer Felix Mendelssohn-Bartholdy. A committed liberal, he directed the Institute for Foreign Policy in Hamburg and was commissioned by the Carnegie Endowment for International Peace to write a book on the war's domestic impact, from which this selection is taken. Though the work is now sixty years old, it still provides one of the best accounts of the erosion of the German civilian government's power owing to the encroaching influence of military authorities.

In the War the Government overreached itself . . . and it may also be said that the War brought out flaws and false pretensions in the Government which had long existed without causing much comment. It is difficult, if not impossible, to say whether that is primarily or mainly due to the peculiar German situation in 1914, or whether it is an innate corollary to war on the great scale in any case and everywhere. No doubt the constitutional arrangement by which, on the outbreak of war and almost automatically,

(2) Excerpt from *War Letters of Fallen Englishmen,* Laurence Housman, ed., Victor Gollancz UK, 1930, pp. 80–81. All attempts at tracing the copyright holders of these letters were unsuccessful.

(3) Excerpt from *The War and German Society* by Albrecht Mendelssohn-Bartholdy, Yale University Press, pp. 108–110. Copyright © 1937 Yale University Press. Reprinted by permission of the publisher.

the executive power is transferred from the civil to the military authorities, did much to raise reasonable doubt as to public administration in the minds of the public, and to make restive and critical those who had, before the War, been patient and long-suffering about public affairs, almost to the point of criminal indifference. Throughout Germany, including Bavaria, in spite of her special prerogatives of sovereignty, the military districts became the administrative districts, in some cases including the territories of several of the smaller central and northern states. The Emperor, as Supreme War Lord, was represented by the general-in-command *(Kommandierender General)* of the district, or, to be more precise, the lieutenant-general-in-command, for the general-in-command himself had to go on active service, and in his place it was usually a retired general who was called upon to reënter service and become the regent of the district. Nor was he a representative official only; he wielded an almost unlimited power in the case of civil administration and political rights generally, as well as in military matters. The conception of his office was essentially different from that of the Cabinet Minister or Secretary of State or Civil Governor *(Regierungspräsident)* whose functions were to be fulfilled by him. It was not service which was expected of him, but command. He was the military commander, *Militärbefehlshaber,* and as such had to exercise civil executive power in its entirety. Civil servants remained at their posts, at least those who had not been called to the colors, and except for the courts of law, the independence of which was strictly maintained, worked under military orders. In addition to this, the general-in-command had a whole staff of officers and officials of military rank. Most of them were retired on grounds of age or disability; and, in the later stage of the War, they were officers who had been wounded or contracted some illness which prevented them from doing active service. It was pure chance if any of these men who formed the government of a district and who, of course, were practically exempt from either ministerial or parliamentary censure or control, was either trained in administration of any kind, or was able to master the technique of civil government by sheer energy of will and quickness of intellect. Many of them were unable to do so, and some of them were unwilling, having their own ideas about the unnecessary fuss trained civil servants used to make about their work, thinking how easy it was for a businessman, or an officer, or any other man with ordinary common sense to administer, if not strict law, then at least a sound measure of equity to everybody concerned.

The people had thus more occasion and likewise perhaps a better opportunity of getting in touch with the authorities and of judging of their impartiality and efficiency. They had to ask all kind of permissions to do things which needed no special permit in times of peace. They volunteered information which they thought was essential; and during the final few months of the War the spy mania gave the information departments of the *Generalkommando* a lot of trouble. People were forced to go to the censor for *imprimaturs* for newspaper items or general literature, and to obtain leave to hold meetings, and so on. Favor or its opposite began to play a rôle it had never played before in administration; and where in peace-time businessmen (and idle men too) had often grumbled about there being too much *Gründlichkeit* — pedantic thoroughness — in the Civil Service or the courts of administration when dealing with petty cases, it became quickly the reverse under the new régime. Decisions were speedy, and, as must be the case with summary decisions, arbitrary; and suspicions of favoritism and petty corruption — there was hardly a case of gross corruption on the part of the military authorities during the whole of the War — grew rife.

Apart from that, some ill will was inevitable in the case of civil servants who were displaced, or who had to carry out orders where they had given them before. It was galling to a man who thought of his work as being a wholly necessary part of an organization that had been perfected through a long period of laborious effort and was admired throughout the world for its honesty and efficiency, to be told that any officer incapacitated for military service, or his non-commissioned subaltern with hardly a full command of German grammar (not to speak of the language of the law), could replace him at a moment's notice. The public — even those who were inclined to be opposed to military supremacy over the civil service — were apt to heap ridicule on those who had believed themselves indispensable for the maintenance of law and order, and who had been suddenly put out of court without any very terrible consequences. Bureaucracy must believe in the necessity of its labors. With this belief shattered, let alone the loss of public favor, it can hardly do its work as it should be done.

On the whole, it was more the system than the men who worked it which made the thing go wrong, and caused the aftereffects with which Germany has had to battle since the War. To my personal knowledge, which was acquired from contacts with two or three *Generalkommandos,* superior military commanders were almost without exception well-intentioned men, and in most cases very anxious to continue the administrative routine of the civil service with the least possible change and to observe the letter as well as the spirit of the law. Incompetence was chiefly noticeable in the censor's office, and in the censorship of private correspondence. The latter should have been left to the public prosecutor's office, and the former might have been entrusted to almost any civil servant versed in literature and newspaper editing rather than to officers or laymen who used their rank as reserve officers to offer voluntary service as heads of information bureaus, as railway station superintendents, commanders of prisoners' camps, and censors. In one of the districts which came to my special notice during the War the owner of a cheap bazaar who had risen to the rank of *Kommerzienrat* and captain in the militia by reason of his officious patriotism, succeeded in wrecking the domestic peace of his town by a few months' tenure of the censor's office; for he read private letters and used their contents to make those who had written or received them both suspect and suspicious. These were, happily, isolated cases. But even if there had been none at all, the system would have led to deplorable results in the end. It was bound to destroy the quiet relation of mutual respect and trust between the civil service and the public which forms one of the firmest bases of public order in a modern community.

4. CENSORSHIP

The first casualty in war, it has been said, is often journalistic freedom. To governments intent on maintaining morale, control of information is as important as control of production. Increased measures of censorship were common in the various combatant nations, though the following catalog of topics prohibited in Germany indicates how stringent such government restrictions could be.

A Memorandum for the Press

Secret

I

The Military Command, in referring to the "Prohibition of Publications about Troop Movements and Means of Defense," issued by the Chancellor, turns in this eventful time to the press as that organ whose works are being spread far beyond the confines of the Reich.

The history of late wars is rich in examples of how easily inadvert reports may disclose to the enemy the marching up of the country's forces and thereby give the course of the war a turn destructive to the Fatherland.

The perfection of news transmission during the last few years has increased the danger of doing injury to the Fatherland by such publications.

More than ever are we being watched by our political adversaries; every inadvert publication is being flashed to them in a thousand ways. Even reports which appear harmless often suffice to give the enemy an accurate picture of our military situation. If we wish to secure for ourselves favorable prospects for a war, then our military measures must be kept secret before the enemy as well as our own country.

Of course, uncertainty and doubt will be felt particularly heavily at this time, but the welfare of the Fatherland demands the sacrifice of strict discretion in all questions pertaining in any way to the German Army and Navy or to the military power of the Allies. Disclosures of military events in all other countries, too, must be refrained from until the clarification of the political affairs, since we do not know what attitude these countries will adopt toward us. As soon as this clarification takes place the press will be informed thereof.

If the press is conscious of its heavy responsibility and the consequence of its reports, it will not light-heartedly become an ally of our enemy. It will give thanks to the War Command when the latter informs it as to what publications would be injurious to the Fatherland. By refraining unselfishly from every report of a military character it will spare the military and naval authorities the necessity of taking legal action against it, the strictest enforcement of which in cases of violations of this prohibition is demanded by interests of state.

The War Command will in its turn do everything to satisfy the legitimate demand of the nation for news. If these reports will have to be at first rather meager, it will be best for the realization of the patriotic effort of the press if it enlightens the nation about the reasons for and the necessity of secrecy and reminds it of its duty.

Through the Press Bureau of the Great General Staff and the Admirals Staff of the Navy reports will be sent out as often as possible to the Generals in Command and the Commanders of Naval Stations for delivery to the publishers of their respective districts. This will be the surer and quicker way for all publishers to get in possession of news than by despatching their own reporters, who can be admitted to the theater of war in only very limited numbers and with restricted freedom of movement.

All requests of the press are to be directed to the local Generals in Command — in case of their removal to the front, to their representatives — to the Commanders of Naval Stations, in Berlin to the Press Bureau of the Great General Staff, Berlin N.W. 40, and to the Admirals Staff of the Navy, Berlin W. 10, Königin Augustastr. 38/42.

II

It is impossible to say beforehand all that which in case of war should be kept secret in the interest of the Fatherland. Tact and insight of the representatives of the press will enable them to form a judgment from the following statements in what matters silence is being dictated until further notice.

Measures the disclosure of which could be injurious to the Fatherland and be of value to the enemy:

1. Formation of troops for the protection of boundary, coast, and islands. The guarding of harbor entrances and mouths of rivers.
2. Measures for the protection of railroads, canals, buildings, etc., and the formation of troops assigned for it.
3. The appearance of our own airships or aëroplanes.
4. Data as to the course of mobilization, the calling of reserves and the Landwehr, and the arriving of ships.
5. The placing of new troop formations and their description.
6. The arrival of detachments in the border districts for the preparation of the quartering of troops.
7. Building of ramps at railroad stations in the border districts by railroad troops and civilians.
8. The establishment of warehouses in the border districts and the purchasing of provisions by the military and naval administrations.
9. The shipment of troops and military authorities, of artillery, munitions, mines, and torpedoes from the garrisons, and the direction of their journey.
10. The journeying or marching through of troops of other garrisons and the direction of journey or march.
11. Arrival of troop divisions from the interior at the border and the naming of the station of their disembarkment and their quarters.
12. Strength and kind of troops advancing toward the frontier.

13. Naming of border districts where there are no troops or from which troops have been withdrawn.
14. Names of the higher leaders, where used, and possible changes in command.
15. Information as to departure and arrival of the higher military authorities at Great Headquarters.
16. Journeys and destination of Princes and other personalities, accompanying the army, as well as the place of their stay upon arrival at the front.
17. Delays of railroad shipments through accidents or the depreciation of railroads and bridges.
18. Work being done on fortresses, coast and inland defenses, in government or private shipyards and other establishments, entrusted with military consignments.
19. The making ready of rolling stock and laborers for purposes of the army or the navy.
20. The launching and damaging of warships.
21. Place of stay and movements of warships.
22. Arrival and sailings of ships of commerce.
23. The preparation and erection of barriers and supplying of ships with mines.
24. Changes of sea code and the extinction of lighthouses.
25. Damaging of ships and their repairs.
26. The garrisoning of places of naval information.
27. Making ready, equipping, and impressing of ships of the merchant marine for naval purposes; change of their crews.
28. The preparing of docks.
29. Publication of letters from people belonging to the army or navy without the consent of the military authorities at home.
30. Publication of lists of losses prior to their release by the military authorities.

The above refers to the allied armies and navies. Publications concerning them in the above sense are forbidden even in the eventuality of an outbreak of war. What countries are to be regarded as "allies" will be announced.

What other information the publishers should be able to find out after the outbreak of war through their foreign correspondents about the armies and navies of our enemies may be published only after the military authorities shall release such publications, since otherwise it will be easier for the enemy to draw conclusions as to our countermeasures. However, in order to utilize in time all reports from abroad, the publishers who come in possession of such reports would earn the praise of their country if they wire them — giving the source of the information — immediately to Great Headquarters in Berlin, in case the information deals with army affairs, or to the Admirals Staff of the Navy in Berlin, in case of naval affairs. The expenses entailed hereby will be borne by the Army and Navy Administrations.

It is desirable that none of these statements under II of this memorandum be published.

As far as is possible every publisher in the Reich has received a copy of this memorandum.

The publication of a forbidden military report in one paper does not absolve other publishers from the observance of the secrecy injunction of the Chancellor.

SUPPLEMENT TO THE MEMORANDUM FOR THE PRESS

It must be emphasized that the attitude of the press and its observance of the rules laid down in the "Memorandum for the Press" so far deserves and finds full appreciation. In spite of that it must be noted that certain papers use now and then a language which is not adapted to the importance of the time. This circumstance forces the War Command, in order to supplement the "Memorandum for the Press," to formulate the following regulations, the observance of which during the duration of the state of war is urgently recommended. The War Command is convinced that the hitherto patriotic attitude of the press is evidence that the press endeavors also in the future to prevent unintentional injuries to our great cause.

1. A questioning of the national sentiment and determination of any German, any one party or newspaper is highly detrimental, because it impairs the impression of German unity and energy.
2. German victory means liberation for many foreign peoples from Russian despotism and English world-hegemony, and does not signify oppression. It would be injurious to our cause if German papers should express a contrary view.
3. The language used against the enemy countries may be harsh. However, an insulting and belittling tone is no sign of power. The purity and greatness of the movement which has gripped our nation demands a dignified language.
4. The foreign policy of the Chancellor, conducted upon instructions from His Majesty the Kaiser, must in this critical moment not be interfered with or hindered by covert or overt criticism. To doubt its firmness injures the prestige of the Fatherland. Confidence in it must be strengthened, and, like the confidence in the military leaders, it too must not be shaken.
5. Demands for a barbaric conduct of war and the annihilation of foreign peoples are repulsive. The army knows where severity and leniency have to prevail. Our shield must remain clear. Similar clamors on the part of the inciting press of the enemy are no excuse for a similar attitude on our part.

Royal Ministry of War

May 14, 1915

Military considerations demand that the press should refrain from discussing the question whether the German Colonial Possessions will be retained or lost or whether any territories outside of Europe might be acquired from foreign powers. Lectures discussing this topic in public are not desirable. Such lectures must not be reported nor should the papers express their own attitude.

May 14, 1915

It is highly desirable that the German press, when arguing the causes which brought about the war, should point to Serbia as the decisive factor. German war literature (for instance, the very title of a whole series of publications, *"The German War"*) has greatly helped persons in Austria who, in good faith or with malicious intent, wish to make it appear that Austria has been made the victim of Germany in the war. All polemics must be avoided, but it must be stressed that the aim of the war is to preserve Austria, an aim which is greatly in the interest of Germany. This will serve to counteract or, at least, to weaken from the very beginning the malicious agitation which is expected to break out in Austria after the war.

5. WAR, PROSTITUTION, AND VENEREAL DISEASE IN GERMANY

State intrusion into the sphere of private life took on increasing importance as the scale and duration of the conflict became apparent. For example, to curtail drunkenness, British authorities sought to limit the hours during which pubs could serve alcohol. Meanwhile, as this selection from the most prestigious British medical journal shows, the German government took steps to grapple with the rise of venereal disease.

The present war has revived the problems of prostitution and venereal disease in an acute form, and, thanks to recent advances in the diagnosis and treatment of venereal disease, the energetic measures adopted in certain of the belligerent countries have given far better results than could have been obtained a few decades ago. But venereal disease remains a greater drain on the fighting forces than any other infectious disease, and the problems associated with it are still far from being solved. . . .

CASUALTIES FROM VENEREAL DISEASE GREATER
THAN FROM WOUNDS

The Germans naturally hark back to the war of 1870 to compare the incidence of venereal disease then and now. Then, as many as 33,538 men, or nearly the equivalent of an army corps, were admitted to military hospitals suffering from venereal disease. This represented 9 per cent. of the total morbidity of the German Army [and] was a surprisingly low proportion, venereal disease in most wars constituting from 17 to 31 per cent.

From "War, Prostitution and Venereal Disease: The Position in Germany," *The Lancet,* 23 Sept. 1916, pp. 567–568.

of all the medical casualties. This author, an Austrian army surgeon, has shown that in most armies in war time from 50 to 300 soldiers per 1000 contract venereal disease every year. It has also been estimated that the dead and wounded in 129 modern battles constituted 79.4 per 1000 of the total strength of the armies concerned. From these figures [it has been argued] that were an army to fight one battle every year its casualties from dead and wounded would barely be as heavy as from infection with venereal disease.

HAS VENEREAL DISEASE AMONG GERMAN SOLDIERS
INCREASED SINCE 1870?

Though complete figures are not yet available, there is already a mass of evidence to prove that venereal disease is still a veritable scourge in the armies of to-day in spite of earlier diagnosis, more effective treatment, stricter discipline, and the regulation of prostitution. In the Prussian Army venereal disease has shown a fairly steady decline for several decades, as shown. . . . The figures in the second column represent the morbidity from venereal disease per 1000 soldiers.

Year	Number of Cases	Year	Number of Cases
1867	53.9	1890–91	27.2
1872	45.1	1900–01	17.8
1873–74	38.4	1909–10	20.8
1880–81	39.2	1910–11	19.9

In 1903–04 the incidence of the three venereal diseases per 1000 in the Prussian Army was 12.4 for gonorrhœa, 4.5 for syphilis, and 2.3 for ulcus molle. Before the war the control of venereal disease in the German Army was so effective that it was less frequent among soldiers than male civilians of the same age. Also, the incidence of venereal disease was higher among recruits than among soldiers already in the ranks. On April 30th, 1900, there were 30,383 men out of 10,000,000 Prussian men under treatment for venereal disease; and . . . this was roughly the number of Germans treated, towards the end of March, 1915, for venereal disease in the military hospitals on the Western Front.

So far it has been shown that for several decades a considerable reduction of venereal disease has been effected in the Prussian army. Has this reduction been maintained in the Prussian and other German armies since August, 1914? Undoubtedly it has not; on the contrary, there is every reason to believe that there has been an alarming increase, not so much in the actual fighting-lines as in the occupied hostile territory behind them. [It has been estimated] that the incidence of venereal disease is bound to rise to about 40 per 1000 in the German Army, and that in an army numbering 7,000,000 men 280,000 would annually contract venereal disease, which in 60,000 cases would be syphilis.

. . . [Further attention has been drawn] to the sad fact that the proportion of married men among the infected has shown a most disquieting rise. Thus, among 653 cases of gonorrhœa and syphilis treated at his hospital in Breslau since the outbreak of the war there were 339 unmarried and 141 married men suffering from gonorrhœa, and 88 unmarried and 85 married men suffering from syphilis. [It has been] estimated the proportion of married to unmarried patients in the German military hospitals at 1 to 3. Another, at first sight, curious fact is the relative frequency of venereal disease among German volunteers and "Landsturm," as compared with the regular troops. This difference is accounted for by the former being largely kept in reserve in garrison towns, while the latter are more frequently employed in the fighting line, where the opportunities for contracting venereal disease are much restricted.

THE CAUSES OF THE GROWTH OF VENEREAL DISEASE IN WAR TIME

The axiom enunciated many years ago, . . . that the incidence of venereal disease rises steadily during a war, and is therefore directly proportional to its duration, is founded on many different factors. Recruits drawn from country districts, where neither prostitution nor venereal disease is known, find the temptations of a garrison town irresistible; the women, the money, and the time unoccupied by military duties all help to lower the rustic's moral sense. Destitution is another common cause, many a previously virtuous woman being driven by dire poverty to maintain life by prostitution. And in the case of both men and women separation from wife or husband, and the resulting loneliness and deprivation of an intercourse which has become second nature, lead to the establishment of extra-marital, promiscuous relations. War brings in its wake a code of morals so utterly at variance with the accepted standard of peace that many men successfully posing as models of probity at home run amuck when constrained only by a so-called military law. It is particularly in hostile, occupied territory that the licentiousness of the German soldier has been given free rein, to judge only by German sources of information. . . . In Poland the distress is so great that the bulk of the women still living there have been driven to prostitution as the only means of existence. In the Balkans the conditions in this respect are little better. Terrible as the fate of these women is, it is safe to say that their sufferings would not have attracted the attention devoted to them by the German military authorities were it not for the ill-effects of this state of affairs on the health of the German Army. . . . In a small village about 135 men of the "Landsturm" contracted gonorrhœa which was traced in every case to the same source, a girl aged 13.

THE GERMAN CAMPAIGN AGAINST VENEREAL DISEASE

Germany has found it necessary to take the gloves off in the fight against venereal disease and to disregard many of the niceties and qualms respected before the war. Well disciplined as the German nation undoubtedly is, the restrictive measures put into force by the higher command would have roused serious opposition were it not for the plea of urgent necessity. As it is, a discussion has already been started in the German medical press on the feasibility of continuing after the war measures which have been found so effective at present; and the opinion is held in many quarters that after the war Germany will not tolerate the moral dragooning submitted to now.

In June 1915, v. Hindenburg issued his now notorious order which aimed at a drastic suppression of venereal disease. Briefly, this order threatened with imprisonment for from two months to one year any woman who cohabited with soldiers or civilians in spite of the knowledge that she was suffering from venereal disease. Prostitutes who failed to register as such with the police were also liable to a year's imprisonment followed by banishment from the occupied district.

PREVENTIVE MEASURES IN BERLIN

The war had not lasted long before the authorities in Berlin realised that energetic measures would be necessary for the restriction of prostitution in an aggravated form. The Chief of Police issued three orders in succession, beginning with the warning that the already existing regulations in connexion with prostitution would be strictly enforced, and that all provocation to immorality would be suppressed. In his second order he forbade all registered prostitutes to attend public places of entertainment, and in his third order he gave 24 hours' notice to barmaids and the like to quit. Thus, in one day about 700 women lost their employment and had to seek work in other and less exposed occupations. Much was done to find employment for these and other women left dependent on themselves by mobilisation.

Much has also been done for the German soldier. In Brussels, for example, a special institution has been organised for the comfort and entertainment of the 4000 Germans of the railway service in which, as might be expected, the incidence of venereal disease is extraordinarily high. On the lines of communication and in many towns reading-rooms and entertainments have been provided as counter-attractions; and whenever it has been feasible billeting on private houses has been avoided. When on the march soldiers are not put up in towns or densely populated districts, and when it is impossible to avoid quarters in a town the soldiers' leave is restricted. An educational campaign among soldiers has been conducted with great thoroughness, but it has been found that a whole sheaf of printed warnings is incomparably less impressive than the demonstration . . . of a severe case of venereal disease. The treatment of venereal disease by quacks has been practically stamped out by certain army commanders, and penalties attached to the concealment of venereal disease have been most conducive to early detection and treatment.

CONTROL OF PROSTITUTION

Judging by the recent utterances [of] authorities . . . , the belief is prevalent in Germany that extensive extra-marital sexual intercourse is an inevitable evil; the moral regeneration of the nation is not practical politics, and every effort should be concentrated on rendering irregular relations as harmless to their patrons as possible. In other words, the dangers of venereal disease from prostitution must be reduced to a minimum, and this aim naturally raises the old arguments for and against brothels under medical supervision. . . .

PROPHYLAXIS OF VENEREAL DISEASE

The decline of venereal disease in the German Navy during the last decades has been largely attributed to compulsory prophylactic measures. These were not compulsory in the army before the war, but in some commands they have subsequently been enforced, and the soldier who contracts venereal disease and is found to have omitted the ritual of prophylaxis is punished.

The æsthetic aspect of this system of prophylaxis seems to have been lost sight of under the stress of war, the suppression of venereal disease at whatever cost being the first thought of the military authorities. Even Germans who before the war were vehemently opposed to the system of prophylaxis and the moral degradation entailed, seem to have come round to the view that nothing short of this unsavoury measure can be expected to check the spread of venereal disease. Many of them now admit that individual prophylaxis is the most powerful weapon against venereal disease yet known. . . . Though the law still penalises the sale of anticonceptional remedies in Germany, her leading military authorities not only countenance but recommend their employment as preventives of venereal disease. It has been calculated that the decline in the birth-rate due to anticonceptional remedies is to a certain extent compensated for by the relative immunity to venereal disease secured by these remedies. And the decline of the birth-rate traceable to venereal disease itself is far from negligible, for it has been estimated that gonorrhœa has reduced the annual number of births in Germany by 200,000 and syphilis by 70,000. Before the war some squeamishness was felt by the medical profession with regard to recommending condoms; as preventives of conception they were viewed with disfavour by the authorities. But this property of the condom has almost been lost sight of during the war. . . . Every facility is given the German soldier to provide himself with this and other devices, and printed leaflets describing their mode of application are distributed broadcast by the military authorities to the soldier. In some commands the soldiers are equipped with small outfits containing calomel or sublimate ointment and solutions of silver nitrate, and it is even reported that these packets have become so popular as to be sent to soldiers as "Liebesgaben an den tapferen Feldgrauen." [gifts for our brave soldiers in field gray]

6. PRINCE LVOV ON RUSSIA'S OPPORTUNITIES AND DIFFICULTIES

Prince Georgi Lvov headed the All-Russian Union of Zemstvos and was a key figure in the subsequent Provisional Government. Established in 1864 as representative institutions for local government, the zemstvos would serve as one focus for organizing popular support for the war effort. Here, late in 1915, in a speech to a congress of representatives of the zemstvos, Lvov discusses the opportunities the war has brought but also the ominously widening gap between the government and the Russian people.

Gentlemen: At the very start of the war, when Russia was confronted with problems that were beyond the administrative capacities of our governmental machinery, and when the unprogressive methods which had become firmly and deeply rooted proved themselves bankrupt in the face of those unexpected, feverish demands of history which suddenly overwhelmed us, — we, men of the Zemstvo, went to work without any hesitation for the good of the State.

We knew that life itself would summon us to this work. To us, the call did not come as a surprise. Recall to your minds the modest proposals made to us at the beginning of the war, that we should take part in the relief of the sick and wounded soldiers, and compare them with our expectations at that time and the present state of affairs. We do not fight, and we do not now have to fight, for the right to take part in the activities of the State. Life itself is giving that right to us, and we have gradually gone ahead in our work, from rendering hospital service to supplying the wants of the army in the trenches, furnishing it with ammunition, preparing shells, constructing lines of defense, and so on. Hospital, commissary, artillery, engineering services, every branch of the life of our army at the front and in the rear, has become near and dear to us. We have actually been welded together with the army. National in its objects, the war has become truly national in the manner of its conduct as well. . . .

Gentlemen, this national war has turned upside down all the old notions, traditions, and old standards. In reality, we have no longer those old divisions and cells among which the component parts of the body politic had been distributed and artificially maintained. All distinctions between the nationalities composing our State, all party differences, are obliterated. The age-old distribution of functions among the different elements of the State is changing. It is true that the force of habit still makes them hold on to the old forms, but the new demands are more powerful than force of habit, and we all feel that life itself is seeking, and finding, a fresh channel for its mighty current. Life is stronger than laws that are written. Life writes its laws in the hearts and in the minds of men before they write them down on paper, and we do not even notice how we enter a different kind of life, and that we are already living under new laws that are still unwritten.

Before us, gentlemen, there are now arising the most weighty and responsible tasks that ever could have confronted the citizens, even of the most perfect political régime. This war has equipped the forces of the public with all kinds of organs for performing the tasks of the State, but we must not ignore the fact that the war demands of us an ever-increasing exertion, and imposes upon us an ever-growing responsibility. We have already abandoned the position of mere passive objects of government. Actual events have in this particular domain far outstripped our fondest wishes. Life has shown that we have to be self-sufficing. Let us, therefore, rely upon ourselves, let us grow strong in our

"Public Criticism of the Government" excerpt from *Documents of Russian History*, ed. by Frank Golder, Peter Smith Publishers, 1964, pp. 146–149.

self-confidence. Only such faith could give us a firm basis for our attitude toward the historical events we are passing through at present.

Upon our conference, gentlemen, history has laid a vast and responsible task. In difficult moments of the national life, the Zemstvos, in their capacity of leading public organization, ought to maintain, like the keel of a ship in the face of the storm, the steady course of the State. The country feels that everything is not as it ought to be, and it is only natural that it should feel alarmed, and that its heart should beat faster. And Russia now expects of you, gentlemen, some weighty word. Speak it calmly, in the full consciousness of your duty: Let not the Russian Land despair because of its sore trials; let not the faith of the Russian people in their might be shaken; and let them have no doubt as to the ultimate happy issue. For us, no peace is possible. No yoke will be accepted by the Russian people. For them, there can be only one issue of this war — complete victory. We are now retreating, yes, but we know that we shall again advance. We are fully aware that our valiant army and our heroic people are conquering, even while retreating. Their valor and their self-sacrifice give strength also to our own spirit, the spirit of the rear. And it is our sacred duty to uphold this spirit, this courage, and to organize for a conquering spirit in the rear. But we must not for an instant forget that the future of our national existence, of our great country, hinges not only upon the issues of the war, but likewise upon the things that happen in the course of the war. We are fully aware that the loftier the ideal we are aiming at, the longer and harder must be the road we have to travel, and the more we shall require endurance and patience.

Our country is longing not only for the resumption of peaceful existence, but for the reorganization of that existence. Never before has the need of solidarity among all the forces of our country, probably, been felt as keenly as at this time. Never before has this unity, which was proclaimed from the heights of the throne as the pledge of a victorious issue, been needed as urgently as now.

We are happy to see how deep this unity has gone among the masses of the people, a unity that has actually welded together all the nationalities of the empire into a single unit with the army. To our regret, however, we fail to observe solidarity between the ruling powers and the people, and this we are bound to declare emphatically to these powers, for that is the only thing that still obstructs our organization of victory.

Exactly three months ago, when it was made clear to the Russian people that our valiant army was forced to retreat before the enemy because it was lacking shells, we, and the whole country with us, unanimously agreed that the lawful popular representatives should take part in the work for the national defense. We believed that it was possible, on the basis of one single, common, sacred purpose — the salvation of our native country — to organize the activities of the public and governmental forces so as to be animated by a spirit of mutual confidence. Today, after two months of work by the State Duma, we feel even more convinced of that necessity.

Like a shining lamp in the dark labyrinth of events along the mysterious paths of history, the State Duma has always been showing the way out. And we cannot help recognizing that this suspension of its sessions throws us back into darkness, that it harms the cause of the national defense, that it weakens our army. So ardently desired by the whole country, the powerful combination of governmental and public effort has not been brought about. But this has by no means rendered the consciousness of the necessity of mutual confidence between the forces of the Government and the public less acute; on the contrary, it has only strengthened it. At the very first indication that a certain section of our government was inclined to look upon the work of the State Duma as superfluous, the whole of Russia experienced something like a shock and declared that a new Government was needed. But we are faced with a fact: the Government itself intends to organize for victory, and considers it unnecessary for the popular representatives to take part.

At moments like these we have to manifest civic courage of a high order, bearing in mind that it is not the Government, but the people, that is fighting the war. The Government may hold itself aloof from the people, but we shall be only still more confirmed in our conviction that the organization of victory is possible only through full union of the Government and people, through their legal representatives, and we regard it as indispensable to have the work of the State Duma resumed as soon as possible.

But in the face of the formidable foe, we must not be dismayed, because of this situation that prevails. Let the purely formal responsibility for the issue of the war and for the fate of our country rest with the Government; upon us will always rest the duty of true sons of our fatherland, and this we are bound to discharge under any circumstances. And so we shall continue unflaggingly to work and to perform our national duty.

7. RUSSIAN EDUCATION

Education was one means of stimulating commitment, of producing the literate graduates essential to an effective economy, and of preparing the next generation for participation in society. The war disrupted education as much as other areas of civilian life, especially in Russia. The selection below suggests the implications for younger pupils, including, temporarily at least, the possibility that entrenched religious discrimination might be mitigated by the new spirit of universal sacrifice.

The academic year 1914–1915 in the secondary schools was marked by considerable change. We may divide the secondary schools into four groups in respect of the direct influence which, during the first few months of the War, the actual or possible proximity of the front had upon them.

To the first group belonged the schools of those regions, which in the course of 1914–1915 were in the actual theater of war. Among these were the schools under the control of the Warsaw educational district, the majority of the schools in the educational districts of Riga and Vilna, part of the Kiev educational district, and a few of those of Odessa and the Caucasus. The board of the Warsaw educational district was transferred

Excerpt from *Russian Schools and Universities in the World War* by Paul Ignatiev, Dimitry Odinetz, and Paul Novgorotsev, pp. 72–77, 83–84. Copyright © 1929 Yale University Press. Reprinted by permission of the publisher.

to Moscow, and the schools under its control in part ceased their activities, and in part were evacuated to different towns, where they found premises for continuing their studies in the buildings of State and private schools during the vacant hours. A majority of the former pupils of these evacuated schools likewise left the threatened zones. They did not, however, in all cases remove to the same towns to which their schools had been transferred. As was natural, they accompanied their parents and not their school. The evacuated school, bereft of most of its pupils, sheltered under a distant roof, forced to carry on its work in evening hours to which its teachers were unaccustomed, was but a mere ghost of its former self.

To the second group belonged the schools of the regions that lay close to the theater of war. These schools, though not as yet evacuated to other towns, were under the imminent threat of evacuation. This group was chiefly composed of the remaining schools of the educational districts of Vilna and Riga and to some extent of that of Kiev. The conditions under which these schools worked were undoubtedly extremely hard. Under the ever present threat of evacuation and its consequent disturbance of their normal life teacher and pupil alike could evidently not pay that attention to school work which is its due in normal times and circumstances. The center of interest had shifted, and the mental atmosphere was entirely unsuitable for school work.

The third group comprised the schools of the adjacent region. In this were included part of the Petrograd, the whole of the Moscow and Kharkov, and the more eastern parts of the Kiev and Odessa educational districts. The schools of this group became the chief refuges of the evacuated schools. In many schools of the central regions, especially in the capitals, the number of refugee pupils received as supernumeraries was very large. In individual schools, such newly received pupils numbered 50 or even as many as 100. The work in such overcrowded schools could be carried on only at the expense of much of its utility.

Finally, to the fourth group belonged the educational districts of Kazan, Orenburg, and Siberia, wholly removed from the sphere of war, and but little affected by the evacuation of schools near the front. To this group we may add the schools of the northern part of the Caucasian educational district. As regards the work of these schools, it proceeded normally, with the exception of some slight disturbance occasioned by the mobilization of teachers not on the permanent staff.

The obstacles to the progress of education caused by the evacuation of schools were not the only ones; similar difficulties arose from the commandeering by the authorities of school buildings for hospital, depot, and other purposes. The requisition of school buildings in the first few months of the War assumed very large proportions. It was frequently conducted entirely without the knowledge of the educational authorities of the district. In the exhaustive memorandum appended to the estimates of 1916, the Ministry took a very serious view of the difficulties encountered by the schools in the year 1914–1915, owing to their evacuation, to the uncertainty of their situation, to lack of accommodation, or to excessive overcrowding. . . .

Apart from the external difficulties which beset the normal course and development of secondary education, the War itself rapidly affected the internal life of the secondary schools.

The rich and varied information contained in the answers sent in by parents and teachers from all over the country to an inquiry published in November 1914 in a number of educational periodicals makes it possible for us to obtain some knowledge of the effects of the War upon the psychology of pupils in the secondary schools.

"War, as may be expected, produced a stronger impression upon children living in towns than upon those living in the country, and among the former a stronger impression upon children living in large cities than on those living in small provincial towns." The senior pupils of secondary schools were now often compelled to think about complex problems which under normal conditions would have been beyond their grasp. The more mature among them, those belonging to the better educated social groups who had more of an opportunity to follow world events and to observe the reaction of them upon their elders, were prone to such valorous discussions as the responsibility for the War, the relative merits of Germany, France, Great Britain, and Russia, the respective values of the civilization of those countries. They drew plans for the defeat of the enemy, drafted conditions to be embodied in the future peace treaty, and remodeled the map of Europe. But generally speaking, the pupils of secondary schools reacted to the War in a manner similar to that of the pupils of elementary schools. This is of course particularly true in the case of the junior pupils.

"My boys are in a state of perpetual war," writes a mother. "The roof of the new attic is their favorite position. . . . Their games are full of hatred and violence." "The games of my boys," writes another mother, "have undergone a complete change. Travels, boats and buildings have now given place to war, the siege of fortresses, the mining of bridges, of fortifications and ramparts. In response to the news of the capture of Tsing-Tao they at once proceeded to the erection of the fortress, its noisy capture and destruction, and then came a triumphant procession with songs and banners through all the rooms, their faces radiant." An exhibition of children's drawings held in Moscow fully supported the view as to the popularity of military subjects.

The spirit of animosity toward the enemy was as common among the pupils of the secondary schools as it was among those in elementary schools. When a mother reports that her boy, eleven years old and a pupil in a gymnasium, "builds prisons for Germans and erects gallows on which to hang them," she gives a vivid illustration of one of the fundamental conditions of the state of the children's minds at that time. "My son, now in the sixth year in a gymnasium and one of the best students in his class," writes another mother, "continues to dwell each day on the destruction of traitors. His eyes flash when he hears the news of the sinking of a German cruiser or of some other loss suffered by the enemy. Among the children the hatred of Germany is growing day by day. Today, for instance, they have decided to petition the school authorities for the removal of their German teacher and the discontinuance of their German lessons." The children of the junior year of one of the *real* schools were asked in 1914 to write a paper on the topic, "My wishes for the New Year." A great many of them replied with bad wishes for William. "I wish William and his sons would become ill." "I want to strangle, to hang William." Perhaps the kindest of them was the following: "I should like to make William a prisoner and put him in jail as an ordinary citizen, and not to hang him, as Grigoriev suggested." . . .

Even M. Kasso in August 1914 issued an ordinance to the effect that "pupils of Jewish religion from schools that have been closed owing to war conditions may, in the course of the current school year, be admitted into other schools, even if the latter have no vacancies for Jewish pupils, provided that the interests of Christian children are not thereby prejudiced."

The necessity for making such modifications in existing regulations, which admitted equality of responsibility but not the equality of rights, furnished an excellent example of the serious practical defects of these regulations, patently obvious even to their supporters. But under the restrictions imposed by M. Kasso, the position of Jewish children whose fathers were at the front was in no way improved. The children of a Jew, if he were killed or wounded, might enter a school only within the quota and, what is more, not on the basis of the marks obtained in examination, but, under M. Kasso's regulation, by lot.

Later, in May 1915, the new Minister, Count Ignatiev, permitted children of Jewish fathers, who had distinguished themselves or had been killed or wounded, to enter the schools not by lot, but by position on the list of marks; they were still admitted, however, only within the Jewish quota.

At the end of July 1915, at the instance of the Minister of Education, the Government sanctioned the unrestricted admission to the schools of Jewish children whose fathers were serving in the army. The new Minister, so far as we can judge from his whole action and the views he expressed, was unable to approve of the disabilities from which the Jews had hitherto suffered in this respect. Owing to general political conditions, however, even his influence was sufficient only to modify the existing regulations, not to secure their complete repeal.

The other amendments of the regulations made toward the end of the school year by the Ministry were still less important. They related chiefly to the conditions under which the final examinations might be taken. But even here small changes were indications of a new policy. Former Ministerial ordinances had shown marked distrust of the school boards, and had entrusted the fundamental control of the school to the authorities of the educational districts and of the headmasters.

B. Economic Mobilization

1. AUSTRIA-HUNGARY'S WAR ECONOMY

The Austro-Hungarian war effort was hampered by bureaucratic inefficiency and nationalist and ethnic rivalries. The Hungarian prime minister, Count Istvan Tisza, had been skeptical of the empire's entry into the war, for reasons outlined in the following document. Ill-preparedness and economic vulnerability led slowly but inexorably to exhaustion, especially once Germany — blockaded and fighting on two fronts — was unable to help sustain the Austro-Hungarian role in the war.

The system of emergency measures was internally linked to the introduction of war economy and to the militarization of the national economy. The governments of the Dual Monarchy had dealt with the possibility of war for several years and had taken some preliminary steps; however, the Monarchy was not prepared for a lasting conflict either militarily or economically. Regarding internal and administrative affairs, a complete system of measures had been worked out. In the field of economy, however, the preliminary measures were much less extensive and only took into consideration a short war.

The law of 1912 on emergency measures also authorized the government to regulate and control economic life. Pursuant to Article 7, the organs of local self-government could, on the government's initiative, fix the maximum prices of staple foodstuffs. The Law of 1912 "On War Services" (Law LXVIII of 1912), passed at the same time as the emergency law, made possible even wider state control over the economy during the war. The Act provided that in a period of mobilization or war the government could demand personal and material services of the civilian population to meet the demands of the army. Able-bodied men up to the age of fifty could be obliged to compulsory labour for military purposes (Article 4). During this time they were subject to military criminal and disciplinary procedure (Article 9). Owners of factories and industrial plants were liable to produce goods corresponding to military demands or to hand over their factories together with the entire staff (Article 18). The Act also regulated compulsory delivery for the army. Another law (Law LXIX of 1912) regulated the delivery of horses and vehicles.

These acts passed before the war did not prove sufficient, and thus during the war the legislation continually extended the regulating role of the state over the economy, for example in the amendment of the Act of Emergency Measures. . . . Complementing Article 7 of Law LXIX of 1912, and Law L of 1914 which further developed, authorized the government to fix centrally the maximum prices of "means of sustenance and other primary consumer goods" (Article 1), furthermore to ordain the declaration, and even the delivery, of surplus reserves of such goods (Articles 2 and 3). The Act enabled the government to ordain the handing over of any factory producing goods of prime necessity, i.e. not only those supplying the army (Article 4). Compulsory labour could be ordered not only for military type of work, but any work of "public utility," to which women could also be compelled (Article 5). The amendment of 1915 (Law XIII of 1915) extended the rights of the government concerning the declaration of reserve stocks. Article 1 of the amendment of the Act on War Services, passed in 1916 (Law VI of 1916) raised the age limit of those liable to compulsory labour to 55 years.

There were other laws, too, passed partly before and partly during the war, which gave the government ample authority to regulate the economy extensively during the war. The state control of the economy, even if limiting to a certain extent the circulation and free action of capital, did not hamper, but rather favoured, the increase of profits for monopolies and banks. The state-monopolistic tendencies, which had been present everywhere before the war, strengthened with the militarization of the econ-

Excerpt from *Hungary and the First World War* by Josef Galantai, Akademiai Kiado, 1989, pp. 80–84. Reprinted with permission.

omy. The same process could be observed in all belligerent countries, and even in the developed neutral countries. It was in Germany that state control of the economy was the most extensive, but it was quite extensive in both countries of the Monarchy as well. The report of the Hungarian Trade Bank made in 1915 also indicates the measures taken by the Hungarian state to this effect: "The entirety of our economic life has been transformed into war economy . . . The most delicate and most flexible internal functioning of the economic system, the scope of individual enterprise until now, is becoming more and more dependent on state supervision and sober control."

The first few months following the outbreak of the war were characterized by considerable economic confusion. Industrial production, especially that of consumer goods, diminished. Thus, in spite of the great number of people called up, unemployment was a serious problem in the first few months. "The labour supply in general exceeded the demand ten times." Already in the autumn of 1914 many basic goods were lacking. . . . In the first month of the war Tisza was still reluctant to fix the prices officially. He was afraid that "fixed maximum prices will in fact immediately become minimum prices, because the official price-list legitimates high prices." Therefore he advised the leading officials of towns to organize the market. This procedure, however, could only be successful if at least minimum supply of markets could be ensured and if there was no hoarding. But both these conditions were lacking, and in November, Tisza also tried fixing the maximum prices. All this resulted in serious provisionment troubles during the first winter, especially in the north-eastern and southern parts of the country, in the towns situated near the operational areas. In February 1915 the municipalities or mayors of certain towns asked the prime minister by wire to take steps immediately. On February 22 Tisza warned the lord lieutenants of the counties to use the reserves "economically," since "we have no more reserve supplies at our disposal," and only in this way could the bread supply be ensured until the next harvest. He promised that the government would also try to do away with the black market. All this brought little help. Therefore, for the sake of more systematic consumption of supplies the government ordered in the spring of 1915 the general use of flour coupons, which was the first step towards the introduction of rationing.

In his book published after the war, János Teleszky, the finance minister of the Tisza government characterized the autumn months of 1914 as "the first shock of the economy brought about by the outbreak of the war." Later, industry switched over to war production, and in many branches production increased, owing to the war boom, and also to state intervention. The period which followed the shock of the first few months, and which lasted until about mid-1916, Teleszky writes, "was characterized by the adaptation of the economy to the war as well as by its growth due to the initial inflation which was hardly even suspected apart from a few initiated." The whole system of war economy was entirely completed in this period. . . .

More rational use of the raw material supply also demanded the extension of war economy. Since the Central Powers were under a blockade which was becoming more and more efficient, there was soon a shortage of raw materials. . . . Following the German model the state encouraged the creation of central organs in the major industries for inventory keeping and purchasing the stocks for the industry in question and for the transaction of the war contracts. This system was also expected to put an end to the abuses connected with the war contracts; serious cases of abuse came to light as early as 1915. . . .

In order to ensure the undisturbed functioning of the war economy as well as an obedient and cheap labour force, the workers of 263 companies were placed under military supervision by the end of October 1915.

In spite of the rising prices, wages did not generally rise in the first year of the war. In the beginning they even decreased in certain branches and certain factories. In vain did the Ironworkers' Trade Union protest that obliging the workers to work in specified factories meant diminishing wages. . . . In the spring of 1915 the trade unions and the social democratic press protested against the treatment which even exceeded the severity of the war services act, but with very little success. In an embittered article published . . . in the summer of 1915 we can read: "Wages are not rising, but even sagging. Food prices have risen by 100 and 200 per cent. With the same wages we can now buy only half, or even less, of what we could buy earlier . . . We cannot bear this any longer!" . . .

The war meant a great financial burden. According to the quota in force, Hungary had to contribute 36.4 per cent of the costs of maintenance of the army. This meant a sum of nearly a hundred thousand crowns in the first three months of the war. Already in the first year the military expenses multiplied, especially after Italy's entry into the war, when the expenses of the navy also rose considerably. The government partly covered these huge surplus expenses by issuing paper money, i.e. by starting inflation. At the end of 1915 the amount of paper money in circulation was already double the amount at the outbreak of the war. In addition, the government also tried to cover the expenses by external and internal state loans. Among the latter, war bonds were the most important. The first ones were issued in November 1914, and they were followed by others every six months. Through inflation and war loans, the bulk of the financial burdens of the war was directly shifted to everyday working people.

In spite of the war boom, agricultural production gradually decreased in the first years of the war. The large-scale drafting and the destruction of the animal and horse stock had a considerable influence on extensive agriculture, since there was a shortage of manpower and draught animals. The Monarchy needed about a hundred million quintals of corn annually. In the five years preceding the war, there had been an average annual surplus of 4,600,000 quintals. In 1914, however, there was a bad harvest, and the yield only covered nine-tenths of the domestic demand. This is why there were difficulties of supply already during the first winter. The results of 1915 were even worse: two-fifths of the demand was already lacking. As to the yield of 1916, it could only cover 63 per cent of the demand. They tried to reduce the manpower shortage by putting prisoners of war to work. There was a good opportunity to do this in the summer of 1915, when the Monarchy took many prisoners on the eastern front. Mechanization also increased, although on a limited scale only: due to the war conditions, the industry was producing fewer and fewer agricultural machines. Exploiting the productive capacity of the soil did not help, but rather hurt the outlook of agriculture. After the rationing of flour, bread rationing started in December 1915.

2. ECONOMIC EXHAUSTION
IN SOUTHEASTERN EUROPE

The following selection provides further evidence, taken from the prestigious series
of studies commissioned after the war by the Carnegie Endowment, of the inability of
the Austro-Hungarian authorities to stave off eventual collapse. Note how the gradual
erosion of economic production prepared the way for both defeat and eventual revolution.

The Four Stages of Economic Exhaustion

The evolution of the economic situation during the War shows for every group of
objects, whether actually used in the conduct of war or in everyday life, a growing and
parallel exhaustion. That process of exhaustion passed in almost every case through four
phases, each of which had its own peculiar characteristics. The first phase lasted from the
outbreak of the War until the beginning of the first winter of war. During that time the
disturbance caused by the conflict in economic life was violent in the extreme. It
showed itself first in the undermining, for various reasons, of certain branches of production. A first reason was the sudden calling up of workers; many undertakings which
were not engaged on war work thus had to close their doors, simply because they did
not see whence they could get the necessary labor. At the same time the usual markets
were utterly upset; exports were almost wholly cut off, and at home trade in anything
but necessaries was at first at a standstill. Again, many industries were faced at once with
a lack of raw materials, not necessarily because there was a shortage of them, but because
the available supplies, having been requisitioned for military purposes, were not to be
had at all, or only at exorbitant cost, for private needs. The conditions of the money
market further contributed to that disturbance. The raising of the bank rate from 5 to 6
and then to 8 per cent had a discouraging effect on industry; so had the moratorium
proclaimed at once at the outbreak of the War, as it impeded the free use of bank
deposits. Moreover, the immediate cessation of all public works also reacted upon industry; and the complete suspension of all private railway traffic as long as the mobilization lasted, that is till the end of August, had, like the sudden departure of the workers,
a bewildering effect both on industry and on agriculture.

The abrupt disturbance caused through these circumstances lasted, however, no
more than a few weeks. By the end of August industry was already recovering from the
first shock. Indispensable skilled workers were being released from military service, and
women began to take the place of the absent men. The loss of foreign markets was made
up for by fresh demand at home, especially from the army, which absorbed almost
everything that any industry could produce. Private industries suffered at first, because
private demand was disturbed, while the army seemed to have everything in excess.

Excerpt from *The Effect of the War in Southeastern Europe* by D. Mitrany, pp. 157–161. Copyright © 1936
Yale University Press. Reprinted by permission of the publisher.

They began to recover as soon as it became clear that the needs of the army could not be satisfied by the few firms which had been producing war material already before the War, and that as large a number of industrial undertakings as possible would have to be enlisted for the production of military supplies. A few months passed, of course, before the readjustment could be made; during that period the army was insufficiently supplied, though in a decreasing measure. The exhaustion of available supplies was not fully over-come till the spring of 1915. During that phase one can distinguish thus three periods. The first was characterized by profusion in the army and shortage in private industry; the second, during the autumn of 1914, on the contrary by profusion in industry and shortage in army supplies; while a state of balance was reached only in the spring of 1915, a period which marked the second phase of war economics. During that first period began the process of inflation; at first it passed almost unnoticed, but later it had an enormous influence on the whole process of exhaustion. At the time one had the impression that the revival in industry had brought with it easier conditions in the money market.

With the spring of 1915 began the second phase. It had all the appearance of a time of economic prosperity. Industry was in full activity, and the needs of the army were being satisfied with relative ease. According to normal economic standards a steady de-mand and a tendency toward rising prices are the tests of a good situation. During that second phase industry enjoyed an almost limitless demand at continually rising prices. Profits were great, new fortunes were rapidly made, and all means and resources were thrown into the process of reproduction so as to exploit those favorable conditions. Little notice was taken at the time of the loss in the internal value of the money thus gained. More and more factories were being placed in the service of the army. A few special materials were getting short, but were replaced with substitutes; coal and iron were still sufficient. The textile industry was working at full speed and the shortage in cotton did not begin to make itself felt until the second half of 1915. Agriculture, espe-cially in Hungary and in the regions which lay outside the battle zone, reached in 1915 nearly the harvest of normal years, notwithstanding the loss of men and animals.

The real nature of that flushed prosperity was not then realized. It had its roots in fact in the enormous increase of the currency in circulation. By that means ready money was always available for the immense orders of the army, and the prices paid for them could be ever higher. . . . This effect was perhaps more powerful in Austria and Hung-ary than in the Western states. As the blockade and other restrictive measures had closed most of the avenues through which money went abroad, the currency was continually coming back into circulation within the country. Inflation and the consequent rise in prices were thus the means through which the necessary sacrifice and limitations were imposed upon the population, and also the means for drawing upon the capital resources of the nation for purposes of war. What on the surface, therefore, appeared as a flour-ishing state of economic life, in reality was a creeping process of destruction of capital values. "Capital resources which were meant to be placed in the service of production were used up for military ends; they were gradually destroyed and could never again serve the ends of production." This phase of fictitious prosperity was also relatively the easiest for the army. Of the three levels of exhaustion — shortage, lack, and want —

only the first was felt at all so far, and even that not generally. It was pointed out with relief that the disturbed conditions which had prevailed at first had been overcome, and that the production of war material had reached a very high level.

Gradually, however, certain ominously dark spots began to appear on the horizon. Among the first and the most serious was the institution of a closer blockade, in March, 1915. By the autumn a number of raw materials were running short, though not all of them. A severe shortage only began to be felt in 1916 — in wool, cotton, leather, iron; coal only in the winter of 1916–1917; animals and special metals by the spring of 1917, when the army also began to have difficulties with man-power. "If 1915 was a year, if only in appearance, of a flourishing economic state, 1916 was a year of growing shortage, 1917 a year of transition from shortage to want, and 1918 a year of extreme want." Taken as a whole, one can identify 1917 with the third phase of war economics. It was characterized by the struggle against exhaustion, which in truth was often no more than a struggle for postponing exhaustion. The supply of corn had become so inadequate that the Monarchy had to be helped by Germany; the worst was for a time warded off by exploiting the occupied territories. The replenishing of the army ranks was also getting difficult. A special office was set up behind the front to weed out every likely man for military service. This led to a shortage of labor and, therefore, to a growing use of prisoners of war. In the textile as well as in the munition industries only substitutes were available as raw materials; the quality was bad, but at least the quantity could still be made up.

Exhaustion began to creep in also in the spirit of the people. It was evident in the feverish atmosphere of the parliamentary bodies, and in a declining enthusiasm for the War. Extreme radical sentiments and slogans began to appear instead, and the people listened with increasing approval to those ideas and men who were least in sympathy with the War. Common sense demanded at that juncture an effort to end the War. The leaders of the Monarchy made indeed the well-known overtures for peace, but they failed. War had assumed the nature of an elemental phenomenon which could not be stopped at will at any given moment.

During 1918 it became logically clear that exhaustion could no longer be avoided. The supply of food was utterly inadequate, and only desperate efforts could keep it even at that low level. In certain regions the shortage had become chronic and was marked by occasional famines. The mortality rate rose rapidly, especially among elderly people and children. "No one will say it, yet everyone knows that they died of hunger." The shortage of food reacted on the production of coal. By the winter of 1917–1918 hundreds of thousands were already living in dark and unheated rooms. The lack of coal in its turn reacted on the production of munitions. At a joint Ministerial Council the head of the General Staff complained that the supply of munitions had fallen to the disastrous level of the autumn of 1914. People were going about in torn and patched clothes that offered scant protection against the weather. The shortage of fats was so acute that all sorts of experiments were tried, such as the attempt to extract fats from wild chestnuts and from rats. Even paper had become so short that the Government instructed all official departments and public institutions to surrender those parts of their archives which were not indispensable.

Nor did the army fare much better. July and August, 1918, were months of real hunger. For days on end the troops saw neither meat nor fats. Sawdust had to be added repeatedly to the available quantities of flour. It came about that whole detachments "deserted" with all their equipment from the base camps to the front line, because there they were entitled to one or two ounces more food. An examination along one section of the Italian front established that the average weight of individual soldiers was no more than fifty kilograms. Hardly a soldier possessed any longer a complete set of clothing. Some had a uniform but no underwear, others had underwear but no uniform; and all of them were in rags.

3. Weakness of the Italian Economy

Though officially bound as a Triple Alliance member to enter the war on behalf of Germany and Austria-Hungary, Italy declined to do so in 1914, claiming that such provisions applied only to a defensive war and that the two Central Powers had in fact been the aggressors in the July crisis. Determined to liberate "unredeemed Italy" from Austrian possession, the Italian government entered the war in 1915 on the side of the Triple Entente. But as even sympathetic observers noted, Italy still lacked many of the attributes of a first-rank power. Sidney Low, an Englishman with firsthand knowledge of Italy, though he is best known as the official biographer of Britain's King Edward VII, offers observations on Italy's economic state in the following selection.

[Italy] had allowed her military establishment to fall as far below the requisite level, judged by the new standard which the Central Alliance had set, as Britain, even though, unlike Britain, she had the system of national service in good working order. But her statesmen, intent upon internal politics and the rivalries of peace, hypnotised, some of them, by the Teuton magic, had never found time to master the elements of modern military science. The arsenals were unequal to a sudden and much increased demand; heavy guns, and machine-guns, and even rifles were utterly insufficient; there were no large reserves of explosives and projectiles. The organisation of all the supply services was antiquated and imperfect. In August, 1914, Italy would have had little to oppose to the well-equipped legions of her enemy except plenty of willing hearts, strong arms, and energetic brains.

Fortunately she was not called upon to plunge into war, like England, at a few days' notice. She allowed herself a breathing space of nearly ten months, and those months were well used. But her disadvantages were numerous and severe. Britain, after all, was the first industrial community of the world, with almost unlimited productive resources, that required to be directed rather than enlarged in order to supply the needs of the armies.

Italy was in a very different position. Her industries had been rapidly increasing during the previous three decades, but she was still not in the front rank, or even barely

Excerpt from *Italy in the War* by Sidney Low, Longmans, 1916, pp. 217–219.

in the second rank, of the great manufacturing nations. In metallic and mechanical production in particular she stood far below Great Britain, the United States, Germany,
France, and even Russia and Belgium. Busy and active as were the Milanese, Turin, and
the Genoese Riviera, there was no Italian "black country," no such tracts seamed with
mines, and scarred with foundries and blast furnaces, as Lancashire, Westphalia, the Sarr
Valley, or the occupied districts of North-Eastern France and Western Russia.

Of coal Italy had next to none; of iron and steel very little; she had fine workshops
and factories but not too many of them.

For her machinery and hardware generally, she had been largely dependent on
Germany. Her engineers are of the best, in some branches of metal work like electric
welding and iron casting she has no superiors, her artisans, mechanics are as skilful,
laborious, and persevering as any in the world. But her industrial army was still weak
and it was cantoned in small portions of the Peninsula.

It was necessary both to extend and to mobilise industry for war purposes. This task,
after the first period of indecision and dissension had gone by, has been pursued in Italy
with a quiet intensity that has borne amazing results. Like all the Latin countries Italy has
suffered from overcentralisation and the excessive power of a bureaucratic hierarchy.
Where "the State" does much it is always easier for the State to do more. The Italian
administrators, when they set to work in earnest to concentrate national activities on the
one indispensable object, did not find themselves brought up at every turn by an inher-
ited distrust of governmental action and a rooted individualism. There was no trouble
in Italy about labour dilution, longer hours, or the control and diversion of output. That
the Government, in the greatest of all emergencies, should dispose of every man's activity and deal at its will with his property did not seem unreasonable to people, trained to
obedience by administrative autocracy, and by the conscription.

4. MOBILIZING ITALIAN WORKERS

As a consequence of deficiencies in industrial development and constitutional authority, the Italian war effort was marked by a strong military presence without a counter-
balancing parliamentary influence. Rampant inflation, work stoppages, and disputes
over harsh discipline are just some of the results outlined by a recent student of
Italian labor history.

Industrial Mobilization

Industrial Mobilization, regulating the development of the economy and industrial relations during the First World War, was established in Italy in 1915 by two decree laws,
i.e. without preliminary parliamentary discussion. These decrees were No. 993 dated 26
June 1915 and No. 1271 dated 22 August 1915 (the IM *Regolamento*). These were car-

"Industrial Mobilization and the Labour Market in Italy During the First World War" by Luigi Tomassini
from *Social History* 16 (1991), pp. 59–64, 68.

ried out by an under-secretariat for Arms and Munitions within the Ministry of War, set up under decree law 9 July 1915 and headed by General Alfredo Dallolio, who had previously been Director General of Artillery and Engineering. Subsequently, in June 1917, a Ministry of Arms and Munitions was established with Dallolio at its head.

The appointment of a military officer as head of the branch of government responsible for Industrial Mobilization (in contrast to the situation in France and England, the main allied powers serving as inspiration for IM) was highly significant. On the one hand, the appointment of a general demonstrated the intention of dealing firmly with labour issues. On the other, it probably reflected the fact that Italian industry was not in a position to exert sufficient corporate leadership to sustain a full-scale war which would absorb all the resources of the nation. This was not only a result of the structural inadequacy of the industrial sector, just emerging from the "take-off" stage and certainly not yet to be compared with that of the other great powers, but also of the marked conflict within the sector itself between hostile financial / industrial groups. This was reflected in the issue of the "naturalization" of industries, which erupted into bitter controversy from the very start of the hostilities.

In this context, the appointment of a military officer to head Industrial Mobilization, along with the fact that IM itself was initially only an administrative branch of the Ministry of War, demonstrated the force of state intervention in this sector. The military had always represented one of the state's strongest components and was a traditional means of affirming state intervention, being to some degree independent of the interests of the political economic sectors and the social groups represented in parliament. Through IM, the state took charge of controlling the overall planning of mobilizing industrial production, centralizing to a large extent decisions relevant to the management of the economy, redistributing of orders, price control and contract terms. Conversely, entrepreneurs were left alone as regards the internal organization of their work. The state refrained from regulating — probably more so than in other nations — the distribution of raw materials and the flow of manpower controlled by Industrial Mobilization, according to criteria linked to productivity (only towards the end of the war was there some revision of this). The system also guaranteed high profits, thus leaving room for marginal enterprises as well as allowing the larger ones to make enormous reinvestments and to achieve, in many cases, a high degree of independence from their traditional borrowing from banks.

All this did not occur automatically or immediately. It was a gradual process, marked by uncertainties and doubts. . . . Initially the Industrial Mobilization projects in Italy closely followed those of the similar agency in France, stressing the organization of private groups, with "group leaders" and with regional committees headed by the chairmen of the chamber of commerce of the most important city (and thus with representatives freely elected by the industrialists). In the end, however, the approved *Regolamento* provided for a series of regional committees (seven in all, with headquarters at Turin, Genoa, Milan, Bologna, Rome, Naples and Palermo), headed by military officers (generals or admirals) with a solid military-style bureaucratic structure. The representatives of the industrialists, nominated by the Ministry, were joined by an equal number of labour representatives. The inclusion of labour representatives is, in itself, an indication of the fundamental importance attached to labour by this new and definitive organization. As is clearly revealed by the statements made by the leaders of Industrial Mobilization, the organization was created "essentially to discipline labour, so that it does not become a disturbing element, but rather a factor for production and progress." The main penalty for industrialists, which was so important in the British case, i.e. requisition, no longer appeared in the regulations, although it had been provided for in the first decree (of 26 June 1915). It was not simply forgotten. As the ministerial report explained, it was decided from the beginning to refrain from applying such severe measures, for the following reasons:

> Requisition should take place when the industrialists refuse to work and to produce of their own accord. . . . Let us not deceive ourselves . . . the government is bound to be a slower, and perhaps even less efficient, industrialist than the private concerns; so that production, in its hands, instead of increasing, would probably decrease and become more expensive.

In other words, from the very beginning Industrial Mobilization directed its controlling and co-ordinating forces toward the labour question much more than toward matters more directly concerning industry.

Several times during the war, and especially toward the end of the conflict, the members of the Central Committee of IM openly deplored the fact that, as one of them put it, the activities of the highest assembly of Industrial Mobilization were limited to those of "mediator between capital and labour." The central and most interesting factor was that, for the first time, a state agency was formed for the purpose of intervening directly and expressly, with continuity and with ample powers, in the relationship between industrialists and workers. This, of course, had obvious consequences for the evolution of the relationship between the social classes involved — especially concerning the labour market.

The first factor to be kept in mind in understanding the type of state intervention which applied in Italy is that, in comparison with other countries, especially those of the chief allied powers (France and England), Italian Industrial Mobilization was marked from the beginning by very strong intervention (to use the terminology of the era) in the "labour issue." For the ruling classes in Italy two questions were of fundamental importance, one more specifically political, the other having important economic and social aspects. The first question derived from the fact that, unlike the other powers mentioned, Italy had entered the war without being able to count on the support of the most important working-class party. It is well known that the position of the Italian Socialist Party, as Lenin himself observed, was very different from that of the other great parties of the Second International. This was the reason for the intense concern felt by the Italian leaders about the possibility of popular dissent, as well as for the severity of Italian Industrial Mobilization regarding the discipline of mobilized labour. The second problem was the need, common to all the great powers involved in the conflict, to conciliate the demands of the armed forces for men to send to the front while leaving industry enough manpower to ensure production of the increasingly larger amounts of materials required for war purposes. In the other nations — France in particular — this problem was not felt initially, provisions being taken step by step as the war went on. The Italian government, which had maintained a neutral stance for almost a year, issued regulations which took account of this requirement. From this came the special interest shown from the very beginning by Italian Industrial Mobilization in the regulation of the labour market. The dual objective was that of keeping skilled labourers in their posts and limiting the mobility of unskilled labour, as well as preventing excessive wage increases.

The Labour Market

According to IM authorities, the "labour problem," as it appeared in the first months of war, consisted mainly of labour market instability, with the "continuous passage of personnel from one factory to another, in search of higher wages, often at the invitation of the industrialists themselves, who thus became each other's worst competitors." Although unskilled labour had always been plentiful in Italy, skilled workers, who were now in great demand due to the sudden expansion of the metallurgical / mechanical sector that accompanied the outbreak of war, were rather scarce. Consequently, steps had to be taken to prevent the "labour manhunt," initiated by industrialists at the outbreak of the conflict, from resulting in excessive imbalances in the labour market in favour of the workers.

The militarization of factory personnel in Italy was used not only to ensure discipline but also to resolve, through coercive measures, the problem of labour market regulation. . . . Essentially this was achieved through the initial provisions of IM, instituted in August 1915, which included a very radical set of measures. The most important of these were militarization of personnel in the "auxiliary" plants, freezing of contracts and abrogation of the right of workers to leave their jobs.

Under these regulations, a worker could no longer leave his job in order to accept work in another company offering better conditions. Labourers could ask for neither wage increases nor better terms, since work contracts were prorogated up to the end of the war. Lastly, although the law did not normally abrogate the right to strike, the workers could not do so. With the militarization of the plants, leaving one's place of work was forbidden, with punishment for desertion dictated by the extremely harsh military penal code. Basically, militarization of the labour force in the auxiliary factories took two forms. The first was that of exoneration which, while formally considering the militarized worker as belonging to the army and subject to its discipline, allowed him to continue to dress in civilian clothes and to lead a normal civilian life. The second was direct militarization of factory personnel, in which the worker could be assigned to a division of the territorial army, obliged to wear uniform, to take his meals in the barracks, and contribute part of his wages to military administration. There was thus a significant difference between exonerated workers and military workers proper, affecting living conditions as well as discipline and wages.

The maximum increase in the utilization of military workers took place during the period from Autumn 1915 to the end of 1916. In January 1917, military workers accounted for more than 40 per cent of total male workers subject to military obligations in the auxiliary plants. During this period, moreover, IM went so far as to consider the advisability of consolidating the various categories of militarized personnel by transforming all of the exonerated workers into uniformed military labourers. A survey was conducted among industrialists, who almost unanimously declared their enthusiasm for the project, mainly for disciplinary reasons, but also because of other advantages such as production and wages.

The Ministry of War was opposed to the plan on the grounds that the advantages for the industrialists did not compensate for the burden placed on the administration of the state. This was one of the first cases in which the interests of the state openly conflicted with those of the industrialists. Thus, for the duration of the war, there were two categories of militarized labourers in Italy, one consisting roughly of those members of the working class who were in the factories at the moment at which they were subjected to the authority of IM (exonerated), the other of those who came later (military workers). . . .

The obligations deriving from militarization were not limited to the militarized workers, however. Workers with no military obligations (minors, women, the elderly) were subject to some degree of military discipline, and were not allowed to leave one job for another, but they could strike without incurring the severe sanctions to which the militarized workers were subject. . . .

In a country such as Italy, which had an extremely fragmented industrial base, this transfer from small- to large-scale industry undoubtedly had a significant modernizing effect, contributing to the formation of a new working class — new not only in its sociological origins but also in its relationship with the more advanced and modern productive processes. Although sufficient statistics are not available it seems that, during the first months of the war, many of the male workers flowing to militarized big industry were craftsmen or journeymen from other sectors. They chose to enter the great factories, the metallurgical and mechanical ones in particular, because the sectors from which they came were in crisis, but also, and chiefly, in order to avoid the prospect of military service at the front. Many of these workers came from very well-paid jobs and often possessed a strong leftist political background, in line with the typical "subversiveness" of the urban working classes, which occurred even outside big industry in Italy at that time. This may help to explain — along with the fact that the exceptional situation of war was a very strong cohesive element, encouraging working-class solidarity — why there was no appreciable conflict between the old skilled labour force and the new one which grew up during the course of the hostilities.

5. RUSSIA'S ECONOMIC SITUATION

Mikhail Rodzianko was president of the Russian Duma, the legislature grudgingly conceded by Nicholas II in the wake of the Revolution of 1905. His recital of the deteriorating domestic situation provides an interesting parallel with the deficiencies in Italy and Austria-Hungary.

Soon after the first battles, shocking reports came from the front of the incompetency of the sanitary department, of its inability to handle the wounded at the front. There was great confusion. Freight trains came to Moscow filled with wounded, lying on the bare floor, without even straw, in many cases without clothing, poorly bandaged, and unfed. At this time my wife was patroness of the Elizabeth Society [Red Cross organization] and it was reported to her that such trains passed the field units of her society, stopping sometimes at the stations, but that those in charge would not allow the sisters to enter the cars. There was a certain amount of undesirable rivalry between the Ministry of War and the Red Cross. Each acted independently of the other and there was no coördination.

The War Department was particularly weak in first aid. Though it had neither carts, horses, nor first aid material, yet it allowed no other organization on the field. There seemed no other course than to bring the state of affairs to the attention of Grand Duke Nicholas Nicholaevich. I wrote him a letter in which I told him that patriotic enthusiasm had called forth a number of volunteer sanitary organizations, but that they could do nothing because of Evdokimov, the head of the sanitary division of the Ministry of War. Realizing that the volunteer organizations were of a higher order than his, and not willing to admit it, Evdokimov was doing everything that he could to block their efforts. But wounded cannot wait; they must be looked after; the fighting line must be provided with first aid. There must be no loss of time. In view of the fact that it was impossible to bring about a working agreement between the sanitary division and the volunteer organizations, it would be well to appoint some one with dictatorial powers to take charge of both and bring about some order.

I went also to see the old Empress, Marie Fedorovna, who lived on Elagin Island. When I told her the situation she was horrified. "Tell me, what should be done?" asked the Empress.

I advised her to send a telegram to Nicholas Nicholaevich urging him to command Evdokimov to put things in order and to allow the Red Cross to go to work. She asked me to write such a telegram in her name.

As a result of these efforts there came a telegram, followed by a letter, from the Grand Duke stating that he agreed with the president of the Duma, and that he would take the necessary measures. Soon after that Evdokimov was called to Headquarters. A little later Prince Alexander Petrovich of Oldenburg was made the head of the sanitary-evacuation division with dictatorial powers.

Grand Duke Nicholas wrote me that he had long before insisted on the removal of Evdokimov, but that it could not be done because he had the protection of Sukhomlinov and the Empress Alexandra Fedorovna. It was said that the young Empress persuaded the Emperor to leave Evdokimov in his place in order to spite the old Empress. . . .

Soon after my arrival at Warsaw in November [O. S.], 1914, I had a call from

"Rodzianko's Memoirs" from Frank Alfred Golder, *Documents of Russian History,* pp. 82–83, 101–102. Peter Smith Publisher, Inc.: 1964 Gloucester, MA. Reprinted with permission.

Vyrubov [V. V.], a representative of the Zemstvo Union, who asked me to go with him to the Warsaw-Vienna station where there were about eighteen thousand men, wounded in the battles near Lodz and Berezina. There I saw a frightful scene. On the floor, without even a bedding of straw, in mud and slush, lay innumerable wounded, whose pitiful groans and cries filled the air. "For God's sake, get them to attend to us. No one has looked after our wounds for five days."

It should be said that after these bloody battles the wounded were thrown into freight cars without order, and thrown out at this station without attention. The only medical aid they received was from Warsaw doctors and nurses, about fifteen in all, belonging to a Polish organization which volunteered its services. . . . I do not know their names, but with all my soul I hope that the hearty thanks of a Russian may reach them, as well as my highest respect and praise. When I was at the station, these good people had been steadily at work for three days without rest. . . .

Conditions in the country went from bad to worse. Profiteering, graft, and the accumulation of great riches by clever people reached enormous proportions. In the cities, the cost of living mounted, due to the disorganized transport service. In the factories doing war work, there were strikes followed by arrests, usually of those who were for order and against quitting work. . . .

With some other members of the Duma, I went to the Putilov works to find out about the war orders and talk to the workmen. The laborers were quite frank. They assured us that the strikes had no political motive, but were due to the fact that the wages were falling below the high cost of the necessaries of life. After we had talked it over with the management, the just demands of the workers were granted. But, as if on purpose, the men with whom we talked were arrested. These arrests led to more trouble, and it was only after urgent demands that the workmen were freed.

At the beginning of December Prince Lvov, head of the Union of Zemstvos, came to Petrograd. He called on me, and we sat up until three in the morning discussing the situation. He told me that Moscow was becoming more and more revolutionary. Some of the most loyal people talked openly of the collapse of the Government and laid the blame on the Tsar and Tsarina.

6. ORGANIZING RAW MATERIALS IN GERMANY

Walther Rathenau, one of Germany's most prominent industrialists, was director of the AEG (the General Electric Company), which his father founded. But it was more than mere nepotism that made him influential, and the energetic Rathenau took the initiative in persuading the German government to consider the economic consequences of total war. He organized and headed the KRA (Raw Materials Section), and the address that follows gives an indication of both the direction of his own thoughts on total war and the inadequacy of existing preparations. Rathenau, a Jew, was equally prominent during the early Weimar Republic and was assassinated by right-wing gunmen in 1922.

The object of my paper is to report to you a new departure in our economic warfare which has no precedent in history, which will have a decided influence on the war, and which in all probability is destined to affect future times. In its methods it is closely akin to communism and yet it departs essentially from the prophecies and demands resulting from radical theories. It is not my purpose to give an account of a rigid system based on theories, but I shall relate how this system grew out of our actual life, first taking concrete form in a small group, then affecting ever widening circles, and finally bringing about a complete change in our economic life. Its visible result is a new department attached to the War Office which places our whole economic life in the service of the war. . . .

"Organization and administration of raw materials!" Abstract terms, lifeless words, and yet terms of great significance if we fully realize their meaning. If we look around us: our tools and building materials, our clothing, our food, our armaments, our means of transportation, all depend on foreign materials, for the economic life of all nations is closely interrelated. . . .

Even more serious is the problem of armament and defense, above all in a country surrounded and blockaded by the enemy. Daily we hear the food question discussed. And yet our country is able to produce 80 per cent of what is needed. Completely surrounded and cut off, we may be restricted, but we cannot be annihilated. The case is totally different regarding the raw materials needed for warfare: to be cut off from all such sources of supply might spell destruction.

Look at a map of Europe and study the location of the Central Powers; it is as though a demon had drawn the boundaries, for only a very few strategic points need to be taken by our enemy, and the colossal area will be cut off. It is true we have access to three seas, but what are they? They are landlocked inland seas. The Baltic is accessible only through a channel; the North Sea is blocked by the English Channel, by the Orkney and Shetland Islands; the Mediterranean Sea is blocked both in the east and in the west. And back of these landlocked seas there is in the north but a poor country unable to give us a plentiful supply of materials needed, and in the south beyond the Mediterranean Sea the desert, not crossed by railways or trade routes that might bring us in contact with the great centers of productivity.

When on August 4 of last year England declared war our country became a beleaguered fortress. Cut off by land and cut off by sea it was made wholly self-dependent; we were facing a war the duration, cost, danger, and sacrifices of which no one could foresee.

When three days had passed after England had declared war I could no longer stand the agony. I called on the Chief of the War Department, Colonel Scheuch, and on the evening of the same day I was kindly received by him. I explained to him that I was convinced that the supply of the absolutely needed raw materials on hand could probably last only a limited number of months. Colonel Scheuch shared my opinion that the

Reprinted from *Fall of the German Empire, 1914–1918,* Vol. II, edited by Ralph Haswell Lutz, pp. 77–84, 90–91, with the permission of the publishers, Stanford University Press. Copyright © 1932 by the Board of Trustees of the Leland Stanford Junior University.

war would be one of long duration, and so I was forced to ask him, "What has been done and what can be done to avert the danger that Germany will be strangled?"

Very little had been done in the past, but much has been done since the interest of the War Department has been aroused. Returning home deeply concerned and worried I found a telegram from von Falkenhayn, then Minister of War, asking me to come to his office the next morning. . . .

Our discussion lasted the greater part of the forenoon, and when it was ended the Minister of War had decided to establish an organization, no matter whether great or small, provided it had authority and was efficient and able to solve the problem which we were facing. . . .

I was about to take leave, but the Minister detained me by making the unexpected demand that I should undertake to organize the work. . . .

The first problem was the question of available supplies. It was necessary to ascertain the period of months for which the country was provided with the indispensable materials. Any further action depended on that. Opinions received from the great industries were quite contradictory.

Having asked the authorities if statistics might be furnished, I was informed that such statistics might be worked out but that it would probably take six months to do so. When I stated that I must have them within a fortnight because the matter was urgent I was assured that that was quite impossible. Yet I had to have them; and I had them within fourteen days.

We were forced to take a daring step, namely, we had to rely on a hypothesis. And this hypothesis proved to be reliable. We started with the assumption that the store of supplies available for the whole country would be approximately equal to the available supply stored by any large group of industries. The War Office did business with some 900 or 1,000 concerns. . . . Few of the materials needed for the army were available in quantities sufficient for a year (and since that time the yearly demands of the army have substantially increased); in most cases they were considerably less.

At first we were concerned with only a small number of materials. The whole fields of foodstuffs and of liquid fuel were excluded; included was everything called "raw materials." The official definition gave the following interpretation: "Such materials as are needed for the defense of the country and which cannot be produced within the country at all times and in sufficient quantities." At first hardly more than a dozen of such indispensable materials were enumerated; the number, however, increased from week to week and has now passed the hundred mark. . . .

Four measures appeared feasible and worth trying out for reconstructing our economic policies so as to afford proper protection for the country.

First: Coercive measures had to be adopted regarding the use of all raw materials in the country. No material must be used arbitrarily, or for luxury, or for anything that is not absolutely needed. The needs of the army are of paramount importance and everything must be directed toward that ultimate end. That was our first and most difficult task. . . .

The third way of solving the problem was through manufacture. Anything indispensable and not procurable must be manufactured within the country. New methods of manufacture had to be invented and developed wherever the old technique was inadequate.

And now the fourth measure: Materials difficult to obtain must be replaced by others more easily procurable. It is not ordained that this or that object must be made of copper or of aluminum; it may be made of some other material. Substitutes must be found. Instead of using the time-honored materials for our household goods, etc., we must use new substances, and articles must be manufactured that do not require so much raw material. . . .

To solve the problems confronting us we needed the co-operation of many bureaus and of the several Federal Governments. During the first few days we received very encouraging replies from the three ministries of war outside of Prussia, expressing their willingness to permit Prussia to establish the organization. That meant considerable simplification. But we had to carry on negotiations with many more bureaus, authorities, and officials.

The very fact that the problem was not understood caused many difficulties. Up to the present the German people believed that the supply of raw materials takes care of itself. The food question is being discussed all day long; the question of raw materials is hardly mentioned. Even now it is hard for us to realize what the situation was at the beginning of the war. For the first six months no one had any idea what we were trying to do. . . .

. . . It was necessary to establish and formulate new and fundamental ideas upon which the reorganization of our economic life could rest. The term "sequestration" . . . was given a new interpretation, somewhat arbitrarily, I admit, but supported by certain passages in our martial law. At a later period our interpretation was sanctioned by law.

"Sequestration" does not mean that merchandise or material . . . is seized by the state but only that it is restricted, i.e., that it no longer can be disposed of by the owner at will but must be reserved for a more important purpose (or, that it must be put at the disposal of a higher authority). The merchandise must be used for war purposes only: it may be sold, manufactured, shipped, transformed; but no matter what is done to it, it always remains subject to the law that it must be used for war purposes only. . . .

Within two months German industrial life was readjusted. It was done quietly, without a breakdown, with self-confidence and energy, and with magnificent efficiency. . . .

So much regarding sequestration. Its effect was the reorganization of our industries. And now I approach the second factor. . . .

. . . New agencies had to be created for gathering, storing, and distributing the material circulating in a new form through the arteries of German commerce. A new system had to be created, that of the *Kriegswirtschafts-Gesellschaften* (War Industries Boards). Today we are as accustomed to them as if they had been handed down from time immemorial. But at first they appeared so paradoxical that, even in our intimate circle, otherwise so harmonious, there was difference of opinion as to the possibility and practicability of this new organ.

On the one hand, it meant a step in the direction of state socialism. For commerce was no longer free, but had become restricted.

On the other hand, it meant the attempt to encourage self-administration of our industries. . . .

The system of war boards is based upon self-administration; yet that does not signify unrestricted freedom. . . .

Their duty is to amass raw materials and to direct the flow of supply in such a way that each manufacturing concern is furnished the needed materials in quantities corresponding to the orders it receives from the Government and at prices fixed for such materials. . . .

The Department of Raw Materials will not cease to function in peace time; it will be made the nucleus of an Economic General Staff *(Wirtschaftlicher Generalstab)*. Names will change. It is possible that the term Kreigswirtschafts-Abteilung will be used, for it is that now. We cannot and must not be drawn again into a war without being economically prepared. The years of peace must be employed with utmost energy for this preparation. We must constantly keep informed of our supplies of essentials. Our stores must be equal to our needs. Depots of enormous size must be maintained. That will require considerable statistical and clerical work. Arrangements must be made for the smooth and automatic readjustment of these organizations in war time, whereas in this war coercion had to be employed. A general economic mobilization plan must be worked out.

If we look at our organization in its totality and inquire how Germany could succeed where England faltered and Lloyd George failed, I may offer the following answer:

First of all, we made an early start. As soon as it was approached, the War Office boldly decided to identify itself with us and that at a time when other economic questions had not yet been touched. And, in fostering us, the War Office has never failed to exert its power and the genius for which it has always been known.

Secondly, our organization has always remained well centralized and unified. It has never been turned over to commissions, committees, or experts. It has never been decentralized by bureaucratic methods. There was a central will endowed with authority. Committees are good when you want advice but not good when you want to create.

The third factor is German idealism. A group of men was found ready to trust a common leader, working without remuneration, without contract, impelled by enthusiasm, offering their strength and their intellect because they knew that their country needed them. Co-operating in the spirit of democratic and friendly companionship, frequently working quite independently, this select group has created a new economic life for Germany. It had the support of our industry, young and elastic, ready to act, equal to the demands of the time, able to perform what had seemed impossible.

The highest and last factor, however, is purely a human trait. For the human soul rises far above mechanical attainments, as it alone has the power to create and to lead onward. I refer to human trust and to human confidence. I have to thank three Prussian Ministers of War for the confidence which they have bestowed upon our men and our work. Such trust is a sign of genius — I might call it ethical genius — and it would be hard to find it in another country. It speaks well for the German and the Prussian system that such human relationship could be given and received in the service of our economic life and in the defense of our country.

7. GERMANY'S FOOD SUPPLY

Although perhaps neither side at first fully appreciated the possibilities and pitfalls of blockade, the conflict certainly offered the opportunity for indirect action against civilians and a nation's food supply as a complement to direct action on the battle front against soldiers. In the autumn of 1914, the German government convened a commission, headed by Paul Eltzbacher, to examine Germany's food supply. The commissioners' optimistic conclusions were belied by subsequent developments, but Eltzbacher's own introduction to the report outlines some of the probable features of a British attempt to interfere with Germany's civilian living standards.

The present world war is being waged with weapons which were unknown to any earlier age. Economic weapons have been added to military means of annihilation. In the forefront stands a scheme from which our opponents hoped great things even before the war, and which is now, after a succession of fearful defeats, doubly important to them. It is the famous starvation scheme. Our flourishing economic life has brought us into the closest connection with every country, and it is apparently only this connection which has enabled us to feed the ever-increasing population within our narrow borders; now our enemies desire to seal us hermetically from the outside world and to tie the veins of our economic life. Our army and fleet having shown themselves a match for half the world, our nation is to be conquered by hunger.

Germany and Austria are for the most part surrounded by hostile countries, the only neutral frontiers being those of Holland, Denmark, Switzerland, Italy, and Roumania. By means of a so-called command of the sea and by influencing our neutral neighbours it is hoped to cut off Germany and Austria from the rest of the world and so force them to their knees. Our enemies suppose that Germany and Austria cannot exist for any length of time without their enormous foreign trade, which in 1913 amounted to 21 milliards of marks (£1,050,000,000) for Germany and to 5 milliards (£250,000,000) for Austria. While much is hoped from tying up the export trade, greater results are expected from hindering the importation of all that we need for manufacture and daily life — wool, cotton, petroleum, copper, and the like, but, above all, food for man and beast. It is believed that we should find it difficult to hold out for any length of time without our exports — and quite impossible without our imports. This plan of campaign was originated by England, who, in her ruthless desire for power, has never hesitated to countenance the use of any weapon, and in her colonial wars has quite forgotten how to fight decently. The concentration camps of the Boer War afford the latest proof that the English gentleman is not ashamed to make war against women and children; now England desires to use this well-tried weapon on a large scale, and would like to make the whole of Germany one vast concentration camp. France, corrupted by her English alliance, has taken up the starvation idea with rapture, though it is little worthy of so chivalrous a nation. . . .

Excerpt from *Germany's Food: Can It Last?* by Paul Eltzbacher, University of London Press, 1915, pp. 1–3, 6–10.

... The English fleet takes care not to attack ours, but strives to impede our trade in every way. Though it is contrary to all modern idea of right, England has stubbornly refused to accede to the demands of the other Powers that she should respect the defencelessness of enemy private property at sea, and now her fleet's most enlightened task consists in crippling German merchant shipping. Even neutral shipping which could contribute to our support is hindered in every way. . . .

... England's special object is to crush our foreign trade, and she hopes to attain that object the more thoroughly the longer the war lasts. Trusting to her insular seclusion, and because she carries on the war by means of a paid mercenary army, she has little to fear from a long war. With her cold business sense, she brought about and began the war, and apparently considers she has more to gain than to lose from a protracted one. . . .

While Germany, in common with Austria, prepares to meet, for years if necessary, the starvation scheme of her opponents by building up an economic state cut off from the rest of the world, a new problem presents itself to the political economist and the statesman — that of the political economy of the isolated German nation.

Not so very long ago it was thought that two new branches of learning should be placed beside political economy — world economics and special economics. World economics investigates the relations of various national political economies to each other rather than the political economy of a single nation; special economics, on the other hand, deals with the separate economies which make up every national economy, the agricultural, the industrial, and the commercial. World and special economics became so much the fashion that national political economy seemed almost in the background.

Now a situation has arisen in which we must remind ourselves that between world and special economics stands the political economy of our nation. Among the great acquisitions for which we have to thank the war, perhaps the greatest is that it has put new life into our national consciousness. Two dangers threatened us: love of everything foreign (or internationalism), and personal egotism (or individualism). In the most diverse paths of life, in art, literature, fashion, German characteristics seemed either to be forgotten in the general admiration of the foreigner, or to have lost all coherence in the strife of self-assertion. The war has changed all this. With our whole hearts we feel ourselves to be Germans. The cults of the foreigner and egotism have fallen from us as if they were unfitted to us. Each sees his highest aim in serving the Fatherland to the best of his ability, and it now seems absolutely natural that world connections as well as private interests should be placed in the background of our economic life, and that we should think only of the economic weal of the German people. Should circumstances compel Germany and Austria to become one isolated State, each one of us will adapt his thought and deeds to the necessity without further ado.

In an isolated State, economic thought experiences a complete transformation. So long as our national economic life was bound up with that of the rest of the world, the idea of production stood in the foreground; if we produced valuable goods no matter of how one-sided a nature, no one doubted the possibility of exchanging them abroad for all that we needed in our daily life. . . .

So long as our economic life was bound up with that of the rest of the world, great personal freedom in our economic demeanour was possible. Even those who had given up the principle of boundless *laisser faire* still feared any far-reaching restrictions of economic freedom; but in the difficult position which has arisen through the sudden isolation of German economic life that fear must disappear. Our economic life is subject to State regulation to an extent hitherto unheard of. The Federal Council has extensive powers to prohibit the export or fix the highest prices of objects of daily necessity, and they can also demand any restrictions of economic freedom which the situation may require. Patriotic feeling has, however, accepted this far-reaching State regulation as absolutely justified. Nowadays everyone is a Socialist, so to speak.

8. Germany's Economic Collapse

When British troops occupied German soil shortly after the armistice of November 1918 to ensure order and German willingness to accept a final peace treaty, they were struck by the deterioration of the civilian economy and the persistence of a black market with prices ordinary workers could not afford. The first extract contains the observations of Brigadier-General H. C. Rees on conditions in Berlin; the second presents the findings of Captain Roddie after a visit to Leipzig; and the third is a letter by a German housewife.

a. *Conditions in Berlin*

General Impressions

1. Germany appears to be completely beaten and disorganized: further hostilities on any appreciable scale are most improbable. The German people are, in my opinion, fully aware of this fact and accept it as a lesser evil than the continuance of the war.
2. The nation as a whole is on the verge of starvation. The scarcity of food is much more pronounced in the large towns than in the country districts, but the reduction of the food ration has been carried out so gradually that the masses are hardly aware of the extent of the reduction.

   N.B. — Good food is still obtainable in big hotels at very high prices.

   The use of substitutes for necessary articles of food has been brought to a high pitch of perfection.
3. Owing to the lack of raw materials, industry is nearly at a standstill, and the thousands of men now disbanded will not be able to find work.
4. The high standard of discipline attained under the old *régime* still holds the nation. The Workmen's and Soldiers' Councils carry very little weight, and are feared by the average citizen as likely to introduce Bolshevism owing to their incapacity as

From *Reports by British Officers on the Economic Conditions Prevailing in Germany, December 1918–March 1919,* House of Commons Sessional Papers, Vol. 53, Cmd. 52.

rulers. For this reason, many in Berlin would be glad to see the capital occupied by Allied troops.

Narrative

I was a prisoner of war at Bad-Colberg, Saxe Meiningen, and, at the request of the senior British officer at the camp, I proceeded to Berlin on the 12th December to endeavour to obtain some information regarding the evacuation of the camp, and also to obtain food supplies from the Red Cross as we were running very short.

At this camp, there was no question in the mind of anybody, and the local people, our camp guard, &c., were fully convinced that Germany had lost the war. In spite of this, every village and town in Germany had been decorated to welcome back the troops. In no sense was this intended to be other than an ordinary welcome. It was not the welcome given to a victorious army.

On leaving Bad-Colberg, we took a guard of one *Feldwebel* with us to Berlin. We took train at Coburg and went to Lichtenfels, where we secured seats in the first express which had been run since the Armistice from Munich to Berlin, reaching Berlin the same night.

The only food available in the restaurant at Lichtenfels was a little soup, two potatoes and a small quantity of macaroni, which was obtainable at 12 noon. Nothing whatever could be bought at other times.

During the journey, we saw crowds of soldiers, but all disbanded; no formed bodies. I saw many men in a state of considerable exhaustion and dirt. From Lichtenfels to Halle (Munich–Berlin main line), we did not pass a single train of any description. On arrival at Berlin, the station was crammed, chiefly with soldiers, but we were not molested in any way while making our way through the crowd. The only point of interest that arose was that our *Feldwebel,* who was wearing a sword, was ordered by a representative of the Workmen's and Soldiers' Council to take it off.

We stayed in Berlin at the Esplanade Hotel. The hotel was well kept up, a good band played every evening, and sufficient food was obtainable, provided that food cards were produced, but at very great cost. The food obtainable was such as *pâté de foie gras,* salmon and turkey. There are three meat days a week; on these days a small quantity of other meat is available.

The market was practically empty. I saw queues of people waiting for fish at 11 A.M. Many of them had been there, on a bitterly cold morning, since 6 A.M. I was told that fish was expected, but there would not be sufficient to supply one-tenth of those waiting.

The people are ill-clothed and underfed, and the younger generation underdeveloped. As elsewhere, the lack of coal is apparent. The town authorities state that they can keep going for another four weeks at the present rate, but that after that the situation will be desperate.

Industry is at little more than a standstill. What can be done with the material on hand is being done, but the lack of raw material and coal prevents any appreciable amount of work being carried out. The people are willing to work. Wages are not so high as in Berlin — about 30 per cent. less. The number of unemployed increases rapidly.

b. Captain Roddie on Leipzig

Leipzig, owing to its geographical position and to the fact that the population of the surrounding country is industrial and not agricultural, is economically in a worse position even than Berlin. Carrots, turnips, dried beans, cabbage and beet have formed the staple diet of rich and poor for months past. The meat supply is not sufficient to give the people the amount to which the rationing system entitles them. I visited the slaughter-house, which is the centre from which all meat is distributed. About 600 cattle per week are killed, and on this the population of 400,000 to 500,000 is fed. Pork was almost non-existent. A number of goats were killed. All scraps, offal and awful, are made into sausages and sold at 3 to 7 marks per pound. Rigid economy is observed.

The cattle were in a terribly emaciated condition, fed principally on straw, as the people are now eating what formerly cows were fed on.

The potato ration has been much reduced since the time of the last report from Leipzig.

I visited seven families, rich, middle class and poor. All were living on practically the same diet. There was plenty of money, but nothing essential could be bought with it.

Leather boots and woollen goods are no longer to be had. *"Kriegstoffe"* — a sort of shoddy — and paper are used for clothing. The former is very expensive and has very little wear in it. Paper and cretonne underclothing are all that can be had by any but the very rich.

c. A German Woman's Petition

Gentlemen,

A housewife takes the liberty to tell how most people that are not able to pay the price of usury must suffer from hunger and want in this terrible times. Rich people or, also, workmen who earn so enormous sums of money, go to the country and pay there great sums for victuals; for instance, 25–30 mark for a pound of butter or bacon, 1 mark for one egg, 100 mark for a goose, and so on.

Such people cannot feel the want and distress of others.

We get here in our town so little victuals that it is not possible to live on. In our family every one is so miser and weak that we are all desperated. The little quantity of bad meat is scarcely sufficient for two meals a week. Thirty or 40 gramm of butter is the

(b) From *Reports by British Officers on the Economic Conditions Prevailing in Germany, December 1918–March 1919,* House of Commons Sessional Papers, Vol. 53, Cmd. 52.

(c) Ibid.

quantity for one person a week. Last week we got no butter, only margarine, that is so bad I could not take it for preparing dinner. I must prepare vegetables only with water and meal. Short time after dinner we are all hungry again, and have nothing to eat. You cannot imagine the distress. How many people have already died of it. Therefore I — and with me thousands of persons — dare asking you to have pity on this need and to cause that our town and especially the less wealthy people get food from other lands. The most important is fat.

You may be sure that we poor Germans are innocent of the war that has ruined us. We were badly lead by our high diplomats, and had been happy if we could have remained friends to the English, American, and to all nations. We must now suffer what others have committed. Hoping and asking that you will have pity on innocent and hungry people, I dared writing these lines. Excuse the bad expressions and mistakes. I wrote as I can remember it from my school time.

A Desperated Wife and Mother

9. FOOD FOR FRANCE

The Allies proved much more successful than the Central Powers in preserving civilian living standards. Their naval supremacy may provide a partial explanation, but much of the answer lies in the more effective coordination of resources by the British and French governments. François Monod, the cabinet chief to the French high commissioner in the United States, highlights his country's achievement in this sphere despite the severe dislocation of the war.

Food for France and Its Public Control

Emphasizing first the decrease of production and the increase in prices, I will thereafter outline the main measures taken in France in order either to make up for the shortage of agricultural workers or to regulate consumption, to remedy the deficiency of production and to provide a sufficiency of the essential foodstuffs.

I. SHORTAGE OF AGRICULTURAL HANDWORK AND DEFICIT
OF NATIVE PRODUCTION

1. In France during the war the whole food situation has been controlled by an extensive and critical shortage of agricultural handwork. Obvious are the reasons accounting for that main fact of the situation. Seven million men up to the age of forty-eight years have been taken in France for army service. It would be difficult to overstate the consequences of such a wholesale mobilization of our manhood amongst a nation which has

Excerpt from "Food for France and its Public Control" by François Monod, *The Annals of the American Academy of Political and Social Science* 74 (1917), pp. 84–91.

been for centuries and which is still foremost a nation of agriculturists, of food produc-
ers. Though accurate statistical data are not easily procurable, I think that a round figure
and safe estimate of the number of agriculturists in the French army during the war
would not prove to be under four or five million men. This includes without exception
all the younger and stronger male peasantry.

Then there is to be taken into account the invasion and long detention of a large
part of northern France by the Germans which means the loss, during the war, up to the
present day, of some of our best managed and most productive wheat growing districts,
and the enforced employment of their agricultural resources and handwork for the benefit of Germany.

South of the invaded districts along the front in the "army zone," that a large acre-
age of agricultural soil is lying uncultivated and idle is another fact not to be overlooked.
Wheat is not grown on a shell-torn ground and the main crops of that long belt from
the French Flanders to the south part of the Vosges, to the border of Switzerland, are
barbed wire. The varying breadth of that belt, extending far behind the actual "no man's
land," is easily several miles.

Then there is to be mentioned last, a deficiency of the essential fertilizers all over
France. The import of nitrates is cut short by the growing contraction of available tonnage and by the scarcity of shipping from the far distant sources of supply in Chile.

2. A heavy decrease of production has unavoidably been following such unsatisfactory conditions of cultivation. Wheat has ever been the staple food of France. Amongst
all classes over the country bread is the main article of consumption, the actual basis of
the French nation's feeding, even more so especially in the case of our peasants, that is
to say of the majority of the nation with whom bread actually takes to the largest extent
the place of meat as a foodstuff.

In peace times the wheat production of France was about equal to our consumption, sometimes slightly inferior to our needs, sometimes slightly superior and allowing
a thin margin of surplus. This meant a crop of about 90,000,000 French cwt. [about
410,000 English pounds] on the average. Since the war, production decreased to:

    82,000,000 French cwt. in 1914
    75,000,000 French cwt. in 1915
    58,000,000 French cwt. in 1916
    38,000,000 French cwt. in 1917 (estimate)

Thus, compared with the normal production, the present wheat production of
France indicates a decrease of *over 50 per cent* in the native supply of the staple food.

As regards *meat* the unavoidable depletion of our resources in livestock has been
made much heavier by the huge needs of the army. In the army the meat consumption
per head amounts to about 400 "grammes," a little less than one English pound, a day.
This means an exceedingly heavy additional burden on our resources in livestock on
account not only of the tremendous consumption of meat at such a rate in any army of
several million men, but on account of the fact that the peasants, contributing the largest
part of the army's establishment are, as already stated, consuming very little meat in
peace time.

In round figures the decrease of the livestock in France since the end of 1913 runs as follows:

End 1913 14,787,000 bovine species
End 1913 16,138,000 ovine species
End 1913 7,035,000 pigs
End 1916 12,341,000 bovine species
End 1916 10,845,000 ovine species
End 1916 4,361,000 pigs

meaning thus, at the end of 1916, a decrease of about:

2,440,000 bovine species
5,700,000 ovine species
2,700,000 pigs

II. INCREASE IN THE PRICES OF FOODSTUFFS

1. The increase in price for *wheat* has been balancing almost exactly the decrease in production.

Average Price of Native Wheat

Before the war	22 francs per French cwt.
1914	30 francs per French cwt.
1915	36 francs per French cwt.
1916	50 francs per French cwt.

which means in 1916 an increase of *over 50 per cent.*

2. The price of meat has been rising in a similar proportion and an *increase of circa 50 per cent* may safely be stated as an index for the rising in the prices of *all the main foodstuffs.*

3. The price of *bread* though shows a comparatively small increase. The peacetime price was 35–40 centimes per kilogram on the average; the war price did not rise over 50 centimes. The explanation of such a paradoxical fact is that the price of bread was artificially and deliberately kept down by the government burdening public finances with a heavy extra war burden. On account of the paramount importance of the question of bread, the French government adopted the policy of paying from public moneys the difference between the prices corresponding to the actual market quotations of wheat and the price of bread as stated above (50 centimes). Thus a steady, abnormal and uncontrollable increase of wages amongst the community at large and other undesirable results which would have followed as regards the price of bread were avoided.

III. SKETCH OF THE PUBLIC MEASURES TAKEN TO CONTROL THE FOOD SITUATION

Important public measures have been taken to make up for the deficiency of agricultural handwork, to regulate or to lessen consumption and to provide supplies.

1. All over France private initiative amongst the agricultural community did wonders in order to keep the production as large as possible. All the people who were not
in the army, the old men, the women, the boys under military age displayed great
physical and moral courage in taking, as regards agricultural work, the place of the
millions of men at the front. They directed the work — many women have themselves
been running even large-sized farms during the war — or they spent themselves tirelessly
in the manual work involved by the daily business of farming; they took care of the
cattle, of the horses; they performed ably the ploughing, seeding, harvesting operations.

Under such trying conditions they went on with the cultivation of the fields as far
as possible even in the zone behind the actual front, many times in shelled districts. Near
villages located behind the trench line I have often seen women or old men, bent in
two, weeding or hoeing without taking notice of the casual landing of shells in the near
fields.

2. This strenuous endeavor has been helped and stimulated by special organizations
created under the authority of the Ministry of Agriculture.

Under the supervision of the communal authorities and with the help of the local
agents of the Ministry of Agriculture, a special local coöperation was organized in the
rural townships, bringing about a local pooling of agricultural resources of machinery,
draught horses, seeds and of handwork to some extent.

Special military measures, besides, were taken for the same purpose. A certain
amount of supplementary agricultural handwork was provided in two ways: first, by
granting, as far as possible long furloughs to soldiers of the older "classes," and second,
of late, by the release of the 1889 and 1890 "classes," aged forty-seven and forty-eight
years. Another kind of military coöperation was extended in the army zone itself in the
villages located behind the line, by the temporary use of smaller groups of soldiers and
of army horses in agricultural work, helping the peasants on the spot and reclaiming part
of the fields left idle since the war began.

Then the German army herself contributed another welcome addition of handwork
— mobile squads of German prisoners put at the disposal of many of our rural communities have been fairly extensively employed by our peasants in various districts. They
were well treated and well fed and the results proved satisfactory. Provided they are kept
under a sufficiently strict military discipline, the German prisoners are submissive and
willing to work.

Last, another addition of hands was offered by importing natives volunteering from
Algeria. The Kabyles, one of the main races of French Northern Africa, are sedentary
peasants. For months squads of turbaned Kabyles have been seen with us, employed not
only as street sweepers in Paris, but in several rural districts, mixing unexpectedly as
agricultural laborers with the old peasantry of France.

3. So much as regards handwork and cultivation. Regarding the regulation of consumption and the victualling, the most important public provision has been the buying
of all wheat imports by the French government. This resulted in regulating automatically the prices of the native wheat and in preventing speculation in the interior market.

Since December, 1916, this organization has been extended and completed by the
creation of a national Ministry of Supplies (Ministère du Ravitaillement).

4. A series of food laws have been further enacted:

(a) Increase of the proportion of the wheat grain used in the bolting for the making of flour.
(b) Institution of two meatless days per week and reduction of the menu of meals in hotels and restaurants to three courses only.
(c) Institution of sugar cards reducing, monthly, the sugar consumption to 750 grammes, and later to 400 grammes per head.

Besides food laws proper, there ought still to be mentioned in connection with them the institution of coal cards regulating the supply of coal for home consumption. This democratic provision is preventing the well-to-do from buying at high prices, thereby increasing the general retail market price for the larger part of the population.

IV. INTERALLIED MEASURES

The carrying out of these national measures has been seconded by a general interallied understanding. An interallied "wheat executive" (December, 1916) and recently a "meats and fats executive" have been appointed by France, Great Britain and Italy, thereby providing an interallied buying and apportionment of imported supplies.

V. AMERICAN COÖPERATION

The aims and results of the food control organized in the United States are well known. The allies are concerned by the national husbanding of American resources and by the controlling of food exports. After provisions are made for the national consumption the available surplus is kept for supplying the needs of the allies.

This American cooperation has been meeting with a very special appreciation in France as regards the supplies provided in the past and in the present to hundreds of thousands of our unfortunate countrymen who are still enslaved under German bondage and oppression in northern France. Those people have been and are under much worse conditions than the Belgians and their pitiful, exceedingly critical situation at present is a matter of grave anxiety. If they have not literally starved, if they have not died out, this was due entirely to the Belgian Relief Commission operating in northern France.

From this standpoint no adequate tribute could be paid to the former Director of the Commission of Belgian Relief, to the present United States Food Controller, Mr. Herbert Hoover, to his genius for organization, to the generous and tireless activities of Mr. Hoover and of his staff, to their firmness in dealing with German authorities in invaded territories and in upholding American rights for the benefit of our countrymen. Amongst many American names forever dear to us, the name of Mr. Hoover will ever be remembered by the French nation with a deep and affectionate gratitude.

VI. Conclusion

The conclusion to be derived from this review of the food situation in France is plain enough. In her sustenance, France has been depending upon imports in an increasing way. Upon an adequate supply of foodstuffs as well as of coal, and of the other main war supply — steel — depends in the present and in the near future the further resistance of our civilian population and the sustenance of our armies, who, after having borne the main brunt of the fight for three years, are still defending about three-quarters of the western front and acting as the main rampart of the allied cause.

Considering the main food supply — wheat — only the needs of France are emphasized by the present condition of crops. Taking 100 as indexing a very good crop, while the crop of 1916 winter wheat was not classed higher than 64, a very poor crop is indicated by this year's probable index 56.

Needless to say an increase in the supply of foodstuffs means finally an increase of the tonnage available for imports in France. For France thus, from the point of view of American coöperation, the supply of tonnage stands out as the vital issue.

C. Dissent, Mutiny, and Revolution

1. Neutralism in Italy

Italy's initial neutrality and subsequent intervention in May 1915 were overseen by its premier, Antonio Salandra, whose territorial ambitions and conservative inclinations made him willing to contemplate military participation. The forces in Italian society ranged against intervention were far from negligible, however, as the excerpt from Salandra's memoirs that follows suggests. Those divisions would provide an opportunity for Mussolini's Fascists in the immediate postwar years.

The forces of neutralism were not to be despised. The imminence of the decision induced them to come out, if cautiously, into the open. It constrained them to cast aside the prudence imposed by the small sympathy felt for their point of view, and to defend their cause against a propaganda which was becoming more and more intense, and penetrating those classes of society who, if not the largest in mere numbers, were most open to patriotic sentiments. I do not believe that anything existed in the shape of a neutralist plot, but the different tendencies amalgamated, not formally but actually, around a centre and a leader. The centre was Parliament, and the leader was the greatest parliamentarian of the time — Giolitti.

Excerpt from *Italy and the Great War: From Neutrality to Intervention* by Antonio Salandra, Edward Arnold Ltd., 1932, pp. 310–314.

Nos numerus sumus might have been said by the Italian Socialists, whose numerical force had been demonstrated in the elections of 1913 and had certainly not diminished since. But in the most solemn moments of history it is not statistics which decide or direct the fate of peoples. . . . [A]ll the highest elements, the most cultured, the most courageous and energetic, had joined the ranks of interventionism; numerically, however, they were not many. The organized masses remained true to the absolute neutrality proclaimed by their leaders and constantly reaffirmed. But their action was confined to words, manifestos, meetings, debates, fiery newspaper articles; little else. They considered whether they should declare a general strike in case of mobilization; the majority were against, they understood the odiousness of fomenting civil war when a real war against the foreigner was pending, and they also knew very well that repression, if not prevention, would have been immediate and severe. There were, indeed, a few strikes, which were easily brought to nothing. Nevertheless, in some provinces and urban centres there was, so to speak, a great reserve of Socialists who had the local administration in their hands. The Government kept these in mind, perhaps more than was necessary. The leaders in Rome sided with the neutralists of a more conservative and constitutional order, but they did so furtively, as both parties wished to avoid any undesirable manifestations of closer partnership. At any rate, neither in industrial centres where the crowds were greatest, nor in rural districts, was there any serious disturbance of the public peace.

Catholic opinion, although uncertain and ill-defined, was against intervention. Let me be explicit: when I speak of Catholics I do not mean the great majority of Italians practising the national religion but strong in their patriotic feelings and political opinions — if they have any. I mean to refer to that minority — not very numerous but increasing, and of high social condition and connections — which had remained (since 1870) organized round the Vatican as centre. These Catholics had never been, never would be, untrue to the Nation and its aspirations. They certainly had, on the outbreak of war, an explosion of Triplicism, provoked more by hatred of the Freemasons of the other camp, however, than by anything else. But they soon changed route, adhering wholeheartedly to neutrality, not without some idea, indeed, that "circumstances might alter the case." To the immediate triumph of interventionism, however, they could not resign themselves. They were logically drawn towards the "parecchio" formula, which made national aspirations appear reconcilable with the conservation of peace. And when, during the final weeks, the struggle resolved itself into "parecchio" *versus* intervention, they were obliged to detach themselves from the Government with whom, until then, they had maintained close contact and friendly relations.

The Vatican could not refrain from taking up a political attitude at so momentous a time. Unlike his predecessor, Benedict XV had not had a purely spiritual sacerdotal training but had combined with it the training for a diplomatic career, and was not lacking in vision, determination, and on occasion a political sense. At first he tried to keep his equilibrium between the two belligerent forces, a painful effort which caused discontent, and exercised on every occasion his peculiar mission, if not of peace then of attenuation of the War. There was nothing in such a mission at variance with his strong desire and, within certain limits, his attempts to prevent a rupture between Italy and the Austro-Hungarian Monarchy. The latter was the country which the Catholic Hierarchy could not forswear, and I recognize that their feelings were sincere; it was, indeed, their home where they did not fear to be disturbed by the uncertain issues of war and internal crises.

[The Nuncio made several efforts] to persuade the venerable Emperor to cede some part of the Hapsburg inheritance. Although they had no success at first, they certainly contributed to the belated offers of later days. It was only natural that an attempt should be made to improve these on the one hand, and to get them accepted on the other. That this was the Pontiff's personal point of view I have no direct proof, but it is logical to suppose that those Italians and foreigners who state that it was so and took advantage of it, were telling the truth. But I am sure that much that went on round and about the Vatican was neither counselled nor authorized, and the same may be said of the intemperate language and, worse still, the secret manœuvres with Italian and foreign neutralist agents. I have reason to believe that there were men — personally disinterested — who made no scruple of accepting foreign subsidies to help a newspaper in favour of the cause they considered just. These are serious words, but I write for History.

Certainly it would not be true to suppose that neutralism was limited to Socialists and Catholics. On the contrary there were many who had not allowed themselves to be influenced by the feelings and reasons which had led to the Government's decision. I have letters from men of high rank, with long experience, independent of any party, some of them old friends of mine, who reported public opinion in the cities and country districts in which they lived as being against the War. "Public opinion" is so indefinite an expression that every one, in good faith, is ready to colour it according to his own views. These people, however, neither invented nor prevaricated. But there could be no halting on the road we had chosen.

Vincenzo Ricci, Minister of Posts, a man with a clear mind and a pure heart, used to keep a diary, which was not destined for publication. After his death his sons allowed me to read it and to make a few extracts. I quote from the page dated May 6.

Having noted repeatedly the visits of eminent people, some of them ladies, who came to advise him, unasked, to avert war and to accept Austria's proposals, he remarks: "This uniformity of opinion makes me thoughtful. Are we mistaken in wishing for war? The fact is that the majority of the Nation is against it. People would much prefer to escape the terrible damage and suffering. But, is that possible? Would it not be a great deal worse if, through inertia, we let the decisive moment escape? For fear of the responsibility dare we compromise Italy's future for whole generations? The fate of future generations is in our hands. And what is our responsibility? We are the tired sons of an industrious, intelligent and active generation; the generation which has made Italy. But we pass on. A new generation follows close behind, already taking a share in public life, stronger, more vigorous than we. Ought we to block the way? Can we arrest the tide of new forces, or forgo the opportunity of completing Italy's unity?"

My friend was right. Any Government, which was held back by the voices of the Present and did not lead the country towards the Future, would fail in the chief of its duties. Were those men who made Italy representative of the numerical majority of the Italians of their time? Not for ourselves, not for contemporaries do we undertake so great a labour. We toil for our deathless country!

Italian neutralists, determined to prevent the Government from taking the final steps, had accepted the help of foreign elements; and in the end this contributed largely to their discomfiture and scarcely honourable defeat.

2. Resignation in the French Villages

How did French civilians cope with the lengthy war, one that on the Western Front was fought largely on French soil? The following selection, from an important study of civilian morale, distinguishes between attitudes of enthusiasm and resignation toward the continuation of the war.

Morale in the villages appears to have fluctuated somewhat less than in industrial centres like Grenoble and Vienne. The survey of village correspondence in fact suggests that morale in rural areas never reached a crisis point, and a good case can be made for the argument that the overall trend of village opinion of the war and all its disruptions was fundamentally no different during 1917 and 1918 from what it had been during 1915 and 1916, and that, while it fluctuated, it continued to avoid the extremes of outright patriotic endeavour on the one hand and revolutionary defeatism or pacifism on the other. Of course, . . . the absence of the better-educated, more articulate and potentially more critical members of village populations helps to account for this. It must also be borne in mind that in the more remote and "backward" villages and hamlets the local *curé, instituteur* or *institutrice* would help to compose and write letters to the front and would be unlikely to express overtly anti-war sentiments. None the less one searches in vain through reports of opened letters from villages to the front, or through the letters of *maires,* village *instituteurs* or private farmers to the *préfet* for any reference to, or evidence of, fundamental discontent with the régime. There were, of course, isolated criticisms of various Government administrations and their conduct of the war but, outside the ranks of extreme political activists and militants, only in the occasional anonymous letter to the *préfet* was the very nature and *raison d'être* of the Third Republic called into question. Indeed, even amongst the *Grenoblois* and *Viennois,* such discontented references were rare and again largely confined to anonymous letters to the *préfet.* It is significant that criticisms and attacks on Government policies almost totally ceased after the appointment of Clemenceau was made known.

A second feature of the correspondence is the very rare mention of death and destruction in both villagers' and townspeople's letters. This is extraordinary considering the large numbers of families affected by bereavement by 1917. The rather matter-of-fact tone of civilian letters, particularly those of villagers, was noted by the Chairman of the *Commission du Contrôle Postal:* "in the main, while the letters of civilians continue

Excerpt from *France 1914–1918: Public Opinion and the War Effort,* P. J. Flood, ed. Copyright © P. J. Flood, 1990. Reprinted with permission of St. Martin's Press, Inc., pp. 157–159, 161.

to complain about the length of the war, prices, rationing, lack of coal and so on, they exhibit an extraordinary stoicism, an acceptance of human sacrifice. It is as if talk of death is a taboo subject." Returning to this theme three months later when, for the second time in the war, the Germans were threatening Paris and the immediate outlook seemed very depressing, he commented on the "ostrich-like" tone of the villagers' letters and remarked that, rather than talk about the deaths and sacrifices of this war, the civilians seemed to be motivated by a kind of "blind faith" in the outcome.

Blind faith or not, there is no doubt that even in the middle of the crisis period of early summer 1917, at the lowest point of morale during the war, expressions of belief in the final victory of France exceeded by far the fears of defeat. Village letters expressing anxiety or uncertainty about the outcome numbered only just over half of those expressing confidence, and "anxiety" soon receded in July and August as another harvest loomed.

This implies that even during *l'Année Terrible* all thoughts in the villages must be directed towards the immediate and vitally important agricultural work. This should not be too surprising: harvest work traditionally dominated the village calendar, farmers' livelihoods were at stake and, in any case, the full weight of Government propaganda, channelled through the local administration, the press and the Education Service, was geared to agricultural production for the war. In this context it is noticeable that reported attempts to sabotage agricultural production in order to shorten the war were almost non-existent in 1917 and 1918. Indeed not even during the last, optimistic month of October 1918 did references to external affairs exceed, in percentage terms, references to local or economic matters.

A third feature of villagers' correspondence, and again this is to a certain extent true of letters from *Grenoblois* and *Viennois,* is the general absence of reference to war aims. On the whole the civilian population of the Isère seems rarely to have asked "why are we fighting?" even during low points in morale. Presumably it was a superfluous question since the priority had never changed since the early days of the war. French people were still fighting to repel the invader and it was almost an article of faith that Alsace and Lorraine would be returned to France. Beyond this, and the assumption that the war would end in a total victory, there were few references to the post-war world until the last month of the war when . . . stories of atrocities caused a wave of *revanchiste* references. There were increased calls at this time for heavy reparations from the Germans but, again, this was nothing really new. . . . Furthermore, while the Germans were still occupying North-East France and the war had yet to be won, there was likely to be little real interest in the more practical proposals of a League of Nations beyond the vague notion that this must be "the war to end wars." . . .

. . . However, if the villagers seemed impervious to anti-war sentiments, it cannot be said that, barring a few exceptions, they exhibited any more pro-war sentiments than they had since 1914. The key word in correspondence here is *"lassitude"* or war weariness, a feeling that the authorities were continuing to demand too much of the villagers. This is particularly noticeable in *maires'* responses to the organisation of *journées* and in the ability and willingness of the inhabitants of their *communes* to receive new quotas of refugees. . . .

3. THE FRENCH MUTINIES

To an extent, the same resignation characteristic of the villages prevailed at the front. Eventually, in the face of repetitious and fruitless attacks, resignation in the trenches turned to frustration. The spring of 1917, in the wake of Russia's February Revolution, which overthrew the tsarist government, was a critical period when discontent escalated into mutiny. The following entries from a French soldier's diary describe the temporary disruption of authority in many army units.

4 April

Many men get drunk. Morale is low. They are fed up with the war. Certain corps court-martial some men for desertion, theft, insolence, etc.; after condemnation (with reprieve in the majority of cases) they are transferred to another corps. My company is infested with them. Special strictly disciplined companies are needed, prison sentences are useless. . . .

1 June

The spirit of the troops is turning sour. There is talk of mutiny and of troops refusing to go to the lines. The "bad hats" amongst them are more vociferous.

3 June

All the companies are in a state of turmoil; the men are receiving letters from friends informing them of the present spirit and urging them not to march; the ringleaders are becoming insolent; others are trying to influence their comrades. My company does not escape this plague: a squad, under the sway of its corporal, refuses to fall in, the men claiming they are ill. Just as we move to take them to the guardroom, they run off in the fields and insult the N.C.O.s [noncommissioned officers]. Some only return the following day.

I have five court-martialled, to get rid of the worst. Alas! that's just what many want — a motive to be court-martialled, so as to spend a year in prison; they are counting on some future amnesty and, during their stay in prison, they will be far from the Front. Once again, it will be the good who will go and get themselves killed and the scoundrels who will be protected.

In addition, a law has just increased the men's pay: first payment today. These men

Excerpt from *A French Soldier's War Diary* by Henri Desagneaux, Elmsfield Press, 1975, pp. 38–40.

who are getting 20–30 francs rush to spend them on drink; drunkenness all along the line. Command becomes difficult.

5 June

I sit in judgement at the court-martial. What a procession of rogues! How stupid they seem in front of their judges. In their company they tried to be smart, insulted their superiors, tried to get their chums to desert; here they are now, sheepish, not daring to look up, full of repentance. . . .

The Army is becoming more and more a prey to this ill-feeling; those on leave on their return home from the front, are assailed by agitators who, going as far as uncoupling the trains, urge them not to return. I must go to Meaux to re-establish order.

7 June

On my arrival at Meaux at 9.30 I organize my troops at the station and in town.

One platoon for the town and hospital (where there's a load of brutes), two platoons at the station, one in reserve, in case of need.

At 3 P.M. the first train of those on leave arrives at the station from the front. As soon as the train enters, you would say a horde of savages, all the doors opening on both sides and the men flooding out on the platforms.

Shouts, insults, threats fly in all directions: death to the shirkers at home, murderers and pigs that they are; long live the Revolution, down with war, it's peace we want, etc. We empty the station to avoid conflict; the station staff don't dare show themselves. That's why I'm here. At La Ferté-sous-Jouarre a company of machine-gunners is on guard. At Chateau-Thierry, a company of light infantry: each division has its zone.

4 P.M., second train. The troops invade a garden. The owner kindly offers to let them pick flowers, provided they don't do any damage. There is one mad rush and everything is destroyed; they attack the house too, the windows are broken and the blinds torn down. They shout the same cries and insults: Death, long live the Revolution, down with war.

5 P.M., third train. As soon as it stops, the troops surge out menacingly. There is an empty train in the station: the men seize stones and break every window. During the journey, a man had fallen on the track and had had his foot cut off. The military superintendent of the station — a lieutenant aged 55 — rushes up with four men and a stretcher to carry him away. Seeing his white band the troops call him a murderer and beat him black and blue. It all happened so quickly that the attack passed unnoticed and we found this officer lying unconscious on the platform after the departure of the train.

Often scenes such as these happen at the last moment, as the train is leaving, so that we can't intervene.

The trains are in a lamentable state; the doors are wrenched off and thrown on the track during the journey; all the windows are broken, and the seats slashed to ribbons.

That's the state of affairs. My men are well-disciplined and will be ready to act at the first signal. I have no fears in this respect. The situation however, is delicate, for how can I intervene, should the need arise, with 30 or 40 men, against a frenzied horde of a thousand individuals, the majority of them in a state of intoxication?

8 June

At La Ferté, same scenes. At Chateau-Thierry a deputy station-master is injured. A general who was on the platform was manhandled and had his képi snatched from his head. The guard intervened and a man was arrested. Immediately all the troops got off and uncoupled the train. They only consented to leave when their comrade had been freed. The station staff are so ill-treated that they go into hiding when these trains arrive and refuse to do their duties.

At Meaux my guard duty passes normally. My men, well turned-out, parade in the town and are a source of admiration to everyone. This is because at Meaux, there are only fatigue sections: bakers, drivers who have no idea of smart turn-out, good discipline.

The day passes with the usual cries of: down with war, death to the slackers, long live the Revolution and that's all, except for a drunk who got out a razor to show how he cut the Boches' heads off; we cart him off to prison.

12 June

The postal service informs me that letters seized are full of threats and plans for revolution. No-one hides the fact things are bad and everyone is fed up.

4. SHATTERED SPIRITS

Resignation and indifference were equally pronounced on the Eastern Front, as indicated by this Austro-Hungarian soldier's lethargic reaction, in 1915, to Germany's breakthrough at Gorlice, which forced Russian troops to withdraw from the Carpathian Mountains.

Balnica—April 1

We have just received confirmation of our great victory at Gorlice which was reported some days ago by telephone. Remarkable that, now that it has become certainty, nobody

Excerpt from *Hussar's Picture Book* by Pal Keleman, Indiana University, 1972, p. 57.

rejoices in the way that people at home might expect. Listless, resigned smiles, a few gray words, and the officers have already settled the matter of victory among themselves.

Everyone here has become indifferent, worn down by the everlasting tension; the shattered spirits cannot recover any more. I feel no sort of news will ever thrill anyone here again, no excited murmurs will run rife among us until the day when new tidings come with the surest, most indisputable proof, proclaiming peace.

5. A SOLDIER'S REFLECTIONS

The "Reflections of a Soldier," which follows, was published anonymously in the British liberal journal, *The Nation,* in October 1916. In fact, the author was R. H. Tawney, later known as a distinguished economic historian and an influential socialist intellectual. Tawney was born in Calcutta in 1880 into the Victorian upper middle class, the son of a Sanskrit scholar and member of the Indian Education Service. After a fairly conventional public school and Oxford education (at Balliol), he engaged in social work among the underprivileged in London's East End and developed a life-long commitment to workers' education. Serving in France during the war, he was wounded in 1916; thereafter he resumed his academic career, which culminated in his tenure as professor of economic history at the London School of Economics. He died in 1962.

It is very nice to be at home again. Yet am I at home? One sometimes doubts it. There are occasions when I feel like a visitor among strangers whose intentions are kindly, but whose modes of thought I neither altogether understand nor altogether approve. I find myself storing impressions, attempting hasty and unsatisfactory summaries to appease the insatiable curiosity of the people with whom I really am at home, the England that's not an island or an empire, but a wet populous dyke stretching from Flanders to the Somme. And then, just when my pencil is on the paper, I realize how hopeless it is. I used to sit at the feet of a philosopher, who thought he had established a common intellectual medium between himself and an Indian friend, till the latter elucidated his position by a hypothesis. "Let us suppose," he said, "that God has chosen to assume the form of an elephant." With the concrete aloofness of that Oriental imagery, my teacher strove in vain: the depth of the dividing chasm was revealed by the bridge.

And somewhat the same difficulty troubles me. As we exchange views, one of you assumes as possible or probable something that seems to us preposterous, or dismisses as too trivial for comment what appears to us a fact of primary importance. You speak lightly, you assume that we shall speak lightly, of things, emotions, states of mind, human relationships and affairs which are to us solemn or terrible. You seem ashamed, as if they were a kind of weakness, of the ideas which sent us to France, and for which thousands of sons and lovers have died. You calculate the profits to be derived from "War after the War," as though the unspeakable agonies of the Somme were an item in

From "Reflections of a Soldier" by R. H. Tawney, *The Nation,* 21 Oct. 1916.

a commercial proposition. You make us feel that the country to which we've returned is not the country for which we went out to fight! And your reticence as to the obvious physical facts of war! And your ignorance as to the sentiments of your relations about it!

Yet I don't think I'm mad, for I find that other soldiers have somewhat the same experience as myself. Not that I profess to speak for the Army! I leave that to the officers who periodically return to Parliament and tell it that the men at the front demand this, or object to that. I say "we," because I find it difficult to separate opinions that I've formed myself from those formed for me by the men with whom I lived, the chance conversation snatched during a slack time in the trenches, or the comments of our mess when the newspapers arrived with George's latest rhapsody about "cheerful Tommies with the glint of battle in their eyes," or the "Times" military expert's hundredth variation on the theme that the art of war consists in killing more of the enemy than he kills of you. . . .

We have drifted apart partly because we have changed and you have not; partly, and that in the most important matters, because we have not changed and you have. Such a cleavage between the civilians who remain civilians and the civilians who become soldiers is, of course, no novelty. It occurred both in the American and in the English Civil Wars. It occurred most conspicuously in the French Armies of 1793 to 1809 or 1810, in which the Revolution survived as a spell that would charm men to death long after it had become an abomination or a curiosity in Paris. And always it seems to have brought something of the shock of an unexpected discovery to those who, not having borne the same life of corporate effort and endurance, forgot that the unquestioning obedience to which soldiers are trained is not obedience to popular opinions, and that the very absence of opportunities for discussion and self-expression tends, like solitude, to lend weight both to new impressions and to already formed mental habits. The contrast between the life which men have left and the unfamiliar duties imposed upon them creates a ferment, none the less powerful because often half-unconscious, in all but the least reflective minds. In particular, when, as has happened in the present war, men have taken up arms not as a profession or because forced to do so by law, but under the influence of some emotion or principle, they tend to be ruled by the idea which compelled them to enlist long after it has yielded, among civilians, to some more fashionable novelty. Less exposed than the civilian to new intellectual influences, the soldier is apt to retain firmly, or even to deepen, the impressions which made him, often reluctantly, a soldier in the first instance. He is like a piece of stone which, in spite of constant friction, preserves the form originally struck out in the fires of a volcanic upheaval. How often, fatigued beyond endurance or horrified by one's actions, does one not recur to those ideas for support and consolation! "It is worth it, because ——" "It is awful, but I need not loathe myself, because ——." We see things which you can only imagine. We are strengthened by reflections which you have abandoned. Our minds differ from yours, both because they are more exposed to change, and because they are less changeable. While you seem — forgive me if I am rude — to have been surrendering your creeds with the nervous facility of a Tudor official, our foreground may be different, but our background is the same. It is that of August to November, 1914. We are your ghosts.

The contrast reveals itself not less in small things than in great. It appears as much in the manner in which you visualize the events of war and interpret to yourselves the duties and moods of your soldiers as in your conception of the principles for which we are fighting, and of the kind of harmony, national and supernational, in which the world may recover stability. But I am wrong in speaking of "small things and great." Clearness of vision and sensitiveness of judgment are not qualities which can be improvised. The ability of men to command them when they need them most is proportionate to the sincerity with which they have habituated themselves to regard matters more accessible and familiar. Therefore I cannot dismiss as trivial the picture which you make to yourselves of war and the mood in which you contemplate that work of art. They are an index of the temper in which you will approach the problems of peace. The war is always beneath your eyes. You read and talk about it, I should say, more constantly than about any other matter. You are anxious to have a truthful account, not of strategy or of other things which are rightly concealed, but of its daily routine and color, the duties and perplexities, dangers and exposure, toil and occasional repose which make up the life of a soldier at the front. You would wish to enter, as far as human beings can enter, into his internal life, to know how he regards the task imposed upon him, how he conceives his relation to the enemy and to yourselves, from what sources he derives encouragement and comfort. You would wish to know these things; we should wish you to know them. Yet between you and us there hangs a veil. It is mainly of your own unconscious creation. It is not a negative, but a positive thing. It is not intellectual, it is moral. It is not ignorance (or I should not mention it). It is falsehood. I read your papers and listen to your conversation, and I see clearly that you have chosen to make to yourselves an image of war, not as it is, but of a kind which, being picturesque, flatters your appetite for novelty, for excitement, for easy admiration, without troubling you with masterful emotions. You have chosen, I say, to make an image, because you do not like, or cannot bear, the truth; because you are afraid of what may happen to your souls if you expose them to the inconsistencies and contradictions, the doubts and bewilderment, which lie beneath the surface of things. You are not deceived as to the facts; for facts of this order are not worth official lying. You are deceived as to the Fact. . . .

Perhaps this judgment is harsh. Yet when I read the pictures of war given every day in your Press I do not think it is. There are in some of them traits which I recognize as not untrue to life. But the general impression given is tragically false. I can forgive you for representing war as a spectacle instead of as a state of existence, for I suppose that to the correspondent who is shepherded into an observation post on a show day it does seem spectacular. But the representation of the human beings concerned is unpardonable. There has been invented a kind of conventional soldier, whose emotions and ideas are those which you find it most easy to assimilate with your coffee and marmalade. And this "Tommy" is a creature at once ridiculous and disgusting. He is represented as invariably "cheerful," as revelling in the "excitement" of war, as finding "sport" in killing other men, as "hunting Germans out of dug-outs as a terrier hunts rats," as overwhelming with kindness the captives of his bow and spear. The last detail is true to life, but the emphasis which you lay upon it is both unintelligent and insulting. Do you expect us to hurt them or starve them? Do you not see that we regard these men who have sat opposite us in mud as the victims of the same catastrophe as ourselves, as our comrades in misery much more truly than you are? Do you think that we are like some of you in accumulating on the head of every wretched antagonist the indignation felt for the wickedness of a government, of a social system, or (if you will) of a nation? For the rest we are depicted as merry assassins, rejoicing in the opportunity of a "scrap" in which we know that more than three-quarters of our friends will be maimed or killed, careless of our own lives, exulting in the duty of turning human beings into lumps of disfigured clay, lighthearted as children in a garden who shoot at sparrows with a new air-gun and clap their hands when they fall, charmed from the transient melancholy of childhood by a game of football or a packet of cigarettes.

Of the first material reality of war, from which everything else takes its color, the endless and loathsome physical exhaustion, you say little, for it would spoil the piquancy, the *verve,* of the picture. Of your soldiers' internal life, the constant collision of contradictory moral standards, the liability of the soul to be crushed by mechanical monotony, the difficulty of keeping hold of sources of refreshment, the sensation of taking a profitless part in a game played by monkeys and organized by lunatics, you realize, I think, nothing. Are you so superficial as to imagine that men do not feel emotions of which they rarely speak? Or do you suppose that, as a cultured civilian once explained to me, these feelings are confined to "gentlemen," and are not shared by "common soldiers"? And behind the picture of war given in your papers there sometimes seems to lurk something worse than, yet allied to, its untruthfulness, a horrible suggestion that war is somehow, after all, ennobling; that, if not the proper occupation of man, it is at least one in which he finds a fullness of self-expression impossible in peace; that when clothed in khaki and carrying rifles, these lads are more truly "men" than they were when working in offices or factories. Perhaps I do you an injustice. But that intimation does seem to me to peep through some of your respectable paragraphs. As I read them I reflect upon the friends who after suffering various degrees of torture died in the illusion that war was not the last word of Christian wisdom. And I have a sensation as of pointed ears and hairy paws and a hideous ape-face grinning into mine — sin upon sin, misery upon misery, to the end of the world.

Oh! gentle public — for you were gentle once and may be so again — put all these delusions from your mind. The reality is horrible, but it is not so horrible as the grimacing phantom which you have imagined. Your soldiers are neither so foolish, nor so brave, nor so wicked, as the mechanical dolls who grin and kill and grin in the columns of your newspapers. No doubt, here and there, are boys to whom the holiday from parents or schoolmasters or employers is an exhilaration, and whose first impressions — how soon worn out! — are printed by credulous editors as representing "the spirit of the Army." Delightful children! To men whose very souls are bleared with mud, they are as refreshing as spring sunshine after endless cold and rain. But in the letters of the rank and file who have spent a winter in the trenches, you will not find war described as "sport." It is a load that they carry with aching bones, hating it, and not unconscious of its monstrosity, hoping dimly that by shouldering it now they will save others from it in the future, looking back with even an exaggerated affection to the blessings of peace.

They carry their burden with little help from you. For an Army does not live by munitions alone, but also by fellowship in a moral idea or purpose. And that you cannot give us. You cannot give it [to] us, because you do not possess it. You are, I see, more divided in soul than you were when I became a soldier, denouncing the apostles of war, yet not altogether disinclined to believe that war is an exalting thing, half implying that our cause is the cause of humanity in general and democracy in particular, yet not daring boldly to say so lest later you should be compelled to fulfil your vows, more complacent and self-sufficient in proportion as you are more confident of victory and have less need of other nations, trusting more in the great machine which you have created and less in the unseen forces which, if you will let them, will work on your side. And you are more prone than you were to give way to hatred. Hatred of the enemy is not common, I think, among soldiers who have fought with them. It is incompatible with the proper discharge of our duty. For to kill in hatred is murder, and we are not murderers but executioners. I know, indeed, how much harder it is for you not to hate than it is for us. You cannot appease the anguish of your losses by feeling, as we feel, that any day your own turn may come. And it is right that there should be a solemn detestation of the sins of Germany, provided that we are not thereby caused to forget our own.

But it is not among those who have suffered most cruelly or where comprehension of the tragedy is most profound that I find the hatred which appals. For in suffering, as in knowledge, there is something that transcends personal emotion and unites the soul to the suffering and wisdom of God. I find it rather among those who, having no outlet in suffering or in action, seem to discover in hatred the sensation of activity which they have missed elsewhere. They are to be pitied, for they also are seeking a union with their kind, though by a path on which it cannot be found. Nevertheless, the contagion of their spirit is deadly. You do not help yourselves, or your country, or your soldiers, by hating, but only by loving and striving to be more lovable.

6. WORKING-CLASS RESISTANCE IN BRITAIN

Labor unrest in Britain was especially pronounced in Scotland, and work stoppages in the Clydeside shipbuilding region (around Glasgow), for example, were notorious. Other issues that prompted working-class organization included rent strikes to protest the escalating cost of housing, and it was within this movement that James Maxton, a subsequent Labour member of Parliament, gained organizational and political experience. His memoirs, from which the following selection comes, provide insight into the formation of a political identity that embraced the Labour party and repudiated the old liberal party in Britain as the advocate for progressive change.

As I sit down to write my recollections of the War years I remind myself that nearly twenty-one years have elapsed since the outbreak of war, and my memory of how I felt

"War Resistance by Working-Class Struggle" by James Maxton, excerpt from *We Did Not Fight,* Julian Bell, ed., Cobden-Sanderson, 1935, pp. 213–222.

and thought at that time is somewhat cloudy. I was twenty-nine years of age and had been a Socialist for about ten years. I was an assistant teacher in a Glasgow Elementary School, Chairman of the Scottish Independent Labour Party [I.L.P.], with a certain reputation as a propagandist and agitator.

When the war broke out I was in the middle of my summer holiday. I found it very difficult to believe that there would be war. I can recall that the incident which jolted the minds of British Socialists into a full realisation of the disturbed state of Europe was the assassination of Jean Jaurès in a Paris café. . . .

The following day I had to go north to Perthshire. A socialist comrade of mine, Robert Nichol, . . . had taken a holiday job as a clerk at a fruit farm to assist the work of picking the raspberry crop. The actual picking was done by a large body of men and women, recruited mainly from the slums of Dundee, Edinburgh and Glasgow. Their wages were the most disgraceful that I have ever had first-hand experience of. Nichol had persuaded them to come out on strike, and wired me to come and give him a hand with the job. I went, and we managed to secure concessions from the employers on all the three matters in dispute. A meeting arranged to be addressed by us . . . on the question of the strike became a huge gathering. . . . The war possibilities were now getting into the minds of the people, and I imagine that the huge meeting was due rather to the war feeling in the air than to the issues of the strike. One or two anti-war utterances by Nichol and myself let us know that our attitude was not fully shared by our hearers. Our strike, however, came to an abrupt end. The war was declared, and the male portion of our army of strikers vanished in twenty-four hours to line up at the recruiting offices to fight for the country which was only giving them the meanest level of existence. Nichol and I were already beginning to learn something of war psychology.

From that time onward the life of a member of the I.L.P. was one of stress and struggle while the war lasted. We were "white-livered curs," bloody pro-Germans, friends of the Kaiser, traitors to our country. A large proportion of our members, particularly elected persons, left us or withdrew from all activities. We had to hold conferences throughout the country with our own members explaining our attitude and encouraging them to stand up to it. At a very early date all of us who were recognised speakers or representative men were asked to take part in joint recruiting campaigns. Refusal to do this roused much public hostility, and when many Labour men in the country agreed to go on recruiting campaigns it made the position of those who refused all the worse. . . .

During this period . . . a Clyde Workers' Committee, consisting of men in the various engineering and shipbuilding works on the Clyde, was organising and directing working-class struggle, not primarily against the war but about industrial and social grievances. . . . One of the first successes of the agitations on the Clyde was the agitation against the attempt of the house owners to raise the rents. This agitation resulted in the passing of the first Rent Restriction Act. Employers had to make wage concessions, but now in our agitational work we had to have regard to the Defence of the Realm Act and the Munitions Act, both of which provided heavy penalties for offences which had to be committed if Socialist or anti-war agitation were to be carried on at all. I remember a fellow teacher, Mr. J. B. Houston, being sentenced to a term of imprisonment with the option of a heavy fine for a sentence or two in a speech which were held to be prejudicial to recruiting. Some ships' joiners in one of the Clyde shipyards were imprisoned for making a demand about wages which was held to impede the production of munitions.

The Clyde Workers' Committee . . . carried on very active agitational work and produced a weekly newspaper which was widely read. One week-end I went to London to attend a meeting of the No-Conscription Fellowship. When I returned to Glasgow on the Sunday morning it was to learn that the active men in the Clyde Workers' Committee had been seized from their homes during the previous night and been carted away somewhere out of Glasgow, no one knew where. I was due to speak that afternoon on Glasgow Green against conscription. I went there, but a large portion of my speech dealt with the deportation of these men. A few days afterwards I also was arrested in the middle of the night, and after a period of some weeks in jail was tried and sentenced to twelve months imprisonment for a breach of the Defence of the Realm Act. . . .

When my time expired I came out and began to adjust myself to the new situation. I was unemployed and without resources. I had been dismissed from my teaching position and there was no chance of a man of my age, reputation and record getting back. Within a few days I was called before the Military Service Tribunal. I told them my grounds for refusing military service, and admitted that they were political and not religious. The Military Representative was good enough to say that he had no particular desire to have me in the army, for reasons which he did not intend to be flattering to myself, and I was given exemption on condition that I found some work of national importance, as it was called. Work was not difficult to get, but people with my attitude to the war had to find jobs which were not directly assisting the work of slaughter. It was impossible to do any work at all that did not help in some way, but I felt that staying in prison helped the progress of the war in so far as it precluded me from carrying on my work of Socialist agitation. I appreciated and understood the attitude of my friends who absolutely declined to do anything, and suffered continuous imprisonment over the whole war period, but it did not suit my philosophy, which demanded active carrying on of class struggle, nor did it suit my temperament to be cribbed, cabined and confined when the urge within me was to be out trying to influence my fellows to use the opportunities presented by war conditions for the purposes of social revolution.

I got a job in a small Clyde shipyard which was not engaged in making warships or troopships, but was engaged in the peaceful task of making barges to be used for the conveyance of cocoanuts and fruit on West African rivers. I had no doubt that the boats would in some way assist the progress of the war, but they would never kill anyone, and the hope of most of my workmates, who were not so anti-war as myself, was that they would be sunk on their way to Africa, so that they would get more to build. I am afraid I am not able to claim that I have been one of the great shipbuilders of the world, but I did get experience of all the unskilled and semi-skilled work around a shipyard, and got to know how ships were built. What was of more importance for my immediate purposes was that I got into close relationships with the manual workers and was able to participate in the struggles of that time as one of themselves.

By this time war weariness was setting in and it was much easier to make anti-war speeches. The workers as a whole had become more vocal, and although work was plentiful and wages higher, the constant grind had aroused a great irritability among them, and the Socialist agitator was listened to with greater appreciation than ever before in my experience. I carried on my usual agitational and propaganda work for the I.L.P., and whereas the early days of the war had seen our membership diminish, now we, in common with other Socialist organisations, found our membership going up. The speeches I made were much more revolutionary and provocative to the authorities than the one that had got me imprisoned, but by this time they did not feel so confident in proceeding with prosecutions. . . .

When the Russian revolution took place we were at first dumbfounded. It was what our Socialist teaching had told us should take place and must take place sooner or later, but it had come sooner than most of us had expected, and it had come in a place where we had not expected it; but when we recovered from our surprise the Revolution was hailed enthusiastically by all sections of the working class movement, and those of us who had held a revolutionary point of view set out forthwith with the idea of seeing similar revolutionary achievement in the various European countries. That did not happen. It came very near to happening in several of them, and in all of them working class consciousness became more strongly developed than ever before. For some years that attitude of mind remained, and then came reaction. Reaction which is still with us, but should this reaction lead the peoples into another world conflict, the experiences of the last struggle justify us in believing that the capitalist system would not survive it. The human race would suffer terribly, but the human race would survive, to build a different social order.

7. THE COST OF CONSCIENCE

The war threw into bold relief not just the dictates of individual conscience but the case of whether the costs incurred in seeking victory might prove too great — that the end might not justify the means. This issue was central to the discussion in Britain over conscientious objection. The following extract from *The Nation* is a classic liberal defense of individual freedom.

With what ideals did we go into this war, and with what realities are we ending it? High principles of international justice, national right, humanity, even in warfare, were on our lips eighteen months ago. Nor were they on our lips alone. Those do their countrymen deep injustice who do not recognize that the cause of Belgium animated tens of thousands of those young men who marched the roads to the tune of "Tipperary" in those golden September days. Beyond the case of Belgium there was a sincere feeling — indeed, we should call it a true perception — that this country stood for the solidarity of human interests, and for the distinctive ideals of Western democracy. This truth —

From *The Nation,* 20 May 1916.

the fundamental truth about the war — has never been shaken by criticism, but has, on the contrary, been fortified by the further revelation of German methods. But there was another kind of sceptical or pessimistic criticism not so easy to meet. "You go to war," it said, "to maintain certain sacred rights. But war is in practice incompatible with right — not only an unjust, as you would admit, but even and equally a just, war. War is an impartial tyrant that forces upon all who yield to it essentially the same system of disregard of primary human obligations. It is not only the laws, as the Romans admitted, which are silent amid arms; but morals, conscience, religion, humanity. You may make up your mind over and over again that it shall not be so. But the facts will be too strong for you. You give yourself over to the drill-sergeant. Even worse, you give yourself over to that thing of terror, the non-combatant. You abandon your political or personal freedom. These things are alien from war, where one must command and all the rest obey. In a word, fighting for liberty, democracy, and right, you inevitably hand yourself over to the control of a spirit which knows liberty, democracy, and right only to hate them and trample them under foot."

The great internal or domestic question of the war has been and will be whether this pessimistic criticism would justify itself. That there would have to be many restrictions on personal liberty was, of course, recognized by the most optimistic; but they would have argued that the crisis was of the gravest, and that restrictions honestly held necessary to preserve the existence of the nation, could not fairly come under the ban. But there have been departures which cannot be justified by this criterion. Of these the treatment of the Conscientious Objector to military service is perhaps the most flagrant. We say nothing for the moment of the general case for or against conscription. But accepting conscription, the Government, like everyone else, was aware that there was a small but perfectly sincere and resolute body of men who would refuse conformity. In the case of the larger section of this body, the Society of Friends, the reasons are familiar to all, and have been familiar for two centuries and more — so familiar that even Hegel, the philosophic sponsor of the Prussian State, suggests that for Quakers and Anabaptists it would be reasonable to find a substitute for military service. It was also matter of current knowledge that besides Quakers there were a few others who, some as Christians, others as Socialists, hold the taking of human life a thing absolutely unlawful, and refuse to take part in it directly or indirectly. Parliament saw the danger of a clash between law and conscience, and saw also that it could be averted. The number to be considered was so small that it could have no sensible effect on our military efficiency. All that was necessary was to have some assurance that the conscientious objection was genuine and not a mere cloak for slackness or for convenience. Unfortunately, the intention of Parliament was haltingly and inadequately expressed, and the tribunals which it set up were, in many cases, unequal to the task of doing justice to opinions which they, like most of us, hold to be in fact mistaken. The result is that in numerous cases, after a most unedifying exhibition of dialectics as to the meaning of some exceedingly plain passages in the Gospels, or as to the probable action of the objector in various imaginary contingencies, his appeal is either refused altogether or he is passed for non-combatant service, which, as a rule, he regards morally on one plane with the actual fighting. Of these men, a number are proving their sincerity, and therefore *ipso facto,* the error of the tribunal, by maintaining their refusal to serve, against the full pressure of military authority. Some have been sent to hard labor, and others — most sinister of all — to France. As to the fate of these men, the question is urgent and critical. The Government makes some vague disclaimers as to the death penalty, but Government disclaimers are valueless. We are launched upon what is, in effect, a religious persecution, and if no adequate protest is made, we may at any moment hear that, for the first time, we suppose, for two centuries under English law, a man has gone deliberately to his death for his religious faith. The peculiar vice of this persecution is that every step it takes proves, out of its own mouth, the sincerity of its victims and the inequity and inconsistency of its own methods. For the principle, accepted by Parliament, upon which the whole scheme of compulsion rests is that the true Conscientious Objector shall be free. Every man persecuted is being threatened, punished, imprisoned, and in danger of death because he has been held not to be a sincere objector, and every threat or act of persecution that he steadily confronts proves the contention to be false, proves the tribunal that refused him exemption to be wrong, proves that he is precisely not that which he is punished for being. . . . The war is not being helped by the diversion of the efforts of various good soldiers from their proper business of fighting the Germans to the futile task of forcibly converting a good citizen into a reluctant non-combatant camp follower. It is a question, not merely of saving innocent lives, but of maintaining our good name and ensuring the hopes and ideals with which we went into the war, and for which, in all good faith, scores of thousands of the best of our sons and brothers have given their blood.

8. BRITAIN'S PARLIAMENT DEBATES CONSCIENTIOUS OBJECTION

In mid-1917 the House of Commons debated the issue of electoral reform. By now it was clear that some extension of the right to vote was necessary, given that many working-class soldiers were excluded from the franchise. As it stood, the property and residential requirements made it hard for some workers to qualify for the vote. No politician argued that those men, who were prepared to lay down their lives, could remain disfranchised. But a significant number of Conservative MPs favored depriving conscientious objectors, who had not shown the same willingness, of the right to vote after the war. These Tories' arguments were countered from within their own party by Lord Hugh Cecil, a talented son of former Prime Minister Lord Salisbury and a staunch advocate of the Anglican church in particular and of spiritual concerns in general.

[Mr. R. McNeill:]
. . . If these conscientious objectors choose to say, "You cannot make us do what your law and your morals may allow to us, and we would rather suffer death or dishonour

From *House of Commons Parliamentary Debates,* June 26, 1917.

than take the life of man, and we are entitled to do so." But why? They are entitled to do so because their action in that case affects no one, injures no one but themselves. Substantially speaking they will be justified in abstaining from taking life under those circumstances, because it is their own concern. But in the case of the conscientious objectors, which we are considering, it is exactly the opposite. The action they take does not injure themselves; in so far as one can see the immediate effect of it is to benefit themselves. They benefit themselves, but they injure everybody else. They benefit themselves by escaping from the burden, or escaping from the obligation, and they injure other people, because the inhabitants are bearing their common burden, and anyone who stands away necessarily imposes a greater burden upon those who are left. They injure the whole community in which they live; they even endanger the State of which they form a part, or, if they do not endanger it, the only reason is because they are not numerous enough to be a serious danger. They are comparatively few. . . .

Let me ask the Committee for a moment to consider — that being, in my opinion, the aspect of their conduct and their conscience — what it means in the eyes of their fellow countrymen. We have at the present time a combination of the most democratic and ethical-minded peoples on the earth, all in complete agreement upon a matter which is a moral purpose, in complete agreement that unless these peoples withstand Germany and fight Germany to defeat her, the only alternative to that is the loss of all the highest ideals of humanity and of civilisation. That has been expressed time after time by the most representative minds in all the nations of the West. Then against that universal conviction of all these combined peoples we have a small handful of men setting up a little circumscribed, ignorant, uninstructed, dogmatism of their own, many of these men being, so far as we can judge from what we have heard in the House and what we read in the papers, almost half crazy, and, so far as I can remember, not one of them a man who has had any past record established to claim to be accepted as either a leader of thought or a guide of conduct in this country. . . .

. . . Then the question comes: Are they to be allowed to exercise the franchise after the War is over? In other words, are they, when this peril is over and when the Army returns and peace is restored, to enjoy all the rights and privileges of the State which they would not lift a hand to preserve? When the ship was in danger these men would not soil their hands by taking a turn at the pumps. Are these men to be allowed not only to have enjoyed immunity from the work we are engaged in, but also to be allowed to share both the honours and the promotions with the men who have brought the ship into port? To do so would [be] an outrage upon all the enlightened conscience of the nation as a whole. . . .

[Lord H. Cecil:]
. . . Unfortunately, I think both from a lower and a higher point of view my hon. Friend's argument is defective. First of all, I think he very much underrated the force of the consideration that what he is really proposing is to impose a retrospective penalty upon persons who have done nothing worse than avail themselves of an exemption which Parliament themselves afforded them. Personally, I think Parliament did right; but whether Parliament did right or wrong, it is at any rate bound in honour by what it

did. To go to people first of all and say, "If you allege a conscientious objection, and the tribunals we have appointed find you are sincere, you shall be exempted," and then to turn round on them after they have done what Parliament has offered and allowed them to do, and say "You have done this thing, you are the basest of mankind, and unfit for the franchise" — to do that without warning them beforehand would seem to me to transgress all the principles of legislation and national justice. My hon. Friend, in an extraordinarily interesting speech, tried to lay down — if I may say so, a very courageous enterprise — a basis on which the State ought to deal with questions of opinion, and he certainly laid down a basis which would have justified the persecution of the Christians in the first days of Christianity, and still more clearly of the Protestants of Holland. . . . Nothing is more foolish than to underrate the virtue of persecutors. They are very sincere people. They thought, and quite correctly, that the institution which was to them much more valuable than life itself was threatened by those they persecuted. They thought, and often quite correctly, that the persons they were persecuting were a small minority, ignorant and defiled by many faults and infirmities. The error they fell into is much more obvious than the one often imputed to arrogance. The error they fell into was in assuming that human beings have the right to impose opinions upon one another. I am following my hon. Friend on that ground, although I do not think it is necessary to traverse it for the purpose of this discussion. I am quite satisfied that the State can only act wisely in respect to opinions by not going into the reasonableness of any opinion whatever, but allowing liberty of opinion, because in the end it is in the interest of truth that liberty of opinion should be allowed. I am quite as certain as my hon. Friend that the conscientious objectors are wrong, but I am also quite certain that, shall we say, Presbyterians are wrong. It is a question of opinion. . . .

[Captain Gwynn:]
. . . I agree with the Noble Lord in his opposition to this Amendment, but I do not know that I could give exactly the same reasons. Substantially, however, I think they are the same. I agree with him that these are people who are not a blight upon the community; they may very probably prove to be, in my opinion, the very salt of the community. I am speaking now as one who has seen war. I think that everybody who has seen war has one governing desire, and that is to see war abolished from the world. I am not at all sure that these people, whom we propose to reject as the outcasts of the State, may not be the best people to help in the fight to make an end of war. There is one thing that nobody can deny them — I am speaking now, as the Noble Lord spoke, of the real conscientious objector, let us put the other people aside — and that is courage, the most difficult form of courage in the world, the courage of the individual against the crowd. That is a courage which every State would do well to protect and guard. That is the courage which, above all others, makes for freedom. It is for that that I desire to see these men electors, and that I vote for giving them votes — just exactly as I would give votes to the soldiers — because they are the people who have shown not merely physical courage, but because they have made civic responsibility their plea. They have shown a spirit of initiative. These people, in refusing to act, must have taken action which must have been extremely difficult to take, and when we are told that the good

of the nation is to be somehow impaired by allowing these men a voice in our national councils, I ask myself, What is "the good of the nation"? Are you going to advance the real interests of this country, or of any country, by stamping out such people from among your full citizens? Progress, as far as I can understand, comes not with the crowd, but with individuals. Freedom in the last resort is won by individuals working against the crowd, and these are the people who make for freedom. It is in the interests of freedom during a war that is fought, at all events professedly, for freedom that I resist this attempt to limit what is the exercise of their legal freedom, and what is, I think with the Noble Lord, the exercise of higher morals.

9. PACIFISM—A POLITICAL CRIME?

Hélène Brion (1882–1962) had the distinction in 1918 of being the only woman pacifist tried for treason by the French government. A nursery school teacher in Paris during the war, with ties to both the women's movement and a socialist teachers' union, Brion distributed pacifist pamphlets, for which she was dismissed from her teaching position and prosecuted for breach of state-imposed censorship. Although she was found guilty, the French government suspended her three-year sentence. Brion's defense of her pacifist position at her trial is reprinted here.

I appear before this court charged with a political crime; yet I am denied all political rights.

Because I am a woman, I am classified *de plano* by my country's laws, far inferior to all the men of France and the colonies. In spite of the intelligence that has been officially recognized only recently, in spite of the certificates and diplomas that were granted me long ago, before the law I am not the equal of an illiterate black from Guadeloupe or the Ivory Coast. For *he* can participate, by means of the ballot, in directing the affairs of our common country, while *I* cannot. I am outside the law.

The law should be logical and ignore my existence when it comes to punishments, just as it is ignored when it comes to rights. I protest against its lack of logic.

I protest against the application of laws that I have neither wished for nor discussed.

This law that I challenge reproaches me for having held opinions of a nature to undermine popular morale. I protest even more strongly and I deny it! My discreet and nuanced propaganda has always been a constant appeal to reason, to the power of reflection, to the good sense that belongs to every human being, however small the portion.

Moreover, I recall, for form's sake, that my propaganda has never been directed against the national defense and has never called for peace at any price: on the contrary, I have always maintained that there was but one duty, one duty with two parts: for those at the front, to hold fast; for those at the rear, to be thoughtful.

I have exercised this educational action especially in a feminist manner, for I am first and foremost a *feminist*. All those who know me can attest to it. And it is because of my feminism that I am an enemy of war.

Excerpt from "L'Affaire Hélène Brion au I^e Conseil de Guerre" by Hélène Brion, 1918.

The accusation suggests that I preach pacifism under the pretext of feminism. This accusation distorts my propaganda for its own benefit! I affirm that the contrary is true, and it is easy for me to prove it. I affirm that I have been a militant feminist for many years, well before the war; that since the war began I have simply continued; and that I have never reflected on the horrors of the present without noting that things might have been different if women had had a say in matters concerning social issues. . . .

I am an enemy of war because I am a feminist. War represents the triumph of brute strength, while feminism can only triumph through moral strength and intellectual values. Between the two there is total contradiction.

I do not believe that in primitive society the strength or value of woman was inferior to that of men, but it is certain that in present-day society the possibility of war has established a totally artificial scale of values that works to women's detriment.

Woman has been deprived of the sacred and inalienable right given to every individual to defend himself when attacked. By definition (and often by education) she has been made a weak, docile, insignificant creature who needs to be protected and directed throughout her life.

Far from being able to defend her young, as is the case among the rest of creation, she is [even] denied the right to defend herself. In material terms she is denied physical education, sports, the exercise of what is called the noble profession of arms. In political terms she is denied the right to vote — what Gambetta called "the keystone of every other right" — by means of which she could influence her own destiny and have at least the resource to try to do something to prevent these dreadful conflicts in which she and her children find themselves embroiled, like a poor unconscious and powerless machine. . . .

You other men, who alone govern the world! you are trying to do too much and too well. Leave well enough alone.

You want to spare our children the horrors of a future war; a praiseworthy sentiment! I declare that as of now your goal has been attained and that as soon as the atrocious battle that is taking place less than a hundred miles from us has been brought to a halt, you will be able to speak of peace. In 1870 two European nations fought — only two, and for scarcely six months; the result was so appalling that throughout all of Europe, terrified and exhausted, it took more than forty years before anyone dared or was able to begin again. Figure that as of now we have fought, not six months, but for forty-four long months of unbelievable and dreadful combat, where not merely two nations are at odds, but more than twenty — the elite of the so-called civilized world — that almost the entire white race is involved in the melee, that the yellow and black races have been drawn into the wake. And you say, pardon me, that as of now your goal has been achieved! — for the exhaustion of the world is such that more than a hundred years of peace would be instantaneously assured if the war were to end this evening!

The tranquility of our children and grandchildren is assured. Think about assuring them happiness in the present and health in the future! Think about some means of providing them bread when they need it, and sugar, and chocolate to drink! Calculate the repercussions that their present deprivation will have on this happiness that you pretend to offer them by continuing to fight and making them live in this atmosphere, which is unhealthy from every possible point of view.

You want to offer freedom to enslaved people, you want — whether they like it or not — to call to freedom people who do not seem ready to understand it as you do, and you do not seem to notice that in this combat you carry on for liberty, all people lose more and more what little they possess, from the material freedom of eating what they please and traveling wherever they wish, to the intellectual liberties of writing, of meeting, even of thinking and especially the possibility of thinking straight — all that is disappearing bit by bit because it is incompatible with a state of war.

Take care! The world is descending a slope that will be difficult to remount.

I have constantly said this, have written about it incessantly since the beginning of the war: if you do not call women to your rescue, you will not be able to ascend the slope, and the new world that you pretend to install will be as unjust and as chaotic as the one that existed before the war!

10. LENIN'S VIEW OF THE WAR

Although many European socialists initially supported the war, some remained adamantly opposed from the outset. Contrast the German Social Democratic party's defense of its willingness to grant war credits in 1914 with the strong condemnation of such actions in this selection. Its author, the Russian Bolshevik leader V. I. Lenin, was the most influential theorist in Russian social democracy — an eminence that forced him to spend much of the war in exile, returning to Russia only after the February Revolution in 1917.

1. The European and World War has the sharp and definite character of a bourgeois, imperialist, and dynastic war. The struggle for markets and the looting of countries, the intention to deceive, disunite, and kill off the proletarians of all countries, by instigating the hired slaves of one nation against the hired slaves of the other for the benefit of the bourgeoisie — such is the only real meaning and purpose of the war.

2. The conduct of the leaders of the German Social Democratic party of the Second International (1889–1914) — who have voted the war budget and who repeat the bourgeois chauvinist phrases of the Prussian Junkers and of the bourgeoisie — is a direct betrayal of socialism. In no case, even assuming an absolute weakness of that party and the necessity of submitting to the will of the bourgeois majority of the nation, can the conduct of the leaders of the German Social Democratic party be justified. In fact, this party leads at present a national liberal policy.

3. The conduct of the leaders of the Belgian and French Social Democratic parties, who have betrayed socialism by entering bourgeois cabinets, deserves the same condemnation.

4. The betrayal of socialism by the majority of the leaders of the Second Interna-

"Theses on the War" by V. Lenin, pp. 140–143. Reprinted from *The Bolsheviks and the World War: The Origin of the Third International* by Olga Hess Gankin and H. H. Fisher with the permission of the publishers, Stanford University Press. Copyright © 1940 by the Board of Trustees of the Leland Stanford Junior University.

tional (1889–1914) means an ideological collapse of that International. The fundamental cause of this collapse is the actual predominance in it of petty-bourgeois opportunism, the bourgeois nature and danger of which has long been pointed out by the best representatives of the proletariat of all countries. Opportunists have long been preparing the collapse of the Second International by renouncing the socialist revolution and substituting bourgeois reformism for it; by renouncing class struggle, with its transformation into civil war, which is necessary at certain moments; by preaching bourgeois chauvinism under the guise of patriotism and defense of the fatherland and by ignoring or renouncing the ABC truth of socialism, expressed long ago in the "Communist manifesto," that workers have no fatherland; by confining themselves in the struggle against militarism to a sentimental Philistine point of view instead of recognizing the necessity of a revolutionary war of the proletarians of all countries against the bourgeoisie of all countries; by turning the necessity to utilize bourgeois parliamentarism and bourgeois legality into a fetish and forgetting that illegal forms of organization and agitation are imperative during epochs of crises. One of the organs of international opportunism, the *Socialist Monthly,* which has long taken the national-liberal stand, is right in celebrating its victory over European socialism.

5. Of the bourgeois and chauvinist sophisms by which the bourgeois parties and governments of the two chief rival nations of the continent, Germany and France, are especially fooling the masses, and which are being slavishly repeated by the socialist opportunists trailing behind the bourgeoisie (the open as well as the covert opportunists), the following should be especially noted and branded: when the German bourgeoisie refers to the defense of the fatherland, to the struggle against Tsarism, to the protection of the freedom of cultural and national development, they lie; for the Prussian Junkerdom, headed by Wilhelm II, and also the big bourgeoisie, have always pursued the policy of defending the Tsarist monarchy, and whatever the outcome of the war, they will not fail to direct their efforts toward supporting that monarchy; they lie, for, in fact, the Austrian bourgeoisie has undertaken a plunder march against Serbia, the German bourgeoisie oppresses the Danes, the Poles and the French (in Alsace-Lorraine) by waging an aggressive war against Belgium and France for the sake of robbing the richer and freer countries, by organizing the onslaught at the moment considered by them to be the most convenient for utilizing their latest improvements of military technique, and on the eve of the introduction of the so-called big military program by Russia. Similarly, when the French bourgeoisie refer to the defense of the fatherland, etc., they also lie; for in reality they defend countries which are backward in their capitalist technique and which develop more slowly, by hiring with their billions the Black Hundred gangs of Russian Tsarism to wage war for the purpose of plundering Austrian and German territories. Neither of the two belligerent groups of nations is behind the other in the cruelty and barbarism of waging war.

6. The task of Social Democracy in Russia consists in the first place in a merciless and ruthless struggle against the Great Russian and Tsarist-monarchist chauvinism, and against the sophistic defense of this chauvinism by Russian liberals, Constitutional Democrats, and others and by some of the Narodniks. From the point of view of the laboring class and the toiling masses of all the peoples of Russia, the lesser evil would be the defeat

of the Tsarist monarchy and its army which oppresses Poland, the Ukraine, and a number of other peoples of Russia and which inflames national hatred for the purpose of strengthening the oppression of other nationalities by the Great Russians and for the stabilization of the reaction and the barbarous government of the Tsarist monarchy.

7. The slogans of Social Democracy at the present time should be: First, a thorough propaganda (to be spread also in the army and the area of military activity) for a socialist revolution and for the necessity of turning the weapons not against brothers, hired slaves of other countries, but against the reaction of the bourgeois governments and parties of all countries — to carry on such propaganda in all languages it is absolutely necessary to organize illegal cells and groups in the armies of all nations — a merciless struggle against chauvinism and the "patriotism" of petty townsmen and against the bourgeoisie of all countries without exception. It is imperative to appeal to the revolutionary conscience of the working masses, which carry the heavy burden of the war and which are hostile to chauvinism and opportunism, against the leaders of the contemporary International, who have betrayed socialism. Second — as one of the immediate slogans — agitation in favor of German, Polish, Russian, and other republics, along with the transformation of all the separate states of Europe into a republican united states.

11. A SOCIALIST APPEAL TO WORKERS

As the war dragged on, those in opposition to it from the beginning saw no reason to revise their opinions. Although the Second International had collapsed as a forum for pan-European socialist and proletarian unity, some more radical socialists attempted to retrieve that spirit while meeting in neutral Switzerland. The following manifesto, stressing the primacy of class commitment over nationalism, illustrates those efforts. Issued in December 1916, it also rejected as halfhearted, or illusory, recent overtures by Germany and President Woodrow Wilson to end the war through a negotiated peace.

The third year of war is now a reality. Two and a half years of uninterrupted slaughter, two and a half years of unprecedented destruction and devastation, are not enough. The beast unchained on August 1, 1914, after several years of systematic preparation on the part of all the capitalist governments, is not yet satiated. New streams of blood must still be shed. Still more refined and cruel methods must be devised to slaughter men. Still heavier sacrifices will be made until Europe is completely impoverished and exhausted.

Why? For what reason?

The causes of this self-destruction of peoples were indicated in the manifestoes of Zimmerwald and of Kienthal. They are: greediness, desire of the capitalist classes for

"An Appeal to the Working Class," pp. 469–471. Reprinted from *The Bolsheviks and the World War: The Origin of the Third International* by Olga Hess Gankin and H. H. Fisher with the permission of the publishers, Stanford University Press. Copyright © 1940 by the Board of Trustees of the Leland Stanford Junior University.

conquest, their imperialist lust, and their criminal desire to augment profits in their own as well as in the conquered countries and to procure for themselves new sources of wealth.

This truth cannot be effaced either by diplomatic lies, by the prevarications of statesmen, or by the chauvinist phrases of ignoble ex-socialists. This truth has been evidenced and confirmed once more by the events of recent months.

Rumania, whose national glory and esteem were supposed to be increased — in reality she is nothing but a pawn on the chessboard of the great imperialist powers — lies broken on the ground. She underwent the fate of Belgium, Serbia, Montenegro, the fate which tomorrow awaits Greece and other yet neutral states. The miserable farce of the "liberation" of Poland, a country which was not worse off even under the Tsar's whip than under the regime of the Austro-German "liberator," proves how little the military victor thinks of anything but complete robbery and pillage. The deportation of Belgian and Polish proletarians for the purpose of putting them at forced labor far from their native lands, the transformation of all the belligerent states into national penitentiaries, the ghastly terror against all those who appeal to common sense and reason in order to terminate the horrible massacre, the prisons overflowing with the best and most courageous of the fighters of the laboring class — all these facts constitute so many reasons for indicting the ruling classes, so many proofs of their military lies and of the vile motives, greediness, and rapacity which underlie both this war and previous wars.

Today this war is passing through a crisis: "No victors, no vanquished — or rather all vanquished, all bleeding, all ruined, all exhausted." The statesmen of belligerent countries, caught in their own traps, dominated by the war, are now staging the comedy of peace. Just as in peacetime they play with the menace of war, so during the war they prostitute the idea of peace.

The Central Powers have offered to open peace negotiations with their adversaries. But how? By arming themselves to the teeth, by placing their last man under the yoke of organized manslaughter, by acclaiming their victories! Really, such negotiations are utter buffoonery, conducted for the purpose of hiding the truth from the peoples. No doubt these peace proposals will be rejected and thus the ferment of national hatred and of chauvinism will be revived.

The reply of the opposing Entente Powers is worthy of the proposition of the Central Powers. The guardians of the bloody Tsar feel at ease in the terrible bath of blood in their own country. The advocates of pogroms prepare for a general European pogrom. In order to extend their power to Constantinople, to the Straits, and to Prussian Poland, they are ready to sacrifice to the last man the youth of Europe, for they have never stopped even at the most disgraceful acts so long as their power could be maintained over the peoples oppressed by Russia.

The renegade Briand seeks by phrases of hatred and contempt to conceal from France the fact that in reality by continuing the war she is spilling her own blood and moving toward destruction and that she is doing this for the Allied Powers. The greatest demagogue of the century, Lloyd George, advances deliberately the false assertion that England is fighting for the complete liberation of the oppressed peoples. Does he, like his friend Briand, forget that England and France, through their diplomacy and war policy, are bound to Russia's war aims? Do they forget what aspirations England is pursuing in the Orient, in Mesopotamia, and in Asia Minor?

And what about the note of the President of the United States? It cannot lose the character, scarcely disguised, of a war note. Very well, if Wilson wishes peace, America should stop every individual, without any exception, from gaining billions on war deliveries and, with that, as proof, appear before the world as an apostle of peace.

Truly, even today the governments do not want peace, because the leaders of the war fear the inevitable settling of accounts which must follow, and others find war profits more attractive than the highest interests and human rights. There is only one power that can force them to conclude peace: the awakened force of the international proletariat, the firm will to turn one's weapons not against one's own brothers but against the internal enemy in every country.

Meanwhile this force is not yet very large. Even endless calamities and terrible blows have not yet opened the eyes of the peoples. However, something is stirring in every nation on earth. There is no country in which the energetic proletariat does not raise the banner of socialism signifying peace and liberty; there is not a state which does not ban these champions from society and persecute them, thus proving that they are feared as the only force in favor of a real and lasting peace.

This struggle of socialist minorities against their governments and against social patriotic hirelings must be continued without truce or delay. The duty toward one's own class, toward the future of mankind, must stand above everything else. To accomplish this task must be the unbreakable resolve of all workers in the belligerent states as well as in the neutral countries, the former by assembling all the forces in every country in order to oppose them to the dominant class, and the latter by supporting with all their moral and financial power the struggle of the minorities.

At an hour when the war has come to an impasse;

At an hour when the diplomats' hypocritical gestures of peace will lead only to still more atrocious massacres if the masses do not prove their will for peace at the price of the greatest sacrifices;

At an hour when the phantoms of want and famine have become realities —

Now it is imperative to act with faithfulness and complete devotion in the spirit of revolutionary international socialism in order to secure a prompt ending of war. It is necessary to fight for the Workers' International, the liberator of the peoples.

Hail the class struggle!

Hail peace!

Hail the Workers' International!

The Socialist International Committee in Berne

12. STRIKES IN BRITAIN

Given the growing scale of industrial unrest and strike activity in Britain in 1916 and 1917, it is hardly surprising that an official commission was appointed to look into the matter. The following selection summarizes the commission's investigation and principal conclusions, which may be compared with the interpretation of labor action evident in Maxton's memoirs from Part III, Section C.

[N]ot quite three years after the beginning of the war a Commission was appointed by the Prime Minister to "inquire and report upon Industrial Unrest and to make recommendations to the Government at the earliest practicable date." . . .

With the aid of the Commissioners' reports it is not very difficult to see what the main causes of the unrest have been.

In the first place we may take the loss of individual liberty. Of course, many of the restrictions imposed by war measures, while irritating enough to the people in general, can scarcely be regarded as causes of "industrial" unrest, inasmuch as they are not directly connected with employment. Such are the liquor restrictions, and the fact is probably the explanation of the sharp divergence of opinion between the various panels of the Commission when they ask themselves whether the liquor restrictions have been a cause of industrial unrest. . . . The Commissioners in general adopt the view very naïvely expressed in the North-Western report, that "the matter should be sensibly dealt with, not from the high ideals of temperance reformers, whose schemes of betterment must be kept in their proper place till after the war, but from the human point of view of keeping the man who has to do war work in a good temper, which will enable him to make the necessary sacrifices in a contented spirit," beer being to many of the best citizens of the country "not only a beverage, but a sacred national institution."

Conscription appears at first sight not to be a distinctively industrial matter, any more than the liquor restrictions, but it becomes so in consequence of the necessary exceptions to its universality. The loss of liberty involved in every man of a certain age being compelled to serve was a popular loss among almost all classes, because the man of military age who was not willing to serve was disliked, but whether or not, it could not have been a cause of specifically industrial unrest. But when it was found that universality was impossible, and the loss of liberty took the form of tribunals deciding who was to go and who to stay, the situation was completely altered. Decisions that this man and that man, though of military age and fitness, shall be allowed to stay at home in safety because they are indispensable to the industry in which they are employed are and must be industrial decisions, and, human nature being what it is, they are absolutely certain to become a cause of industrial unrest. Moreover, the Army itself, though its efforts are directed to the destruction of the enemy, is an industrial organisation, and offers great variety of occupation: the selection of men for the various occupations is entirely in the hands of the military authorities, and would be far from giving universal satisfaction, even if those authorities were perfectly wise. As things are, it is not surprising to hear from the Scotch Commissioners that "the whole system of the operation of the Military Acts is, in the opinion of the great bulk of the working classes, an exhibition of bungling incompetence and of exasperating dilatory methods," and that the opinion generally held of the unfair working of the Acts is "a great cause of unrest."

While willing to submit to the loss of liberty involved in universal military service,

Excerpt from "Industrial Unrest," *The Economic Journal* (December 1917), pp. 454–459.

the working classes to a man were strenuously opposed to "industrial conscription." Now it is true that no man has been industrially conscribed in the sense of being directly compelled to take some particular employment, but a great deal of what may be called negative industrial conscription has been introduced by restricting men's freedom to abandon their employment, either by way of strike or in order to take other employment. As the West Midlands Commissioners say, "The Munitions of War Acts have revolutionised industry. In normal times the workman is free to leave his employment, whether to secure better wages or on personal grounds; now he can do neither unless his employer consents or the Munitions Tribunal grants a certificate. . . . In normal times wage changes are settled by collective bargaining; now they are settled by the State. In normal times the employer disciplines his own men; now discipline is enforced publicly in a criminal court. Lastly, the Trade Unions have fought, rightly or wrongly, and in the engineering trades have fought successfully, for the principle that certain men or certain unions alone were entitled to certain work. Now this has been swept away, and men and women of rival unions, or of no unions at all, work alongside skilled craftsmen. These changes are strongly resented as infringements of personal liberty, to which men are deeply attached." . . .

. . . The eight panels of the Commission are unanimous in regarding the opinion of the working classes, that they have been exploited by the rise of food prices, as the universal and most important cause of industrial unrest.

The other great reason for the failure of the rise of money wages to placate the wage-earners has been the fitfulness of its distribution. . . . The war changes have not only altered the distribution of earnings between different industries, but have altered the distribution between different classes of workers inside each industry at haphazard, so that individuals working in the same shop have seen their relative positions reversed. . . .

. . . The war caused changes which can be grouped under three heads: —

"*First,* the introduction of semi-skilled and unskilled men and women into work previously regarded as skilled men's work.

"*Second,* the largely increased output of existing processes giving a greater earning power for the same piece rate, and

"*Third,* the introduction of many new processes easily learnt and yielding a high wage at the agreed piece rates. To this must be added the great speeding-up which the beginning of the war called out, and the fact that it was very wisely determined that piece rates existing before the war should not be reduced. The result has been as great a revolution in industry as any similar period has witnessed. The output has been vastly increased, old processes have been scrapped, and new and more efficient ones introduced. Our industries stand on a different plane from the pre-war period. Now the effect of increased production coupled with a fixed piece rate has been a great increase of the earning power of workers doing repetition work. The rates were fixed in peace time, when not only were conditions more leisurely, but orders were received in dozens and grosses where they are now received in thousands and tens of thousands. Hence the machine can now be worked for a longer productive period, the output is enormously increased, and the wages earned have reached a height hitherto undreamt of. In the engineering trade four pounds a week for [a] man or woman, who has entered the trade since the war, is not an unusual wage; whilst in many cases the wage reaches six, eight, and ten pounds a week or even more, all, be it understood, by workers with no previous experience. At the same time the tool-maker and the gauge-maker, both skilled men whose skill is the basis on which the machine operates, are still working on a pre-war rate, plus the bonuses and advances received since the war, but taking all these into account, are receiving considerably less than the piece-worker.

"The result may be imagined. The skilled man with a life's experience behind him sees a girl or youth, whom perhaps he himself has taught, earning twice as much as he does. The injury to his self-respect is as great as that to his pocket." . . .

The discontent which exists takes the form of anger with the Government, not in the sense of the particular group of politicians who happen to form the Cabinet or the Ministry, but the whole machine. The Government is directly employing an astonishingly large proportion of the whole population, and a large proportion of the remainder are employed by firms which are mere puppets in the hands of the Government. We hear no more of grandmotherly legislation; dropping that, the State has become the Grand-employer, and the employees do not like it in that capacity. The Commissioners for the North-Eastern and the South-Western divisions, indeed, do not seem to have been much impressed by the feeling against the Government, but the other six panels have no doubt of its strength and importance. The machine is regarded as slow, stupid, and untrustworthy in all the six divisions. The two of them which have the most independent life of their own — Scotland and Lancashire — think it too remote, and demand more local autonomy; but in the London area, within easy call of Whitehall, there is but "a fading confidence in Government departments," and "a distinct opinion amongst both employers and workmen that the Government has intervened to a much greater extent than is desirable or useful in the relations between employers and employed"; in the West Midlands the distrust of Government "is both widespread and deep"; in the Yorkshire and East Midland division, not only the skilled engineering and electrical trades, but members of a dozen less skilled unions "all alike without a single exception expressed distrust in, and total indifference to, any promise the Government may make, while some referred to 'Russia,' and openly declared the one course open for Labour was a general 'down tools' policy to secure reforms that constitutional action was failing to effect"; and the South Wales Commissioners say: "An outstanding feature of our inquiry has been the unqualified hostility on the part of witnesses, both on the men's and the employers' side, to Government interference."

13. REBELLION IN IRELAND

When war broke out, Britain had been deeply divided over the Irish Question (whether British rule in Ireland should or could be maintained), but many Irish political leaders (notably John Redmond, leader of the Irish Nationalist party) wasted little time in pledging Ireland's loyalty. British troops need not be diverted from the Western Front to secure Ireland, they promised. Moreover, some 200,000 Irishmen volunteered for service against Germany. Yet republican elements within Ireland, who scorned any compromise measures of Home Rule (limited provision for self-government) that might emerge after the war and sought complete independence instead, believed that Britain's absorption on the Western Front marked their opportunity to cast off the yoke of British rule in Ireland. The eventual result was an armed uprising by some 2,000 Irish in Dublin on Easter Monday in April 1916. Their proclamation of the republic follows. The harsh British response to the so-called Easter Rising, which was defeated within a week, made many initially skeptical Irish citizens more sympathetic to the ideal of complete independence from British rule.

Poblacht na h-Eireann
The Provisional Government of the Irish republic to the people of Ireland

Irishmen and Irishwomen: In the name of God and of the dead generations from which she receives her old tradition of nationhood, Ireland, through us, summons her children to her flag and strikes for her freedom.

Having organized and trained her manhood through her secret revolutionary organization, the Irish Republican Brotherhood, and through her open military organizations, the Irish Volunteers, and the Irish Citizen Army, having patiently perfected her discipline, having resolutely waited for the right moment to reveal itself, she now seizes that moment, and, supported by her exiled children in America and by gallant allies in Europe, but relying in the first on her own strength, she strikes in full confidence of victory.

We declare the right of the people of Ireland to the ownership of Ireland, and to the unfettered control of Irish destinies, to be sovereign and indefeasible. The long usurpation of that right by a foreign people and government has not extinguished the right, nor can it ever be extinguished except by the destruction of the Irish people. In every generation the Irish people have asserted their right to national freedom and sovereignty; six times during the past three hundred years they have asserted it in arms. Standing on that fundamental right and again asserting it in arms in the face of the world, we hereby proclaim the Irish republic as a sovereign independent state, and we pledge our lives and the lives of our comrades-in-arms to the cause of its freedom, of its welfare, and of its exaltation among the nations.

The Irish republic is entitled to, and hereby claims, the allegiance of every Irishman and Irishwoman. The republic guarantees religious and civil liberty, equal rights and equal opportunities to all its citizens, and declares its resolve to pursue the happiness and prosperity of the whole nation and of all its parts, cherishing all the children of the nation equally, and oblivious of the differences carefully fostered by an alien government, which have divided a minority from the majority in the past.

Until our arms have brought the opportune moment for the establishment of a permanent national government, representative of the whole people of Ireland, and elected by the suffrages of all her men and women, the Provisional Government, hereby

From *The Times,* 1 May 1916.

constituted, will administer the civil and military affairs of the republic in trust for the people. We place the cause of the Irish republic under the protection of the Most High God, whose blessing we invoke upon our arms, and we pray that no one who serves that cause will dishonour it by cowardice, inhumanity, or rapine. In this supreme hour the Irish nation must, by its valour and discipline, and by the readiness of its children to sacrifice themselves for the common good, prove itself worthy of the august destiny to which it is called.

Signed on behalf of the provisional government,

Thomas J. Clarke, Sean MacDiarmada, Thomas MacDonagh, P. H. Pearse,
Eamonn Ceannt, James Connolly, Joseph Plunkett

14. A WARNING FROM THE SPD

The German Social Democratic party, or SPD, began to reevaluate its earlier stance supporting the war effort. The initial sense of civic unity, the so-called *Burgfrieden*, had worn off, and as socialist deputy Hugo Haase warned in the Reichstag — the German legislature — the government could not expect socialist workers to sacrifice themselves for their country if they were to remain subject to political discrimination and contempt at the hands of the state.

Gentlemen, the idea that actuated the Social-Democratic Party at the outbreak of war was that it is our duty to do everything for the protection of our own country. *[Applause from Social-Democrats.]* These endeavors are not thwarted by public criticism; on the contrary, they are strengthened by criticism of the right sort. The Social-Democratic Party has never thought of asking for any presents in return for its vote of August 4. . . . It is not considering and has never considered its vote as a trade transaction. But we cannot approve of the Government on the whole presenting nothing but the budget to a Reichstag gathering in the eighth month of a war that has upset the whole world. The sacrifices which our people are bearing are overwhelming. Our brothers in the field, facing death every moment, are doing their duty with an almost superhuman strength *["Quite right!" — S.D.]*, all of them equally; and under such circumstances the Government must no longer evade its task of seeing to it that the amount of political rights should be equal to the amount of the duties. *[Hearty assent from S.D.]* It is quite unbearable that all citizens, without difference of class, party, religion, and nationality, are not being granted full equality. *[Renewed assent by S.D.]*

Gentlemen, the workmen's organizations have supplied more than 20 army corps from amongst their members. *["Hear, hear!" — S.D.]* On the battlefields and at home they have done great things, as the Government itself has acknowledged, and now is a session of the Reichstag to pass, without doing away with the exceptional regulations concerning the rights of coalition which are directed against them? What we ask for is equality in all respects *["Quite right!" — S.D.]*, not only as a reward for the immense sacrifices but also as the fulfilment of an undeniable claim. *["Quite right!" — S.D.]* Gentlemen, it is always being put forward that our chief care must be not to lower the sentiment of our brothers in the front ranks who are doing wonders in bearing privations and sufferings; but those who want to act thus must first see to it that our brothers, when they come home, are not looked upon one day longer as citizens of lesser rights in empire, state, and parish. *[Hearty assent by S.D.]* Nothing will hurt the masses more deeply than consciousness of the fact that those who on account of the war are restricted in their earning power will on that account be marked as citizens of lesser rights. *["Quite right!" — S.D.]* There is no more room within the German Empire for class suffrage.

If the Government will actively set its mind to it, it will, with the aid of our people, overcome all obstacles. The more openly and decisively it acts, the more easily it will reach its goal. . . .

We shall again put forward a motion to that end, and if the Government will maintain its reluctant and evasive position, the soldiers coming back from the war, together with those of their comrades who stayed at home, will claim their rights impetuously. *["Quite right!" — S.D.]* We must not close our eyes to the fact that after the blood and health of hundreds of thousands of men have been sacrificed for the protection of the Empire, the fight for equal rights and the democratization of organizations will be continued with more stress than ever. *[Assent by S.D.]*

With growing discontent we are watching the restrictions and even the destruction of the liberties already won, for instance, the rights of association and assemblage, as also those of the press. The present state of affairs is not based on the constitution of our Empire. The latter only allows the declaration of the state of war in case the public safety of one of the Federated States is threatened. But hardly anyone would venture to say that in the whole German Empire the public safety is in danger. Our people have waited in vain for the end of the state of siege in the interior of the Reich, as was promised at the outbreak of the war; but the restrictions on the contrary have been rather increased and have caused growing discontent, the importance of which the authoritative circles evidently do not grasp. *["Quite right!" — S.D.]* In various districts even the closed meetings must be sanctioned and supervised by the police and the speakers are obliged to submit their manuscripts for approval to the Censor, before the meeting is allowed to be held.

How the censorship is being handled! The fate of political lectures and papers is laid in the hands of censors who have never before had anything to do with politics and accordingly have no understanding of the matter. The reasons for which newspapers have been prosecuted and prohibited indeed defy all description. . . .

Gentlemen, the reference to the so-called "party truce" frequently becomes a nuisance. The party truce, as it has been proclaimed, requires that, in the political struggle, attacks against parties or religions in a hateful personal form should be avoided; but it should not lead to a denial of principles or to the renunciation of a Weltanschauung. It would be a misfortune for our people if the party truce should lead us to the peace of a cemetery. *["Quite right!" — S.D.]*

When *Vorwärts* was suppressed, the Censor expressly permitted that during the party truce every newspaper should be able to discuss all happenings of public life and of the world in the light of its Weltanschauung. Only under this reservation did *Vorwärts* declare that it would not touch on the theme "Class Struggle and Class Hatred" during the war. It gave assurance that it would abstain from every hateful polemic against any class, which, by the way, it had done even before its suppression.

Gentlemen, the question arises now whether the newspapers have actually been given full scope of expression. Nobody will be able to assert that. Week after week new regulations are being given out. Only yesterday meetings for women were forbidden *["Hear, hear!" — S.D.]*, an action which demands the same criticism. The Chancellor wants the German people to be a free people. The condition just described is not worthy of a free people and should be cleared away immediately. A free people deserve free speech. *[Hearty assent by S.D.]* This is especially requisite as soon as the war approaches its end. The German people should not allow themselves to be pushed aside when the fateful question of their future is being settled. *[Hearty assent by the S.D.]* They have the right to take part in discussions and preparations.

Gentlemen, in all countries dread of the war makes itself felt more every day. It is natural that the longing arises everywhere to put an end to the terrible butchery of the nations. To express this is not a sign of weakness and can least of all be looked upon as such by us. For our military successes are indisputable; our social life, stimulated by the war industry, has been revived in a surprising manner; our finances have proved themselves to be strong. It is just the strong who may first hold out the hand of peace. My party as representative of international socialism has always been the peace party, and it knows that this is the case for the Socialists of other countries as well. Our desire is for a lasting peace, such a one as does not include new difficulties and does not contain seeds of future quarrels. That can be obtained if the nations do not oppress each other *[approval by S.D.]* and if the peoples see the advantage of the peaceful exchange of culture. The delusion that the German people can be annihilated has been destroyed. *["Quite right!" — S.D.]* Our people are not to be annihilated any more than any other nation which defends its independence and self-reliance with all its strength. Until the bloody struggle has come to a close, we in Germany have the great task to fulfil that in any case the feeding of the people be made safe. Our people cannot be forced to their knees by hunger; that is our conviction. The food will have to be regulated without regard to special interests. Up to now much has been done amiss. We cannot save the Government this reproach. My "Fraktion" has already in the middle of August, and since then, continually drawn the attention of the Government to taking the necessary measures in conformity with this proposal. A timely embargo on wheat would have greatly increased our store of food. The high prices of bread-grains, . . . were not necessary. The timely slaughter and conserving of pigs would have saved great quantities of potatoes for human food. The unfortunate idea of establishing economical housekeeping by raising the price of potatoes deserves the strictest condemnation. *[Hearty assent by S.D.]*

The task of the Government is to make safe what food we have for the people, and to distribute it appropriately at moderate prices to the consumer. No interest should come before that of the consuming population. *[Approval by S.D.]* He who withholds food with the intention of profiteering should be dealt with severely and should be held in contempt by everybody. *[Applause by S.D.]* At a time when our best people are dying on the battlefields it is more than ever our duty to prevent the population which remains behind from becoming weak by underfeeding. It is more than ever our duty to see to it that a healthy, strong generation grows up. Besides other regulations, as for instance weekly assistance for women during confinement, it is necessary to procure food at moderate prices for the whole population, especially for the poorer classes. The increase of prices, which is not to be avoided anyhow, makes it a duty also to raise the money for this purpose. At the same time the law concerning the maintenance of military persons and their survivors will have to be amended. . . .

. . . Gentlemen, never before has the Reichstag had its ordinary session in such difficult times as now. It has great tasks to accomplish. We shall strive to the end that effective and successful work may be rendered and that these tasks may be brought to a favorable solution. *[Lively applause by S.D.]*

15. REVOLUTIONARY SENTIMENT IN GERMANY

The following three documents chronicle the growing disillusion in Germany with the country's prospects of victory and the military leadership's legitimacy in that struggle. In the first selection, the War Office's exhortations to German workers to reject strike action betray a certain desperation, as do the exaggerated claims of the success of the U-boat campaign. Within both the work force (the second selection) and the navy, as demonstrated in the third selection by seaman Richard Stumpf, war weariness, defeatism, and discontent were growing enormously.

a. Proclamation of the War Office at Leipzig to the Workers, April 20, 1917

WORKERS!
THE DECISION OF THE WORLD-WAR IS IMMINENT
THE GREATEST BATTLE IN THE HISTORY OF THE WORLD IS
RAGING IN THE WEST

The iron ring with which our U-boats surround the enemy presses them ever closer. Defeat in the three years' struggle which they forced on us stares them in the face.

Despair urges them to seek a decision on the battlefield in these weeks. They hope to break through our lines at the present time or else they are lost.

Reprinted from *Fall of the German Empire, 1914–1918,* Vol. II, edited by Ralph Haswell Lutz, pp. 221–222, with the permission of the publishers, Stanford University Press. Copyright © 1932 by the Board of Trustees of the Leland Stanford Junior University.

But with iron fist our fathers, husbands, brothers resist their raging onslaughts; they repel the foe, preserve our homes and fields from devastation, protect our women and children from want, death, and dishonor.

IN FUTURE, TOO, THE ENEMIES' FIERCEST EFFORTS
WILL BE USELESS

But this depends on vast supplies of munitions and war material of every kind. Day by day you and we and all of us must work early and late, to stand by our dear ones at the front, to help them to decide the present final battle in our favor.

EVERYONE MUST DO HIS BIT

None of you want to attack your fathers, husbands, brothers from behind. That is what you do if you idly fold your hands, if you strike or urge others to strike. That is what you do if in these iron times you trouble yourselves with things which could be postponed till times of peace.

You have all, both men and women, done your duty loyally for almost three years; your dear ones at the front confidently expect you to do so in the future.

Do not betray your dear ones; follow the example of the workers at Berlin and the other industrial centers of Germany! They all stopped striking yesterday and today, and went back to the furnace, the lathe, and the machines. They are working busily to make weapons and war material for our fellow-countrymen at the front.

Follow their example; don't cripple your power of resistance.

You will be assured of the gratitude of the Fatherland, your children, and grandchildren.

War Office, Leipzig

b. The Demands of the Strike Directorate in Berlin, January 29, 1918

A strike movement has been again initiated by the workingmen themselves without any suggestion or instruction from any directing body. The strike of yesterday corresponds to the spontaneous movement which arose in April 1917, when the bread ration was reduced. It was only after the workers had left the factories in great numbers that they proceeded to the appointment of a Strike Directorate at a meeting held yesterday afternoon in the Trade Unions Hall. A representative of the Social-Democratic Party was also allowed to address the meeting, as was a representative of the Independent Social-

Reprinted from *Fall of the German Empire, 1914–1918,* Vol. II, edited by Ralph Haswell Lutz, pp. 232–233, with the permission of the publishers, Stanford University Press. Copyright © 1932 by the Board of Trustees of the Leland Stanford Junior University.

ists. The meeting elected a Strike Directorate consisting of delegates of the strikers and representatives of both Socialist parties.

The meeting formulated the following demands: (1) The speedy bringing about of peace without annexations or indemnities, on the basis of the self-determination of peoples in accordance with the principles formulated by the Russian People's Commissioners in Brest-Litovsk. (2) Delegates of the workers of all countries to be invited to participate in the peace negotiations.

As regards Germany in particular: (3) More liberal food supply by the control of food stocks in places of production and in warehouses, for the purpose of insuring an even distribution among all classes of the people. (4) The immediate revocation of the state of siege. The complete restoration of the right of assembly as well as that of free discussion in the press and at public meetings. The restoration, without delay, of the laws for the protection of women and children. The cancellation of all measures of the military authorities which interfere with the activity of trade unions and the prohibition of all fresh restrictions. (5) The abolition of the military control of industrial undertakings. (6) The immediate release of all persons convicted or arrested for political action. (7) The drastic democratization of the entire state organism in Germany, beginning with the introduction of the general, equal, direct, and secret vote for all men and women of over 20 years for the Prussian Diet.

The meeting adopted the following resolution also: As only the most complete solidarity can insure success, we solemnly undertake to defend our leaders, representatives, and commissioners with all our force, against all punitive measures. We urgently call upon the proletariats of Germany and of other belligerent countries, as a whole, to adopt mass strikes, as our colleagues in Austria have already successfully done; for only the joint international class struggle will definitely procure for us peace, freedom, and bread.

c. Mutiny and Revolution in the German Fleet

Today's date is August 2. It is the third anniversary of the declaration of war on France and Russia. I tried to recapture the spirit of 1914 by recalling my impressions. The feverish excitement which then gripped our emotions has vanished completely. I still tremble whenever I think of the events of three years ago. Those who were the most enthusiastic supporters of the war are now to be found in the camp of the pessimists and defeatists. On August 2 we regarded such great events as the outbreak of a two-front war as unimportant in relation to the fateful question: what will England do? It seems almost incredible to remember that at the time we felt "that the war would be no fun without England."

However now the war is no fun even "with" England. All of us ought to beat our breasts and confess *mea culpa*. I am utterly convinced that England is no more responsible for the war than we. We provided England with the best rationale for its intervention by our injustice to Belgium.

All the statesmen who participated in igniting the powder keg are no longer in office. The Kaiser's well-intentioned servant, the honorable philosopher of Hohenfinnow,[1] resigned recently. He has been succeeded by a Bismarckian mind [Georg Michaelis], a man who is deadly earnest in [his intention to] obtain an early and honorable peace. In his most impressive speech he stated: "I do not know what will happen. But I cannot conceive of the misery resulting from an unexpected announcement that Germany does not have enough food to last until the next harvest!" These words from such an important source electrified all of Germany. He was Director of the War Wheat Control Administration. In my opinion, this is the only organization which has completely fulfilled its responsibilities without mismanagement. He is Germany's first bourgeois chancellor.

If I were called upon to render a medical diagnosis of the present state of feelings among the enlisted men, it would read something like this:

> High state of excitement caused by a total lack of confidence in the officers. Persistence of the fixed notion that the war is conducted and prolonged solely in the interests of the officers. Manifestations of bitter anger due to fact that the enlisted men are starving and suffering while the officers carouse and roll in money.

Is it therefore any wonder that the men should now inevitably turn to revolt as a means of improving their sordid lot? As far as I have been able to tell, the mutiny raged most strongly on the ships of the *Kaiser* class, especially on *Prinzregent Luitpold* and *König Albert*. Apparently the Captain bears most of the blame. He arrested a stoker for collecting subscriptions to *Vorwärts*.[2] The joint protests of two crews of stokers compelled the Captain to set him free again. The next morning the Captain was missing, his body was found later floating near the submarine nets. . . . No one knows what happened; whether it was murder, suicide, or an accident. At any rate, it constitutes a warning to all officers.

These unpleasant events were discussed at a commanders' meeting on the *Posen* on Friday morning. Afterward our Captain assembled the crew on deck and gave an explanation. Some very unfortunate things had occurred on *Prinzregent Luitpold,* he said. "Three days ago one of the watches was scheduled to go to the theater, but for some reason the production did not take place. Instead they were to see a film. As the showing began the projector failed to function properly. Since it was too late to start anything else, the next day's schedule was substituted. The men were marched to the drill field for military exercises. A large number of the crew refused to obey and left the field without permission. Later on, 350 of the men were found at Fort Schaar. They rested there, got hungry and returned to their ship. There is evidence that foreign agents were involved (outraged muttering from the men). At a time when thousands of your comrades lay down their lives for the Fatherland in Flanders and are about to drive the

---

[1] Stumpf is referring to Chancellor Theobald von Bethmann-Hollweg (1909–1917).

[2] The official newspaper of the Majority Socialist party.

Russians out of Galicia, it is tragic that you should entertain such ideas. This is precisely what our enemies desire. Our internal dissension and hatreds will give them what they could not achieve in honorable battle. I feel sorry for these unfortunate, misguided people; they will suffer the full consequences of the law. Dismissed!" . . .

How Did It Happen?

This question should not have been placed here, but at the beginning of my diary. By "it" I mean the mutiny or revolution, which is greeted with horror by most people, by many as the fulfillment of their ideals and by a small group as the reward for their work. Now the revolution has arrived! This morning I heard the first flutter of its wings. It came like lightning. Unexpectedly it descended with one fell swoop and now holds all of us in its grip.

Even though I was in the midst of things, I did not realize how quickly word spread this morning to "prepare to demonstrate on shore." The Division Officer, the First Officer and the Adjutant came down to our quarters and asked us in a crestfallen manner what it was that we wanted. We replied, "We have nothing against our officers. Nevertheless we shall parade in the streets to obtain our rights." However each one of us looked upon these "rights" as the fulfillment of his own wishes. Since things seemed to be getting interesting, I put on my parade uniform and went along. "I can't stop you," the First Officer commented with resignation.

Hardly any of the men stayed behind. At the Old Port Barracks a long line of marines armed with rifles stood assembled. At our approach they broke out in a loud shout of joy and gave three hurrahs. People streamed in from all sides. Within a matter of minutes a huge crowd of sailors had gathered on the parade grounds. Occasionally someone tried to address the crowd. At last we decided to march to the flagship in order to enlist its crew in our demonstration. The only interesting part of the entire story occurred at this point. A verbal duel ensued between the Captain of the ship and several spokesmen of the demonstrators. The crew of the *Baden,* which stood assembled on the top deck, would be the reward for the victor. Had the Captain been a reasonably accomplished speaker, our spokesmen would have been forced to depart without a single man. However both the deathly pale officer and the Sailors' Council handled themselves badly. Consequently roughly a third of the crew joined our ranks.

Later on I saw more. Since it was difficult to maintain order in the huge mob, loud calls for music rang out. The harbor band and several of us fetched our instruments and played the old military songs and marches. The mighty throng, more or less inspired [by the music] moved along the docks. At the Peterstrasse we were met by a forty-man patrol led by an officer. The men came over to our side with their weapons. It was very comical to watch the lieutenant when he realized suddenly that he was all alone. Because of the music we received large reinforcements from all directions. At first I thought that we would release the imprisoned sailors at the jail. But I soon realized that we lacked leadership and that the crowd was driven along by sheer mob instinct.

The great gate at the Marine Barracks was bolted. In an instant the gate was off its hinges. An elderly major blocked the way. He thrust a pistol against the first sailor who broke in. He was disarmed immediately, hands reached for his sword while others tried to tear off his epaulettes. My sympathy went out to this unfortunate man who courageously tried to do his duty, and disgust at such brutality rose in my throat. I felt like shaking his hand.

The seemingly endless procession moved along the sides of the great drill field and joined at the center. Hastily a speaker's platform was erected. Then all at once twenty men began to speak. It was an excellent opportunity to study the thoughtlessness of the mob in action. Even the most ridiculous demands were greeted with stormy applause. A demand to hang the Kaiser could easily have been pushed through. I must admit, however, that there were also repeated demands for order and discipline. This is somewhat encouraging. It indicates that the radical, irresponsible elements have not yet gained the upper hand. I hope it remains this way. Then I will not be sorry that I participated.

We next moved in the direction of the Torpedo Division. I was able to observe the gradual rise of bestiality [in the mob]. Every woman was greeted with coarse remarks and whistles. Incredibly red cloths waved in the air. In the place of a banner someone carried a red bedsheet on a pole. It was certainly no great honor to march behind this dirty rag. But because it was the first day of our new freedom we gladly ignored these superficialities.

It was evident that we received little support from the townspeople in their windows. Surely the shortage of handkerchiefs alone could not have been responsible. The townspeople understood quite well that the collapse of the fleet meant the end of the growth of their city. In the future Wilhelmshaven will remain an insignificant medium-sized town.

Relentlessly the procession moved across the drill field toward the Teichbrücke and the torpedo boats. Everyone there applauded us but no one joined us because — it was lunch time. When the mob began to grumble at this, a crew member yelled across to us: "Calm down, friends. We've put out the fires long ago, but now we're having lunch." Lunch — everyone began to feel pangs of hunger. In nervous and planless haste we moved on.

An hour later we stood assembled in front of the Station Headquarters. A statue of Admiral Coligzy [Coligny?], drawn dagger in hand, towered over us. Breathless silence prevailed when a speaker arose from the crowd. He announced that Admiral Krosigk had agreed to accept the demands of the Kiel Sailors' Council. Rousing applause. "All political prisoners in the fortress are to be released." The mob resisted: "We want all [prisoners] released, all! Down with Kaiser Wilhelm." The speaker handled all these protests very effectively by ignoring them.

Now a dockworker stepped up to speak. The man had a typical, classic criminal face, I thought. Only from such a face could come the demand for the establishment of a "Soviet Republic." I felt sorry for the fellow even moreso for the crowd which applauded these stupidities.

When the first speaker rose again and suggested that we return to our posts immediately, he was met with resounding laughter. But then everyone disappeared in the direction of the nearest kitchen. The revolution had triumphed bloodlessly.

In order to stage a proper celebration, a great triumphal meeting was organized the next day. Although the [rest of the] fleet had still not arrived and its attitude was still questionable, we ignored these problems. Our representatives wrangled throughout the night about which of them should be elected to the so-called Council of Twenty-One. It was not a pretty scene. Naturally each of them wanted to see his signature affixed to some proclamation, especially since no risk was involved. Early the following morning a broadsheet listing all the gains we had already made was distributed.

This time I scornfully refused to join the demonstration and went into town all by myself. Things were even more hectic than on the previous days. This time most of the demonstrators were civilians and shipyard workers, but I also noticed some officials and a sprinkling of deck officers without their swords. Red flags abounded and they were in better condition than yesterday. In order to simplify the matter [of identification] each of the flags indicated the organization it represented. The procession lasted for twenty-eight minutes. A speaker in a flowing cloak and with gesticulating hands was already talking in the square. Could it be [Reichstag] Deputy Noske?[3] But no. In his first sentence I heard him say that the Reichstag deputies had accepted bribes from food speculators and the war profiteers. "I also know their names," shouted the speaker. "Yes, I know who they are. Deputy [Giesberts of the Centrist Party] is one of them." At that point I began to realize who had instigated the whole uproar. There was a long pause while the band played a few selections. In the meantime a Seaman First Class amused the gathering by reciting his family secrets and personal problems. Today a soldier's wife with her five children had been to see him. Her application for an increased allowance had been rejected. "All of you must be aware of whom I mean?" A voice from the rear, "The mayor!" "Yes, indeed, he is the one." (The same voice again) "Away with him! Away with him! Pfui, pfui!" echoed the voices of thousands in the audience. I was astonished at the patience of the crowd, for it allowed the loudmouth to repeat the story all over again. But when he attempted it for a third time, the band drowned him out ingloriously.

Thereupon a sailor stepped onto the platform and informed the "honorable party members, comrades and workers" that the principal objective [of the revolution] had thus far not been implemented and that the Kaiser and all the federal princes should herewith be deposed. "True, true!" they shouted to the sky with the same sort of fervor they had manifested over the misdeeds of the mayor. All those who accepted this demand were told to raise their right hands to signify their approval. About one half [of the people in the crowd] managed to raise their hands, the same hand which had once sworn loyalty and obedience to the head of state. Now I was overcome with disgust. I wandered around for a while longer and then departed.

While I was busy recording these impressions, a terrific noise interrupted my thoughts. Someone stuck his head through the door and bellowed: "All hands to receive rifles and ammunition!" I stopped the first man I met and asked, "What's going on? Why the rifles?" "Treason," he gasped, foaming with rage. "The loyalists are firing on us at Rüstringen!" Someone else shouted, "The Tenth Army Corps is marching

---

[3] Gustav Noske, who belonged to the right wing of the German Socialist party, was sent by the government in Berlin to quell the rebellion in the northern port city of Kiel.

288   State and Society in Crisis

against us. We shall shoot them down like dogs!" That I would like to see. The uproar was terrific. Everybody called for the Executive Officer and the armorer. Then the first men carrying rifles and bayonets came out. I said to myself, this means blood will be spilled; these people are absolutely insane. The streets were like a madhouse. Armed [men] ran through the gates from all directions; there were even a few women dragging cases of ammunition around. What madness! Is this the way it has to end? After five years of brutal fighting, shall we now turn our guns against our own countrymen? Since even the most reasonable and stable of the men I saw were in a state of semihysteria, only a miracle could prevent a disaster.

But the miracle occurred. With the same care of planning and direction that had gone into spreading the rumor, the "Soldiers' Council" now saw to it that order was restored. Men in cars and on bicycles spread the word that it had all been a "false alarm." Later on one of the representatives even admitted that this was merely a stratagem to obtain possession of the weapons. At any rate it was certainly not a proper way to behave. It was an unbelievably reckless playing with fire. By evening, however, everything was peaceful and quiet once more. 8 November 1918.

Within the past two days an unbelievable change has taken place within me. [I have been converted] from a monarchist into a devout republican. . . .

(I find that I can no longer devote even fifteen minutes to my work. Spectacular events occur in bewildering succession. This veritable witches' sabbath has completely upset my mental equilibrium. Never before has Wilhelmshaven looked like this! Thousands upon thousands of flaring rockets rise in the air, all the sirens howl, the searchlights gleam by the dozen, the ships' bells clang madly and the guns of the fort roar out their salute. This is really too much all at once.) 10 November 1918.

I think that the time has come for me to reorganize my thoughts. But since my mood keeps vacillating every hour between extreme exultation and deathlike despair, I find it extremely difficult to narrate my impressions and feelings in a sensible order. Although I wrote earlier that I have become a convinced republican, I came to regret my decision within a matter of hours.

November 10 may perhaps turn out to be the most significant day of this war. At least this is the way I felt on Sunday morning as I gazed down upon a mob of "a hundred thousand." For the first time I felt somewhat solemn. A springlike sun was shining and the happy and gay faces of the men indicated that they welcomed the arrival of the new era with open arms. Although the procession had already lasted two hours, a constant stream of new battalions of sailors and soldiers came streaming from the center of town. Amidst wild cheering Stoker First Class Kuhnt introduced himself as the first president of the Republic of Oldenburg. Low-flying aircraft dropped down bundles of handbills. To the thunderous applause of the mob, the huge Imperial war flag was lowered and the red flag of liberty, equality and fraternity rose up over the barracks. I could no longer resist and was swept along by the mass hysteria.

All my qualms of conscience evaporated when the Kaiser abdicated and my Bavaria proclaimed itself a Republic. I felt as if a heavy weight had suddenly been lifted from my heart, particularly when I learned that the revolutionary movement had spread to the French-Italian front. This automatically signified the conclusion of an armistice. The proletarians of all nations would embrace each other and the capitalists, of course, they would pay the price. . . . Was this not an exhilarating and an infectious prospect?

16. THE ROLE OF WOMEN IN A NEW GERMANY

A supporter of the conservatively oriented German National Liberal party *(National-liberale Partei)* and a contributor to women's journals, Emma Stropp voiced her opinions just following the Revolution of 1918. The following selection emphasizes the importance of political awareness for bourgeois women.

A new era has arrived; the storms of November have swept away everything we honored and held dear. In these weeks, many of our companions face the crumbling of hopes that seemed certain of fulfillment; they look into a country that is shrouded by heavy veils of mist. Will the sun ever again shine upon Germany? Will any new shoots and young blossoms follow this pitiless winter's night? Such anxious questions make our hearts tremble.

Surely Longfellow's great image "that above the clouds the sun is shining" is true also for us, the more so since all German forces in both country and city are prepared to work upon the land which is now so barren and lies before us in ruins. New fruit must and will thrive upon the land, but it will require hard and devoted labor to prepare the land, the hard and devoted labor of men and women.

Yes, women too, because through the collapse of the old regime women have gained a new right — a right that thrusts a new responsibility upon their shoulders. They now have a duty to participate in the elections and vote upon constitutional organization of the National Assembly and upon the future parliament and the basic form and development of the building of the new state, which will ensure our care and safety and that of our children.

Some country women who lived far from politics and found full satisfaction in their domestic activity will say: "What is the new right to us? We didn't want it!" And they add indignantly: "Politics is men's business."

No, it is no longer men's business. That dream has been dreamed long enough, that dream of a protected and sheltered womanhood, concerned only with its domestic duties involving the family and the care of the sick and needy. The delicate veil that screened big events from your view and shielded your ears from the conflicts of the day has been whisked away. That veil was torn away from the dreamers most harshly and violently on the ninth of November. The twenty-one and a half million women who will go to the polls to determine the future of Germany, with only eighteen million men, find themselves in a new era. The figures speak for themselves and emphasize the great excess of women's votes over men's. And there is another figure. At the last election 40% of all votes were cast for the Social Democrats. Who will not admit that since

Excerpt from "Die deutschen Frauen und ihr neues Recht" by Emma Stropp, 1918.

that time the followers of this party have multiplied infinitely, owing to their support of many past occurrences and to a most dedicated and effective canvassing. This canvassing was conducted not only by men, but by social democratic women who have long been politically organized and who have used the full weight of their extremely important influence in their homes and families in order to fill the ranks of their party members ever more solidly.

Meanwhile, what have bourgeois women done in politics? Almost nothing at all. Only about 800,000 of them who are incorporated in the Union of Women's Federations are politically organized. This is not to offer reproaches, but merely to answer the question: "Why should I be concerned with politics?"

Whoever asks this question today does not recognize the seriousness of the times; she lays upon herself a heavy burden of guilt which neither can nor will ever be forgiven. Red flames leap sky-high from the devastated house. And in the light of these flames, who dares to say, "How does this concern me?"

Whether women have previously opposed or approved of female suffrage is now irrelevant. Today *all* bourgeois women must vote; we cannot have elections that *strengthen our political opponents.*

The time remaining to us before the great day of the battle between two world views must be used by German women in preparation for that day. So that they may be armed, not as "voting beasts" — forgive this crude expression — but as far as possible in this short time to vote from their own convictions, with their votes as women.

Opportunities to educate oneself for that day are being promoted in the cities and in the country. The great women's organizations are tirelessly at work stimulating and spreading discussion and understanding of the most important current economic and political questions, through education courses, through civic and political lectures. We must take advantage of these opportunities.

Housewives and mothers should avail themselves of these opportunities; they should try to take along their female domestics as well as those young people who are not yet of voting age. What women have missed, whether through their own fault or not, must not be neglected in their daughters, for they will soon be citizens with full political rights. Unfortunately, the good intentions of the present government have set the voting-age limit extremely low. Twenty-year-old women comrades in working circles know very well for which party they will vote. However, among rural domestic servants we shall find many girls who are completely naïve politically, but whose ballots have the same impact as those of more knowledgeable women. Therefore, they should not be contemptuously neglected but rather one should try to persuade them and to counsel them tactfully, and through friendly discussion awaken their understanding of the great duty they must discharge.

Wives of owners of country estates and their daughters must also not neglect to find political and economic instruction in the newspapers. They must read leading articles in the news section, before the short stories and miscellaneous material; they must get to know and think through the programs of individual parties; they must become members of whatever bourgeois party speaks to their own interpretation of what must be pursued and what can be achieved. This entry into a specific political organization must not be

undervalued; it offers a feeling of belonging that strengthens and vitalizes. This is especially necessary for women who are newcomers to political life and who are still largely
prey to emotions that might influence purely practical evaluation of thought. In addition, the economic strength and thus the power and sphere of the party's canvassing
activity grows even through minimal membership dues. One should consider what the
working woman has done for her party with her annual contribution of 12 marks or
more, and should ask oneself what one has done personally to further one's political
conviction.

Thus, through their new rights, German women are charged with a number of
duties. They may be compared to tools for sharpening the plough that will furrow the
desolated acres so that fruitful seeds may take root. The seeds themselves, however, are
the votes cast by men and women for the national assembly — there must be no empty
kernels. It is the duty of German women in city and country to ensure this; in their
hands lies the future of Germany. Let them be fully aware of the great responsibility that
their new rights have laid on them.

17. THE RUSSIAN REVOLUTION

The Russian Revolution remains the clearest example of the link between the strain
of total war, military defeat, and the collapse of the existing regime. The following four
documents do not examine the revolution from the familiar perspective of Petrograd
or the intentions of the Bolsheviks; rather, they illustrate the inability and, more important, the unwillingness of the Russian army to prolong the struggle or to preserve
the old order. The first two selections embody the complaints of Russian army and
naval officers that they could no longer find sufficient recruits, that Russia's traditional quantitative advantage was dwindling. A common refrain, explicit in the third
extract, concerns the suspicion of pro-German influence at the court, that the war
was not being directed properly at the highest levels. The final selection continues
Botchkareva's story, the odyssey of a female soldier in the Russian ranks.

a. Army State of Mind

1. Recruiting

(A) MEETING OF THE COUNCIL OF MINISTERS

August 17, 1915

Scherbatov: I should say that recruiting is going from bad to worse. The police is unable
to handle the slackers. They hide in the forest and in the grain fields. If it should become

Excerpt from *Documents of Russian History,* ed. by Frank Golder, Peter Smith Publishers, 1964, pp.
220–221.

known that the recruits of the second class are called out without the approval of the Duma I fear, that under the present conditions, we would not get a single man. . . .

(B) MEMOIRS OF POLIVANOV

. . . The following letter of July 31, 1915, General Ianushkevich [Chief of Staff of Grand Duke Nicholas] wrote to me [General Polivanov, Minister of War]. . . .

> We get information that in the villages the new recruits are being advised, under the inspiration of the left parties not to fight to the point of getting hurt but to surrender in order to live. If we should have two or three weeks of drilling with one rifle for every three or four men in addition to this kind of teaching it will be impossible to do anything with such troops. His Majesty has already confirmed two measures: (1) that the families of those who surrender of their own free will shall be deprived of Government support, and (2) that at the end of the war such [returned] war prisoners will be sent to colonize Siberia. It would be exceedingly desirable to impress upon the population that these two measures will be rigidly enforced, and that the land portion [of those who surrender] will be transferred to the landless men honestly doing their duty. . . .

b. *The Baltic Fleet*

November 30, 1915

Dear Sir, Ivan Loginovich:
[Goremykin, Prime Minister]

I have the honor to bring to the attention of Your Excellency the information, which has been laid before me by agents, on the state of mind of the men in the Baltic Fleet.

Humbly yours,
A. Khvostov, [Minister of Interior]

Our recent temporary failures on land have had a bad effect on the sailors of the Baltic Fleet. The seizure by the enemy of large parts of the Vistula and Baltic regions and his reconquest of Galicia from us, as well as certain shortcomings in our naval forces, are attributed, by the sailors, to the traitorous acts of our military leaders of German origin. . . .

Among the factors which tend to work on the sailors are: the dismissal of the State Duma and the criticism of the Government by the radical legal press, . . . especially the "Riech" which is widely read by the rank and file. . . .

Excerpt from *Documents of Russian History,* ed. by Frank Golder, Peter Smith Publishers, 1964, p. 221.

The excited state of mind of the sailors is evidenced (1) in their interest in the activities of the left parties of the Duma, (2) in open expression of dissatisfaction with the inactivity of the Russian Government, which, according to their opinion, has done little to win the war and, in contrast to the German Government, has done nothing for winning the war in the course of the year, and finally (3) in their indignation at the weak efforts made to root out German domination by the Government which, they say, is in the hands of the German party at Court. . . .

c. War Management at Court

[A journalist interviews General Alexeev in late-1916]

Alexeev: I can get nothing from them [ministers]. My supplies are decreasing. . . . It is even necessary to think about bread. We are already cutting down the rations. They have forgotten about food for the horses. . . .

Journalist: What are you going to do about it?

A: What shall I do? With these people there is nothing that can be done.

J: Have you said anything to the Tsar about it?

A: I have . . . but it does no good.

J: Why?

A: While you talk to him he pays attention, gets worked up, is eager to do something . . . but as soon as he leaves you he forgets about it. All kinds of pressure are brought to bear upon him; he is not a free man.

J: Is it true that the Tsarina has much influence?

A: It is only too true. Her influence is irresistible. What is worse, she never comes out in the open. She interferes with everybody, but works behind their backs. You never can tell what she will do next. Every time she comes here she makes new trouble.

J: Do the ministers ever consult you?

A: They come, they talk. What can they do? The honest men leave and the worthless remain. . . . If it were not for the war I should resign too. If I should leave, what would not they do with the army? Do I not understand that Sturmer and Company are thinking only of an alliance with Germany? . . . The home situation is serious. They [Sturmer and Company] are purposely instigating hunger disturbances in order to provoke a revolution so as to have an excuse for breaking away from the Allies and end the war. Our army is now in condition to crush Germany, without which there can be no real peace in Europe. But a permanent peace is not desired by Sturmer and Protopopov; they wish to keep the people under the heel of a strong Germany. Apart from the Germans no one will protect them from the revolution. The pity of it all is that at the head of the government there still are men who are interested in crushing the people.

Excerpt from *Documents of Russian History,* ed. by Frank Golder, Peter Smith Publishers, 1964, p. 226.

d. The Revolution at the Front

The first swallow to warn us of the approaching storm was a soldier from our Company who had returned from a leave of absence at Petrograd.

"Oh, my! If you but knew, boys, what is going on in the rear! Revolution! Everywhere they talk of overthrowing the Tsar. The capital is aflame with revolution."

These words spread like wildfire among the men. They gathered in knots and discussed the possibilities of the report. Would it mean peace? Would they get land and freedom? Or would it mean another huge offensive before the end of the war? The arguments, of course, took place in whispers, behind the backs of the officers. The consensus of opinion seemed to be that revolution meant preparation for a general attack against the Germans to win a victory before the conclusion of peace.

For several days the air was charged with electricity. Everybody felt that earthquaking events were taking place and our hearts echoed the distant rumblings of the raging tempest. There was something reticent about the looks and manners of the officers, as if they kept important news to themselves.

Finally, the joyous news arrived. The Commander gathered the entire Regiment to read to us the glorious words in the first manifesto, together with the famous Order No. 1. The miracle had happened! Tsarism, which enslaved us and thrived on the blood and marrow of the toiler, had fallen. Freedom, Equality and Brotherhood! How sweet were these words to our ears! We were transported. There were tears of joy, embraces, dancing. It all seemed a dream, a wonderful dream. Who ever believed that the hated régime would be destroyed so easily and in our own time?

The Commander read to us the manifesto, which concluded with a fervent appeal to us to hold the line with greater vigilance than ever, now that we were free citizens, to defend our newly won liberty from the attacks of the Kaiser and his slaves. Would we defend our freedom? A multitude of throats shouted in a chorus, that passed over No Man's Land and reverberated in the German trenches, "Yes, we will!"

Would we swear allegiance to the Provisional Government, which wanted us to prepare to drive the Germans out of Free Russia before we returned home to divide the land?

"We swear!" thundered thousands of men, raising their right hands, and thoroughly alarming the enemy.

Then came Order No. 1, signed by the Petrograd Soviet of Workmen and Soldiers. Soldiers and officers were now equal, it declared. All the citizens of the Free Russia were equal henceforth. There would be no more discipline. The hated officers were enemies of the people and should no longer be obeyed and kept at their posts. The common soldier would now rule the army. Let the rank and file elect their best men and institute committees; let there be Company, Regimental, Corps and Army committees.

We were dazzled by this shower of brilliant phrases. The men went about as if

Excerpt from *Yashka. My Life as Peasant, Officer and Exile* by Maria Botchkareva, Frederick A. Stokes, 1919, pp. 139–145.

intoxicated. For four days the festival continued unabated, so wild with the spirit of jubilation were the boys. The Germans could not at first understand the cause of our celebration. When they learned it they ceased firing.

There were meetings, meetings and meetings. Day and night the Regiment seemed to be in continuous session, listening to speeches that dwelt almost exclusively on the words of peace and freedom. The men were hungry for beautiful phrases and gloated over them.

All duty was abandoned in the first few days. While the great upheaval had affected me profoundly, and the first day or two I shared completely the ecstasy of the men, I awoke early to a sense of responsibility. I gathered from the manifestoes and speeches that what was demanded of us was to hold the line with much more energy than before. Wasn't this the concrete significance for us of the Revolution? To my questions the soldiers replied affirmatively, but had no power of will to tear themselves away from the magic circle of speech-making and visions. Still dazed, they appeared to me like lunatics at large. The front became a veritable insane asylum.

One day, in the first week of the revolution, I ordered a soldier to take up duty at the listening-post. He refused.

"I will take no orders from a *baba*," he snorted, "I can do as I please. We have freedom now."

I was painfully stunned. Why, this very same solider would have gone through fire for me a week before. And now he was sneering at me. It seemed so incredible. It was overwhelming.

"Ha, ha," he railed. "You can go yourself."

Flushed with chagrin, I seized a rifle and answered:

"Can I? I will show you how a free citizen ought to guard his freedom!"

And I climbed over the top and made my way to the listening-post where I remained on duty for the full two hours.

I talked to the soldiers, appealing to their sense of honor and arguing that the revolution imposed greater responsibilities upon the man in the ranks. They agreed that the defense of the country was the most important task confronting us. But didn't the revolution bring them also freedom, with the injunction to create their own control of the army, and the abolition of discipline? The men were in a high state of enthusiasm, but obedience was contrary to their ideas of liberty. Seeing that I could not get my men to perform their duties, I went to the Commander of the Company and asked to be released from the army and sent home.

"I see no good in sticking here and doing nothing," I said. "If this is war, then I want to be out of it. I can't get my men to do anything."

"Have you gone insane, Yashka?" the Commander asked. "Why, if you, who are a peasant yourself, one of them, beloved by all the rank and file, can't remain, then what should we officers do? It is the obligation of the service that we stay to the last, till the men awake. I am having my own troubles, Yashka," he confided, in a low voice. "I can't have my way, either. So you see, we are all in the same boat. We have got to stick it out."

It was abhorrent to my feelings, but I remained. Little by little things improved.

The soldiers' committees began to function, but did not interfere with the purely military phases of our life. Those of the officers who had been disliked by the men, or who had had records typical of Tsaristic officials, disappeared with the revolution. Even Colonel Stubendorf, the Commander of the Regiment, was gone, retiring perhaps because of his German name. Our new Commander was Kudriavtzev, a popular officer.

Discipline was gradually reestablished. It was not the old discipline. Its basis was no longer dread of punishment. It was a discipline founded on the high sense of responsibility that was soon instilled into the gray mass of soldiery. True, there was no fighting between us and the enemy. There were even the beginnings of the fraternization plague that later destroyed the mighty Russian Army. But the soldiers responded to the appeals from the Provisional Government and the Soviet in the early weeks of the spring of 1917. They were ready to carry out unflinchingly any order from Petrograd.

Those were still the days of immense possibilities. The men worshipped the distant figures in the rear who had brought them the boon of liberty and equality. We knew almost nothing of the various parties and factions. Peace was the sole thought of the men. They were told that peace could not come without defeating or overthrowing the Kaiser. We, therefore, all expected the word for a general advance. Had that word been given at that time nothing in the world could have withstood our pressure. Nothing. The revolution had given birth to elemental forces in our hearts that defied and ever will defy description.

Then there began a pilgrimage of speakers. There were delegates from the army, there were members of the Duma, there were emissaries of the Petrograd Soviet. Almost every day there was a meeting, and almost every other day there were elections. We sent delegates to Corps Headquarters and delegates to Army Headquarters, delegates to a congress in Petrograd and delegates to consult with the Government. The speakers were almost all eloquent. They painted beautiful pictures of Russia's future, of universal brotherhood, of happiness and prosperity. The soldiers' eyes would light up with the glow of hope. More than once even I was caught by those enticing traps of eloquence. The rank and file were carried away to an enchanted land by the orators and rewarded them with tremendous ovations.

There were speakers of a different kind, too. These solemnly appealed for a realization of the immediate duty which the revolution imposed upon the shoulders of the army. Patriotism was their keynote. They called us to defend our country, to be ready at any moment for an attack to drive the Germans out and win the much-desired victory and peace. The soldiers responded to these calls to duty with equal enthusiasm. They were ready, they would swear. Was there any doubt that they were? No. The Russian soldier loved his Mother Country before. He loved her a hundred-fold now.

The first signs of spring arrived. The rivers had broken, the ice fields had thawed. It was muddy, but the earth was fragrant. The winds were laden with intoxicating odors. They were carrying across the vast fields and valleys of Mother-Russia tidings of a new era. There was spring in our souls. It seemed that our long-suffering people and country were being born for a new life, and one wanted to live, live, live.

But there, a few hundred feet away, were the Germans. They were not free. Their souls did not commune with God. Their hearts knew not the immense joy of this unusual spring. They were still slaves, and they would not let us alone in our freedom. They stretched themselves over the fair lands of our country and would not retire. They had to be removed before we could embark upon a life of peace. We were ready to remove them. We were awaiting the order to leap at their throats and show them what Free Russia could do. But why was the order postponed? Why wait? Why not strike while the iron was hot?

Yet the iron was allowed to cool. There was an ocean of talk in the rear; there was absolute inactivity at the front. And as hours grew into days and days into weeks there sprang forth out of this inactivity the first sprouts of fraternization.

"Come over here for a drink of tea!" a voice from our trenches would address itself across No Man's Land to the Germans. And voices from there would respond:

"Come over here for a drink of vodka!"

For several days they did not go beyond such mutual summons. Then one morning a soldier from our midst came out openly into No Man's Land, announcing that he wanted to talk things over. He stopped in the center of the field, where he was met by a German and engaged in an argument. From both sides soldiers flocked to the debaters.

"Why do you continue the war?" asked our men. "We have thrown over the Tsar and we want peace, but your Kaiser insists on war. Throw over your Kaiser and then both sides will go home."

"You don't know the truth," answered the German. "You are deceived. Why, our Kaiser offered peace to all the Allies last winter. But your Tsar refused to make peace. And now your Allies are forcing Russia to continue in the war. We are always ready for peace."

I was with the soldiers in No Man's Land and saw how the German argument impressed them. Some of the Germans had brought vodka along and gave it to our boys.

A Flanders Field War Memorial
(© FPG International)

Part IV

The Aesthetic War

In cultural terms as well as political terms, the Great War left an indelible mark. Like the myriad faces of war, the literature and art generated by the conflict expressed contradictory national moods. While some purveyors of culture justified and glorified the euphoria accompanying its outbreak with images of Dionysian celebrations and tales of heroism, others, tempered by the reality of battle, offered more sobering and somber portrayals of humanity at its most animalistic. No longer could art be considered for art's sake alone; it, along with other cultural venues, had become politicized, manipulated by supporters and opponents of the conflict alike to deliver a specific message. The fear that the pen was mightier than the sword prompted Europe's governments to employ artists and authors in propaganda campaigns designed to elicit public cooperation and maintain order. Posters, broadsheets, and circulars were used more extensively in the First World War than ever before for this purpose.

The benefits of propaganda were already known to nineteenth-century figures such as France's Napoleon III, whose successful presidential campaign in 1848 (before he proclaimed himself emperor) was aided by an impressive array of placards, buttons, and other such paraphernalia. As European politics took on a mass character in the late nineteenth century, the use and dispensation of propaganda increased. Not only did posters carry easily remembered slogans or catch phrases, but their visual appeal served to reinforce their message. One need only recall what might well be the most famous (and most recognizable) of all American war posters — that of Uncle Sam as a military recruiter. Dressed in patriotic red, white, and blue, this fatherly and wise figure sternly pointed his finger at males of enlistment age to take up the call to arms and thereby serve and protect their country and its values. This poster was based on a similar British appeal, featuring the bewhiskered and martial-looking Lord Kitchener. Indeed, all European governments commissioned posters that glorified recruitment: young men were pictured in uniform, showered with the adulation of beautiful young women and adoring crowds; prospective soldiers were reminded, if only indirectly, of the horrors of war that could befall their innocent mothers, wives, and children should they spurn the call to arms. Images of the bestial Hun or Cossack were invoked as barbarous threats.

In view of food shortages and other hardships caused by inevitable disruptions in supply and demand, and so as to ensure the continued cooperation of civilians and soldiers alike for the war effort, Europe's governments increasingly accepted the need to disseminate propaganda that often contained only a modicum of truth but whose impact proved devastating for their opponents. Above all, Germany's invasion of neutral, "defenseless" Belgium and its ruthless destruction of cathedrals, libraries, and other buildings served the Allied propaganda machine extraordinarily well. Claims of German barbarism against property and women (many of them exaggerated) enabled Germany's enemies to exonerate their participation in the war and served to reinforce the idea of a holy Christian war waged against the German heathen barbarians. British admiral Sir John Fisher's offhand remark that in war anything was permissible if used against one's enemies came to haunt the Germans.

In response to accusations of German atrocities in Belgium, the British government in August 1914 engaged Charles Masterman, former literary editor of the *Daily Chronicle* and a member of Parliament, as head of the War Propaganda Bureau. Masterman enlisted the assistance of some of Britain's most prominent literary figures, among them Arnold Bennett, G. K. Chesterton, Sir Arthur Conan Doyle, John Galsworthy, H. G. Wells, and Rudyard Kipling, in placing their pens in the service of the Crown. The efforts of Wellington House and its proprietors in publishing inexpensive pamphlets aimed at convincing neutral countries such as the United States of the efficacy of the war, demonstrating the evils of German militarism and documenting German atrocities, and countering pacifistic appeals all proved fruitful. Since Britain did not have a conscript army until 1916 and thus relied on citizens' sense of responsibility to the nation, Wellington House contributors were instrumental initially in recruiting volunteers. In fact, Rudyard Kipling's pamphlet "To Arms!" in which he appealed to the patriotism of the nation's able-bodied men, was likely the inspiration behind one of Britain's most famous and successful recruiting posters, that of Lord Kitchener.

The most infamous (and fictitious) piece of propaganda concerning German atrocities during the war, one fabricated by Wellington House, was the "Corpse Conversion Factory Story" of 1917. According to the story, which was printed in numerous Allied newspapers, Germans were using a factory in the Belgian city of Liège to distill human cadavers into oils. The mere thought that any nation would commit such outrages was sufficient to place the Germans at the lowest level of humanity. Only after the war did it become known that the British had transposed two separate photographs and captions, one of a train transporting dead soldiers from the front for burial, the other depicting horse cadavers being brought by train to fertilizer factories. The German government failed, despite its own best propaganda efforts, to quell the accusations. German propagandists for their part played on their compatriots' fear of British and French colonial troops, fabricating accounts of incidents in which Hindu soldiers stole into army camps under the cover of darkness to slit German soldiers' throats and drink their blood, and Africans who cannibalized innocent men.

Germany was also especially sensitive to the use of art, cinema, and literature in shaping domestic attitudes toward the war. German censorship was not new; it had been applied before the war to various aspects of German culture deemed inappropriate by Germany's ruling monarchs. Cinema or writings thought to be either risqué (such as sexual "pulp literature") or too violent (crime novels) were either banned or rewritten to suit German sensibilities. Censorship tightened with the outbreak of war. As of July 31, 1914, all literature, cinema, and other popular culture became subject to strict control by local authorities, who could legally read and pass judgment on any cultural contribution before it was released to the general public.

While governments churned out propaganda posters and literature denigrating their enemies, peace advocates and disillusioned soldier-writers also used literature and the visual arts to convey their version of the war. State censorship, however, often blunted the impact of such dissent. The expressionist movement in literature and the graphic arts celebrated emotions over rationalism, utopianism over materialism, and called for a new social order to replace the old, dysfunctional one. An eclectic group, expressionists comprised both confirmed pacifists and those for whom the idealism and patriotism of the August Days waned rapidly under the reality of trench life. Franz Werfel, for example, joined the Austrian army but did his best to undermine the efforts of officers to maintain a sense of order and morale among the troops. His disgust at war and sense of despair emerges in his collection of poetry, *Der Gerichtstag* (The Day of Judgment), written while serving in the trenches between 1915 and 1917. The dramatist and professional officer Fritz von Unruh initially welcomed the war by penning patriotic songs; but by the autumn of 1914 he had undergone a spiritual transformation, most evident in his *Vor der Entscheidung* (Before the Decision) and *Opfergang* (The Way of Sacrifice).

France's Henri Barbusse was among the more celebrated wartime authors to challenge French censors and the government's sanitized version of war. A journalist and published author before the outbreak of the war, Barbusse wrote the novel *Under Fire* (Le Feu) from the trenches. Published in 1916, it surprisingly escaped French censors and made an impression not only within France but on foreign readers in countries where the book was translated. Barbusse's portrayal of the horrors of war was so compelling that his style has been compared subsequently to that of the great realist Emile Zola. The novel's antiwar message and its sympathy with the fate of all soldiers, including enemy ones, reflected the author's socialist sympathies. More important, however, it revealed Barbusse's conviction that wars, especially those waged for the sake of nationalism and imperialism, were immoral and unjust.

Roland Dorgelès, who fought as a corporal, published his version of trench warfare as *Wooden Crosses* in 1919, while a physician with a literary penchant, Georges Duhamel, produced two novels, *The New Book of Martyrs* (1917) and *Civilisation 1914–1917* (1918), based on his four years as a medical officer in the French army. Only Romain Rolland remained true to his original pacifist outlook, choosing to stay in Switzerland for the duration of the battle, where he assisted the Red Cross in ministering to prisoners of war and wrote numerous journal articles decrying France's participation in the war. The collection entitled *Above the Battle* contains many of his most famous antiwar appeals.

The poetry and prose of British writers Edmund Blunden, Rupert Brooke, Ford Maddox Ford, Wilfred Owen, Isaac Rosenberg, and Siegfried Sassoon, who volunteered for active service at different phases of the war, reflected their trench experiences as well their social backgrounds. (All, with the exception of Rosenberg — a first-generation British working-class Jew — and Sassoon, had roots in the British middle class.) Soldiering amid enormous brutality in a life-and-death struggle, they, like their working-class counterparts, were forced to rely on the support and compassion of their fellow fighting men. Their poetry, couched in pastoral or religious imagery, reinforced the idea of war as a great equalizer; death did not discriminate among social classes or age cohorts. Influenced by the nineteenth-century romantics and pre-Raphaelites, their verse was distinguished by the new vocabulary of twentieth-century war as well, one that expressed the horrors of the technology of modern warfare.

If poetry seemed to be the most characteristic and enduring British response, its soldiers nonetheless produced prose that movingly evoked the same themes. Siegfried Sassoon, for example, in his memoirs chronicled his transformation from an idle, fox-hunting country gentleman into a veteran infantry officer decorated for bravery. Frederic Manning's *The Middle Part of Fortune* provided a sensitive exploration (albeit in crude language) of the psychological impact of soldiering, especially the strain preparing and waiting for an attack. Surely the best-known example of the genre was by Robert Graves. He was only nineteen when he entered the war with a commission as a second lieutenant in the Royal Welsh Fusiliers (one of the best units in the British army). Although he was wounded, his experience left more than physical scars, and his autobiographical account, *Goodbye to All That,* points out the military incompetence and the absurdity of war that he saw all around him. Beyond that Graves was outraged that so many Englishmen, in an atmosphere of supposed universal sacrifice, clung steadfastly to class pretensions and social conventions. Eventually, unable to stomach life in postwar England, he said "goodbye to all that" and settled on the Spanish Mediterranean island of Majorca.

Female authors left their recollections as well, as in Vera Brittain's haunting *Testament of Youth* and Helen Zenna Smith's provocative *Not So Quiet,* which convey the anguish of war for women and men alike. Written in 1933, *Testament of Youth* records Brittain's experiences as a volunteer nurse in London, Malta, and France. Brittain abandoned her dream of attending Somerville College, Oxford, to enlist in the nursing corps; although she considered herself a pacifist, socialist, and feminist, the diaries she kept revealed her elitist and even patriotic side. Nonetheless, *Testament of Youth* illustrates the reconstruction of gender relations in wartime Britain. Although less known than Brittain, Evadne Price, who wrote under the name Helen Zenna Smith, in *Not So Quiet* (1930) produced an intriguing novel recounting the wartime experiences of six English female field ambulance drivers. The French accorded the book, which they believed "promoted international peace," one of their most prestigious literary awards.

One of the most poignant and widely read postwar novels remains Erich Maria Remarque's *All Quiet on the Western Front.* In stark contrast to Ernst Jünger's ode to war *Storm of Steel,* Remarque's *All Quiet* (1928) exposed the futility of war. Remarque condemned the conflict not only for inflicting physical scars on Germany's youth but also for spawning a "Lost Generation" of young men, who were subsequently alienated from the corrupt political and social order for which they had fought. *All Quiet* was based in part on its author's limited war experience; in 1916, at the age of eighteen, Remarque was conscripted, subsequently wounded, and sent to recuperate in a military hospital, where he spent the remainder of the war. Despite his limited military duty, he clearly saw death all around him, a theme omnipresent in the novel.

Artists created a visual testimony to the war in their paintings. In France, cubism remained the dominant style by many artists at the front. Dissonant, irreverent, and disassociated from the past, cubist paintings portrayed the helter-skelter nature of modern warfare, unlike — and more destructive than — anything earlier. But on the French home front, artists preferred a more traditional, even conservative approach. This classicist revival, which began in earnest after 1917, was a result, in part, of Italy's entry into the war in 1915 on the Allied side. Italy's association with classical civilization, humanism, and Christianity served as a counterpoise to Germany's "barbarism"; thus, the Allies could justify their war against Germany as one waged to preserve Western civilization. And since France was part of the Latin tradition, French artists in particular responded to the call with portraits of Roman ruins, protective ancient goddesses hovering above wounded soldiers, and well-known figures such as Dante urging combatants to persevere against a heathen enemy. French artists rejected the lascivious and frivolous caricatures of prewar Orientalism (its depictions of harems, seduction, and sexuality), not only out of deference to the serious nature of the conflict but also because of Turkey's alliance with Germany. In reaffirming their belief in the superiority of France's Western heritage, these artists revived the traditional Latin *commedia dell'arte,* which emphasized popular and collective elements. Mandolins, harlequins, and punchinellos, for example, featured prominently in the portraits of the great master Pablo Picasso, a Spanish refugee, Juan Gris from Spain, and Gino Severini of Italy.

Paintings, posters, and picture cards were used to reinforce the conservative, patriotic message evoked by the war. The image of the mother provided an especially symbolic quality. Both Severini and Frenchman Lucien Lévy-Dhurmer painted portraits of mothers suckling children, themes evoking France's preoccupation with its declining birthrate. The mythical symbol of the French Revolution, Marianne, often classically robed, once again led her countrymen into battle or comforted wounded soldiers. One famous poster of 1917, "For the War Loan, the Sacred Union," extolled giving birth as tantamount to fighting, farming, and contributing to the war effort. Even in the image of the mother as procreator of future progenies and dutiful supporter of the war effort, France echoed Italy's concern for the propagation of the traditional maternal role.

Germany's expressionist artists, who drew on cubism and futurism, exposed the most venal aspects of the war. Captivated by the writings of the philosopher Friedrich Nietzsche, Otto Dix eagerly joined the ranks in 1914 and served on both the Western and Eastern fronts. After the war, Dix's paintings captured the bestiality and violence of war with his depictions of crippled soldiers. *Flanders,* painted between 1934 and 1936, evokes a horrid scene in which the physical destruction of the landscape is matched by the disintegration of the soldiers themselves, in which rotting corpses blend with putrefying tree stumps and fetid pools of water. Austrian artist Oskar Kokoschka also volunteered for service in the Austrian cavalry in 1914. He was subsequently wounded, but returned as an observer on the Italian front only to suffer from shell shock.

The artistry of the enigmatic and bizarre Georg Grosz expressed the absurdities of both war and German society as he saw it. Born in Berlin in 1893, Grosz disdained the German bourgeoisie, detested the Prussian military ethic, and felt only contempt for Germany's obsession with materialism. Although he served in the army during the war, his two tours of duty were brief, both interrupted by bouts of illness, possibly feigned. While with the colors, Grosz's disgust for the German hierarchical structure, for incompetent and inconsiderate military physicians, officious officers, boastful bureaucrats, and deceitful profiteers, found form in his artwork. These pillars of bourgeois society not only appeared surrounded by lowly street prostitutes and knife-wielding murderers but were also themselves portrayed as orgiastic perverts, power-hungry egotists, and exploiters of the underclasses. In 1916 he contributed briefly to an antiwar journal, *Neue Jugend* (New Youth), which was banned by government censors one year later. Grosz's art, with its grotesque, lurid characters and its emphasis on the darker elements of society, evolved from expressionism to dadaism by 1917. The horrors and futility of war convinced Grosz and fellow artists that German bourgeois society and culture were irredeemable; they were to be degraded, scorned, and ultimately destroyed. As a dadaist, Grosz embraced the idea of a socialist revolution along Sparticist lines.

Indeed, the German revolution of 1918 gave expressionist artists renewed hope that a new order was on the horizon, promising an artistic freedom denied to them under Wilhelm II and repudiating the values of the "philistine bourgeoisie." Artists formed revolutionary councils to put forward their demands, but on the whole most expressionists refused to be drawn into the political aspects of the revolution, preferring instead to remain, as the aesthetically conservative author Thomas Mann put it, "unpolitical men." Even artists whose paintings and etchings revealed particular sympathy for the proletariat still relied on the patronage of the bourgeoisie they despised. Expressionism, like the German revolution itself, ultimately succumbed to bourgeois values of law and order.

Russian cubo-futurist artists welcomed the war and the subsequent Revolution of 1917 as a vindication of their views on industrialization and the tsarist government. Bold geometric shapes dominated their works, which benefited from international exhibitions and an exchange of ideas with European artists. Many Russian artists, who had been abroad practicing their trade, including Marc Chagall, Natan Altman, Zhenia Bogoslavskaya, and Georgi Yakulov, came home at the outbreak of war.

Pavel Filonov, whose artistry has been compared to Paul Klee's and which contained elements of dadaism (especially his *People–Fishes,* c. 1915), fought for three years on the Romanian front, while Georgi Yakulov was severely wounded in 1917. Artists who remained on the home front held exhibitions to aid wounded soldiers. With the revolution unleashed beginning in 1917, these artists eagerly threw themselves into creating a vivid new order. They established museums throughout Russia to exhibit their abstract art, decorated streets and city squares with cubo-futurist designs, and organized street pageants in which Russian citizens reconstructed the Bolshevik seizure of power — a kind of living art celebration.

British postimpressionist/cubist artists sought to unleash an artistic revolution of their own, one that would serve to reconcile national art with its industrial heritage. Initially inspired by the technological advances of the "machine age," C. R. W. Nevinson, one of Britain's most well-known and more radical war artists, became disillusioned with technology as the war progressed. Although poor health precluded him from soldiering, Nevinson served in the Red Cross and the Royal Army Medical Corps until 1916, when a bout with rheumatic fever forced him to resign. In June 1917 the army hired him to portray British soldiers in combat. Two of his paintings, *A Group of Soldiers* and *The Paths of Glory,* received a cool reception from his military supervisors, who feared that their realistic portrayals of disillusioned and dying soldiers would undermine morale. Other English artists such as Eric Kennington *(The Kensington's at Laventie),* Paul Nash *(We Are Making a New World),* and Mark Gertler *(Merry-Go-Round),* also captured the devastation and dehumanization of war.

Artists, writers, and poets, serving their governments as purveyors of propaganda or expressing their humble convictions borne out of active duty, memorialized the Great War for survivors and future generations. Those who perished in battle would, it was hoped, live on in spirit through the cemeteries and monuments commissioned by Europe's governments and constructed by their architects. The visual impressions of the First World War would not be forgotten, even if the conflict's lessons were ignored.

A. War of Words

1. WOMEN'S PERSPECTIVE

Students of the war sometimes assume that moving poetry evoking the war's deeper tragedies was solely the preserve of male writers experiencing the war at the front. In fact, women were neither oblivious to nor fully insulated from the horrors of the conflict. And so for every whimsical poem like Nina MacDonald's evocation of the topsy-turvy world around her (the first selection), there were somber reflections about what it meant for women to participate in a struggle that extinguished life. The other two poems in this section probe that dilemma: Mary Gabrielle Collins' anguish over the use of the munitions so many women proudly made and then Eleanor Farjeon's call for love to replace hate in "Peace."

a. "Sing a Song of War-Time"

Sing a song of War-time,
Soldiers marching by,
Crowds of people standing,
Waving them "Good-bye."
When the crowds are over,
Home we go to tea,
Bread and margarine to eat,
War economy!

If I ask for cake, or
Jam of any sort,
Nurse says, "What! in War-time?
Archie, cert'nly not!"
Life's not very funny
Now, for little boys,
Haven't any money,
Can't buy any toys.

Mummie does the house-work,
Can't get any maid,
Gone to make munitions,
'Cause they're better paid,
Nurse is always busy,
Never time to play,
Sewing shirts for soldiers,
Nearly ev'ry day.

Ev'ry body's doing
Something for the War,
Girls are doing things
They've never done before,
Go as 'bus conductors,
Drive a car or van,
All the world is topsy-turvy
Since the War began.

"Sing a Song of War-Time" by Nina MacDonald from *War and Nursery Rhymes,* Routledge and Kegan Paul, 1918.

b. *"Women at Munition Making"*

Their hands should minister unto the flame of life,
    Their fingers guide
The rosy teat, swelling with milk,
To the eager mouth of the suckling babe
Or smooth with tenderness,
    Softly and soothingly,
The heated brow of the ailing child.
Or stray among the curls
Of the boy or girl, thrilling to mother love.
    But now,
Their hands, their fingers
Are coarsened in munition factories.
Their thoughts, which should fly
Like bees among the sweetest mind flowers,
Gaining nourishment for the thoughts to be,
Are bruised against the law,
    "Kill, kill."
They must take part in defacing and destroying the natural body
Which, certainly during this dispensation
Is the shrine of the spirit.
    O God!
Throughout the ages we have seen,
    Again and again
    Men by Thee created
    Cancelling each other.
And we have marvelled at the seeming annihilation
    Of Thy work.
But this goes further,
    Taints the fountain head,
Mounts like a poison to the Creator's very heart.
    O God!
Must It anew be sacrificed on earth?

"Women at Munition Making" by Mary Gabrielle Collins from *Branches unto the Sea*, Erskine Macdonald, 1916, p. 24.

c. "Peace"

I

I am as awful as my brother War,
I am the sudden silence after clamour.
I am the face that shows the seamy scar
When blood has lost its frenzy and its glamour.
Men in my pause shall know the cost at last
That is not to be paid in triumphs or tears,
Men will begin to judge the thing that's past
As men will judge it in a hundred years.

Nations! whose ravenous engines must be fed
Endlessly with the father and the son,
My naked light upon your darkness, dread! —
By which ye shall behold what ye have done:
Whereon, more like a vulture than a dove,
Ye set my seal in hatred, not in love.

II

Let no man call me good. I am not blest.
My single virtue is the end of crimes,
I only am the period of unrest,
The ceasing of the horrors of the times;
My good is but the negative of ill,
Such ill as bends the spirit with despair,
Such ill as makes the nations' soul stand still
And freeze to stone beneath its Gorgon glare.

Be blunt, and say that peace is but a state
Wherein the active soul is free to move,
And nations only show as mean or great
According to the spirit then they prove. —
O which of ye whose battle-cry is Hate
Will first in peace dare shout the name of Love?

"Peace" by Eleanor Farjeon from *Sonnets and Poems*, B. H. Blackwell, 1918, pp. 36–37.

2. "A WORKING PARTY"

Siegfried Sassoon was born into a comfortable existence in the southern English county of Kent in 1886. He attended Cambridge University but did not take a degree, and until the war's outbreak he lived as a country gentleman, filling his ample leisure time with sports, hunting, and writing. He volunteered for service on the Western Front, where he soon distinguished himself by his conspicuous bravery and apparent disregard for his own life. Decorated for heroism, Sassoon earned the nickname "Mad Jack," but his enthusiasm for the war soured and he published a pacifist appeal in 1917. Only the intervention of his friend Robert Graves prevented a court-martial. Sassoon was thus diagnosed as suffering from shell shock and sent home as an invalid. He never seemed to feel fully at ease in postwar Britain, and he dwelt obsessively in the past, writing and rewriting his wartime experiences.

Three hours ago he blundered up the trench,
Sliding and poising, groping with his boots;
Sometimes he tripped and lurched against the walls
With hands that pawed the sodden bags of chalk.
He couldn't see the man who walked in front;
Only he heard the drum and rattle of feet
Stepping along the trench-boards, — often splashing
Wretchedly where the sludge was ankle-deep.

Voices would grunt, "Keep to your right, — make way!"
When squeezing past the men from the front-line:
White faces peered, puffing a point of red;
Candles and braziers glinted through the chinks
And curtain-flaps of dug-outs; then the gloom
Swallowed his sense of sight; he stooped and swore
Because a sagging wire had caught his neck.
A flare went up; the shining whiteness spread
And flickered upward, showing nimble rats,
And mounds of glimmering sand-bags, bleached with rain;

Then the slow, silver moment died in dark.
The wind came posting by with chilly gusts
And buffeting at corners, piping thin
And dreary through the crannies; rifle-shots

"A Working Party" by Siegfried Sassoon from *The Old Huntsman and Other Poems,* E. P. Dutton, 1918, pp. 27–29.

Would split and crack and sing along the night,
And shells came calmly through the drizzling air
To burst with hollow bang below the hill.

Three hours ago he stumbled up the trench;
Now he will never walk that road again:
He must be carried back, a jolting lump
Beyond all need of tenderness and care;
A nine-stone corpse with nothing more to do.

He was a young man with a meagre wife
And two pale children in a Midland town;
He showed the photograph to all his mates;
And they considered him a decent chap
Who did his work and hadn't much to say,
And always laughed at other people's jokes
Because he hadn't any of his own.

That night, when he was busy at his job
Of piling bags along the parapet,
He thought how slow time went, stamping his feet,
And blowing on his fingers, pinched with cold.
He thought of getting back by half-past twelve,
And tot of rum to send him warm to sleep
In draughty dug-out frowsty with the fumes
Of coke, and full of snoring, weary men.

He pushed another bag along the top,
Craning his body outward; then a flare
Gave one white glimpse of No Man's Land and wire;
And as he dropped his head the instant split
His startled life with lead, and all went out.

3. "THE DEAD"

The poet Rupert Brooke, whose war poems were written largely at the beginning of the conflict, served in the Mediterranean with the Royal Naval Division. Ironically, he fell victim not to enemy bullets but to blood poisoning in April 1915.

These hearts were woven of human joys and cares,
   Washed marvellously with sorrow, swift to mirth.
The years had given them kindness. Dawn was theirs,
   And sunset, and the colours of the earth.
These had seen movement, and heard music; known
   Slumber and waking; loved; gone proudly friended;
Felt the quick stir of wonder; sat alone;
   Touched flowers and furs and cheeks. All this is ended.

There are waters blown by changing winds to laughter
And lit by the rich skies, all day. And after,
   Frost, with a gesture, stays the waves that dance
And wandering loveliness. He leaves a white
   Unbroken glory, a gathered radiance,
A width, a shining peace, under the night.

4. Suffering on the Eastern Front

"War," by Russian writer V. Ladizhensky, provides a moving indictment of the apparent aimlessness of the conflict. The second and third poems are by Austrian-born pharmacist and expressionist poet Georg Trakl, who served as a reserve lieutenant pharmacist with the Austrian army on the Eastern Front. In November 1914 at the age of twenty-seven, after being unable to relieve the suffering of soldiers injured during the battle of Grodek in Galicia (southern Poland), Trakl attempted suicide. He was sent to a military hospital in Krakow for observation, where he finally managed to take his own life with a drug overdose. The mental anguish Trakl endured as he witnessed the carnage of battle is overwhelmingly present in his two poems.

a. "War"

Dim is the twilight of raw winter's day,
Hamlets lit up by a flash
Stand out ablaze, then again die away.
Hark! Cannons thunder and crash!
All this is war. Crisp white snow on the ground,
Long rows of trenches I see.

---

(3) "The Dead" by Rupert Brooke from *Collected Poems of Rupert Brooke,* John Lane, 1918, p. 110.

(a) "War" by V. Ladizhensky from *Poems Written during the Great War 1914–1918,* Bertram Lloyd, ed., George Allen and Unwin, 1918, p. 63.

Real work of life, full of tasks fair and sound,
How far off you seem to me!
In the village near by the children play,
To guns accustomed their ear;
Out of the twilight the spent horses neigh,
Their trampling dimly I hear.
All this is war. If an answer you seek
To the question, What is war's aim?
I will say nought. Endless suffering shall speak,
Cruelty, torment, and shame.
I will say nought, but I will shed a tear
With the mother for her lad,
Or with the children in anguish and fear,
Homeless and hungry and sad.

b. "In the East"

Like the wild organs of the winter storm
Is the people's gloomy rage,
The purple billow of battle
Of stars leaf-stripped.

With broken brows, silvery arms
The night beckons to dying soldiers.
In the autumnal ash-tree's shade
The spirits of the fallen sigh.

A thorny wilderness surrounds the town.
From bleeding stairs the moon
Chases the startled women.
Wild wolves have burst in through the gates.

c. "Grodek"

At nightfall the autumn woods cry out
With deadly weapons and the golden plains,

(b) "In the East" by Georg Trakl from *In the East,* translated by Michael Hamburger, The Latin Press, Cornwall. Reprinted with permission of Michael Hamburger.

(c) "Grodek" by Georg Trakl from *Georg Trakl: A Profile,* Carcanet Press, Manchester, 1984. Reprinted with permission of the translator, Michael Hamburger.

The deep blue lakes, above which more darkly
Rolls the sun; the night embraces
Dying warriors, the wild lament
Of their broken mouths.
But quietly there in the willow dell
Red clouds in which an angry god resides,
The shed blood gathers, lunar coolness.
All the roads lead to blackest carrion.
Under golden twigs of the night and stars
The sister's shade now sways through the silent copse
To greet the ghosts of the heroes, the bleeding heads;
And softly the dark flutes of autumn sound in the reeds.
O prouder grief! You brazen alters,
Today a great pain feeds the hot flame of the spirit,
The grandsons yet unborn.

5. THE DESTRUCTION OF YOUTH

The eldest son of a lower-middle-class Welsh family, Wilfred Owen, born in 1893, found solace in literature and the earth sciences. Uncertainty about his career plans — whether to become a vicar or poet — led him to enlist in 1915 as a cadet in the British army's Artists' Rifles. After a year of additional training at the end of 1916, the army sent Owen to France for active duty in the trenches. This experience provided him with further inspiration for his poetry. Hospitalized twice, once for a concussion and once for shell shock, Owen finally succumbed to enemy fire on November 4, 1918, only a week before the armistice. War as a destroyer of youth, a pervasive theme of Owen's wartime poetry, is very much evident in his "Disabled" (1917) and "Mental Cases" (1918).

a. "Disabled"

He sat in a wheeled chair, waiting for dark,
And shivered in his ghastly suit of grey,
Legless, sewn short at elbow. Through the park
Voices of boys rang saddening like a hymn,
Voices of play and pleasures after day,
Till gathering sleep had mothered them from him.

About this time Town used to swing so gay
When glow-lamps budded in the light blue trees,
And girls glanced lovelier as the air grew dim, —
In the old times, before he threw away his knees.
Now he will never feel again how slim
Girls' waists are, or how warm their subtle hands;
All of them touch him like some queer disease.

There was an artist silly for his face,
For it was younger than his youth, last year.
Now, he is old; his back will never brace;
He's lost his colour very far from here,
Poured it down shell-holes till the veins ran dry,
And half his lifetime lapsed in the hot race,
And leap of purple spurted from his thigh.

One time he liked a blood-smear down his leg,
After the matches, carried shoulder-high.
It was after football, when he'd drunk a peg,
He thought he'd better join. — He wonders why.
Someone had said he'd look a god in kilts,
That's why; and may be, too, to please his Meg;
Aye, that was it, to please the giddy jilts
He asked to join. He didn't have to beg;
Smiling they wrote his lie: aged nineteen years.

Germans he scarcely thought of; all their guilt,
And Austria's, did not move him. And no fears
Of Fear came yet. He thought of jewelled hilts
For daggers in plaid socks; of smart salutes;
And care of arms; and leave; and pay arrears;
Esprit de corps; and hints for young recruits.
And soon, he was drafted out with drums and cheers.

Some cheered him home, but not as crowds cheer Goal.
Only a solemn man who brought him fruits
Thanked him; and then enquired about his soul.

Now, he will spend a few sick years in institutes,
And do what things the rules consider wise,
And take whatever pity they may dole.
Tonight he noticed how the women's eyes
Passed from him to the strong men that were whole.
How cold and late it is! Why don't they come
And put him into bed? Why don't they come?

b. "Mental Cases"

Who are these? Why sit they here in twilight?
Wherefore rock they, purgatorial shadows,
Drooping tongues from jaws that slob their relish,
Baring teeth that leer like skulls' teeth wicked?
Stroke on stroke of pain, — but what slow panic,
Gouged these chasms round their fretted sockets?
Ever from their hair and through their hands' palms
Misery swelters. Surely we have perished
Sleeping, and walk hell; but who these hellish?

— These are men whose minds the Dead have ravished.
Memory fingers in their hair of murders,
Multitudinous murders they once witnessed.
Wading sloughs of flesh these helpless wander,
Treading blood from lungs that had loved laughter.
Always they must see these things and hear them,
Batter of guns and shatter of flying muscles,
Carnage incomparable, and human squander,
Rucked too thick for these men's extrication.

Therefore still their eyeballs shrink tormented
Back into their brains, because of their sense
Sunlight seems a blood-smear; night comes blood-black;
Dawn breaks open like a wound that bleeds afresh.
— Thus their heads wear this hilarious, hideous,
Awful falseness of set-smiling corpses.
— Thus their hands are plucking at each other;
Picking at the rope-knouts of their scourging;
Snatching after us who smote them, brother,
Pawing us who dealt them war and madness.

6. THE SOLDIER AS READER

Reading provided soldiers with an escape from the drudgery and danger of war. French soldiers indulged themselves in *Vie Parisienne,* the most popular trench magazine replete with handdrawn pinups of voluptuous women. German and English soldiers also had their own variations of such magazines, as well as trench journals, and detective and adventure novels. But literature of a more exalted sort could be found in possession of the soldier "Mr. Thomas Atkins," a generic name for the British enlisted man. This selection surveys the cultural impact of the war by trying to divine the reading habits of British servicemen. Note the suggested relationship between the soldier's social status and the kind of literature he read.

Is it possible to discover and set down the psychology of the British soldier, old and new, as a reader of books? Not fully, perhaps, not in a resolved way. . . .

. . . The war has brought us a stiffening of moral fibre, a larger outlook in affairs, a quickening of intellectual interests, a finer moral vision. Mentally we are more alert than we were before it, spiritually we are more active than we have been for a generation or two. This wave of war inspiration has touched all our life, elevated it, and some of the consequences are reflected in the new mentality of the soldier. But that does not make him a book-lover, much less a book-worm, and it may not even make him a reader for recreation. He lives his inspiration, he is gathered into the terrible strife, as something far greater, far nobler, than any book can be. A knight of the air flies his own epic every other day. His experiences, feelings, sensations are on so high a note of actuality that life pictured in a book is distant and cold beside them. . . .

Does all this convey how, perfectly naturally, the soldier is first moved by the stir of the times, then engrossed by the drama of his own "bit" in the war, and finally left just a wandering spirit, so far as the printed page is concerned? It is needful to understand conditions, for they maketh men, men at one moment indifferent to the world of real literature, at another moment oddly grateful for bare scraps of reading, such as the popular, well-embellished magazine holds in plenty. He is a new sort of reader altogether, this British soldier of Armageddon, governed by its huge circumstances, but always he answers to the call of the blood, English, Scotch, Irish, or Welsh, Canadian, Australian, Greater British somehow, the Commonwealth in arms.

The grand parade began with the old army, with the soldier who deliberately chose the uniform as his colour of calling. He was not usually a reader, at all events not a real reader, though there was, no doubt, the exception to prove the rule. Then came the Territorial Army, the man whose civilian life had enabled him to keep easily in touch with books if he had a taste that way. The Territorial carried "light and leading" in his knapsack, as he carried a possible commission, that is to say the pocket edition was familiar among his goods and chattels of campaigning. Next there marched the great New Army, as we now know it, and in its multitudinous ranks the book-reader is what

Excerpt from "The Soldier as a Reader" by James Milne, *Fortnightly Review* 111 (May 1919), pp. 752–756.

he is in the ranks of the nation, very much in the same proportion except that a reign of war lies over the world, not a state of peace, which means, however, a mighty difference.

The natural reading of Mr. Thomas Atkins, who held the bridge for civilisation at Mons, at the Marne, at "Wipers," was light, very light. He had not been brought up on books, unless, indeed, the drill-book, and the louder news of the day and the half-spoken gossip of the evening, with a liking for sport and a weakness for sensational trials, mostly formed his faring in print. But he knew Mr. Nat Gould for his racing stories, and in that fact, perhaps, gave him the start which has made him clearly the first favourite, as a writer, among our mass of men in arms. . . . He could not help knowing something of that master of the detective craft, Sherlock Holmes, because Mr. Atkins has a bold curiosity for the unravelling of bad deeds, a manly anxiety to bring all villains to justice. He even had a distant acquaintance with Mr. Rudyard Kipling, because he wrote the "Barrack Room Ballads" and understood soldier human nature.

When the Territorial shouldered his gun and crossed to France he took with him some knowledge of French and a varied, nay, often a rich, acquaintance with English literature. A man who likes poetry is a man who has the soul of a reader, even, it may be, the soul of letters in him. It was surely the Territorial who inspired, without thinking about it, the remarkable revival of English poetry which has characterised this wartime. When the call broke upon us, the poets responded in rhyme and blank verse, but that might have remained merely a chorus to the gods of war, if it had not been for the Territorial. He carried with him, in his stored mind and his tunic pockets, the raw materials from which the first flowers of the new muse blossomed. He not only read Shakespeare and Coleridge, Robert Burns, and Walter Scott's *Marmion* by the camp fire, but he made verse himself. Do we not still remember the first thrills of it, how it set our hearts aglow and kept them strong? Clearly the Territorial, in his love for the old poets and his own frequent making of a new one, was the true begetter of the dower of poetry which the literary historian will inscribe as a wonderful monument of Armageddon.

When the Canadians and the Australians came over the seas to help the Old Mother, grimly at bay, they brought with them another impulse towards the war "boom" in poetry. Here were men who loved the open-air song of Robert Service and Adam Lindsay Gordon, men who found the very form of poetry an easy form of reading. They took with them the flame of many a Poets' Corner in the backwoods of Canada, of many another on the cattle-runs and sheep-stations of the Australian bush. Their first love was for their own poets, but they knew ours, enough of them, anyhow, to want to know more, so the light of the burning bush of English poetry grew in the war. . . . Anyhow, the soldier of our full national hour will ask in one letter for a "Nat Gould," and in another for a handful of verse, ballads preferably, certainly things with cheerfulness and a lilt in them. This is a reflection, in print, of his fondness for a "sing song" such as rises nightly from a billet "somewhere in France" or anywhere in England.

Nationality, meaning tradition, custom, outlook, and geography, meaning the scenic and weather colour of one's up-bringing, have much to do with the reading of the soldier. A Scotsman will actively engage a book which an Englishman of the sunny south would think heavy, dull, hardly understandable. An Englishman of the north will stand half-way between them and, perhaps, choose an historical novel. A countryman, who, by reason of the rural life, is thrown into some sort of company with books, is likely to be a better reader than a townsman who has a music-hall at his door and a football field round the corner. The soldier of the spacious Dominions oversea has not been accustomed to "snippets," or the surprising adventures of "Nick Carter," and therefore has no use for either. But he has an endless desire for reference books, as well as for poetry, which suggests that he is keeping an open eye on the Old World.

Now, having made these excursions, without alarums, let us get down rather more intimately to the soldier as a general reader. He says, in effect, "Tell me a story." That is the primitive curiosity of all humanity since the world began, the impulsive desire of humanity at all stages of life, the child in the cradle, the youth, the man, the dotard on the edge of the grave. The British soldier is a simple personality, good-natured, good-hearted, a gentleman of sentiment. Therefore he likes a story to be simple, to have a worthy hero and a virtuous, beautiful heroine. He does not want what he would call "frills," delvings into the wells of human nature, and a "problem novel" would merely bore him. His own psychology is on the surface, and he expects that of his heroes and heroines to be also sun-clear. If you like, he does not understand psychology, and he does not want to understand it, this average soldier reader.

Perhaps he comes out of a home where newspaper paragraphs about people of title, members of the world of fashion, lights of the vaudeville stage, have been favourite reading, because that is to sail briefly into the azure of a higher world of gold and lace. Certainly he himself, unless he is country-bred, has been a pretty constant patron of the cinema, and has come to regard it as telling his brand of story, swift action, short turnings to the desired end, a general sense of bustle and go, all leading, with soft music, to the desired happy ending. Naturally those two schools of training do much to determine the kind of reading, in particular the kind of tales, that the soldier in general finds suitable. Unless he be a habitual reader, he follows no plan in his reading, but takes what comes along and likes it or "lumps" it. Primarily he just wishes to be amused, to be taken out of himself, to be "bucked up." These are the signs of a fully healthy physical nature, and the British soldier has, fortunately for us, such a nature.

Parade the classics before him! He shakes his head, most likely, and reasons with them instead of reading them. Were they not written long ago, and is it not better to "Let the dead bury their dead?" No; give him the topical yarn-teller, the up-to-date fellow, and others may have the dead masters. Give him something with blood in it and at least an occasional peal of thunder, no matter that it is made on the stage. . . .

As the war grows older, the English soldier grows younger in years, and so the young taste in reading increases. It is not always good to push forward the clock of age, for the pendulum may snap. "Don't send us stiff books; send us the Bull Dog Breed Series and more Nick Carter and Sexton Blake Detective Stories." This was an actual request from an actual Mr. Atkins somewhere in the far-flung fighting line. His half-articulate cry would really have been better satisfied by *Robinson Crusoe, The Swiss Family Robinson,* or *Tom Cringle's Log,* but either he had read these romances as a boy or he had never known their alluring pages. Their spirit of adventure, with *Treasure Island* added as a modern instance, is the reading for which the general soldier-man craves.

7. ON KEEPING A DIARY

In this extract from his *Copse 125*, Ernst Jünger explains the significance of maintaining a wartime diary. While such a practice would promote fuller self-awareness and mental preparation for the rigors of war, also note Jünger's emphasis on the historical value of such diaries.

I would advise anybody who takes part in a war or any other unusual experience for a long period, to keep a consecutive diary, if it be only a succession of jottings which serve later on to give memory its clues. Such records have a value even for posterity, for it is only thus that the line of fate, still for us the secret of the future, can be recognized; for then the passions of to-day will have no more than a historical importance. In this way a number of written monuments are fashioned which add to family tradition and to the sense of one's country's destiny. This would be of service to people at large; for they have too little history in them, too little feeling for the higher social responsibility that lays less emphasis on the passing individual and his small concerns than on the race in whose history the individual is no more than an organic link binding the future with the past.

Apart from this, memoranda of this kind have an immediate personal value. They force the writer of them to seize upon the essence of his experiences and to get above — if only for a few minutes a day — the familiar surroundings and to put himself in the position of a spectator. The daily experience will appear in a new light, just as a well-known landscape changes as soon as you try to sketch it. And lastly, there is a certain comfort to be derived from even the simplest representation of things, a release through expression; and in this sense a diary is a confession, a confidence made to oneself.

As things are, nearly every volunteer goes to the front with a notebook, of which a page or two perhaps is written up before it is left behind in some billet after the first battle. I have often seen them. In some of them is to be read in large letters on the front page "War Diary"; and after that a few notes, addresses, card scores, and a lot else scribbled during the kit-inspections. I hope at least that letters from the front will be kept by the relations who receive them. It takes more energy than one might think to put a few facts together day by day when it is not a matter of life and death. I myself have made time for it, without missing a day scarcely, during the last year or two, though certainly I do not lay claim to extraordinary energy on that account. It is from inclination. Sometimes I am afraid I do too much of it, for nothing is more repulsive to me than the literary man who must immediately display every emotion and every experience to its best advantage and stick it on paper. . . . And if we survive the war, may the temper to which we are accustomed preserve us from writing a line to which we are not driven by an inward compulsion. For us — there will be more important work to do.

Excerpt from *Copse 125* by Ernst Jünger, Chatto & Windus, 1930, pp. 67–68, 102–109. Reprinted by permission of Random House UK Limited.

8. PROPAGANDA

It was widely believed that effective government use of information made a difference in the war effort and that the use of such material was often disingenuous. Hence some official statements, laced with exaggerations or outright lies in the effort to persuade, and thus deviating from truth, were labeled with the relatively new term *propaganda*. Moreover, it was generally believed after the war that the Allies had disseminated more effective propaganda. The selection that follows is from one of the first scholarly efforts to discuss critically whether the role of propaganda actually bore out the widespread perceptions of its value.

A study of the leaflets, books, and pamphlets issued by the Allies against the enemy reveals that the propaganda material went through five fairly well-defined stages. Each of these stages had a definite aim, and all led up to the final aim: the destruction of the German Empire. Although it is impossible to state exactly when one stage left off and the other began, the five types of propaganda material are quite clearly distinguishable in the following order: (1) propaganda of enlightenment; (2) propaganda of despair; (3) propaganda of hope; (4) particularistic propaganda; and (5) revolutionary propaganda. . . .

PROPAGANDA OF ENLIGHTENMENT

In time of war no nation gives out information regarding the military or political situation which would be detrimental to the fighting power of the country or disheartening or depressing to its population. France, by the law of August 5, 1914, forbade the publication of any news of a military or diplomatic nature that might have the effect of weakening the morale of the people. Only such military or diplomatic news could be printed as came from the War Department. In England the Defense of the Realm Act regulated the printing and distribution of pamphlets and leaflets. This act made it an offense for any person by word of mouth or by writing or by means of any printed book, pamphlet, or document to spread reports or make statements "calculated to cause disaffection to His Majesty or prejudice His Majesty's relations with foreign powers." . . .

The press of Germany was no less restricted than that of the Allies. The German General Staff set up the "Kriegspresseamt," which supplied the press with war news. In all of the warring nations, therefore, there were restrictions on the type of news that could be printed, and war news emanated from official sources only.

This restriction meant that facts of a military nature were withheld from the public.

Excerpt from *Allied Propaganda and the Collapse of the German Empire in 1918* by George Bruntz, Stanford University Press 1938, pp. 85–89, 102–104, 106–107, 109. Reprinted with permission of the publisher.

If the Germans failed to tell their people of their military defeats, the English failed to report all of the ships lost in the submarine campaign. If the Germans neglected to inform their people of the actual size of the American forces coming to the aid of France, the French failed to report the full facts of the military situation before the coming of the Americans. In other words, none of the warring nations allowed facts that would weaken the people's will to fight to be published. . . .

The first task of the Allied propagandists was, therefore, to impart to the German people those facts which their military leaders kept from them. A "Trench Newspaper" was published by the British and distributed to the German troops. This was a single-page "newspaper" which told of the victories of the Allies; it also illustrated the advances of the British from month to month by means of maps. The French issued the *Truppen Nachrichtenblatt,* which, though it was only a small leaflet, contained such pointed statements as these: "Foch Leading New Attack," "Entente Armies Press Forward on Another Wide Front," "Turkish Army in Palestine Destroyed," "No Further Opposition to English Expected," "20,000 Prisoners Taken."

Charts and diagrams showing plainly the number of prisoners taken and the number of dead and wounded on each side were sent to the German trenches. . . .

PROPAGANDA OF DESPAIR

The second phase of the propaganda campaign aimed to bring despair to the Germans. The leaflets stressed the horrors of war and announced the intention of the Entente to fight to the bitter end. One leaflet was addressed "To you in the fields of death!" The German troops were told that wherever they marched there was death. "Look about you! All that you can see is the work of death!" The Allies then asked "Why are you here with the dead? Why are you marching over the dead?" And at the end of the leaflet the propagandists told the German soldier, "You will lie where your comrades are lying — in the field of death." . . .

A great deal of propaganda of despair had in it a touch of sentimentalism. It called attention to the suffering of the wives and children of the soldiers. . . .

Cartoons were also used to bring home to the German soldiers the situation at home. The French, for example, published a drawing in *Die Feldpost* in December 1915 which showed the kitchen of a German family. The table was bare, and two emaciated children were staring pitifully at the empty table. The father, nothing but skin and bones, remarks to his spouse, who still has a little life in her, "My insides are rumbling with hunger." Whereupon the wife replies, "Then don't go on the street or you will be arrested for disturbing the peace." . . .

Another method of promulgating the propaganda of despair was to paint a picture of the rewards of the crippled soldiers after the war. Stories were circulated that veterans of the war of 1870 died of hunger in the parks of Berlin while begging from the rich who scorned their pleas for help. One leaflet shows a picture of a poor crippled soldier standing at the entrance of a large restaurant or hotel. Fat men and buxom women, dressed in the richest evening clothes, are coming out of the place with a look of contentment and happiness on their faces. Not one of them notices the war-exhausted, hungry cripple. The inference was that such a reward awaited the soldiers who were wounded while fighting for the Fatherland. . . .

PROPAGANDA OF HOPE

It was not enough to bring to the attention of the German troops the fact that they were fighting a losing battle, that they were the slaves of the military and Junker classes. They had to be given something better to strive for. The soldiers were told that they were being mistreated, and forced to fight for the wealthy aristocrats of Germany. But where would they be treated better? They were told that they were certain to meet death if they continued to fight for their militarists. But what else could they do? They were reminded that the war was taking away their best, that it was destructive of their economic life and ruinous to the common people. But if they made peace, what assurance had they that the Allied peace conditions would not be equally as destructive to their economic life as the war? Here, then, was the task for the propaganda of hope.

One way by which the German soldier could hope to save his life, and perhaps return to his family unmaimed, was by surrendering to the Allies. Propaganda purporting to come from the German prisoners already in the Allied camps was used most extensively. These leaflets contained letters supposedly from prisoners in France or England which told of the good food, the comfortable quarters, and the fine treatment that they were receiving at the hands of their captors.

One of these letters from "a German prisoner" to his comrades still in the trenches said:

Comrades!

From the war prisons we are sending you a few words and hope that they will meet with a little success and bring the end of this war a little nearer.

First. Do not believe those who tell you that you will be treated cruelly in prison. On the contrary we can assure you that we get more to eat in one day than you get from your murderous leaders in three.

Second. Warm clothing and shoes and kind treatment from the English officers such as a German soldier can hardly imagine.

Third. For whom are you taking your hide to market? For whom are your wives and children suffering? For the Hohenzollerns and Junkers. . . . Don't you hear them laugh? . . .

Still other letters lament the fact that their German comrades at the front continue to fight for the Hohenzollerns whose "thirst for blood is not yet quenched." They appeal to the men to think of their wives and children at home. "For you do not know why you are fighting," says one appeal, "while the French are fighting to recover their fatherland and for the rights of humanity. Come over! Break the bonds that hold you down, and see for yourselves how a free man is treated in a free land."

9. German Atrocities

In an attempt to expose the transgressions of German troops against Allied soldiers and civilians, J. H. Morgan, a professor of constitutional law at the University of London and former Home Office commissioner with the British Expeditionary Force, gathered the oral testimonies of British soldiers who had witnessed German atrocities in France during the war. He interviewed more than two thousand British soldiers over the course of the winter of 1914–1915 and submitted the results confidentially to the Bryce committee, whose primary interest lay in verifying German atrocities in Belgium and whose conclusions were embodied in the famous Bryce Report of 1915. Morgan's investigation generated the same basic conclusion: that German soldiers had systematically violated the laws of war.

A German military writer of great authority predicted some years ago that the next war would be one of inconceivable violence. The prophecy appears only too true as regards the conduct of German troops in the field; it has rarely been distinguished by that chivalry which is supposed to characterise the freemasonry of arms. One of our most distinguished Staff officers remarked to me that the Germans have no sense of honour in the field, and the almost uniform testimony of our officers and men induces me to believe that the remark is only too true. Abuse of the white flag has been very frequent, especially in the earlier stages of the campaign on the Aisne, when our officers, not having been disillusioned by bitter experience, acted on the assumption that they had to deal with an honourable opponent. Again and again the white flag was put up, and when a company of ours advanced unsuspectingly and without supports to take prisoners, the Germans who had exhibited the token of surrender parted their ranks to make room for a murderous fire from machine-guns concealed behind them. Or, again, the flag was exhibited in order to give time for supports to come up. It not infrequently happened that our company officers, advancing unarmed to confer with the German company commander in such cases, were shot down as they approached. The Camerons, the West Yorks, the Coldstreams, the East Lancs, the Wiltshires, the South Wales Borderers, in particular, suffered heavily in these ways. In all these cases they were the victims of organised German units, *i.e.* companies or battalions, acting under the orders of responsible officers.

There can, moreover, be no doubt that the respect of the German troops for the Geneva Convention is but intermittent. Cases of deliberate firing on stretcher-bearers are, according to the universal testimony of our officers and men, of frequent occurrence. It is almost certain death to attempt to convey wounded men from the trenches over open ground except under cover of night. A much more serious offence, however, is the deliberate killing of the wounded as they lie helpless and defenceless on the field of battle. This is so grave a charge that were it not substantiated by the considered

Excerpt from *German Atrocities. An Official Investigation* by J. H. Morgan, T. Fisher Unwin, 1916, pp. 46–58.

statements of officers, non-commissioned officers, and men, one would hesitate to believe it. But even after rejecting, as one is bound to do, cases which may be explained by accident, mistake, or the excitement of action, there remains a large residuum of cases which can only be explained by deliberate malice. No other explanation is possible when, as has not infrequently happened, men who have been wounded by rifle fire in an advance, and have had to be left during a retirement for reinforcements, are discovered, in our subsequent advance, with nine or ten bayonet wounds or with their heads beaten in by the butt-ends of rifles. Such cases could not have occurred, the enemy being present in force, without the knowledge of superior officers. Indeed, I have before me evidence which goes to show that German officers have themselves acted in similar fashion. Some of the cases reveal a leisurely barbarity which proves great deliberation; cases such as the discovery of bodies of despatch-riders burnt with petrol or "pegged out" with lances, or of soldiers with their faces stamped upon by the heel of a boot, or of a guardsman found with numerous bayonet wounds evidently inflicted as he was in the act of applying a field dressing to a bullet wound. There also seems no reason to doubt the independent statements of men of the Loyal North Lancs, whom I interrogated on different occasions, that the men of one of their companies were killed on December 20th after they had surrendered and laid down their arms. To what extent prisoners have been treated in this manner it is impossible to say; dead men tell no tales, but an exceptionally able Intelligence Officer at the head-quarters of the Cavalry Corps informed me that it is believed that when British prisoners are taken in small parties they are put to death in cold blood. Certain it is that our men when captured are kicked, robbed of all they possess, threatened with death if they will not give information, and in some cases forced to dig trenches. The evidence I have taken from soldiers at the base hospitals on these points is borne out by evidence taken at the Front immediately after such occurrences by the Deputy Judge-Advocate General, an Assistant Provost Marshal, and a captain in the Sherwood Foresters, and in the opinion of these officers the evidence which they took, and which they subsequently placed at my disposal, is reliable.

THE PROOFS OF POLICY

The question as to how far these outrages are attributable to policy and superior orders becomes imperative. It was at first difficult to answer. For a long time I did not find, nor did I expect to find, any documentary orders to that effect. Such orders, if given at all, were much more likely to be verbal, for it is extremely improbable that the German authorities would be so unwise as to commit them to writing. But the outrages upon combatants were so numerous and so collective in character that I began to suspect policy at a very early stage in my investigations. My suspicions were heightened by the significant fact that exhaustive inquiries which I made among Indian native officers and men in the hospital ships in port at Boulogne, and at the base hospitals, seemed to indicate that experiences of outrage were as rare among the Indian troops as they were common among the British. The explanation was fairly obvious, inasmuch as many of these Indian witnesses who had fallen into German hands testified to me that the German officers seized the occasion to assure them that Germany was animated by the most friendly feelings towards them, and more than once dismissed them with an injunction not to fight against German troops and to bring over their comrades to the German side. For example, a sepoy in the 9th Bhopals testified to me as follows:

> I and three others were found wounded by the Germans. They bound up our wounds and invited us to join them, offering us money and land. I answered, "I, who have eaten the King's salt, cannot do this thing and thus bring sorrow and shame upon my people." The Germans took our chupattis, and offered us of their bread in return. I said, "I am a Brahmin and cannot touch it." They then left us, saying that if we were captured again they would kill us.

There was other evidence to the same effect. Eventually I obtained proofs confirming my suspicions, and I will now proceed to set them out.

On May 3rd I visited the Ministry of War in Paris at the invitation of the French military authorities, and was received by M. le Capitaine René Petit, Chef du Service de Contentieux, who conducted me to the department where the diaries of German prisoners were kept. I made a brief preliminary examination of them, and discovered the following passage (which I had photographed) in the diary of a German N.C.O., Göttsche, of the 85th Infantry Regiment (the IXth Corps), fourth company detached for service, under date "Okt. 6, 1914, bei Antwerpen" [October 6, 1914, near Antwerp]:

> . . . The Captain called us to him and said: "In the fortress [*i.e.,* Antwerp] which we have to take there are in all probability Englishmen. But I do not want to see any Englishmen prisoners in the hands of this company." A general "Bravo" of assent was the answer. . . .

. . . I now come to the most damning proofs of a policy of cold-blooded murder of wounded and prisoners, initiated and carried out by a whole brigade under the orders of a Brigadier-General. This particular investigation took me a long time, but the results are, I think, conclusive. It may be remembered that some months ago the French military authorities published in the French newspapers what purported to be the text of an order issued by a German Brigadier-General, named Stenger, commanding the 58th Brigade, in which he ordered his troops to take no prisoners and to put to death without mercy every one who fell into their hands, whether wounded and defenceless or not. The German Government immediately denounced the alleged order as a forgery. I determined to see whether I could establish its authenticity, and in February last I obtained a copy of the original from M. Mollard, of the Ministry of Foreign Affairs, who is a member of the Commission appointed by the French Government to inquire into the alleged German atrocities. The text of that order was as follows:

> . . . Army Order of 26 Aug., 1914, about 4 P.M., such as was given to his troops as a Brigade or Army Order by the leader of the 7th Company of the 112th Regiment of Infantry at Thionville, at the entrance of the wood of Saint Barbe.
> To date from this day no prisoners will be made any longer. All the prisoners will

be executed. The wounded, whether armed or defenceless, will be executed. Prisoners, even in large and compact formations, will be executed. Not a man will be left alive behind us.

Taking this alleged order as my starting-point, I began to make inquiries at British Head-quarters as to the existence of any information about the doings of the 112th Regiment. I soon found that there was good reason to suspect it. Our Intelligence Department placed in my hands the records of the examination of two men of this regiment who had been captured by us. One of them volunteered a statement to one of our Intelligence Officers on November 23rd to the effect that his regiment had orders to treat Indians well, but were allowed to treat British prisoners as they pleased. This man's testimony appeared to be reliable, as statements he made on other points, *i.e.* as to the German formations, were subsequently found to be true, and his information as to discrimination in the treatment of Indians entirely bore out the conclusions I had already arrived at on that particular point. The German witness in question further stated that 65 out of 150 British prisoners were killed in cold blood by their escort on or about October 23rd on the road to Lille, and that the escort were praised for their conduct. Other German prisoners have, I may add, also made statements that they had orders to kill all the English who fell into their hands. . . .

The cumulative effect of this evidence, coupled with the statements of so many of our men who claim to have been eye-witnesses of wholesale bayoneting of the wounded, certainly confirms suspicions of the gravest kind as to such acts having been done by authority. Neither the temperament of the German soldier nor the character of German discipline (*furchtbar streng* — "frightfully strict" — as a German prisoner put it to me) makes it probable that the German soldiers acted on their own initiative. It would, in any case, be incredible that so many cases of outrage could be sufficiently explained by any law of averages, or by the idiosyncrasies of the "bad characters" present in every large congregation of men.

TREATMENT OF CIVIL POPULATION

The subject-matter of the inquiry may be classified according as it relates to: (1) ill-treatment of the civil population, and (2) breaches of the laws of war in the field. As regards the first it is not too much to say that the Germans pay little respect to life and none to property. . . . Here it is clear that the treatment of civilians is regulated by no more rational or humane policy than that of intimidation or, even worse, of sullen vindictiveness. As the German troops passed through the communes and towns of the arrondissements of Ypres, Hazebrouck, Bethune, and Lille, they shot indiscriminately at the innocent spectators of their march; the peasant tilling his fields, the refugee tramping the roads, and the workman returning to his home. To be seen was often dangerous, to attempt to escape being seen was invariably fatal. Old men and boys and even women and young girls were shot like rabbits. The slightest failure to comply with the peremptory demands of the invader has been punished with instant death. The curé of Pradelle, having failed to find the key of the church tower, was put against the wall and shot; a shepherd at a lonely farmhouse near Rebais who failed to produce bread for the German troops had his head blown off by a rifle; a baker at Moorslede who attempted to escape was suffocated by German soldiers with his own scarf; a young mother at Bailleul who was unable to produce sufficient coffee to satisfy the demands of twenty-three German soldiers had her baby seized by one of the latter and its head dipped in scalding water; an old man of seventy-seven years of age at La Ferté Gaucher who attempted to protect two women in his house from outrage was killed with a rifle shot.

I select these instances from my notes at random — they could be multiplied many times — as indications of the temper of the German troops. They might, perhaps, be dismissed as the unauthorised acts of small patrols were it not that there is only too much evidence to show that the soldiers are taught by their superiors to set no value upon human life, and things have been done which could not have been done without superior orders. For example, at Bailleul, La Gorgue, and Doulieu, where no resistance of any kind was offered to the German troops, and where the latter were present in force under the command of commissioned officers, civilians were taken in groups, and after being forced to dig their own graves were shot by firing parties in the presence of an officer. At Doulieu, which is a small village, eleven civilians were shot in this way; they were strangers to the place, and it was only by subsequent examination of the papers found on their bodies that some of them were identified as inhabitants of neighbouring villages. If these men had been guilty of any act of hostility it is not clear why they were not shot at once in their own villages, and inquiries at some of the villages from which they were taken have revealed no knowledge of any act of the kind. It is, however, a common practice for the German troops to seize the male inhabitants (especially those of military age) of the places they occupy and take them away on their retreat. Twenty-five were so taken from Bailleul and nothing has been heard of them since. There is only too much reason to suppose that the same fate has overtaken them as that which befell the unhappy men executed at Doulieu. I believe the explanation of these sinister proceedings to be that the men were compelled to dig trenches for the enemy, to give information as to the movement of their own troops, and to act as guides (all clearly practices which are a breach of the laws of war and of the Hague Regulations), and then, their presence being inconvenient and their knowledge of the enemy's positions and movements compromising, they were put to death. This is not a mere surmise. The male inhabitants of Warneton were forced to dig trenches for the enemy, and an inhabitant of Merris was compelled to go with the German troops and act as a guide; it is notorious that the official manual of the German General Staff, *Kriegsbrauch im Landskriege,* condones, and indeed indoctrinates, such breaches of the laws of war. . . .

In this connexion it is important to observe that the German policy of holding a whole town or village responsible for the acts of isolated individuals, whether by the killing of hostages or by decimation or by a wholesale *battue* of the inhabitants, has undoubtedly resulted in the grossest and most irrelevant cruelties. A single shot fired in or near a place occupied by the Germans — it may be a shot from a French patrol or a German rifle let off by accident or mistake or in a drunken affray — at once places the whole community in peril, and it seems to be at once assumed that the civil inhabitants are guilty unless they can prove themselves innocent. . . .

OUTRAGES UPON WOMEN — THE GERMAN OCCUPATION
OF BAILLEUL

. . . Outrages upon the honour of women by German soldiers have been so frequent
that it is impossible to escape the conviction that they have been condoned and indeed
encouraged by German officers. As regards this matter I have made a most minute study
of the German occupation of Bailleul. This place was occupied by a regiment of German Hussars in October for a period of eight days. During the whole of that period the
town was delivered over to the excesses of a licentious soldiery and was left in a state of
indescribable filth. There were at least thirty cases of outrages on girls and young married women, authenticated by sworn statements of witnesses and generally by medical
certificates of injury. It is extremely probable that, owing to the natural reluctance of
women to give evidence in cases of this kind, the actual number of outrages largely
exceeds this. Indeed, the leading physician of the town, Dr. Bels, puts the number as
high as sixty. At least five officers were guilty of such offences, and where the officers set
the example the men followed. The circumstances were often of a peculiarly revolting
character; daughters were outraged in the presence of their mothers, and mothers in the
presence or the hearing of their little children. In one case, the facts of which are proved
by evidence which would satisfy any court of law, a young girl of nineteen was violated
by one officer while the other held her mother by the throat and pointed a revolver,
after which the two officers exchanged their respective rôles. The officers and soldiers
usually hunted in couples, either entering the houses under pretence of seeking billets,
or forcing the doors by open violence. Frequently the victims were beaten and kicked,
and invariably threatened with a loaded revolver if they resisted. The husband or father
of the women and girls was usually absent on military service; if one was present he was
first ordered away under some pretext; and disobedience of civilians to German orders,
however improper, is always punished with instant death. In several cases little children
heard the cries and struggles of their mother in the adjoining room to which she had
been carried by a brutal exercise of force. No attempt was made to keep discipline, and
the officers, when appealed to for protection, simply shrugged their shoulders. Horses
were stabled in salons; shops and private houses were looted (there are nine hundred
authenticated cases of pillage). Some civilians were shot and many others carried off into
captivity. Of the fate of the latter nothing is known, but the worst may be suspected.

The German troops were often drunk and always insolent. But significantly
enough, the bonds of discipline thus relaxed were tightened at will and hardly a single
straggler was left behind.

Inquiries in other places, in the villages of Meteren, Oultersteen, and Nieppe, for
example, establish the occurrence of similar outrages upon defenceless women, accompanied by every circumstance of disgusting barbarity. No civilian dare attempt to protect
his wife or daughter from outrage. To be in possession of weapons of defence is to be
condemned to instant execution, and even a village constable found in possession of a
revolver (which he was required to carry in virtue of his office) was instantly shot at
Westoutre. Roving patrols burnt farm-houses and turned the women and children out

into the wintry and sodden fields with capricious cruelty and in pursuance of no intelligible military purpose.

B. The Visual War

1. KÄTHE KOLLWITZ'S DIARY

Born in 1867 into a religious family in Königsberg, East Prussia, Käthe Schmidt-Kollwitz received early encouragement from her father to pursue a career as an artist. She studied art in both Berlin and Munich and her first major work — a series of etchings and lithographs — depicted the miserable existence of Silesia's weavers and their uprising in 1844 and reflected her impressions of dramatist Gerhard Hauptmann's controversial play, *The Weavers*. This highly acclaimed series marked her as an artist of the underdog — the proletariat. Upon the outbreak of the First World War, Kollwitz's second son, Peter, motivated by youthful enthusiasm, enlisted in the army at the age of eighteen. On October 22, 1914, Peter was killed in action. His death nearly plunged Kollwitz into the depths of despair, but she revitalized herself by dedicating her artwork — images of peace and portrayals of the plight of the downtrodden — to his memory. Although sympathetic to the revolutionary socialist ideals of 1918, Kollwitz maintained no party affiliation. In 1919, with the creation of the Weimar Republic, the new socialist government honored her contributions to the art world by installing her as the first female member of the highly prestigious Prussian Academy of Arts. In 1923 Kollwitz completed her antiwar portfolio, *Seven Woodcuts About War*. The diary entries that follow reveal her innermost thoughts on war and art.

August 27, 1914

In the heroic stiffness of these times of war, when our feelings are screwed to an unnatural pitch, it is like a touch of heavenly music, like sweet, lamenting murmurs of peace, to read that French soldiers spare and actually help wounded Germans, that in the franctireur villages German soldiers write on the walls of houses such notices as: Be considerate! An old woman lives here. — These people were kind to me. — Old people only. — Woman in childbed. — And so on.

A piece by Gabriele Reuter in the *Tag* on the tasks of women today. She spoke of the joy of sacrificing — a phrase that struck me hard. Where do all the women who

Excerpt from *The Diary and Letters of Käthe Kollwitz,* Northwestern University Press, 1988, pp. 62–63, 68, 72–74, 156–157.

have watched so carefully over the lives of their beloved ones get the heroism to send them to face the cannon? I am afraid that this soaring of the spirit will be followed by the blackest despair and dejection. The task is to bear it not only during these few weeks, but for a long time — in dreary November as well, and also when spring comes again, in March, the month of young men who wanted to live and are dead. That will be much harder.

Those who now have only small children . . . seem to me so fortunate. For us, whose sons are going, the vital thread is snapped.

September 30, 1914

Cold, cloudy autumnal weather. The grave mood that comes over one when one knows: there is war, and one cannot hold on to any illusions any more. Nothing is real but the frightfulness of this state, which we almost grow used to. In such times it seems so stupid that the boys must go to war. The whole thing is so ghastly and insane. Occasionally there comes the foolish thought: how can they possibly take part in such madness? And at once the cold shower: they *must, must!* All is leveled by death; down with all the youth! Then one is ready to despair.

Only one state of mind makes it at all bearable: to receive the sacrifice into one's will. But how can one maintain such a state?

[Peter Kollwitz was killed on October 22, 1914.] . . .

February 21, 1916

Read an article by E. von Keyserling on the future of art. He opposes expressionism and says that after the war the German people will need eccentric studio art less than ever before. What they need is realistic art.

I quite agree — if by realistic art Keyserling means the same thing I do. Which refers back to a talk I had recently with Karl [Dr. Karl Kollwitz, her husband] about my small sculptures.

It is true that my sculptural work is rejected by the public. Why? It is not at all popular. The average spectator does not understand it. Art for the average spectator need not be shallow. Of course he has no objection to the trite — but it is also true that he would accept true art if it were simple enough. I thoroughly agree that there must be understanding between the artist and the people. In the best ages of art that has always been the case.

Genius can probably run on ahead and seek out new ways. But the good artists who follow after genius — and I count myself among these — have to restore the lost connection once more. A pure studio art is unfruitful and frail, for anything that does not form living roots — why should it exist at all? . . .

August 22, 1916

Stagnation in my work.

When I feel so parched, I almost long for the sorrow again. And then when it comes back I feel it stripping me physically of all the strength I need for work.

Made a drawing: the mother letting her dead son slide into her arms. I might make a hundred such drawings and yet I do not get any closer to him. I am seeking him. As if I had to find him in the work. And yet everything I can do is so childishly feeble and inadequate. I feel obscurely that I could throw off this inadequacy, that Peter is somewhere in the work and I might find him. And at the same time I have the feeling that I can no longer do it. I am too shattered, weakened, drained by tears. I am like the writer in Thomas Mann: he can only write, but he has not sufficient strength to live what is written. It is the other way round with me. I no longer have the strength to form what has been lived. A genius and a Mann could do it. I probably cannot.

For work, one must be hard and thrust outside oneself what one has lived through. As soon as I begin to do that, I again feel myself a mother who will not give up her sorrow. Sometimes it all becomes so terribly difficult. . . .

October 11, 1916

Everything remains as obscure as ever for me. Why is that? It's not only our youth who go willingly and joyfully into the war; it's the same in all nations. People who would be friends under other conditions now hurl themselves at one another as enemies. Are the young really without judgment? Do they always rush into it as soon as they are called? Without looking closer? Do they rush into war because they want to, because it is in their blood so that they accept without examination whatever reasons for fighting are given to them? Do the young want war? Would they be old before their time if they no longer wanted it?

This frightful insanity — the youth of Europe hurling themselves at one another.

When I think I am convinced of the insanity of the war, I ask myself again by what law man ought to live. Certainly not in order to attain the greatest possible happiness. It will always be true that life must be subordinated to the service of an ideal. But in this case, where has that principle led us? Peter, Erich, Richard, all have subordinated their lives to the idea of patriotism. The English, Russian and French young men have done the same. The consequence has been this terrible killing, and the impoverishment of Europe. Then shall we say that the youth in all these countries have been cheated? Has their capacity for sacrifice been exploited in order to bring on the war? Where are the guilty? Are there any? Or is everyone cheated? Has it been a case of mass madness? And when and how will the awakening take place?

I shall never fully understand it all. But it is clear that our boys, our Peter, went into the war two years ago with pure hearts, and that they were ready to die for Germany.

They died — almost all of them. Died in Germany and among Germany's enemies — by the millions.

When the minister blessed the volunteers, he spoke of the Roman youth who leaped into the abyss and so closed it. That was one boy. Each of these boys felt that he must act like that one. But what came of it was something very different. The abyss has not closed. It has swallowed up millions, and it still gapes wide. And Europe, all Europe, is still like Rome, sacrificing its finest and most precious treasure — but the sacrifice has no effect.

Is it a breach of faith with you, Peter, if I can now see only madness in the war? Peter, you died believing. Was that also true of Erich, Walter, Meier, Gottfried, Richard Noll? Or had they come to their senses and were they nevertheless forced to leap into the abyss? Was force involved? Or did they want to? Were they forced? . . .

April 22, 1917

My dear Hans! . . . You know how at the beginning of the war you all said: Social Democracy has failed. We said that the idea of internationalism must be put aside right now, but back of everything national the international spirit remains. Later on this concept of mine was almost entirely buried; now it has sprung to life again. The development of the national spirit in its present form leads into blind alleys. Some condition *must* be found which preserves the life of the nation, but rules out the fatal rivalry among nations. The Social Democrats in Russia are speaking the language of truth. That is internationalism. Even though, God knows, they love their homeland.

It seems to me that behind all the convulsions the world is undergoing, a new creation is already in the making. And the beloved millions who have died have shed their blood to raise humanity higher than humanity has been. That is my politics, my boy. It comes from faith.

2. HOSPITAL ORDERLY FELIXMÜLLER

Born in 1897 into a working-class family in Dresden, Conrad Felixmüller studied at the Dresden Academy of Fine Arts until 1915. By 1917 he had abandoned his earlier apolitical stance toward the war, joining the antiwar Expressionist Working Group of Dresden. During that year he was drafted but avoided active military duty in the German army by serving instead as a military hospital orderly in the city of Arnsdorf. Felixmüller's experience in that hospital, formerly a mental asylum, led to the publication of the following essay, originally printed in an antiwar journal, *Menschen,* in May 1915. His lithograph, *Soldier in the Lunatic Asylum,* which accompanied the nightmarish description of life in the hospital ward, depicted a deranged patient clasping an envelope with the sender's name, Felixmüller, written on it. By the end of the war Felixmüller had gravitated toward the far left of the political spectrum and was actively involved in reconciling art with a form of utopian socialism.

Am now here, military hospital orderly Felixmüller. Emphasize, however, *sick* and Felixmüller. Want first to examine myself and my sick ones. Kindness, sympathy and feeling restore health. Still have heart and soul with which to feel after all. It is night. In twenty beds around me sick soldiers are laid out. Sick in mind, epileptics, madmen, cripples, wounded. All men like me. Flesh, body, bones — strange forms, sometimes weak, sometimes strong. Pains everywhere, above all in the head (three days ago the doctor battered my head with a small hammer, i.e., I have splitting pains). Everything is steeped in blood. Glowing red like molten iron. Lungs, breast, the whole body with capillaries full of these microscopic, fine details. Distended stomach traversed by the blue and red of these thin, swelling capillaries. Green, sulfurous, gleaming intestines, endlessly long, filled with swollen pulp, of flesh like my flesh, permeated with animal blood. Loathing (I feel full) rises up — disgusts me — would like to vomit — cannot. A truck runs over my limbs.

And I make every effort with this body to serve other like bodies, sick, wounded, insane. Laid out in twenty beds. Suddenly all these men are before me enveloped in carbolic clouds, foggy and for a time lost in bloody, festering bandages. Am now everything myself in order to understand and help: am sick, wounded, insane, feverish, and have ice packs in my legs. Have everywhere a red burning rash. It grows fast enough to watch from speck-size to palm size — eventually I am only a single burning rash. And cannot lie, nor sleep. Day dreams. First in combat loaded with rounds of ammunition, almost crushed to death — and soon in a speeding Red Cross express train. Rumbling pause. Lie in ghostly white. Red Cross nurses, white-smocked orderlies and doctors in front of my large-swollen face — consumed, all feeling vanished. [I] howl in a deep, dark infinity. Still hear beautiful cracklings like glass from a knife cutting through skin into flesh, shredding sinews like leather. Sawing leg bones like wood — Off! — blood spurts in a red arc toward the window over cities, villages, fields. Shreds of field bandage fly past, bind up my stump. And howl with the train in the dark red tunnel. Always deeper — watch out — head off — it tears off — plunges down into the abyss until — I feel bed. Terror convulses me. . . .

So beautiful is blood — ?! it can flow so beautifully, drip!

If — only — I — could give — all — 20 comrades — this — same — joy with my silver needle? bring to them a liberating release from head pain. Extinguish their consciousness just so. If, one after another, I could push my silver steel needle blue, now colored over blood red, into the temple.

Why not then? After all, I have shed no blood so far. After all, I have thrust no bayonet into the intestines — offal stomachs! Knocked no skulls in with rifles!?

So I'll do it at once. If only everyone would sleep peacefully. Should be surprised in the morning. Each lying in his delicate little stream of blood.

"Military Hospital Orderly Felixmüller" by Conrad Felixmüller, pp. 169–170. Reprinted with permission of G. K. Hall & Co. an imprint of Macmillan Publishing Co. from *German Expressionism: Documents from the End of the Wilhelmine Empire to the Rise of National Socialism,* edited by Rose-Carol Washton Long. Copyright © 1993 by G. K. Hall & Co.

It is good that night is over — and comrade orderly summons [us] to wash up. . . .

Deranged by an agitated night. The whole night an attack of madness. First one bed — then two close by — then four beds — all beds, and the big orderly — rest.

Two days ago they brought a comrade into the compartment — now they bring him back again still completely high on cocaine . . . after an unsuccessful effort to escape. He tells me of his discovery of a fire window — window bars broken by a strong thrust, lowered on the bedsheet to escape! I flee along with [him]. Am, however, not crazy! . . .

Everyone would immediately become healthy and happy if one said to them: "War is over" said to them: "we delivered you from it through us — because we knew and recognized that thou and thou art our fellow man, hast consumed our guilt for us, art raving and insane." If one were to say to them: "We love you, fellow creatures, — and put an end to it." . . .

Warm the walls of ice-cold hearts with love! Burst the obstinate egoism of capitalist liars for these men here in this sink of iniquity that is Europe.

No man is your enemy — in an insane bloody stump thou shouldst still recognize thy fellow man, thou thyself — because thou art the insane one, the raving one, the raging one, the *murderer* in the war!

3. An Appeal to Solidarity

Ludwig Meidner's enthusiasm for the war, as depicted in some of his earlier paintings such as *French Soldiers* (1914), which showed French troops making a hasty retreat while abandoning their wounded, waned by the autumn of 1915. During 1916 he was associated with the antiwar cause but soon found himself drafted into the German army as a translator for captured French prisoners. His interaction with "the enemy" led him to compose a number of pacifistic tracts, among them the "Hymn of Brotherly Love," written in 1917. In his desire for greater cooperation among peoples, Meidner abandoned his earlier apocalyptic scenery for religious imagery and wrote an appeal, "To All Artists, Musicians, Poets," which appeared in the January 1919 issue of the art journal *Das Kunstblatt*.

a. *"Hymn of Brotherly Love"*

The rattle of machine guns on sunny, high monoplanes. . . . Men's curses, venal, explode the sunny day. Oh horror that flows out of all mouths. . . . Thou high ark of God,

August day in morning glow — and thou pain-torn? earth of the prison camp. Human suffering, inexpressible, of thee must I exult loudly and finally confess my love, deep love.

I am frightened away from barren, scattered court-yards. What turmoil there on a warm human day. Races of Europe and Africa; colored pinions and faces whitened with pain. . . . Oh humanity, thou turnest thy eyes towards me. Thou hast faces like me, with noses, hairs and thin-sorrowful cheeks, human faces calling for help.

Thou Frenchman before me, in bright blue uniform, thy tanned, friendly look, thy casual bearing, arms hanging deep in the pockets of wide trousers, thy mischievous head full of jests, ironies and good jokes, thy heart full of poetic fever and longing for life and withheld fury, thou exuberant Frenchman, thou artist-man and true poet; no, how like you are to me. Art thou not the very closest to me?! come and allow me to call thee my best friend and brother.

Come, ye Englishmen, elegantly built and unaffected as young boys. Thou slandered, much-maligned, how I delight in thee. The books and papers of this time are full of your evil, cunning, self-seeking and treachery. But I need only to see thy free, manly look and friendly and simple bearing. Yes, thou art true, nothing other than true friends. Thou hast in thee the grand simplicity and justice of the sea. Thou art near to me, as only my dear brothers and sisters.

And ye Russians! thou comest yet nearer to me, ye dear Russians! Shyness, hesitancy speak well of thee, thou fundamentally good, thou beloved of God, thou deep, loving human beings. May I step in thy midst and speak with thee, for yes, thou art clearly shy and do not trust me. Oh, how thou hast all come down in the world, wasted by the terrible winters and pestilential summers. Thy silhouettes, how shattered and unsteady! Ye emaciated and crippled, . . . and scrofulous ones — Oh, that I could help you! Thy faces are indeed grown wild, scarred, and sticky from the daily round of days of imprisonment; trampled down and tread upon by insults and hate. . . . Ye humble, god-fearing Russians, ye beloved, beloved Russians and men! . . .

Ye Arabs, colored and pious, what fabulous past one sees in thy gentle and collected gaze. What passionate gestures surround you. Ancient heroic people, great in fervor and moral power. Is it not as though I had always known ye? To me ye have been trusted friends since my fairy tale days of childhood. . . . ye sonorous Moroccans, hot from the carnivore sun of Africa and — ye noble, deeply noble Negroes!

What should I say first to thy glory!? Show me one more beautiful among all the men in these courtyards! . . .

. . . Humanity! White, brown, and black. Broken and upright. Brothers, brothers; all brothers, all equally near to me. How I understand each one of thee. Oh, thou art as miraculous as I myself. Human rock rising up resounding monuments on fleshy legs. Mysterious as I myself and unfathomable. . . . Oh, I know ye are full of folly, spite, and cunning; are cowardly, arrogant, selfish, and full of hate. Let's not speak of that. I am not one whit better. I know, no grain of my soul stands above ye. But I have recognized my love in time. Yet, I have cleared away all foolishness, all evil instincts and now surrender myself completely to my overflowing heart. Now I also turn myself to you.

Let us forget hatred and all the wickedness of the recent years that ye inflicted on one another. . . . Ye have listened to the evil ones. Ye ran screaming after the gaudy banners of empty phrases. See the fiery August summer. Open your heart and let it in. Open your hearts' floodgates and inundate the world with warm humanity. . . .

Come out! Come out! Hearts of my brothers, arise, awake and live.

b. "To All Artists, Musicians, Poets"

So that we no longer have to be ashamed before the heavens, we must finally get busy and help establish a just order in government and society.

We artists and poets must join in the first ranks.

There can be no more exploiters and exploited!

It can no longer be the case that a huge majority must live in the most miserable, disgraceful, and degrading conditions, while a tiny minority eat like animals at an over-flowing table. We must commit ourselves to socialism: to a general and unceasing so-cialization of the means of production, which gives each man work, leisure, bread, a home, and the intimation of a higher goal. Socialism must be our new creed!

It must rescue both: the poor out of the humiliation of servitude, oppression, bru-tality, and malice — and the rich it will deliver forever more from merciless egotism, from their greed and harshness.

Let a holy solidarity ally us painters and poets with the poor! Have not many among us also known misery and the shame of hunger and material dependence?! Do we have a much better and more secure position in society than the proletariat?! Are we not like beggars dependent upon the whims of the art-collecting bourgeoisie!

If we are still young and unknown, they throw us alms or leave us silently to die.

If we have a name, then they seek to divert us from the pure goals with money and vain desires. And when we are finally in the grave, then their ostentatiousness cov-ers our undefiled works with mountains of gold coins — painters, poets, composers, be ashamed of your dependence and cowardice and join as a brother with the expelled, outcast, ill-paid menial!

We are not workers, no. Ecstasy, rapture — passion is our daily work. We are free and knowing and must, like guiding banners, wave before our strong brothers.

Painters, poets. . . . who other than we should then fight for the just cause?! In us the world conscience still throbs powerfully. Ever anew the voice of God breathes fire into our rebellious fists. . . .

Painters, poets! let us make common cause with our intimidated, defenseless brothers, for the sake of the spirit.

The worker respects the spirit. He strives with powerful zeal for knowledge and learning.

"To All Artists, Musicians, Poets" by Ludwig Meidner, pp. 175–176. Reprinted with permission of G. K. Hall & Co. an imprint of Macmillan Publishing Co. from *German Expressionism: Documents from the End of the Wilhelmine Empire to the Rise of National Socialism,* edited by Rose-Carol Washton Long. Copyright © 1993 by G. K. Hall & Co.

The bourgeois is irreverent. He loves only dalliance and aesthetically embellished stupidities and hates and fears the spirit — because he feels that he could be unmasked by it.

The bourgeois knows only one freedom, his own — namely to be able to exploit others. That is the pale terror that goes about silently, and millions collapse and wither early.

The bourgeois knows no love — only exploitation and fraud. Arise, arise to battle against the ugly beast of prey, the booty-hungry, thousand-headed emperor of tomorrow, the atheist and Anti-Christ!

Painters, architects, sculptors, you whom the bourgeois pays high wages for your work — out of vanity, snobbery, and boredom — listen: on this money sticks the sweat and blood and life juices of thousands of poor, overexerted people — listen: that is an unclean profit. . . .

Listen further: we must take our conviction seriously, the new wondrous belief. We must join with the workers' party, the decisive, unequivocal party. . . .

Socialism is at stake — that means: justice, freedom, and human love at stake — at stake, God's order in the world!

4. "AN APPEAL FROM RUSSIAN ARTISTS"

"An Appeal from Russian Artists" appeared in the February 1919 issue of the expressionist art journal, *Neue Blätter für Kunst und Dichtung* (New Journal for Art and Poetry), edited by the unemployed German architect and art critic Hugo Zehder. Although the author of the appeal was the Russian artist David Sterenberg, who resided in Paris from 1906 until the Russian Revolution, the commentary preceding the appeal was likely that of Zehder, whose hope for a better society was nurtured by the possibility of greater cooperation among Europe's expressionist artists.

Let's not forget that the Russians under Kandinsky[1] were the strongest storm troops of Expressionism. Their work, with its striking and intelligibly formulated theories, inasmuch as it was not disturbed, has continued to have a powerful impact. They triumphed before the bloody deluge occurred. But what has happened since? In European coun-

"An Appeal from Russian Artists" by D. P. Sterenberg, pp. 227–228. Reprinted with permission of G. K. Hall & Co. an imprint of Macmillan Publishing Co. from *German Expressionism: Documents from the End of the Wilhelmine Empire to the Rise of National Socialism,* edited by Rose-Carol Washton Long. Copyright © 1993 by G. K. Hall & Co.

---

[1] Wassily Kandinsky (1866–1944), born in Russia, immigrated to Munich in 1896. He founded, along with German expressionist artist Franz Marc, the Blaue Reiter movement, which promoted modernism in art.

tries, no one denies any longer that Expressionism is the truest expression of the spiritual need of its time, and that its originators had the most delicate sense of what lay ahead. That helped Expressionism to victory everywhere. That made it possible to survive the deluge and hold the course. But there, in the East, where salvation came from? What fate awaited the new art there? After the frontline cut the nation off in the summer of 1914, all too little was heard of what the leaders of the most decisive art movement were accomplishing. Since the revolution tore up the front, nothing has improved. Yet, whoever believes in the power of this art, whoever is aware of its metaphysical sources and, not taken in by the fragmentary and arbitrary reports of the daily press, suspects that the momentous events in a Russia not yet desecrated are also of metaphysical origin, will not doubt that there, too, a radical youth has seen its ideals disembark from the rescuing ark on this side of our new time. And now, there is the further message that the men, who are turning from scientific socialism back to utopia in Russia and are attempting to realize this goal by intuitively comprehending the essence, power, and meaning of artistic youth, officially favor them over the older generation. The revolution in art goes hand in hand with the revolution of public life as a whole. The Russian revolutionaries had barely received the news of the German overthrow when they were suddenly overcome by a feeling of spiritual solidarity. They are the harbingers of an international appeal from all the arts that is marching toward us! An appeal from the Russian vanguard, unknown in Germany until now, perhaps suppressed, has been transmitted to us. It reads as follows:

Moscow, November 30, 1918

Appeal

From the Progressive Russian Visual Artists to German Colleagues!

The new Russian government has called upon all young creative talent to establish a new life, and it has turned over national direction of artistic matters *to the new progressive tendencies*. For only the new creative work, done shortly before the worldwide upheavals, is able to harmonize with the rhythm of the newly developing life.

At last there is the prospect of communal creative work, which will transcend a more narrow, national consciousness and serve international communication.

To start with, the Russians are turning to their closest neighbors, their German colleagues, and asking them to advise and to exchange news within the framework of artistic possibilities. As a practical measure to bring about such relationships, we propose a congress of representatives of German and Russian artists, which will serve as the beginning of a future world conference on art, and which will immediately initiate artistic communication between the two nations about far-ranging projects such as exhibitions, publications, theater productions, and music.

Chairman of the Board of Artists in Petersburg and Moscow
(signed) D. P. Sterenberg
(signed) (Signatures of members of the International Office of Painters)

On Using Posters as Evidence

Posters were a prominent feature of each nation's effort to secure its population's support for the war. Like photographs, posters are illustrative evidence, but they do not so much reflect reality as "package" or advertise a view of the conflict for popular consumption. Accordingly, the interpretation of posters as evidence requires as much care as the use of any other type of source material.

Refer, for example, to the poster *Learn to Make Munitions* (page 96), which was intended to help recruit women for the unfamiliar, arduous, and dangerous task of producing munitions. Obviously, given its purpose, the poster does not allude to the dangers involved, such as TNT poisoning (which turned hair and hands a bright orange) or explosions. It does not, therefore, reflect the full reality of munitions making. Yet while concealing these hazards, the poster emphasizes the sense of women's service to the war effort, "doing their bit." Furthermore, it captures very strikingly the potentially liberating implications of such employment; note the artist's effort to convey equivalence between the male soldier's jaunty salute and the female worker's similar gesture. In that sense, the poster testifies to popular attitudes and aspirations in a unique way. One should approach the other posters in a similar light for the particular insights they can provide.

Германскій антихристъ

The German Anti-Christ, *1914 (Russia)*
"THE GERMAN ANTICHRIST Emperor Wilhelm, the tyrant of Europe, last of the Hohenzollerns . . . War with the Germans — a holy war for freedom, truth, and justice, for the Faith, the Tsar, and the Russian People."
(Hoover Institution Archives)

Once a German, Always a German *by David Wilson, 1918 (Great Britain)*
(Imperial War Museum, London)

In Front of the Ruins of the Colosseum *by G. Quesnel, 1915 (France)*
"I didn't know, Gretchen, that our troops had passed through Rome. . . ."
"But Fritz, they haven't passed through here. . . ."
"Well, then, who began their work?"
(Cover of Le Pêle-Mêle magazine, November 14, 1915)

Red Cross or Iron Cross? *by David Wilson (Great Britain)*
(Hoover Institution Archives)

The Greatest Mother in the World *by Alonzo E. Foringer, 1918 (U.S.A.)*
(Imperial War Museum, London)

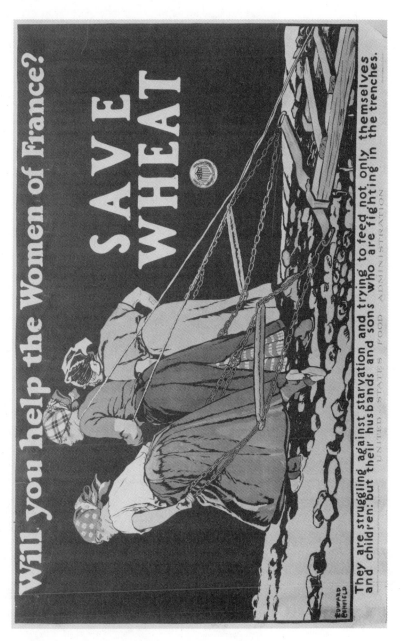

Will You Help the Women of France? *by Edward Penfield, c. 1918*
(Boston Athenaeum)

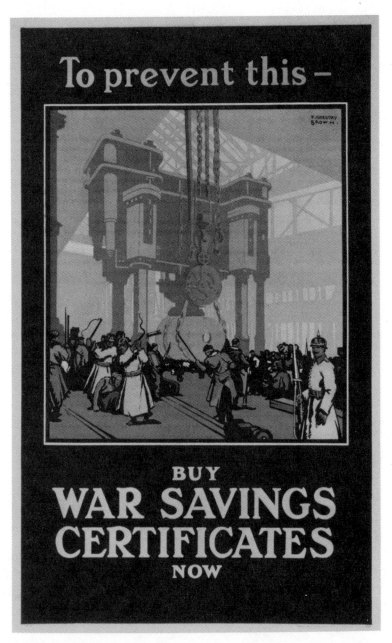

To Prevent This — Buy War Savings Certificates Now *by F. Gregory Brown, 1918 (Great Britain)* (Hoover Institution Archives)

Subscribe to War Bonds *by Alfred Offner, 1917 (Austria)*
(Imperial War Museum, London)

For the Flag! *by Georges Scott, 1917 (France)*
(Imperial War Museum, London)

Flanders *by Otto Dix, 1934–1936 (Germany)*
(Courtesy Bildarchiv Preussischer Kulturbesitz, Berlin)

Gassed Men *by Maurice Rétif, 1918 (France)*
(Archipel © SPADEM, Courtesy Musée d'Histoire Contemporaine, BDIC, Hotel National des Invalides, Paris)

We Are Making a New World *by Paul Nash, 1918 (Great Britain)*
(Imperial War Museum, London)

Troops Resting *by C. R. W. Nevinson, 1916 (Great Britain)*
(Imperial War Museum, London)

C. War and Memory

1. WHY MEN FOUGHT

Belgian socialist Hendrik de Man served as an infantry private in the trenches. His *The Remaking of a Mind: A Soldier's Thoughts on War and Reconstruction,* published in 1919, dwelled less on the details of his experience as a soldier than on the new ideals emerging from the war and his hopes of promoting them in the postwar period. In the following passage from the book, de Man offers a number of suggestive reasons why men went to war in 1914.

The love of my native country played but a part in my life. It is true that, when the war broke out, I found that something in the subconscious impulses which are after all the mainspring of even an educated man's actions, was particularly associated with the land of my birth and childhood. These fundamental impulses, that really make a man what he is, can no more be obliterated by later attempts to identify oneself with the soul of other nations, than having learnt foreign languages can make one forget the sound of the mother tongue. This sound, the images associated with it, and the instinctive likes and dislikes formed in those early years remain paramount. It takes a strong cause, which, like dreaming or death agony, releases the strings of self-consciousness, to make one realise how much more of these impulses remain present and active than one would think.

Yet although they are associated with one's native language and the recollections of childhood, they have little to do with nationality as such. They are an essential part of national feeling, but no more identical with it than are the topographical boundaries of home, or, at the utmost, of the native town, with the frontiers of the country. This is especially the case with Belgium, where several languages are spoken, and where my native Flemish tongue, or, more particularly still, my local dialect, does not identify itself with the existence of the State. So though my instinctive patriotism would link me with my home, with my family, with the customs and manners of my class, and with the aspect of the small part of the country where I received my impressions as a child, it would not do so with the country as a whole.

In so far as patriotism means attachment to the institutions and the national spirit of a country, I candidly confess that in the ordinary sense of the term, I never was much of a Belgian patriot. If I were asked whether the fact that I have fought for years with the Belgian army, and shared its glory and its sufferings as well as those of the whole nation, has not created a new tie between me and my countrymen, I am afraid that I could only to a limited extent answer in the affirmative. There is certainly a very strong sympathy between me and those whose sufferings I have shared, but as far as it is really a bond of feeling, that is, based on actual and personal experience, it only applies to that very small

Excerpt from *The Remaking of a Mind: A Soldier's Thoughts on War and Reconstruction* by Hendrik de Man, Scribner's, 1919, pp. 4–7, 154–157, 166–169.

portion of the army with which I have actually been in touch, my own men, and my own comrades. On the other hand, as far as military solidarity is the outcome of conscious thinking, it is not at all confined to my own countrymen, for I naturally extend it to all soldiers who have fought for the same cause. My intellectual sympathy goes out to the poilu, the Tommy and the Sammy and all their allies, as well as to the Belgian soldier, and to every one of them in direct ratio not so much of their sufferings and their courage as of the extent to which their purpose in fighting was identical with mine. Otherwise I might include the German soldiers as well, who certainly have fought as bravely and suffered as much as most of us. But this is another story. My point for the moment is that military solidarity created by the war is either too narrow or too broad a feeling to add much strength to the patriotism of a man who never looked upon the war from a purely national viewpoint. . . .

. . . [W]ar should be opposed as destructive of some of the higher impulses which are necessary to the progress of mankind. For the kind of hatred necessitated and generated by a war like this is not the enlightened passion that only sees in men the victims or the instruments of a system. Nor is it the enlightening passion that, through fighting these men, leads to discernment and hatred of the system; for experience shows, on the contrary, that the fighting tends to inure to that system the very men who have set out to fight it.

I hope that in all belligerent countries there will be found a sufficient number of combatants with the courage to emancipate themselves from the sentimental and ethical cant that has been brought into fashion with the public by a conventional literature, and to say what, if they dare look it in the face, they know to be the truth of their experience. My conclusion is that the impulses which actuated most of the combatants had very little to do with the ethical motives, preached by the leaders of public opinion, for or against certain systems of government. They were accepted as more or less mythical symbols, that is all. The masses everywhere *started* fighting because they were forced to do so, or led to believe — whether rightly or wrongly, need not concern us here — through the machinery by which a leading minority makes public opinion, that they were to defend their homes, their families and their possessions against an enemy bent on taking all this away from them. And they *went on* fighting, because fighting itself created, by the action of military discipline, the additional impulses without which it could not have lasted, to wit: the inculcation of the sense of duty, solidarity and comradeship; the suggestive power of the instincts of imitation, emulation and pride; and, chiefly, the spirit of revenge. It is obvious that all these impulses are *blind*, that is, their working is independent of the motives of the minority that disposes of the machinery through which they are created. Experience has shown that this machinery was equally effective in all European countries, whether the motives of the men at the rudder were ethically good or bad; at any rate, it was so for four years, both in the armies of the Central Powers and those of the Entente. . . .

In Europe also, ethical motives played a large part in war propaganda. Above all, the violation of the neutrality of Belgium stirred what is conventionally called the public mind in many countries. This especially applies to England. There the war would hardly have been popular enough in the first days had it not been for the appeal to her chivalry that was answered by the sending of an expeditionary force to redress the wrong done to Belgium. But important though this motive was, it was only with a minority of the combatants that it was strong enough to act as an actual impulse to fight.

There is, of course, a mutual reaction between what the people at home think and what the combatants at the front do. However, I am not dealing here with the motives of nations at large — which are a problem by themselves, and a very complicated one, too — but merely with the passions that make the combatant minority do the actual fighting. They are two quite different questions. It is easier to make a civilian in Chicago who reads his newspaper at breakfast curse the Kaiser and wish he could throttle the Crown Prince, than to make a soldier cross a bit of ground swept by machine-gun bullets, to go and kill people whom he has never seen and against whom he has no individual grudge. If you talk from a soap-box to a crowd at home in order to incense it against the enemy, there is no nonsense you can not make it swallow, provided that you appeal to the sense of morality and chivalry which it will take a childish pride in demonstrating. . . .

There is another fundamental instinct of man that makes him willing to fight the more the longer the fighting lasts: his desire to retaliate for blows he has suffered himself, or has seen inflicted on his comrades.

In this connection I remember an incident that throws a characteristic light on soldiers' psychology in trench warfare. It happened in March, 1917, in the Belgian lines in front of Dixmude, where I was then in position with my trench mortar battery, a short distance in rear of our first line. The latter was only about thirty-five yards away from the enemy, who held the opposite bank of the Yser. Things had been fairly quiet for some time, except for desultory bombardments in the rear and the usual machine-gun and rifle fire at night. The natural consequence was that the fighting *morale* of the infantry fell rather low. I must add that there was a certain amount of discontent on account of various extraordinary hardships that had resulted from a long spell of severe cold. Perhaps, also, the news of the revolution in Russia and of the fraternisations on the Eastern front had suggested imitation in the minds of a few light-headed boys. Be that as it may, for a few days in succession there had been a kind of tacit truce along the first line, with several attempts at communication. They were timid at first, and mostly consisted in the throwing over of jocular messages. Then some Belgian soldiers threw letters across with the request to send them on to their families in occupied territory. Finally a few men got up on the parapet on both sides and talked to each other as well as they could. As far as I could make out, the contents of their conversation were quite harmless, and mostly in the nature of jocular remarks about the duration of the war and similar subjects of common interest. Yet, needless to say, the whole trend of affairs was such as to expose the culprits to severe disciplinary punishment, though it probably escaped the notice of their officers, who were some distance away, as the first line was but a system of outposts very thinly held. I overheard some of the remarks of my own men, who were, like myself, watching events from the rear, and others were reported to me later on. They were all more or less to this effect: "What's the harm, after all, in talking to these chaps? They've been pretty decent of late. They haven't thrown over no grenades for more than a week. They are poor blokes like us. Their positions aren't a rap more comfortable than ours, you know, and the frost must have cut off their supplies of potatoes just like ours. They say their officers are brutes. . . . They say their women and children are hungry. . . . Aren't they men like us? I bet they care for their own people, and want to get back home just as much as us!"

Suddenly a shot rang out from our line, and reports say that a man dropped from the German parapet. A Belgian officer, whose action, by the way, was diversely judged by his comrades, had fired it. The Germans retaliated with a few grenades, and after a couple of minutes the whole place was as "lively" as ever before. Blood had flowed, and called for blood. Pale faces and drawn features told of hatred inflamed by the spirit of revenge. Everything that had been said about "those poor blokes over there" was forgotten. They were "Boches" and "grey vermin" once again. I think if I had allowed my men to send a few "flying pigs" over to them — for which there was no tactical need — they would have kissed my hands.

Then it struck me that the shot that had created such a revulsion of feelings was like a symbol of the first shot that, on the first day of the war, had hit a man somewhere in Europe, and awakened his comrades' thirst for revenge.

2. WAR CEMETERIES

Shortly after the conclusion of the armistice in November 1918, an Imperial War Graves Commission assembled in London to discuss plans for the erection of war cemeteries in France to honor British and imperial soldiers. To reconcile its members' divergent opinions on this matter, the commission appointed the director of the British Museum, Sir Frederic Kenyon, to advise them on the aesthetic and religious concerns related to the construction of the cemeteries. Kenyon's recommendations follow, based on his observations of French cemeteries and discussions with military and religious officials as well as with relatives of the fallen soldiers. The report offers a unique insight into how the commission sought to commemorate the ideal of sacrifice in an appropriately spiritual way while not trespassing on sensitive social, racial, and religious convictions.

Report

Your Royal Highness, My Lords and Gentlemen

I have the honour to lay before you the following report on the subject referred to me by the resolution of your Commission on 20th November, 1917.

In accordance with the instructions contained in that resolution, and in order to carry out the task entrusted to me, I visited France on two occasions. I was able to see a considerable number of cemeteries of various types; large base cemeteries . . . ; large

Excerpt from "War Graves: How the Cemeteries Abroad will be Designed" by Sir Frederic Kenyon, HMSO, 1918, pp. 3–14.

independent cemeteries . . . ; cemeteries which form adjuncts to French communal cemeteries . . . ; cemeteries adjoining or amalgamated with French military cemeteries . . . ; small isolated cemeteries . . . ; and finally, an immense number of single burials, as over the whole area of the battles of the Somme. . . . I was able to visit cemeteries along all parts of the front . . . , and thereby was able to form an idea of the variety of problems arising in connection with their arrangement, decoration and upkeep.

I have also had opportunities, both abroad and at home, of consulting representatives of the principal interests involved — the Army, the relatives of the fallen, the religious denominations, and the artists and others whose judgment may be of value in a work demanding imagination and taste and good feeling. . . . Among others, I have made a point of obtaining opinions from those who are qualified to speak for India and for the Dominions which have sent so many of their sons to lie in the graves which for generations to come will mark the line of our front in France and Flanders. My endeavour has been to arrive at a result which will, so far as may be, satisfy the feelings of relatives and comrades of those who lie in these cemeteries; which will represent the soldierly spirit and discipline in which they fought and fell; which will typify the Army to which they belonged; which will give expression to those deeper emotions, of regimental comradeship, of service to their Army, their King, their Country and their God, which underlay (perhaps often unconsciously) their sacrifice of themselves for the cause in which they fought, and which in ages to come will be a dignified memorial, worthy of the nation and of the men who gave their lives for it, in the lands of the Allies with whom and for whom they fought. . . .

And while dealing with this part of the subject, it may be as well to remind some who may read this report that of many who have fallen in this war there can be no identified grave. Many bodies are found but cannot be identified; many are never found at all; many are buried in graves which have subsequently been destroyed in the course of fighting. This is especially the case in areas such as that of Ypres, where the same ground has been contested for three consecutive years, and the whole countryside has been blasted and torn with shell fire. Therefore, whatever may be done in the way of placing individual monuments over the dead, in very many cases no such monument is possible. Yet these must not be neglected, and some memorial there must be to the lost, the unknown, but not forgotten dead.

EQUALITY OF TREATMENT

The Commission has already laid down one principle, which goes far towards determining the disposition of the cemeteries; the principle, namely, of equality of treatment. . . . As soon as the question was faced, it was felt that the provision of monuments could not be left to individual initiative. In a few cases, where money and good taste were not wanting, a satisfactory result would be obtained, in the sense that a fine individual monument could be erected. In the large majority of cases either no monument would be erected, or it would be poor in quality; and the total result would be one of inequality, haphazard and disorder. The cemetery would become a collection of individual memorials, a few good, but many bad, and with a total want of congruity and uniformity. The monuments of the more well-to-do would overshadow those of their poorer comrades; the whole sense of comradeship and of common service would be lost. The Commission, on the other hand, felt that where the sacrifice had been common, the memorial should be common also; and they desired that the cemeteries should be the symbol of a great Army and an united Empire.

It was therefore ordained that what was done for one should be done for all, and that all, whatever their military rank or position in civil life, should have equal treatment in their graves.

It is necessary to face the fact that this decision has given pain in some quarters, and pain which the Commissioners would have been glad to avoid. Not a few relatives have been looking forward to placing a memorial of their own choosing over the graves which mean so much to them; some have devoted much time and thought to making such a memorial beautiful and significant. Yet it is hoped that even these will realize that they are asked to join in an action of even higher significance. The sacrifice of the individual is a great idea and worthy of commemoration; but the community of sacrifice, the service of a common cause, the comradeship of arms which has brought together men of all ranks and grades — these are greater ideas, which should be commemorated in those cemeteries where they lie together, the representatives of their country in the lands in which they served. The place for the individual memorial is at home, where it will be constantly before the eyes of relatives and descendants, and will serve as an example and encouragement for the generations to come. A monument in France (and still more if further afield) can be seen but seldom; a monument in the parish church or churchyard is seen day by day and week by week, from generation to generation.

If any further argument is needed, I would say that the contrast now presented between the military and communal cemeteries, where they adjoin one another, provides it. The communal cemeteries are a jumbled mass of individual monuments of all sorts and sizes and of all variety of quality, packed much more closely than the monuments in an English churchyard; and the result is neither dignified nor inspiring. Side by side with these, the military cemeteries, whether French or English, with their orderly rows of crosses (the French ones bearing, in addition, a tricolour *cocarde*), have both dignity and inspiration. It is this impression which it is sought to perpetuate in the treatment now proposed for permanent adoption.

HEADSTONES

The principle of equality and uniformity of treatment having been adopted, there are two main alternative methods by which it may be carried out: (1) either the individual graves will be undistinguished (except perhaps by an inconspicuous number), and the names of the dead will be commemorated on a single inscription, placed in some convenient position in the cemetery; or (2) each grave will have its own headstone, of uniform dimensions, on which the name of the dead will be carved, with his rank, regiment, and date of death.

In the first alternative, the cemetery would have the appearance of a small park or garden, composed of turf or flower beds divided by paths, planted with such shrubs or trees, and in no way recognizable as a cemetery, except by the presence of some central monument or monuments (of which more will be said later).

In the second alternative, the cemetery (besides such central monument or monuments) will be marked by rows of headstones of uniform height and width, though perhaps with some variety of pattern, as indicated below. The graves themselves might, in principle, be either separate mounds or a continuous flat surface. In practice I strongly recommend the latter, as being both easy to maintain and (especially where graves are so crowded as they necessarily are in these cemeteries) more satisfactory in effect, and also better adapted for decoration by flowers.

Of these two alternatives, my recommendation is definitely in favour of the second, for the following reasons: —

(a) The headstones clearly indicate the nature of the enclosure, that it is a cemetery and not a garden. Although it is not desired that our war cemeteries should be gloomy places, it is right that the fact that they are cemeteries, containing the bodies of hundreds of thousands of men who have given their lives for their country, should be evident at first sight, and should be constantly present to the minds of those who pass by or who visit them.

(b) The rows of headstones in their ordered ranks carry on the military idea, giving the appearance as of a battalion on parade, and suggesting the spirit of discipline and order which is the soul of an army. They will perpetuate the effect, which all who have seen them feel to be impressive, of the present rows of wooden crosses.

(c) The existence of individual headstones will go far to meet the wishes of relatives, who above all things are interested in the single grave. Many of them, as indicated above, will be disappointed that they are not allowed to erect their own monument over their own dead; but they will be much more disappointed if no monument except a mere indication number marks that grave at all. The individual headstone, marking the individual grave, will serve as centre and focus of the emotions of the relatives who visit it.

(d) Although opinion is not unanimous, it is my impression from all the interviews and conversations which I have had on the subject, that a large majority of those whose opinions are most entitled to consideration (including soldiers, relatives and artists) would be in favour of the use of headstones.

I recommend that the headstones should normally be 2 ft. 6 in. in height and 1 ft. 3 in. in width; not so large as to be cumbrous and oppressive, but large enough to convey the effect desired. Subject to this latter consideration, the smaller the dimensions the smaller will be the expense, and the less will be the difficulty of accommodation in the more crowded cemeteries. . . .

Regimental Patterns of Headstones

In order to secure a certain amount of variety in uniformity, and at the same time to gratify the regimental feeling which is so strong a characteristic of the British Army, it is proposed that each regiment, or other convenient unit, should have its own pattern of headstone, incorporating the regimental badge, which will be erected over the grave of every man of that regiment, wherever he may be buried. It is desirable that regimental feeling should be consulted as to the design of these headstones, and consequently (the approval of the Commission having been given to the principle) a circular has, I understand, been issued to units inviting suggestions or designs from men of artistic knowledge and experience. In the case of British regiments, the circular is being issued through the Colonels of regiments; in the case of other units, through such channels as are most in accordance with military practice. The designs, when received, will be submitted to a committee representing artistic taste and experience, and one will be selected to serve as the regimental pattern for each unit. . . .

Inscriptions on Headstones

The inscription carved on each headstone will give the rank, name, regiment and date of death of the man buried beneath it. There is some difference of opinion as to whether leave should be given to relatives to add anything further. It is clearly undesirable to allow free scope for the effusions of the mortuary mason, the sentimental versifier, or the crank; nor can space be given for a lengthy epitaph. On the other hand it would give satisfaction in many individual instances to be allowed to add an appropriate text or prayer or words of dedication. . . .

Central Monuments

The question of the central monument (I mean by this central in interest, not necessarily in position) in each cemetery which will strike the note, not only of the cemetery itself, but of the whole of this commemoration of the fallen, is one of great importance, and also of some difficulty. It is essential that it should be simple, durable, dignified and expressive of the higher feelings with which we regard our dead. In order to do this, it must have, or be capable of, religious associations, and while it must satisfy the religious emotions of as many as possible, it must give no reasonable ground of offence to any. The central sentiment of our commemoration of the dead is, I think, a grateful and undying remembrance of their sacrifice; and it is this sentiment which most persons will wish to see symbolised in the central monument. . . .

One suggestion was made at an early stage . . . which has been received with a considerable amount of approval. This was to the effect that the main memorial in every British cemetery should be "one great fair stone of fine proportions, 12 ft. in length, lying raised upon three steps, of which the first and third shall be twice the width of the second; and that each stone shall bear, in indelible lettering, some fine thought or words of sacred dedication." This stone would be, wherever circumstances permit, on the eastern side of each cemetery, and the graves will lie before it, facing east, as the Army faces now. It would have the character of permanence, as much as any work of man can hope for it. It would meet many forms of religious feeling. To some it would merely be a memorial stone, such as those of which we read in the Old Testament. To others it would be an altar, one of the most ancient and general of religious symbols, and would serve as the centre of religious services. As an altar, it would represent one side of the idea of sacrifice, the sacrifice which the Empire has made of its youth, in the great cause for which it sent them forth. And wherever this stone was found, it would be the mark, for all ages, of a British cemetery of the Great War.

The idea and symbolism of this great memorial altar stone go far to meet our requirements, but they do not go all the way. It lacks what many (probably a large majority) would desire, the definitely Christian character; and it does not represent the idea of self-sacrifice. For this the one essential symbol is the Cross; and I have no doubt that great distress would be felt if our cemeteries lacked this recognition of the fact that we are a Christian Empire; and this symbol of the self-sacrifice made by those who lie in them. The Jews are necessarily intermixed with their Christian comrades; but it is believed that their feelings will be satisfied by the inclusion of their religious symbol (the double triangle, or "Star of David") in the design of their headstones, and that they would not be offended by the presence of the Cross in the cemetery. For the great majority the Cross is the symbol of their faith, which they would wish to see in the cemeteries where their comrades or their kinsmen lie. One large and important class must be dealt with separately. It will be understood that where our Mohammedan, Hindu, and other non-Christian fellow subjects lie (and care has always been taken to bury them apart) their graves will be treated in accordance with their own religious beliefs and practices, and their own religious symbol will be placed over them. . . .

My recommendation, therefore, after much consideration and consultation with representatives of many points of view, definitely is that these two forms of monument should be combined; that in every cemetery there should be, on the east side, unless local conditions render it impracticable, a memorial stone . . . ; and elsewhere in the cemetery a cross. The cross should not be of the bare pattern, which would provoke comparison with the crucifixes habitually found in French cemeteries, but rather of the nature of the crosses found in many English country churchyards, or the Celtic crosses characteristic of northern Britain. The size, pattern, and position would be left to the artist who designs each cemetery. The cross and stone combined would be the universal mark of the British war cemetery. . . .

OTHER BUILDINGS

Besides the cross and stone, some form of building will, for practical reasons, be required in all except the smallest cemeteries. In every cemetery a register of graves will have to be kept; in most some form of tool-house will be required. But beyond these needs, it will be convenient to have some shelter for visitors from the weather, some place where simple religious services may be held. . . . In general it may be worth while to emphasise the fact that the buildings, like the other features of the cemetery, should be as durable as possible, and should involve as little cost in upkeep as possible. Permanence should be the note of our cemeteries, but we desire both the lessons of the war and the expressions of our gratitude to those who gave their lives in it to be permanent. . . .

SUMMARY OF PRECEDING RECOMMENDATIONS

If the recommendations made in the preceding portion of this Report are carried out, the general appearance of a British cemetery will be that of an enclosure with plots of grass or flowers (or both) separated by paths of varying size, and set with orderly rows of headstones, uniform in height and width, but with slight difference of shape. Shrubs and trees will be arranged in various places, sometimes as clumps at the junctions of ways, sometimes as avenues along the sides of the principal paths, sometimes around the borders of the cemetery. The graves will, wherever possible, face towards the east, and at the eastern end of the cemetery will be a great altar-stone, raised upon broad steps, and bearing some brief and appropriate phrase or text. Either over the stone, or elsewhere in the cemetery, will be a small building, where visitors may gather for shelter or for worship, and where the register of the graves will be kept. And at some prominent spot will arise the Cross; as the symbol of the Christian faith and of the self-sacrifice of the men who now lie beneath its shadow.

. . . Different parts of it appeal differently to different persons, but there appears to be a general consensus of opinion that the scheme, carried out under good artistic guidance, will give a dignified and harmonious result, and that future generations will not be ashamed of what will be regarded as the characteristic British memorial of the Great War. It leaves ample scope for the display of artistic talent in adapting the scheme to the details of the ground in each particular instance, and the credit for satisfactory results will rest with the designer. All that is desired here is to ensure that all the designers shall work on a common plan. Each cemetery, it is hoped, will be beautiful, or at least satisfying, in itself; but their effect becomes cumulative if all, under whatever circumstances, have the same main features and express the same ideas, and so typify the common spirit of the nation, the common purpose of the Army, and the common sacrifice of the individual.

Epilogue

In a very real sense, the war's effects persisted long after the guns fell silent. Despite the widespread desire for a "return to normalcy," voiced in President Warren Harding's famous (and mangled) phrase, efforts to resume life as though nothing had changed over the past four years were as illusory as those undertaken by the architects of the Restoration after the defeat of Napoleon a century before.

No issue received greater attention (or subsequent condemnation) than efforts to fashion a lasting peace settlement. Germany's military collapse occurred rapidly in late-1918 after four years of war fought almost exclusively on foreign soil. The collapse lent apparent credence to the utterly unjustified accusation that German soldiers had not lost the war but had been "stabbed in the back" by pacifist politicians and profit-hungry financiers who "lacked the stomach" to continue the conflict. Thus, even before a peace conference convened, politicians faced a difficult task in forging an agreement acceptable to all victors.

The peacemakers — or, more accurately, the victors, for Germany was only summoned to *accept* a treaty — met outside Paris at Versailles to settle the framework for postwar Europe. In attempting to do so, they were guided by their interpretation of the war's origins. In practice, that meant recognizing the rights of subject nationalities to self-determination (nationalist and ethnic rivalry having destabilized southeastern Europe and prompted the July crisis) and stripping the defeated Germany (presumed to have been the principal aggressor) of its colonial empire and much of its military capacity. The result was a redrawn map of Europe from which the collapsed Austro-Hungarian and Ottoman empires disappeared. A series of new states arose in eastern Europe that, the peacemakers anticipated, might also provide a buffer between democratic Europe and Soviet Russia. In retrospect, these new states were often divided by ethnic rivalries and proved too small to withstand German and Soviet expansion in the late 1930s.

The enormous cost of the war and the prospect of tangible rewards for cooperating in the war effort (in response to an appeal by governments seeking to preserve morale) encouraged the discussion of reparations, namely, financial restitution to be paid to the victors by the losers. While not a new concept — reparations had figured, for example, in the settlement of the Franco-Prussian war in 1871 — they took on a particular importance in the Versailles treaty. The famous "War Guilt" clause 231 assigned Germany full responsibility for the war's outbreak and for the damages incurred in its conduct. Clause 231 unwittingly strengthened the hand of German extremists who contended that the Allies maintained a double standard: careful to recognize the rights of nations in so many cases but eager to trample on those of Germany. Assigning Germany the financial burden of the war proved both unrealistic — though the required payments were scaled back and further reduced through inflation — and unwise in saddling that nation's first democratic government, the Weimar Republic, with an economic and emotional albatross.

Just as the immediate impact of the war reached far beyond the battlefields, so too its legacy stretched beyond Versailles. Issues of religion, gender, the work ethic, the nature of authority, social conventions, and moral and civic responsibilities all collided on the battlefield and the home front. If the First World War initiated change with respect to international relations and geographic boundaries, it also reinforced or accelerated political and social trends already under way before August 1914. For example, states now bore even heavier social-welfare responsibilities, including the payment of veterans' pensions. The entry of women in the workplace, a crisis of masculinity, and social and religious discrimination all quickened as a result of the war.

Ultimately, the war imparted to all participants a heightened sense of the importance of self-preservation. Whether for the soldier in the trenches or the civilian on the production lines, the death and deprivation that enveloped them for four years led to a search for order where chaos had ensued, and for respectability and dignity where before there had been paternalism and exploitation. This quest for stability, rationality, and compassion from their fellow citizens, employers, and the state would not, however, be fulfilled.

In the end, Sir Edward Grey's prophecy on August 4, 1914, proved correct — the lamps of European civilization as he had known it were not relit within his lifetime. The war proved to be a great watershed in European affairs. Most nations' economies had suffered harsh blows from which they did not fully recover, as would be revealed in the prolonged fiscal crisis from 1929 onward. Liquidated investments, accumulated debts, and disrupted trade patterns all bore witness to the conflict's dislocating effects. But in a deeper philosophical sense, too, the war had changed something. Liberalism, which had seemed so confident of progress over the course of the nineteenth century, appeared powerless to deal with the postwar realities of the twentieth. Promoting the rational mediation of disputes had not forestalled the war (as again it would not in 1939), and the elevation of the responsible, sovereign individual as the basic unit of society withered in the face of the slaughter and a vast extension of state authority. After 1918, ideologies extolling group identities, collective action, and the liberating role of violence proved the more influential, most notably fascism and communism.

Finally, the entry of the United States into the conflict and its crucial financial role in the war and the postwar settlement reflected a shifting of gravity in political and economic affairs. Despite persistently strong isolationist sentiment at home, the United States was now inextricably linked to Europe. If one appreciates the importance of the war in hastening revolution in Russia, it becomes clear how the polarization of European superpowers in the aftermath of the Second World War owed so much to the impact of the First. In that sense, too, perhaps in a way Grey did not anticipate, Europe would never look the same again.

Suggestions for Further Reading

General

Berghahn, Volker. *Germany and the Approach of War in 1914*. 2nd ed. New York: St. Martin's, 1993.

Evans, R. J. W., and H. Pogge von Strandmann, eds. *The Coming of the First World War*. Oxford: Clarendon Press, 1988.

Ferro, Marc. *The Great War 1914–1918*. London: Routledge Kegan Paul, 1973.

Fischer, Fritz. *Germany's Aims in the First World War*. New York: Norton, 1967.

Joll, James. *The Origins of the First World War*. London: Longman, 1984.

Offer, Avner. *The First World War: An Agrarian Interpretation*. Oxford: Clarendon Press, 1989.

Robbins, Keith. *The First World War*. Oxford: Clarendon Press, 1984.

Schmitt, Bernadotte, and Harold Vedeler. *The World in the Crucible*. New York: Harper and Row, 1984.

Stevenson, David. *The First World War and International Politics*. Oxford: Clarendon Press, 1988.

Winter, J. M. *The Experience of World War I*. New York: Oxford University Press, 1989.

Part I The Challenge of Mobilization and Stalemate

Ashworth, Tony. *Trench Warfare 1914–1918*. London: Macmillan, 1980.

Beckett, Ian F. W., and Keith Simpson, eds. *A Nation in Arms: A Social Study of the British Army in the First World War*. Manchester: Manchester University Press, 1985.

Bidwell, Shelford, and Dominick Graham. *Fire Power*. London: Allen and Unwin, 1982.

Bond, Brian, ed. *The First World War and British Military History*. Oxford: Clarendon Press, 1991.

Bourne, John M. *Britain and the Great War 1914–1918*. London: Edward Arnold, 1989.

French, David. *British Strategy and War Aims, 1914–1916*. London: Allen and Unwin, 1986.

Giraudoux, Jean. *Campaigns and Intervals*. Providence: Berghahn, 1994.

Haber, Lutz. *The Poisonous Cloud*. Oxford: Clarendon Press, 1986.

Halpern, Paul G. *A Naval History of World War I*. Naval Institute Press, 1994.

Hough, Richard. *The Great War at Sea*. Oxford: Oxford University Press, 1983.

Keegan, John. *The Face of Battle*. London: Allen Lane, 1975.

Leed, Eric J. *No Man's Land. Combat and Identity in World War I.* New York: Cambridge University Press, 1979.

MacDonald, Lyn. *They Called It Passchendaele.* London: Michael Joseph, 1978.

———. *Somme.* London: Michael Joseph, 1983.

Middlebrook, Martin. *The First Day of the Somme.* London: Allen Lane, 1971.

Morrow, John Jr. *The Great War in the Air.* Washington, DC: Smithsonian Institution Press, 1993.

Simkins, Peter. *Kitchener's Army.* Manchester: Manchester University Press, 1988.

Stone, Norman. *The Eastern Front 1914–1917.* London: Hodder and Stoughton, 1975.

Travers, T. H. E. *The Killing Ground: The British Army, the Western Front and the Emergence of Modern Warfare 1900–1918.* London: Allen and Unwin, 1987.

———. *How the War Was Won: Command and Technology in the British Army on the Western Front, 1917–1918.* London: Routledge, 1992.

Turner, John, ed. *Britain and the First World War.* London: Unwin Hyman, 1988.

Wildman, Allan K. *The End of the Russian Imperial Army.* Princeton: Princeton University Press, 1980.

Wilson, Trevor. *The Myriad Faces of War.* Oxford: Polity Press, 1986.

Winter, Denis. *Death's Men.* London: Allen Lane, 1978.

Wohl, Robert. *The Generation of 1914.* Cambridge, MA: Harvard University Press, 1979.

———. *A Passion for Wings: Aviation and the Western Imagination, 1908–1918.* Vol. 1. New Haven: Yale University Press, 1994.

Part II   Society Under Stress

Becker, Jean-Jacques. *The Great War and the French People.* Leamington Spa: Berg, 1986.

Braybon, Gail. *Women Workers in the First World War.* London: Croom Helm, 1981.

Coetzee, Frans, and Marilyn Shevin-Coetzee, eds. *Authority, Identity and the Social History of the Great War.* Providence: Berghahn, 1995.

Frevert, Ute. *Women in German History.* Leamington Spa: Berg, 1988.

Fridenson, Patrick, ed. *The French Home Front.* Providence: Berg, 1992.

Higonnet, Margaret, et al., eds. *Behind the Lines. Gender and the Two World Wars.* New Haven: Yale University Press, 1987.

Kent, Susan Kingsley. *Making Peace. The Reconstruction of Gender in Interwar Britain.* Princeton: Princeton University Press, 1993.

Kocka, Jürgen. *Facing Total War.* Cambridge, MA: Harvard University Press, 1984.

Marwick, Arthur. *The Deluge. British Society and the First World War.* 2nd ed. Houndmills, Basingstoke: Macmillan, 1991.

McMillan, James F. *Housewife or Harlot: The Place of Women in French Society.* Brighton: Harvester, 1981.

Panayi, Panikos. *The Enemy in Our Midst: Germans in Britain during the First World War.* Providence: Berg, 1991.

———, ed. *Minorities in Wartime.* Providence: Berg, 1993.

Roberts, Mary Louise. *Civilization Without Sexes: Reconstructing Gender in Postwar France, 1917–1927.* Chicago: University of Chicago Press, 1994.

Vincent, C. P. *The Politics of Hunger: The Allied Blockade of Germany, 1915–1919.* Athens, OH: Ohio University Press, 1985.

Wall, Richard, and J. M. Winter, eds. *The Upheaval of War: Family, Work and Welfare in Europe, 1914–1918.* Cambridge: Cambridge University Press, 1988.

Whalen, Robert Weldon. *Bitter Wounds. German Victims of the Great War, 1914–1939.* Ithaca: Cornell University Press, 1984.

Winter, J. M. *The Great War and the British People.* Houndmills, Basingstoke: Macmillan, 1986.

Woollacott, Angela. *On Her Their Lives Depend: Munitions Workers in the Great War.* Berkeley: University of California Press, 1994.

Part III   State and Society in Crisis

Barnett, L. Margaret. *British Food Policy during the First World War.* London: Allen and Unwin, 1985.

Burk, Kathleen, ed. *War and the State.* London: Allen and Unwin, 1982.

———. *Britain, America and the Sinews of War 1914–1918.* London: Allen and Unwin, 1985.

Carsten, F. L. *War against War: British and German Radical Movements in the First World War.* Berkeley: University of California Press, 1982.

Ceadel, Martin. *Pacifism in Britain, 1914–1945: The Defining of a Faith.* Oxford: Clarendon Press, 1980.

Dewey, Peter. *British Agriculture during the First World War.* London: Royal Historical Society, 1989.

Feldman, Gerald. *Army, Industry and Labor in Germany, 1914–1918.* Princeton: Princeton University Press, 1966. Reprinted by Berg Press, 1992.

———. *The Great Disorder: Politics, Economics and Society in the German Inflation, 1914–1924.* New York: Oxford University Press, 1993.

Fitzpatrick, Sheila. *The Russian Revolution.* Oxford: Oxford University Press, 1982.

Flood, P. J. *France 1914–18. Public Opinion and the War Effort.* London: Macmillan, 1990.

Godfrey, John. *Capitalism at War: Industrial Policy and Bureaucracy in France, 1914–1918.* Leamington Spa: Berg, 1987.

Grieves, Keith. *The Politics of Manpower, 1914–1918.* Manchester: Manchester University Press, 1988.

Haimson, Leopold, and Charles Tilly, eds. *War, Strikes, and Revolution.* New York: Cambridge University Press, 1988.

———, and Giulio Sapelli, eds. *Strikes, Social Conflict and the First World War.* Milan: Annali della Fondazione Feltrinelli, 1993.

Hardach, Gerd. *The First World War.* Berkeley: University of California Press, 1976.

Hinton, James. *The First Shop Stewards' Movement.* London: Allen and Unwin, 1973.

Horn, Daniel, ed. *War, Mutiny and Revolution in the German Navy: The World War I Diary of Seaman Richard Stumpf.* New Brunswick: Rutgers University Press, 1967.

Horne, John. *Labour at War. France and Britain, 1914–1918.* Oxford: Clarendon Press, 1991.

Kaiser, Daniel, ed. *The Workers' Revolution in Russia: The View from Below.* New York: Cambridge University Press, 1987.

Koenker, Diane, and William Rosenberg. *Strikes and Revolution in Russia, 1917.* Princeton: Princeton University Press, 1989.

MacLean, Ian. *The Legend of Red Clydeside.* Edinburgh: John Donald, 1983.

Offer, Avner. *The First World War: An Agrarian Interpretation.* Oxford: Clarendon Press, 1989.

Rae, John. *Conscience and Politics.* London: Oxford University Press, 1970.

Robbins, Keith. *The Abolition of War: The Peace Movement in Britain, 1914–1919.* Cardiff: University of Wales Press, 1976.

Rubin, Gerry. *War, Law and Labour: The Munitions Acts, State Regulation and the Unions, 1915–1921.* Oxford: Clarendon Press, 1987.

Smith, Leonard V. *Between Mutiny and Obedience: The Case of the French Fifth Infantry Division During World War I.* Princeton: Princeton University Press, 1994.

Stromberg, Roland. *Redemption by War. The Intellectuals and 1914.* Lawrence: The Regents Press of Kansas, 1982.

Swartz, Marvin. *The Union of Democratic Control in British Politics during the First World War.* Oxford: Clarendon Press, 1971.

Turner, John. *British Politics and the Great War.* New Haven: Yale University Press, 1992.

Vellacott, Jo. *Bertrand Russell and the Pacifists in the First World War.* New York: St. Martin's Press, 1980.

Waites, Bernard. *A Class Society at War: England 1914–1918*. Leamington Spa: Berg, 1987.

Part IV   The Aesthetic War

Audoin-Rouzeau, Stéphane. *Men at War 1914–1918. National Sentiment and Trench Journalism in France during the First World War*. Providence: Berg, 1992.

Eksteins, Modris. *Rites of Spring. The Great War and the Birth of the Modern Age*. New York: Anchor, 1990.

Fuller, J. G. *Troop Morale and Popular Culture in the British and Dominion Armies 1914–1918*. Oxford: Clarendon Press, 1991.

Fussell, Paul. *The Great War and Modern Memory*. New York: Oxford University Press, 1975.

Hynes, Samuel. *A War Imagined*. New York: Atheneum, 1991.

Kavanagh, Gaynor. *Museums and the First World War: A Social History*. New York: St. Martin's Press, 1994.

Lewis, Beth Irwin. *George Grosz. Art and Politics in the Weimar Republic*. Princeton: Princeton University Press, 1991.

Mosse, George. *Fallen Soldiers*. New York: Oxford University Press, 1990.

Pick, Daniel. *War Machine: The Rationalization of Slaughter in the Machine Age*. New Haven: Yale University Press, 1993.

Prost, Antoine. *In the Wake of War. "Les Anciens Combattants" and French Society 1914–1939*. Providence: Berg, 1992.

Sanders, M. L., and Philip Taylor. *British Propaganda during the First World War*. London: Macmillan, 1982.

Silver, Kenneth E. *Esprit de Corps. The Art of the Parisian Avant-Garde and the First World War, 1914–1925*. Princeton: Princeton University Press, 1989.

Weinstein, Joan. *The End of Expressionism. Art and the November Revolution in Germany, 1918–19*. Chicago: University of Chicago Press, 1990.

Wohl, Robert. *The Generation of 1914*. Cambridge, MA: Harvard University Press, 1979.